AF286632

Max Teichert

The interest rate risk of banks

Max Teichert

The interest rate risk of banks

Current topics

Würzburg
University Press

Dissertation, Julius-Maximilians-Universität Würzburg

Wirtschaftswissenschaftliche Fakultät, 2017

Gutachter: Prof. Dr. Peter Bofinger, Prof. Dr. Martin Kukuk

Impressum

Julius-Maximilians-Universität Würzburg
Würzburg University Press
Universitätsbibliothek Würzburg
Am Hubland
D-97074 Würzburg
www.wup.uni-wuerzburg.de

© 2018 Würzburg University Press
Print on Demand

Coverdesign: Jule Petzold, Max Teichert

ISBN 978-3-95826-070-2 (print)
ISBN 978-3-95826-071-9 (online)
URN urn:nbn:de:bvb:20-opus-153669

 Except otherwise noted, this document—excluding the cover—is licensed under the
Creative Commons License Attribution-ShareAlike 4.0 International (CC BY-SA 4.0):
https://creativecommons.org/licenses/by-sa/4.0/

 The cover page is licensed under the Creative Commons License
Attribution-NonCommercial-NoDerivatives 4.0 International (CC BY-NC-ND 4.0):
https://creativecommons.org/licenses/by-nc-nd/4.0/

Acknowledgments

The German National Academic Foundation (Studienstiftung des deutschen Volkes) supported me financially during my work on this dissertation. In addition, it got me in touch with many outstanding people.

My supervisor Prof. Dr. Peter Bofinger provided extremely helpful guidance and support throughout the entire process. This dissertation was shaped by our intense discussions and its completion would not have been possible without him.

The Deutsche Bundesbank supported me through a joint research project. Special thanks go to Dr. Christoph Memmel and Dr. Atilim Seymen who co-authored a research paper with me that is also a part of this dissertation.

Words of thanks also go to my closest friends for motivating as well as for distracting me whenever the one or the other was necessary. Julius gave me a home, Niklas and Philipp made sure I eat well.

Last but not least, I owe particular thanks to my family. My daughters Martha and Ida were always there to put things in perspective. And words fail me to express my gratitude toward my wife Nina. I love you.

Max Teichert

Abstract

This dissertation produces three main results. First, from publicly available statistics, it can be inferred that the interest rate risk from on-balance sheet term transformation of banks in Germany exceeds the euro area average and is bound to increase even further. German banks push for shorter-term funding and hardly counteract the increased demand for longer-term loans. Within Germany, savings banks and cooperative banks are particularly engaged. Second, the supervisory interest rate shock scenarios are found to be increasingly detached both from the historic and the forecasted development of interest rates in Germany. In particular, German banks have been exposed to fewer and smaller adverse changes of the term structure. This increasingly limits the informative content of mere exposure measures such as the Basel interest rate coefficient when used as risk measures as is common practice in banking supervision and economic research. An impact assessment further supports the conclusion that the least that is required is a more comprehensive set of shock scenarios. Third and finally, there is a reasonable theoretical rationale and there is strong empirical evidence for banks' search for yield in interest rate risk. In addition to the established positive link between the term spread and the taking of interest rate risk by banks an additional negative link can be explained theoretically and there is significant empirical evidence for its existence and relevance. There is even a threshold of income below which banks' search for yield in interest rate risk surfaces openly.

Zusammenfassung

Die vorliegende Dissertation beschäftigt sich mit dem Zinsänderungsrisiko von Banken. Sie bearbeitet Themen mit hoher aktueller Relevanz angesichts gegenwärtiger Entwicklungen in der Geldpolitik, der Volkswirtschaftslehre und der Bankenregulierung.

Im ersten Teil werden vier Grundlagen gelegt. Erstens wird die moderne Auffassung des Bankgeschäfts vorgestellt, der nach Banken Geld in Form von Ersparnissen schaffen, wenn sie Kredite gewähren. Mit dieser Auffassung gehört die Übernahme von Zinsänderungsrisiken zum normalen Bankgeschäft. Zweitens wird ein Überblick über die Mikroökonomie des Bankgeschäfts gegeben, in dem der jüngst vollzogene Wechsel zum Paradigma des Risikos dargestellt wird. Unter diesem Paradigma sind Banken wesentlich Risikonehmer auch von Zinsänderungsrisiko. Drittens wird die Geldtheorie der Transmissionskanäle zusammengefasst, wobei der Fokus auf dem zuletzt starke Beachtung findenden Risikoneigungskanal liegt. Dieser Transmissionskanal stellt auch eine Verbindung zwischen der Geldpolitik und der Übernahme von Zinsänderungsrisiko durch Banken her. Viertens werden Ansätze und Spezifika der Behandlung des Zinsänderungsrisikos von Banken in der ökonomischen Forschung zusammengetragen. Das ist das Handwerkszeug für die Erarbeitung neuer Forschungsbeiträge.

Im zweiten Teil werden drei Erweiterungen entwickelt. Die erste Erweiterung begegnet dem nahezu vollständigen Fehlen von spezifischen Daten zum Zinsänderungsrisiko von Banken in Deutschland mit einer umfassenden Auswertung allgemeiner, öffentlich verfügbarer Statistiken. Es zeigt sich, dass das Zinsänderungsrisiko von Banken in Deutschland über dem Durchschnitt des Euroraums liegt und einem steigenden Trend folgt, der sich insbesondere aus einer Verschiebung hin zu kurzfristigerer Refinanzierung speist. Von den unterschiedlichen Arten von Banken in Deutschland präsentieren sich Sparkassen und Genossenschaftsbanken als besonders exponiert. Die zweite Erweiterung untersucht die Veränderungen der Zinsstruktur in Deutschland und nimmt damit die zweite Komponente des Zinsänderungsrisikos neben der Position der Banken in den Blick. Analysen historischer sowie prognostizierter Veränderungen weisen auf ein sinkendes Zinsänderungsrisiko hin. Auch auf Basis einer ergänzenden Szenarioanalyse ergeben sich konkrete Kritikpunkte an jüngst auf internationaler Ebene beschlossenen regulatorischen Standards sowie genaue Vorschläge zur Ergänzung im Rahmen ihrer Implementierung. Die dritte Erweiterung adressiert ein mögliches Streben nach Rendite (search for yield) von Banken bei der Übernahme von Zinsänderungsrisiko, die geringere Profitabilität zu höherer Risikoübernahme führen lässt. Ein theoretisches Modell führt dieses Verhalten auf eine plausible Nutzenfunktion von Bankmanagern zurück. Eine empirische Untersuchung belegt die statistische Signifikanz und ökonomische Relevanz mit Daten aus Deutschland.

Contents

List of Figures

List of Tables

List of Abbreviations

BaFin	Bundesanstalt für Finanzdienstleistungsaufsicht
BAKIS	Bankaufsichtliches Informationssystem
BBK	Deutsche Bundesbank
BCBS	Basel Committee on Banking Supervision
BilMoG	Bilanzmodernisierungsgesetz
BIS	Bank of International Settlements
BoE	Bank of England
bps	Basis points
CAPM	Capital asset pricing model
CEBS	Committee of European Banking Supervisors
EA	Euro area
ECB	European Central Bank
EMIR	European Market Infrastructure Regulation
EU	European Union
FED	Federal Reserve System
GER	Germany
ICAPM	Intertemporal capital asset pricing model
ifo	ifo Institut
IMF	International Monetary Fund
KWG	Kreditwesengesetz
MFI	Monetary financial institution
pos.	positions
rem.mat.	remaing maturity
UK	United Kingdom
US	United States of America
ZEW	Zentrum für Europäische Wirtschaftsforschung

Chapter 1 Introduction

The interest rate risk of banks is a topic of current high relevance for three main reasons: current developments in monetary policy, in economic research, as well as in banking regulation.

In the United States of America (US) an interest rate turnaround is taking place presently. The Federal Reserve System (FED) ended its series of large-scale asset purchases after six years in October 2014. And after seven years with a target for the federal funds rate of nearly zero, the FED increased this target for the first time in December 2015 and again in December 2016.[1] Contrastingly, in the euro area (EA) interest rates are kept low for now. The European Central Bank (ECB) decreased the interest rate on the main refinancing operations to zero in March 2016. And the ECB increased the average monthly volume of its expanded asset purchase program also in March 2016 from €60 billion to €80 billion and extended the programme in December 2016.[2] Even though an interest rate turnaround does not seem to be immediately imminent in the EA, it may well be the case that the current developments in the US map out the future course. These two developments in monetary policy make the exposure of banks to changes in interest rates, and thus banks' interest rate risk, a topic of current high relevance: the present interest rate turnaround in the US, and the medium-term prospect of an interest rate turnaround in the EA as well.

In monetary economics, the research on the transmission of monetary policy has recently started to produce substantial output on the risk-taking channel. Through this transmission channel, monetary policy affects the risk-taking of lenders, and thus of banks. While this new branch of research initially focused entirely on monetary policy's influence on banks' taking of credit risk, most recently the influence on banks' taking of interest rate risk has started to attract attention. In the microeconomics of banking, there just has been a shift from the paradigm of asymmetric information to the paradigm of risk. According to this new paradigm of risk, banks are considered to be quintessential risk-takers also of systematic risks. And these systematic risks include interest rate risk. The paradigm shift in the microeconomics of banking links in with a modern understanding of banking gaining momentum in economics research. According to the traditional understanding, which has been the orthodoxy of economic research until now, banking is the intermediation of loanable funds. This understanding is goods-based, as a bank is considered to collect resources from one group of clients in the shape of deposits for example, and to distribute these resources to another group of clients in the shape of loans for example. In contrast, according to the modern understanding, banking is financing through money creation. This understanding is money-based, as a bank is considered to create a deposit, and hence a form of money, as it makes a loan in the interaction with the same client. A key difference is that asset transformation in the shape of maturity transformation is a much more natural part of banking according to the modern understanding than of banking according to the traditional understanding. This occurs because a difference in maturity between the loan and the deposit is what makes the interaction with the bank worthwhile for the client in the first place. And since maturity transformation is the primary source of interest rate risk as far as the classical banking activities such as taking deposits and making loans are concerned, the taking of interest rate risk also becomes a much more natural part of banking when the traditional understanding is replaced by the modern understanding. These three developments in economic research, make the interest rate risk of banks a topic of current high relevance: the emergence of research on the

---

[1] The relevant press releases by the Board of Governors of the FED are Board of Governors (2014), Board of Governors (2015), and Board of Governors (2016).

[2] The relevant press releases by the ECB are ECB (2016b), ECB (2016c), and ECB (2016a).

influence of monetary policy on banks' taking of interest rate risk, the shift to the new paradigm of banks as quintessential risk takers also of interest rate risk, and the modern understanding of banking gaining momentum which includes banks' taking of interest rate risk naturally.

At the moment, the banking regulation concerning the taking of interest rate risk is undergoing substantial change. After close to 12 years, the Basel Committee on Banking Supervision (BCBS) published new regulatory standards for interest rate risk in the banking book in April 2016.[3] Around the world, these new standards are currently transposed into supranational and national regulation. In Germany, the Bundesanstalt für Finanzdienstleistungsaufsicht (BaFin) initiated a consultation process on the future treatment of interest rate risk in the banking book, with the publication of a draft regulation in November 2016.[4] In contrast to the new standards by the BCBS, the draft regulation by the BaFin even includes specific capital requirements. These two developments in banking regulation, make the interest rate risk of banks a topic of current high relevance: the new global regulatory standards by the BCBS for interest rate risk in the banking book which are now in the process of implementation as well as accompanying supranational, and national initiatives such as the recent publication of draft regulation by the BaFin on the future treatment of interest rate risk in the banking book.

This dissertation picks up on the current developments, with both its focus and the open tasks it approaches. In basic terms, as far as their trading business is concerned, banks usually benefit from increased volatility in prices, which includes changes in interest rates. In contrast, through classical banking activities, which take the form of borrowing short and lending long, many banks build up sizeable negative exposures to specific types of changes of the term structure. Along these lines, the current developments in monetary policy suggest focusing on the part of interest rate risk that comes with the classical banking activities. And since this part of the interest rate risk of banks coincides more or less with the interest rate risk in a bank's banking book, current developments in banking regulation suggest the same focus. The interest rate risk in the banking book is currently on the top of the regulators' agenda, and its future treatment has been the subject of an intense debate. As a result of this debate, the new regulatory standards by the BCBS only include non-uniformly increased disclosure requirements and still do not feature capital requirements. In the face of this, two open tasks can be identified. First, it is still worth making every effort to increase the transparency of banks' taking of interest rate risk through classical banking activities and in their banking books. This remains a valuable contribution to guiding supervisors' attention as well as to enhancing market discipline. Second, the new interest rate shock scenarios defined by the BCBS are undoubtedly worth being examined thoroughly. In particular and given the changing interest rate environment, an empirical assessment of their adequacy is in order. Current developments in economic research also suggest focusing on banks' interest rate risk from classical banking activities. The interest rate risk the taking of which can be explained naturally, given the modern understanding of banking, is of this type. And since the paradigm shift in the microeconomics of banking, this is the type of interest rate risk that banks are considered to be quintessentially taking. Finally, the risk-taking channel, which is currently investigated intensively in monetary economics concerns risk-taking of lenders, not of traders. Here, a third open task can be identified. The few already existing contributions to the research on the risk-taking channel, in so far as it concerns banks' interest rate risk, are all one-dimensional, in that they only accommodate a positive link between the term spread and banks' maturity transformation. Until now, a possible search for yield in interest rate risk has not been taken into account. This research gap is worth addressing.

This dissertation focuses on the interest rate risk of banks from classical banking activities and in their banking books. Also it approaches the open tasks identified. It increases the transparency

---

[3] The relevant publication is BCBS (2016).
[4] The publications referred to here is BaFin (2016).

of banks' taking of interest rate risk in an investigation built on publicly available statistics. Additionally, it empirically assesses the adequacy of past, current and future supervisory interest rate shock scenarios in Germany. Finally, it addresses the research gap of a possible search for yield of banks in interest rate risk.

This dissertation has two main parts. The first part covers the foundations, while the second presents the extensions. These two main parts are preceded by the introduction at hand in Chapter 1 and are followed by the conclusion in Chapter 9. The introduction motivates this dissertation and provides an overview. The conclusion summarizes the key results and points to policy implications. The two main parts are built up as follows:

The first main part covers the foundations and is made up of four chapters. Chapter 2 provides the most important definitions. Chapters 3 and 4 review the literature of the two main strands of research this dissertation builds upon, namely the microeconomics of banking and the monetary economics of the transmission channels, and identify points of reference as well as research gaps. Chapter 5 then uncovers specifics of the treatment of interest rate risk in economics and sets the stage for the extensions.

The second main part assembles the extensions and consists of three chapters each approaching one of the open tasks identified. Chapter 6 investigates what publicly available statistics tell us about the interest rate risk of banks in Germany. Chapter 7 empirically assesses the adequacy of supervisory interest rate shock scenarios in Germany. Finally, Chapter 8 develops a theoretical rationale for banks' search for yield in interest rate risk and searches for empirical evidence for German banks. On a chapter level, the structure of this dissertation is presented in Figure 1.1.

Building on the foundations, the extensions in this dissertation produce new results. On the highest level of aggregation, these new results can be summarized as follows: First, from publicly available statistics, it can be inferred that the interest rate risk from on-balance sheet term transformation of banks in Germany exceeds the euro area average and is bound to increase even further. German banks push for shorter-term funding and hardly counteract the increased demand for longer-term loans. Within Germany, savings banks and cooperative banks are particularly engaged. Second, the supervisory interest rate shock scenarios are found to be increasingly detached both from the historic and the forecasted development of interest rates in Germany. In particular, German banks have been exposed to fewer and smaller adverse changes of the term structure. This increasingly limits the informative content of mere exposure measures such as the Basel interest rate coefficient when used as risk measures as is common practice in banking supervision and economic research. An impact assessment further supports the conclusion that the least that is required is a more comprehensive set of shock scenarios. Third and finally, there is a reasonable theoretical rationale and there is strong empirical evidence for banks' search for yield in interest rate risk. In addition to the established positive link between the term spread and the taking of interest rate risk by banks an additional negative link can be explained theoretically and there is significant empirical evidence for its existence and relevance. There is even a threshold of income below which banks' search for yield in interest rate risk surfaces openly.

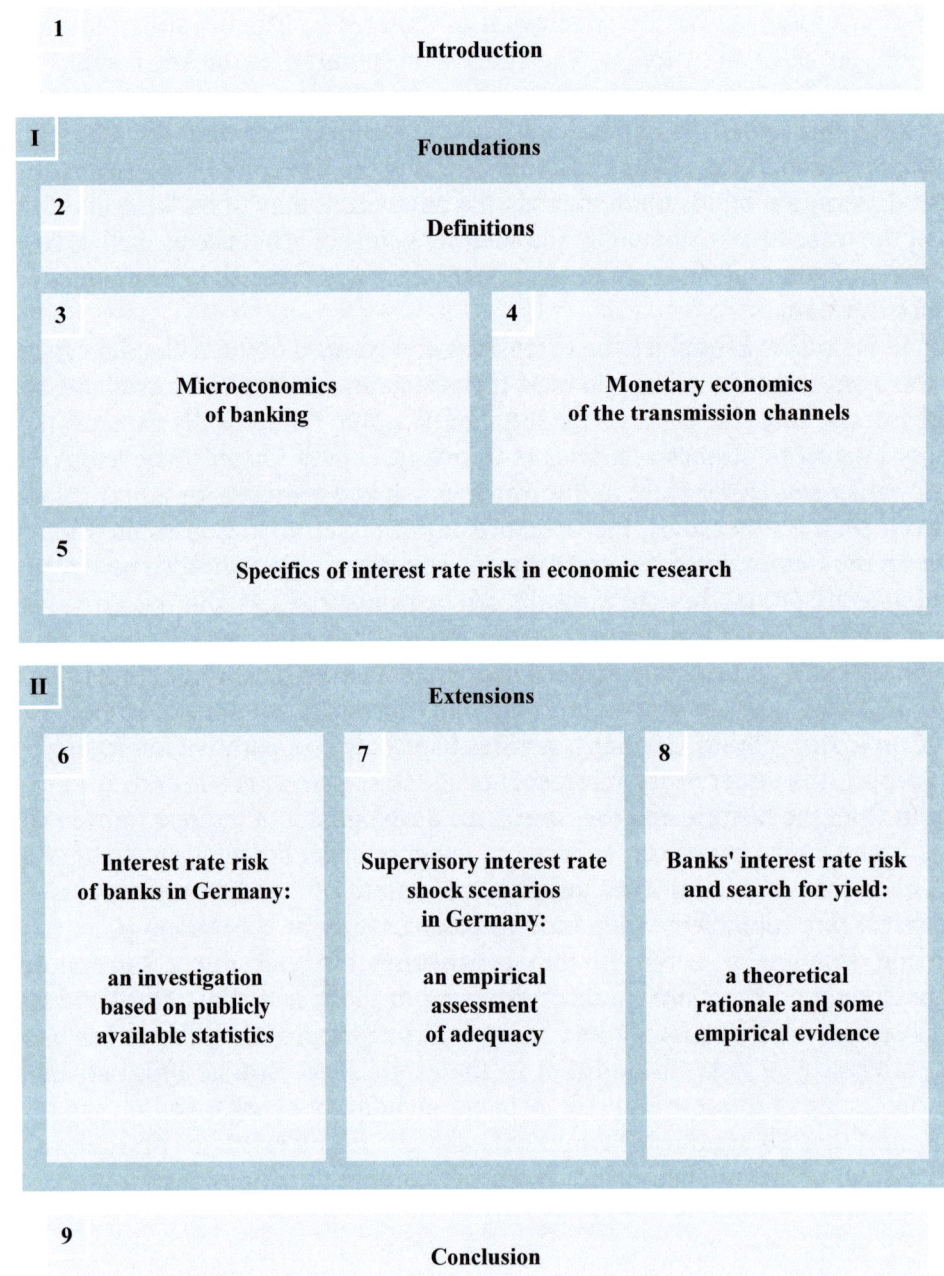

Figure 1.1: Structure of this dissertation on the chapter level.

I Foundations

Chapter 2 Definitions

This scientific investigation starts with providing the definitions of the key concepts involved. These key concepts include the concept of a bank, the concept of interest rate risk, and the concept of the term spread. Providing definitions for these key concepts promotes understanding and limits ambiguity. The three definitions are presented in turn. For banks a traditional and a modern definition are distinguished.

2.1 Defining banks: traditional version

A generally accepted definition of a bank does not exist. However, there is a legal definition that captures very well what may be regarded as the traditional understanding of banks. This is the definition of a credit institution as provided by the European Union. It is presented below. The understanding of banks this definition captures is traditional in the sense that it has been the dominant understanding of banks both in economics and in the educated public for a long time now.

2.1.1 Characterizing activities and other ventures

The European Union (EU) defines a credit institution as an "undertaking the business of which is to take deposits or other repayable funds from the public and to grant credits for its own account" (Regulation (EU) No 575/2013 Article 4). First, this definition does not restrict the scope of activities of a credit institution. It identifies two activities, such that if and only if these are among the core activities of an institution, it is a credit institution. But doing so, it permits every other activity as a further core or non-core activity of a credit institution.[5] Second, the definition through the core activities of taking deposits or other repayable funds and granting credits for its own account characterises a credit institution as performing a particular kind of financial intermediation. Taking deposits or other repayable funds and granting credits for its own account implies that a credit institution sells and buys financial claims and conducts what is called asset transformation. With respect to both of these specifications, financial intermediation can also be performed differently.[6] Third, by pointing to the public for depositors or providers of other repayable funds the definition characterises a credit institution as interacting with a possibly large number of non-professional individuals in at least one of its core activities. Commonly, this is seen as extending to the other core activity as well, namely that credit institutions grant credits to the public. Traditionally, the involvement of the public has played an important role in discussions about granting privileges and inflicting burdens.[7] Granted privileges include access

---

[5] The non-restrictive nature of this definition of credit institutions becomes particularly apparent where they are delimited from investment firms. An investment firm is defined as "any legal person whose regular occupation or business is the provision of one or more investment services to third parties and/or the performance of one or more investment activities on a professional basis" (Direktive 2004/39/EC Article 4) with three exceptions one of which excludes credit institutions (Regulation (EU) No 575/2013 Article 4). Credit institutions may hence conduct the activities of investment firms.

[6] The German Banking Act, the Kreditwesengesetz (KWG), defines credit institutions more inclusively in two ways. First, both taking deposits or other repayable funds and granting credits are individually sufficient conditions for an undertaking to be a credit institution. Second, neither taking deposits or other repayable funds nor granting credits is a necessary condition for an undertaking to be a credit institution. The KWG includes nine other activities that are each sufficient conditions but of which none individually is a necessary condition for an undertaking to be a credit institution (KWG Article 1).

[7] Note that this involvement of the public is commonly cited by economists to justify the claim that credit institutions provide a public good (Freixas and Rochet 2008, pp. 1).

to central bank liquidity and to safety nets such as public deposit insurance. Inflicted burdens include regulation and oversight in order to ensure consumer protection and overall financial stability.

The EU definition of a credit institution suggests to distinguish activities conducted on a credit institution's own account from activities conducted on account of its customers.[8] And from a business perspective, the numerous activities actual credit institutions conduct are usually clustered into commercial banking and investment banking (Choudhry 2012, pp. 8-9).[9] Commercial banking most prominently includes activities related to performing credit intermediation, which are the defining activities of credit institutions, namely taking deposits as well as other repayable funds and granting credits, on the credit institution's own account. But commercial banking also extends to activities on account of the customers such as payment transactions, brokerage of securities, and custody of valuables. Investment banking most prominently includes activities related to assisting clients in raising funds in financial markets, which are facilitating the issuance of securities on account of the customer as well as underwriting and market making on the credit institutions own account. As further activities on account of the customer, investment banking comprises facilitating mergers and acquisitions plus asset management. And as another activity on account of the credit institution, investment banking contains proprietary trading. Furthermore, the two distinctions also allow to locate the sources of the three basic types of income of credit institutions. Commercial banking activities conducted on the credit institution's own account yield the net interest income. Investment banking activities conducted on the credit institution's own account yield the trading income.[10] And activities conducted on the account of the customer yield fees and commissions irrespective of them being commercial or investment banking activities. Finally, it should be noted that the scopes of activities of actual credit institutions differ and that a credit institution does not necessarily conduct activities in any category other than commercial banking on its own account. This definition of a credit institution by the EU captures the traditional understanding of banks is very well. According to this understanding banks may be engaged in very diverse activities. But the defining activity of banks is financial intermediation through selling and buying financial claims by taking deposits and granting credits from and to the general public, respectively.

2.1.2 Financial intermediation and asset transformation

Universally, financial intermediation consists in arranging for one external party to sell a financial claim and for another external party to buy a financial claim (Greenbaum and Thakor 2007, pp. 43-50). Two distinctions allow to demarcate the main particularities of taking deposits or other repayable funds and granting credits, i.e. of the defining core activities of a credit institution, as an instance of financial intermediation. First, the financial transaction between the external parties may be direct or indirect. In the former case, the financial intermediary merely engineers the transaction, i.e. the selling and buying by the two external parties are two sides of the same transaction with one another. In the latter case, the transaction happens via the financial intermediary, i.e. the selling and buying by the two external parties are each one side of two separate transactions with the financial intermediary which itself in turn buys and sells the financial claim. Now, taking deposits or other repayable funds and granting loans clearly is

---

[8]   Note that aiming at accommodating the variety of activities actual credit institutions conduct, the CRR standardised framework maps 21 distinct activity bundles to eight business lines (Regulation (EU) No 575/2013 Article 317).

[9]   Note that the distinction between commercial banking and investment banking was coined by the U.S. Banking Act of 1933, commonly referred to as the Glass-Steagall Act. This act separated commercial banks and investment banks through detailed provisions regarding the (domestic) securities operations of the former (Benston 1990, pp. 1-2, 6-14).

[10]   Note that there is one noteworthy ambiguity. Interest payments received as a result of holding debt securities might be treated as adding to the trading or alternatively to the net interest income (Choudhry 2012, pp. 3-6).

an instance of the latter case. Second, the financial claims transacted may be equal or unequal. Obviously, the financial claims can only be unequal, if the transaction between the external parties is indirect such that there are two separate transactions with the financial intermediary. In this case, the financial intermediary can sell one financial claim and buy a different one, i.e. conduct what is called an asset transformation. Now, putting deposits or other repayable funds to use for granting credits usually comes with such a mismatch of financial claims.

Every mismatch between the financial claims a credit institution buys and sells constitutes an asset transformation. But traditionally volume transformation, maturity transformation, and risk transformation are highlighted as the three main dimensions (Arnold 2013, pp. 30-31). Another common dimension is currency transformation. Asset transformation accompanies many activities, and it is obvious in the financial intermediation consisting in taking deposits and granting credits. Volume transformation occurs, if the lot sizes differ, e.g. if many small deposits are put to use for one large credit. Maturity transformation occurs, if the possible timings of cash-flows differ, e.g. if sight deposits are put to use for a ten year mortgage. In a strict sense, maturity transformation refers to a difference in timing of the last associated cash flows. However, the term is also commonly used to refer to differences in duration or repricing dates. The duration depends on the timing of all associated cash flows and not only of the last ones. And the repricing dates in the form of interest rate reset dates on either side can be sooner than the last associated cash flows. Risk transformation occurs, if the risk-return profiles differ, e.g. a deposit account at a bank usually has both a lower risk and a lower return than a non-top tier corporate bond. Last but not least, currency transformation occurs, if currencies differ, e.g. if deposits denominated in EUR are put to use for a credit denominated in USD. Now, it should be noted that the prices for which the financial claims are bought and sold may also differ, and usually do, as this is a way for financial intermediaries to generate income. Nevertheless, this sort of mismatch does not constitute an asset transformation, since it does not concern the financial claims but their prices.

2.1.3 Granted privileges and inflicted burdens

Commonly, credit institutions enjoy the privilege of access to central bank liquidity and the safety net of public deposit insurance.[11] With access to central bank liquidity a credit institutions can borrow money from the central bank for a defined interest rate, for a short period of time, and given that it provides high quality collateral.[12] Covered by public deposit insurance the deposits at a credit institution are protected up to a certain level or in full and its membership in the deposit insurance is not at the discretion of the credit institution.[13] But credit institutions are also subject to a large number of regulations and oversight through dedicated authorities. The recent financial crises was generally perceived as showing that regulation and oversight had been insufficient. Since then, numerous initiatives have aimed at improvements, resulting in stricter regulations and enhanced oversight.

---

[11] Note that the Federal Reserve System (FED) as well as the Bank of England (BoE) have extended the range of financial institutions with excess to central bank liquidity significantly in the recent past. In 2008 the FED introduced the Primary Dealer Credit Facility available to all primary dealers (see Board of Governors (2008)). And since 2014 the BoE includes broker-dealers and central counterparties in its Sterling Monetary Framework (see BoE (2014)). Still, shadow banks are sometimes defined as entities conducting credit intermediation of some sort (see FSB 2014, p. 1) without access to central bank liquidity or public deposit insurance (Pozsar et al. 2013, p. 1). For an overview of definitions of shadow banking that can be found in the literature (see IMF 2014, p. 91).

[12] The most prominent examples for instruments used to allow certain financial institutions access to central bank liquidity are the FED's discount window credit and the ECB's marginal lending facility.

[13] For example, the Federal Deposit Insurance Cooperation in the US covers deposits up to $ 250.000 (Dodd-Frank Act Section 335) and the EU deposit guarantee scheme covers deposits up to €100.000 (Directive 2014/49/EU Article 6).

2.2 Defining banks: modern version

According to the traditional understanding, the core business of banks consists in the intermediation of loanable funds. Banks take deposits and make loans by collecting loanable funds from one group of agents and lending them out to another. Loanable funds are first produced by non-banks through saving and finally used up by other non-banks through spending. Banks channel loanable funds in-between. And the amount of loanable funds handed in to banks limits the amount they can hand out.

This traditional understanding of the core business of banks is fundamentally goods-based. Loanable funds are seen as just another type of goods. In particular, they are considered to be a scarce resource. And banks are seen as just another type of intermediaries. That is, they are considered to function as conduits for goods. Accordingly, the core business of banks as traditionally understood can be illustrated with tangible goods as loanable funds. Bofinger (2015), for example, uses coconuts.

But there also exists an alternative understanding of the core business of banks according to which it consist in financing through money creation. This understanding is essentially money-based.[14] This alternative understanding is modern in two respects. First, it arguably captures what modern banks actually do. This is shown by Werner (2014). Second, it is gaining momentum and might replace the traditional understanding as the orthodoxy of economic research. This is partly due to McLeay et al. (2014).[15]

2.2.1 Money creation

The modern understanding of the core business of banks centers around the following insight. When a bank makes a loan to one of its customers, it credits this customer's deposit account. The bank makes two matching bookkeeping-entries, one for the new loan on the asset side and one for the new deposit on the liability side of its balance sheet. And by doing so the bank creates money since bank deposits can be used to repay any debt including taxes.[16] Recently, Werner (2014), McLeay et al. (2014), and Jakab and Kumhof (2015) have called attention to this fact.[17] Even though it has long been recognized, it has so far shaped neither economic research nor the public debate.[18]

Just like the bank creates money when it makes a loan, the customer destroys money when he repays the loan. On the balance sheet of the bank two matching bookkeeping-entries disappear, the repaid loan on the asset side and the deposits used for repayment on the liabilities side. But the making and repaying of loans are not the only ways in which money is created and destroyed in the interaction between banks and non-banks, that is the government, firms, and households.

---

[14] There are different terms in use in the literature to name these two different understandings of the core business of banks. The terms "intermediation of loanable funds" and "financing through money creation" are borrowed from Jakab and Kumhof (2015). The alternative terms "financial intermediation theory of banking" and "credit creation theory of banking" are used by Werner (2014).

[15] This BoE Quarterly Bulletin article attracted attention even from mainstream media such as theguardian.com (Graeber (2014)).

[16] As is explained below, one exception is debt between banks which can only be repaid with reserves.

[17] The following exposition mainly draws on these three sources.

[18] Werner (2014) and Jakab and Kumhof (2015) present extensive collections of quotes to establish that the modern understanding of the core business of banks is not new. They show that it has been around at least since the middle of the nineteenth century and spread at the beginning of the twentieth century in the writings of Macleod (1855) and Wicksell (1906). They also try to find out how this understanding became a heterodoxy with the orthodoxy being the understanding of the core business of banks according to which they intermediate loanable funds. They point to the influential works of Keynes (1930, 1936) and Gurley and Shaw (1955, 1956) as milestones in this development. It is particularly interesting to note that according to Werner (2014) Keynes (1930, 1936) seems to agree with the understanding of banks as intermediaries of loanable funds in contrast to his earlier writings.

A bank creates money whenever it buys an asset from a non-bank, for example a government bond. And a non-bank destroys money whenever it buys an asset from a bank, for example a government bond.

In order to fully comprehend the modern understanding of the core business of banks it is necessary to distinguish different types of money. The money created by banks in the form of deposits is called book money. The money created by the central bank in the form of reserves and currency is called central bank money.[19] Deposits and currency make up the money that is in circulation in the economy and which is referred to as broad money. And reserves only circulate as money between banks and between banks and the central bank and are referred to as base money. Last but not least, a bank can exchange reserves for currency at the central bank and vice versa.

There are three basic options for what happens with the money a bank creates by crediting one of its customer's accounts with a deposit.[20] First, the money may remain in this account or be transferred to another account at the same bank. In this case the balance sheet of the bank does not change. Second, the money may be withdrawn in the form of currency. In this case the bank exchanges some of its reserves for currency which it then hands out and hence its reserves decrease along with deposits. Third, the money may be transferred to an account at another bank. In this case the bank transfers a matching amount of reserves to this other bank[21] and hence again its reserves decrease along with deposits.

The insight that banks can create money raises many questions. Two particularly interesting are, what determines the amount of money banks create, and, what does this imply for economic research. The first of these two questions arises naturally, when one considers the three basic options for what happens with the money a bank creates. Indeed, bank reserves are a frequently referred to supposedly limiting factor for banks' money creation. The second of these questions is posed in view of the fact that economic research has long been shaped by the hence so called traditional understanding of the core business of banking. Both questions are briefly addressed below.

2.2.2 Determining factors

According to the traditional understanding of the core business of banks, banks cannot create money individually or as a system. Banks simply channel money from one group of non-banks to another group of non-banks. According to the modern understanding of the core business of banks, banks can create money individually. A bank makes a loan to a non-bank or buys an asset from a non-bank and in this process deposits come into existence through a bookkeeping-entry. Now there is a third view that says that banks cannot create money individually but can as a system. This view rests on what is usually called the deposit multiplier.[22]

The deposit multiplier story runs as follows. A bank keeps a certain fraction of the deposits of its customers as reserves and uses the remaining funds to make loans. These loans again end up as as deposits at banks and these banks again keep a fraction of these deposits as reserves and use the remaining funds to make loans. As this process continues, the initial deposits are multiplied by being lent out repeatedly, reduced only by the reserves kept by banks when making

---

[19] One might alternatively distinguish between reserves in the form of deposits banks have in their accounts at the central bank and reserves in the form of currency they store in vaults.

[20] To be precise, these three basic options apply to all money in a bank's customer accounts, that is not only the money created by the bank itself but also to money created by other banks and then transferred.

[21] This is called settling the transaction.

[22] Again, the term "deposit multiplier" is taken from Jakab and Kumhof (2015). Werner (2014) calls the view the "fractional reserve theory". Werner (2014) also provides the standard reference for this delimitation of the three understandings or views.

a new loan. Commonly, this story is told assuming a fractional reserve requirement.[23] But it may also be told referring to the self-interest of banks to hold some reserves for covering deposit withdrawals and transfers. The deposit multiplier story suffers from the same deficit as the traditional understanding of the core business of banks. It features loanable funds that behave like goods and not like money.[24]

However, the deposit multiplier story also leads to the following reasoning. If the central bank controls the amount of reserves, and if there is a fractional reserve requirement, then this limits the amount of book money banks can create. Now it is true that, if an amount equivalent to a certain fraction of deposits has to be held in reserves, the required amount of reserves puts a limit to the amount of deposits. But at least in advanced economies and normal times is not true that the central bank controls the amount of reserves. Instead the central bank targets an interest rate. The central bank usually conducts open market operations to bring this interest rate about and in this process buys or sells assets from and to banks injecting or extracting reserves. But the central bank does not simply supply some fixed amount of reserves and controls this amount. Instead, the central bank supplies that amount of reserves at which the interest rate charged between banks for the inter-bank lending of these reserves meets the targeted interest rate. This interest rate is the parameter the central bank targets and aims to control. The amount of reserves necessary to be supplied is determined by the inter-bank market and hence an endogenous variable.

That the central bank supplies an amount of reserves which is determined endogenously is not to say that reserves are not a scarce resource. On the contrary, the interest rate targeted by the central bank comes about as a market price that expresses the scarcity of reserves. As described above, the reserves of an individual bank are reduced when deposits are withdrawn in the form of currency and when deposit are transferred to another bank. Inversely, the reserves of the bank are increased when deposits are paid-in in the form of currency and when deposits are transferred from another bank. At this point some part of the traditional understanding of the core business resurfaces. In the typical fragmented banking sector, it is more likely than not that the deposit created by a bank in the curse of making a loan is transferred to another bank. The bank that made the loan is then left with the same amount of deposits as before but with less reserves. And a natural way for the bank to increase its amount of reserves again is to induce transfers of deposits from other banks. Along these lines, making a loan leads to a demand for deposits, and this might be seen as resembling the traditional understanding on the individual bank level, that is on the micro level. The actual determining factor for the size of the core business of a bank these considerations point to is its profitability. The amount of money a bank creates in the form of deposits in the process of making loans is determined by the lending opportunities available and the borrowing conditions prevailing. Under typical market conditions, a bank has to lower the interest rates it charges on loans to increase its loan volume and raise the interest rate it pays on deposits in order to attract transfers of deposits from other banks. And at some point, a lower bound of the net interest income is reached and a further increase of its core business would be unprofitable for the bank. Besides profitability there are two other determining factors. The second one is risk. For example, instead of lowering the interest rate it charges on loans, a bank can also change its lending standards or terms and conditions in order to increase its loan volume. If the bank makes loans to less creditworthy borrowers, it increases its credit risk. If the bank makes loans with a longer maturity or repricing period, it increases its liquidity risk or its interest rate risk. Of course, the liquidity risk and interest rate risk of the bank are also affected by changes to the liabilities side of its balance sheet. The third one is regulation. In particular, there are capital and liquidity requirements. The classic reference for these three determining factors for the money creation, hence for the core business of banks, is Tobin (1965).

---

[23] Such a reserve requirement is in force today in the US and the euro area but not in the UK, for example.
[24] Put differently, it features deposits but no book money.

2.2.3 Research implications

It is natural to expect that a shift from the traditional to the modern understanding of the core business of banks has important research implications for macroeconomics and for monetary economics in particular. Jakab and Kumhof (2015) develop a DSGE model in which banks finance through money creation and compare it to a DSGE model in which banks intermediate loanable funds. They find that in their model, shocks have a larger and faster effect on banks' balance sheets and ultimately a more pronounced impact on the real economy. They trace this back to the fact that creating money can happen instantaneously and discontinuously while accumulating loanable funds must happen slowly and continuously since these funds have to be produced first.

It is less clear what a shift from the traditional to the modern understanding of the core business of banks implies for research in microeconomics. As discussed above, the determining factors for the individual bank are profitability, risk, and regulation. And as for the individual bank deposits behave like a scarce resource, the traditional understanding of banks resurfaces. There is a market and mainly depending on the interest rate a bank offers it attracts more or less payment-ins in the form of currency or transfers of deposits from other banks. At least this makes clear that under the modern understanding a microeconomic model cannot plausibly feature a binding volume constraint of deposits. A more general research implication is that it becomes natural to see banks as essential risk-takers because their core business consists in producing mismatching claims. Asset transformation is not some feature that needs to be explained by further assumption but rather the reason for customers to interact with a bank in its core business. With respect to the taking of interest rate risk by banks, the shift from the traditional to the modern understanding of the core business of banks has an obvious research implication. Under the modern understanding the difference in maturities of deposits and loans is a natural result. A customer takes out a loan precisely because he needs financing he can only pay back later. Under the traditional understanding the fact that deposits have a shorter maturity than loans can only be explained with reference to liquidity preferences on the side of the depositors and some long run investment projects on the side of the borrowers.

2.3 Defining interest rate risk

There exists a general accepted definition of interest rate risk. It is the definition of interest rate risk provided by the Basel Committee on Banking Supervision which is presented below. This definition features three dimensions of interest rate risk, namely the dimensions of shock, exposure, and effect. The dimension of shock concerns possible changes in interest rates. The dimension of exposure concerns the actual positions of a bank. And the dimension of effect concerns the impacts of a possible changes in interest rates given the actual positions of a bank.

Conducting the traditional banking activities of taking deposits and granting loans, most commonly in the form of borrowing short and lending long, a bank does not only take interest rate risk but also liquidity risk and credit risk. These other two risks and their links to interest rate risk are also presented below.

2.3.1 Dimensions of interest rate risk

The Basel Committee on Banking Supervision (BCBS) defines interest rate risk as the "exposure of a bank's financial condition to adverse movements in interest rates" and effectively continues to distinguish between three kinds of shocks, three types of exposure, and two sorts of effect (BCBS 2004, pp. 5-7).[25]

The first kind of shock is a parallel shift of a yield curve. Here the yield for every maturity is increased or decreased by the same delta. The second kind of shock is a change in shape of a yield curve. Here the deltas vary between maturities. And the third kind of shock is a movement of yield curves relative to one another. This is the result of one of the first two kinds of movements of one yield curve with another yield curve not moving in exactly the same way.

The first type of exposure is a timing mismatch. Here the roll-over or repricing dates of assets and liabilities and of corresponding off-balance sheet items differ and thus different maturities are relevant. The second type of exposure is a basis mismatch. Here the relevant interest rate denominations differs and thus different yield curves are relevant.[26] And the third type of exposure is optionality. This stands for all options including embedded ones, such as the right of a customer to withdraw all money from his current account at any point in time. Such options possibly worsen any of the first two types of exposure as a customer rationally exercises an option only if doing so is advantageous for him.

The first sort of effect is the impact on economic value. The net present value of future cash flows depends on the presently prevailing interest rates.[27] Thus, a change in interest rates can result in an instant change in economic value. And the second sort of effect is the impact on earnings. The rolling-over and repricing of assets and liabilities and of corresponding off-balance sheet items requires to make business given the current interest rates. Hence, a change in interest rates can result in a progressive change in earnings.[28] Obviously, the time profile of such a progressive change in earnings can take various forms. It is possible that a certain change in interest rates initially has a positive net effect and later has a negative net effect on the period earnings of a bank. A certain business model can first become more profitable only to become less profitable as a critical share of the portfolio is rolled over or repriced.[29]

2.3.2 Interest rate risk and liquidity risk

Two types of liquidity risk are distinguished by the BCBS (BCBS 2008, p. 1). First, funding liquidity risk is the "risk that the firm will not be able to meet efficiently both expected and unexpected current and future cash flow and collateral needs without affecting either daily operations or the financial condition of the firm". Second, market liquidity risk is the "risk that a firm cannot easily offset or eliminate a position at the market price because of inadequate market depth or market disruption".

Funding liquidity risk is the risk that a not further defined cause has the effect that a firm cannot meet its financial obligations as they come due. As what may be called an "effect-risk" it is of the same type as solvency risk, that is the risk of a negative equity value. And market liquidity risk is the risk that that the current inability to obtain a normal market price has a not further defined effect on a firm. As what may be called a "cause-risk" it is of the same type as normal

---

[25] Actually the BCBS does explicitly distinguish between shocks and exposures but lists four sources of interest rate risk, namely repricing risk, yield curve risk, basis risk, and optionality. But these in effect represent different combinations of kinds of movements of interest rates and certain positions a bank can take.

[26] Note that this kind of mismatch is sometimes inaccurately called interest rate mismatch.

[27] Note that the presently prevailing or current interest rates are the interest rates at this point for all maturities and claims. In particular, the misunderstanding should be avoided that only short-term interest rates are referred to.

[28] Hellwig (1994) introduces two sub-types of interest rate risk, namely valuation risk and reinvestment opportunity risk, to cover these two sorts of effect.

[29] For example, a change in the form of an downward shift and flattening of the relevant yield curve might at first make it more profitable to fund long-term assets by short-term liabilities (downward shift of the yield curve). But as more and more of the long-term assets mature, this simple business model of maturity transformation becomes less profitable (flattening of the yield curve).

market price risk, which includes the risk of adverse movements in interest rates. When market liquidity risk induces funding liquidity risk this is commonly referred to just as liquidity risk.

Besides interest rate risk, liquidity risk is the second major risk that stems from a mismatch between assets and liabilities plus possibly associated off-balance sheet items.[30] For this reason interest rate risk and liquidity risk are the two focal points of banks' asset liability management. How closely interest rate risk and liquidity risk are related becomes particularly apparent in the case where borrowing short and lending long is the common source. This commonly involves both a timing mismatch in a possible adjustment of interest rates and a timing mismatch in roll-over dates. And of these timing-mismatches the first constitutes an interest rate risk exposure and the second a liquidity risk exposure.

The interaction of interest rate risk and liquidity risk as well as liquidity risk in isolation are the topics of some well known contributions to economic research, of which the following two are the most prominent. Hellwig (1994) adds technology induced interest rate risk to the model of Diamond and Dybvig (1983), which already features liquidity risk, and derives the resulting risk allocation between agents. Diamond and Rajan (2001) build on the incentive structure developed by Diamond (1984) and advance a theoretical framework that features the liquidity risk of a bank as a source of financial instability that aligns incentives in such a way that liquidity creation becomes possible.

2.3.3 Interest rate risk and credit risk

The BCBS defines credit risk as "the potential that a bank borrower or counterparty will fail to meet its obligations in accordance with agreed terms" (BCBS 2000, p. 1). Defined as such, credit risk concerns the asset side of the balance sheet only but does not only stem from credits or loans the borrowers may default on but from all agreements the counterparties may default on. For this reason it is also frequently referred to simply as default risk.

One phenomenon that receives particular attention in the economic literature on credit risk is credit rationing. Credit rationing is a credit market outcome in which interest rates do not equate demand and supply but in which credit demand exceeds credit supply. Most prominently, Stiglitz and Weiss (1981), elaborated on at length by Jaffee and Stiglitz (1990), and Williamson (1987), and presented in brief by Freixas and Rochet (2008), identify the classical problems resulting from asymmetric information as the underlying causes for this phenomenon and provide explanations for credit rationing as an equilibrium solution in the presence of adverse selection and moral hazard or costly state verification, respectively. They develop rationales for what is today established as the backward-bending credit supply function. This concept captures the important insight that the expected return of a credit can be a non-monotonic function of the interest rate. More specifically, an increase of the interest rate beyond a certain threshold does not further increase but reversely decreases the expected return of the credit because it increases the credit risk excessively.

The economic literature on credit rationing already features a link between interest rate risk and credit risk implicitly. After all, the explanations this literature provides build on movements in interest rates leading to changes in credit risk. More recent publications address the relationship between interest rate risk an credit risk explicitly. Among the first, Drehmann et al. (2010) and Alessandri and Drehmann (2010) analyze banks' overall exposure to both types of risks with a particular focus on their interaction. They establish two further links between interest rate risk and credit risk. They do not only account for the dependency of credit risk on changes in interest rates, but they also account for common macroeconomic risk factors that drive both interest rate risk and credit risk. Furthermore, they account for the impact of credit risk on the net interest

---

[30] Another risk of this kind that is particularly relevant for international banks is foreign exchange risk.

income. The common macroeconomic risk factors such as the rate of economic growth influence the probabilities of default of borrowers as well as reference and more generally market interest rates. The impact of credit risk on the net interest income is not limited to actual defaults but also stems from accounting for possible defaults in the setting of interest rates.

Summing up, the three links between interest rate risk and credit risk so far established in the economic literature are the following. First, there is a possible trade-off between higher interest rates charged and higher credit risk. Second, interest rate risk and credit risk at least in part depend on the same economic developments. Third, interest rate risk and credit risk both influence the net interest income to some extend. Crucially, the trade-off between higher interest rates charged and higher credit risk as featured in the first of these links easily translates into a trade-off between higher interest rate risk and higher credit risk. For example, it is easy to think of a scenario in which a bank shields a borrower from changes in interest rates by providing a long-term fixed-rate loan and in turn is rewarded with an increased probability of full repayment. In this scenario the bank decreases its credit risk but other things being equal increases its interest rate risk.

2.4 Defining the term spread

The profitability of the traditional banking activity of taking deposits and granting loans, most commonly in the form of borrowing short and lending long, critically depends on the term spread. For the interest rate risk of banks it is of utmost importance. But it also receives a lot of attention more generally. The term spread measures the slope of a yield curve the importance of which is underlined by the fact that it is the only shape parameter the classical characterizations of yield curves refer to. Four hypothesis have emerged as governing the literature that aims at explaining the term spread of the default-free yield curve which is the basis for any yield curve that includes some default-risk premium. A macroeconomic application of the term spread is its use as an indicator with predictive content for changes in macroeconomic variables particularly for changes in the output growth. Understanding the term spread as a measure is an essential prerequisite for the main analysis. Touching on hypothesis that explain the term spread and its use in forecasting primarily serves the purpose of shedding some light on how the it features in other parts of economic research.

2.4.1 Slope measure

An interest rate is the price for a provision of funds for a given period of time expressed as a fraction of the principal and usually in per annum terms (see ECB 2004, p. 225). The period of time the funds are provided for is called the maturity and the schedule of interest rates across maturities is known as the term structure of interest rates or the yield curve (Hull 2012, p. 159).[31] Factors other than the maturity that interest rates depend on mark separate yield curves.[32]

The term spread of a yield curve measures its slope as the difference between long-term and short-term interest rates. Therefore, any yield curve can be described by as many term spreads as there are pairs of long-term and short-term interest rates. And it is indeed necessary to select two concrete maturities if one is interested in the precise numerical value of the term spread. Nevertheless, it is also common to speak of the term spread of a given yield curve without referring to two definite maturities for making qualitative instead of quantitative statements. Because in so far as a yield curve steepens or flattens term spreads across large parts of the

---

[31] Some contributions to the literature reserve the term structure of interest rates for the functional relationship and the yield curve for its graphic representation. But since this distinction is not very common, it is not adopted here.

[32] For example, different yield curves exist for different default probabilities of the borrower.

relevant yield curve move in the same way and hence may collectively be referred to as the term spread.

The common basic categories employed in the categorization of a yield curve only refer to its slope, that is its term spread. A yield curve is characterized as upward sloping or downward sloping or flat, that is as having a positive or a negative or no term spread. Referring to the frequency of observations, an upward sloping yield curve is called normal and a downward sloping yield curve is called inverted. Other less commonly used parameters for the description of a yield curve are its level and its curvature.

2.4.2 Governing hypotheses

The default-free yield curve is of particular interest because every yield curve that embodies some non-zero default risk can be analyzed into the default-free yield curve and a risk premium. The default-free yield curve features the dependency of interest rates on maturity in isolation and therefore its term spread measures a relationship of fundamental economic importance. A common proxy for the default-free yield curve is the yield curve of government bonds with the highest rating from the economic area of interest.

Existing theories of the term spread of the default-free yield curve are generally categorized under one of four governing hypothesis (see e.g. Cox et al. 1985). First, according to the expectation hypothesis current long-term rates can be explained as cumulated current and expected future short-term rates. In its basic form, this hypothesis equates the return of a long-term investment and the expected return of successive short-term investments with the same total maturity. Second, the liquidity preference hypothesis builds on the expectation hypothesis but adds the assumption of risk aversion which systematically increases long-term rates. In its standard form, this hypothesis implies a liquidity premium as a mark-up on long-term rates, due to risk aversion, that increases with maturity as uncertainty of future interest rates increases with the distance of the future. Third, according to the market segmentation hypothesis investments with different maturities are no substitutes but traded on distinct markets. In its pure form, this hypothesis entails that interest rates for different maturities are unrelated since the preferences of investors have sharp time profiles. Fourth, the preferred habitat hypothesis softens the market segmentation hypothesis and understands investments of different maturities as imperfect substitutes. In its common form, this hypothesis features the further assumption that shorter maturities are generally preferred and that that investors need to be compensated for accepting longer maturities.

These hypothesis explain the positive term spread of a normal default-free yield curve differently. According to the expectation hypothesis it implies rising short-term rates. According to the liquidity preference and the preferred habitat hypothesis it may or may not imply rising short-term rates depending on the liquidity premium or compensation demanded by investors, respectively. The market segmentation hypothesis does not explain the fact that the term spread is usually observed to be positive.

2.4.3 Predictive content

The term spread of the default-free yield curve has been observed to have predictive content for important macroeconomic variables. Most prominently, changes in the output growth have been documented to be predicted by the level of the term spread. Indeed the claim that a low level of the term spread predicts a decrease in the output growth has by now gained the status of a "stylized fact" (Benati and Goodhart 2008, p. 1237) that is to be accommodated in theoretical models.

There exists a large number of empirical studies on the forecasting relationship between the term spread and the output growth and there are also various reviews of this literature available (see e.g. Wheelock and Wohar 2009). Earlier studies examine the link between the term spread and output growth with a particular focus on the effective forecasting period and the marginal predictive content of the term spread. These studies detect that a low term spread predicts changes in the output growth up to two years in advance and also does so if other influencing factors such as the monetary policy rates are controlled for. More recent studies investigate the stability of the predictive content of the term spread for the output growth through time. Some of these studies find evidence for a deterioration of the forecasting relationship at least for the US since the mid-1980s. A parallel strand of studies focusses on the evaluation of a extraordinary low term spread as an indicator for an outright economic recession. These studies marshal empirical evidence that suggests a high reliability of this forecasting relationship.

Several other noteworthy points emerge from the literature about the term spread and its link to output growth (see e.g. Estrella 2005). The most reliable forecasts build on the level of the term spread, not on its change, and accordingly it is irrelevant to what extend a particular level of the term spread is reached due to a change in short-term or long-term rates. The predictive power of the term spread for the output growth is shown by some research contributions to depend critically on the monetary policy, that is on the reaction function of the central bank. Finally, some theoretical as well as some empirical analyses suggest that the forecasting relationship between the term spread and the output growth is bidirectional.

Chapter 3 Microeconomics of banking

One of the main topics of the microeconomics of banking is to explain what a bank is and does. Three paradigms with successive periods of largest influence on research can be identified, namely the paradigm of transaction costs, the paradigm of asymmetric information, and the paradigm of risk. Each of these three paradigms has shaped distinct explanations for why banks exist, why and how banks coexist with financial markets, and how banks compete with one another. The current paradigm of risk for the first time produces an understanding of banks as quintessential risk-takers also of systematic risks including interest rate risk. This understanding is of particular interest.

Under the assumption of general access to complete financial markets, banks are redundant institutions. The equilibrium allocations with and without banks turn out to be payoff-equivalent. Hence, it has to remain essentially unexplained what banks are and do. Credit for establishing this negative result explicitly is usually given to Fama (1980). Against this, the first paradigm of the microeconomics of banking explains banks on the basis of market imperfections in the form of transaction costs. Banks produce the means for intra-temporal and inter-temporal consumption rearrangement at minimal transaction costs. They benefit from various forms of scale economies that cannot be replicated on financial markets without incurring higher transaction costs. The canonical rationale of this paradigm of transaction costs is presented by Benston and Smith (1976). Judging classical transaction costs alone to be of insufficient magnitude, the second paradigm explains banks as alleviating market imperfections that result from asymmetric information. Banks mitigate problems of adverse selection, moral hazard, and costly state verification and facilitate investment and insurance. They buy and sell financial claims and ensure that information is credible and appropriable. The seminal justification for the shift to this paradigm of asymmetric information is given by Leland and Pyle (1977).

The largest part of the existing research on what a bank is and does is still governed by the paradigm of asymmetric information. Interest rate risk does not play a significant role in this body of literature. And this is not a coincidence. Two fundamental results oppose the meaningful treatment of this topic. Each of these results is linked to one of the most influential models of the microeconomics of banking under the paradigm of asymmetric information. The first result is linked to the model of banks as facilitating delegated monitoring drawn up by Diamond (1984). Given that investors can learn the returns of a risky technology, operated by entrepreneurs, through costly monitoring only, delegating this task to a bank is preferable, provided that the bank is sufficiently diversified. Now Diamond (1984) distinguishes unobservable and observable risks, and shows that a bank can efficiently hedge all observable risks completely, including its interest rate risk. The second result that opposes the meaningful treatment of interest rate risk is linked to the model of banks as providing liquidity insurance developed by Diamond and Dybvig (1983). In the face of a privately observed and as such uninsurable risk of a liquidity shock, the competitive solution falls short of, but a deposit contract enables optimal risk sharing between risk averse consumers. Hellwig (1994) extends this model to include technology-induced interest rate risk, and shows that in the equilibrium a bank does not bear any interest rate risk, but that this is completely allocated to its depositors or the market.

Allen and Santomero (1998) fire the starting gun for the shift to the third paradigm. They collect empirical evidence for an increase in financial intermediation despite a decrease in transaction costs and asymmetric information. And they draw the conclusion that those activities that should rather be the focus of the microeconomics of banking prominently include the management of risk. Schmidt et al. (1999) and Allen and Santomero (2001) add further supportive empirical evidence from Europe and the United States, respectively. Hellwig (1998) identifies the explanation of the actual allocation of risks as the most pressing challenge for the microeconomics of banking. Scholtens and van Wensveen (2000, 2003) expand on the lessons to be learned for future research. They conclude that the absorption of risks has to be accounted for as the central function of banks and that this function is not limited to idiosyncratic risks such as counterparty credit risk but extends to systematic risks such as interest rate risk. Banks create value through qualitative asset transformation that bridges a risk mismatch between savings and investments. Hence, an explanation of what a bank is and does has to center around risk-taking and since banks actually take systematic risks including interest rate risk this also has to feature in any comprehensive explanation.

Hakenes (2004) develops a model that explains a bank as conducting risk management. This model features risk management as including not only risk controlling, that is the supply of risk hedging tools, but also risk analysis, that is the production of information about risks. Crucially, the model rationalizes economies of scope between this comprehensive form of risk management and lending and in this way explains banks. Through this, the model answers the call for a change of focus by Allen and Santomero (1998). Unfortunately, since risk-taking of banks is not accommodated, the model does not go as far as demanded by Scholtens and van Wensveen (2000, 2003).

A disclaimer is in order. The following literature review is not meant to be encyclopedic. Instead, its aim is to present the most fundamental and relevant ideas in a comprehensive way. To this end it focuses on the most influential contributions. And the presentation of these contributions focuses on their explanations for why banks exist, why and how banks coexist with financial markets, and how banks compete with one another. Further topics are covered only selectively. References to cursory overviews are provided.

3.1 Paradigm of transaction costs

Whereas the second and the third paradigm of the microeconomics of banking were developed with dismissive reference to previous paradigms, the first paradigm of transaction costs emerged against the backdrop of the general framework of complete markets. Fama (1980) proves that the assumption of access to complete financial markets implies that banks are redundant institutions. In doing so, he sets the bar for an explanation of what a bank is and does.

The microeconomics of banking under the paradigm of transaction costs explain banks on the basis of market imperfections in the form of transaction costs. Market imperfections are built on in order to overcome the negative result of financial intermediation being redundant. Transaction costs lend themselves naturally to an explanation of intermediation, since an important aspect of intermediation involves the facilitation of transactions. The nowadays most readily cited literature review of the microeconomics of banking under the paradigm of transaction costs is the one by Baltensperger (1980). It is of particular interest, in so far as it allows to trace back the origin of the microeconomics of banking. Two main lessons can be drawn. First, the microeconomics of banking emerge as a specific part of the much greater effort of the microeconomic foundation of macroeconomics. Second, the early microeconomics of banking draw on two main sources, namely, the theory of the firm and theory of portfolio choice.

Benston and Smith (1976) spotlight transaction costs the "raison d'être" of financial intermediation and offer an explanation of banking that exemplifies the paradigm of transactions costs in the microeconomics of banking in its most comprehensive form. Instead of developing a formal model and deriving analytical solutions, they provide a coherent line of argument that covers the most fundamental points explicitly and is designed for easy extendability. As such, their reasoning offers the natural framework for the following exposition.

3.1.1   Irrelevance of banks

In his fundamental contribution Fama (1980) shows that under the assumption of access to complete financial markets the equilibrium allocations with and without banks are payoff-equivalent. Hence, banks are irrelevant and their existence cannot be explained. The underlying reasoning makes use of the theorem by Modigliani and Miller (1958) and presupposes access to complete financial markets in the form of a classical Arrow-Debreu setting.

Freixas and Rochet (2008) illustrate the same point with a simple model. The economy consists in a representative household, a representative firm, and a representative bank and lasts for two periods. The household derives utility from consumption in both periods and starts with an endowment. The firm features a production technology and requires input in the first period to produce output for the second period. The bank can take deposits and grant loans in the first period that are paid back plus interest in the second period. Now all three agents have access to a financial market. The household can make an investment in the form of deposits or bonds. The firm can receive an investment in the form of loans or bonds. The bank can cover the delta between deposits and loans with bonds. Now the financial market is complete. The household is indifferent between deposits and bonds as means for making an investment in the first period and for collecting this investment plus interest in the second period. The firm is indifferent between loans and bonds as means for receiving an investment in the first period and for paying back this investment plus interest in the second period. The bank then turns out to provide an investment-channel completely equivalent to the financial market. Both channels can be used to channel the investment from the household to the firm in the first period and the investment plus interest from the firm to the household in the second period. Furthermore, both investment-channels are perfect substitutes for the household and the firm. Thus in the equilibrium the interest rates of deposits and loans both have to be equal to the interest rate of bonds. Hence payoffs do not depend on the volumes of deposits and loans. So payoffs are the same with or without deposits and loans. Therefore the existence of banks cannot be explained. Consequently the coexistence of banks with financial markets and the competition of banks among one another cannot even be investigated.

The lesson that is readily drawn from this reasoning is that in order to explain the existence of banks, the assumption of access to complete financial markets has to be abandoned. And this is precisely the route the development of the microeconomics of banking took.

3.1.2   Consumption rearrangement

In their seminal contribution Benston and Smith (1976) formulate a general explanation of a bank as facilitating intra-temporal and inter-temporal consumption rearrangement. Both forms of consumption rearrangement bring possible consumption closer to desired consumption. Intra-temporal consumption rearrangement concerns earnings and preferences at any one point in time. Inter-temporal consumption rearrangement concerns the time-profile of earnings and the time-profile of preferences. The main idea is that even though using non-financial commodities is also possible for both forms of consumption rearrangement, using financial commodities minimizes transaction costs and therefore leads to preferred results.

Existence of banks

Just like firms from other industries, Benston and Smith (1976) understand banks as producing commodities. But unlike the commodities produced by firms from other industries, the financial commodities produced by banks cannot be consumed in a way that yields utility. Yet, they can be exchanged for other commodities the consumption of which yields utility. And therefore there can be a derived demand for financial commodities. The basis for this derived demand is that financial commodities can be converted into other commodities at minimal transaction costs. Because, and this may be understood as their defining characteristic, financial commodities make barters superfluous and allow for precise sizing and timing. This makes financial commodities advantageous for intra-temporal and inter-temporal consumption rearrangement, with the latter necessarily involving the former.

The general idea of a bank as a producer similar to firms from other industries is the starting point for the theory of the banking firm as advanced by Sealey and Lindley (1977), Klein (1971), and Monti (1972) among others. This theory identifies inputs and outputs as well as forms and steps of production. And it analyses upstream and downstream markets as well as types of competition and effects of government intervention. The theory of the banking firm builds on and is complemented by the theory of bank portfolio choice as developed by Porter (1961), Tobin (1965), and Pringle (1974) and many more. This theory explores the optimal structure of the asset and the liability side of the balance sheet of a bank in detail. And in doing so, it trades-off risk and return in all sorts of ways.

As Benston and Smith (1976) continue to reason, financial commodities produced by an intermediary such as a bank are in general preferable to financial commodities that can be produced by firms from other industries or even households. Banks produce financial commodities for making payments as well as for deferring and for bringing forward consumption in particular in the form of deposits and loans. While demand deposits allow making payments, time deposits offer favourable terms for deferring consumption. And loans are the classical instrument to bring forward consumption. Now banks have a competitive advantage producing these financial commodities for three reasons. First, a bank achieves economies of scale through a reduction of search costs. Interacting with many borrowers and lenders allows to efficiently serve the demand of any new customer. Second, a bank achieves economies of scale through an increase of specialization. Handling a sufficiently large amount of business of a certain type allows an efficient division of labor and the employment of efficient technical solutions. Third, as an intermediary a bank can offer a certain form of discretion or confidentiality. And this might be required by agents that can also produce financial commodities themselves.

The fundamental idea behind the supposed preferability of financial commodities produced by a financial intermediary such as a bank can be traced back to Gurley and Shaw (1960). Suppose the needs of borrowers and lenders do not match. In this case a bilateral trade would come at terms, a bank could improve on. To this end the bank produces two financial commodities that better meet the needs of the borrower and the lender respectively. And in trading these with the borrower and the lender both get more favorable terms. Hence, the bank can make a profit that may be high enough to compensate it for the risk associated with the mismatch of claims it incorporates. Now Baltensperger (1972) identifies scale economies in taking risks. Holding reserves is costly, but the larger is the number of depositors with an independent probability of withdrawal, the smaller is the amount of reserves as a share of deposits that is required at any accepted level of risk to ensure liquidity. Similarly, holding capital involves opportunity costs, but the larger the number of debtors with an independent probability of default, the smaller the amount of capital as a share of loans is required at any level of risk to ensure solvency. And Freedman (1977) points to transaction costs as preventing a similarly efficient diversification by individual borrowers and lenders through a multilateral trade.

The theoretical accommodation of economies of scale in banking is motivated, at least to some extend, by empirical findings. Benston (1964) and Bell and Murphy (1968) find empirical evidence for economies of scale on the product level. Many products associated with any side of the balance sheet, such as demand deposits and real-estate loans, incur costs the average of which decreases in total volume. Yet, some products, such as time deposits and business loans, exhibit decreasing or no economies of scale. Benston et al. (1982) construct a measure of total bank output and empirical evidence for economies of scale for smaller and diseconomies of scale for larger banks, that is a U-shaped average cost curve.

Coexistence with financial markets

Benston and Smith (1976) distinguish three types of financial intermediaries. The sophisticated type produces financial commodities. The medium type trades in financial commodities. And the basic type provides a market place for financial commodities. Typical examples are a bank for the sophisticated type, a broker-dealer for the medium type, and a stock exchange for the basic type. Now financial intermediaries of all three types exist because they reduce transaction costs. And depending on the precise consumption rearrangement aimed for, it can be advantageous to conduct it via a financial intermediary of either of these three types. For example, one might prefer buying stocks to making a time deposit for the purpose of deferring a certain amount of consumption for a certain period of time given the risk and return characteristics of both options including the respective necessary transactions. Along the same lines, one can also rationalize special setups in which financial commodities produced by firms from other industries or even households are preferable to the ones produced by banks or other sophisticated financial intermediaries. These may even be traded by medium type financial intermediaries and on the market places provided by basic type financial intermediaries. Hence, banks and financial markets may in general coexist and transaction costs situational tip the scales.

Townsend (1983) offers an extensive analysis of intermediation in general and traces it back to transaction costs and other market frictions. Their specification turns out to be key for any specific explanation of intermediaries. Stigler (1967) addresses the issue of readily supposed imperfections focussing on the capital market. Many apparently puzzling observations can in fact readily be explained without attributing them to imperfections. In an effort that exemplifies this reasoning, Baltensperger (1976) rationalizes certain aspects of relationship banking as standard outcomes of perfect competition. This is achieved by accounting for the amount of equity of the borrower.

Competition among banks

The all-encompassing transaction cost reasoning is also used by Benston and Smith (1976) to rationalize competition among banks. Even though economies of scale imply an advantage for larger banks, this does not entail a natural monopoly. Because other transaction costs can be large enough to offset these economies of scale. For example the difference in costs associated with traveling to a smaller bank nearby or to a larger bank further away can be large enough to offset the difference in efficiency. And difference in location is just one of any number of possible distinguishing features between banks. Another factor to be taken into account are economies of scope. Diversification can reduce risk costs for the bank and search costs for its customers. And since the results of trading-off scale against scope can differ between banks depending on their individual features, competition among banks with different product profiles can emerge.

Klein (1971) and Monti (1972) develop the classical monopoly model of banking. Ali and Greenbaum (1977) adopt the seminal model of Hotelling (1929) to model oligopolistic competition of banks in the form of spatial competition. Gilbert (1984) surveys the empirical literature. Other prominent topics in this context include the effects of government interventions as treated by Kalish and Gilbert (1973).

3.2 Paradigm of asymmetric information

The microeconomics of banking under the paradigm of asymmetric information features explanations of banks as alleviating market imperfections that result from asymmetric information. These explanations build on the fundamental results of the economics of information as decisively shaped by Akerlof (1970), Spence (1973), and Stiglitz (1975). And as James (1987) highlights, these explanations succeed in capturing banks as distinct from normal firms.

There is a large number of literature reviews that cover the microeconomics of banking under the paradigm of asymmetric information. The following five are prominent examples. Santomero (1984) identifies various types of models and is one of the first to cover asymmetric information. Allen (1990) includes an comprehensive overview of advances toward solving the reliability problem. Bhattacharya and Thakor (1993) identify six main puzzles and find that individual contributions collectively point to possible solutions. Van Damme (1994) organizes contributions by some classical problems from the economics of information. Swank (1996) focusses on contributions toward explaining bank behavior rather than existence.

The three most important contributions, that exemplify the paradigm of asymmetric information in the microeconomics of banking, are the ones by Leland and Pyle (1977), Diamond (1984), and Diamond and Dybvig (1983). They feature the leading explanations of banks as facilitating indirect co-investment, delegated monitoring, and liquidity insurance, respectively. The following exposes the takes of these explanations on why banks exist, why and how banks coexist with financial markets, and how banks compete with one another.

3.2.1 Indirect co-investment

With their pioneering contribution, Leland and Pyle (1977) introduce the paradigm of asymmetric information into the microeconomics of banking. They take transaction costs alone to be of insufficient magnitude to be the primary reason for the existence of banks. Instead, they focus on informational asymmetries for an explanation of banking. Specifically, they reason as follows. There are two preconditions. First, investment opportunities exist about which some relevant information can only be produced at a cost. Second, producing this information is subject to some economies of scale. Given these preconditions hold, some organization can be explained as exploiting economies of scale in producing information about investment opportunities. But as a mere information provider, this organization faces two problems. First, making use of the produced information by selling it in some form requires some credibility. Second, preventing free-riding in any form, in particular for non-rivalrous information, requires some appropriability. Now in the form of a bank the organization can overcome both problems. To this end two characteristics are critical. First, with some equity involved the credibility of the information can be signalled. At a level of equity sufficiently high, it is in the self interest of the bank to produce information and make use of it in a way that is also in the interest of investors. Second, by selling financial claims of some sort the appropriability of the information can be secured. By co-investing indirectly through the bank, investors pay for the production of information and receive a rivalrous good in return. Now the bank uses the proceeds from selling financial claims to fund investment opportunities. And in buying and selling financial claims that do not necessarily match perfectly it conducts what one might call classical banking. Two further points are noteworthy. First, the lower the risk of the total return of the investments of the bank is, the lower its equity level can be. With lower risk, signalling can still be achieved at higher leverage. Second, as entrepreneurs with better investment opportunities can benefit more from the production of information, financial markets may be substituted in an unbalanced way. If any investment opportunities remain available for direct investment, these are likely to be of lower quality.

Leland and Pyle (1977) do not build a formal model. Still, their contribution is nongeneric. They do not only herald the paradigm shift toward asymmetric information in the microeconomics of banking. But they also offer one specific explanation of banks instantiating this new paradigm. Their explanation presents a bank as offering indirect co-investment. The bank offers co-investment in the sense that it offers investors to co-invest with the bank that invests its own equity. And this investment is indirect as investors do not invest in the investment opportunities directly but through the bank.[33]

Campbel and Kracaw (1980) and Boyd and Prescott (1986) build formal models that capture the specific explanation of banks given by Leland and Pyle (1977). Campbel and Kracaw (1980) explicitly connect to Leland and Pyle (1977). Accordingly, the relatedness is apparent. Boyd and Prescott (1986) do not explicitly mention Leland and Pyle (1977). Nevertheless, the relatedness is striking. In the following the key lessons from both models are presented to shed more light on the reasoning of Leland and Pyle (1977).

Existence of banks

The explanation of the existence of banks by Leland and Pyle (1977) has three main components. These are the economies of scale in producing information, the signalling of credibility by investing equity, and the ensuring of appropriability by selling financial claims.

Campbel and Kracaw (1980) accommodate all three components in a straight forward way. Economies of scale make the technology used for the production of information effectively binary. If the technology is put to use efficiently, information about all projects is produced, not about some subset only. The producers of information differ only in the total costs incurred. Now the signalling of credibility requires a certain level of investment and this level depends on the efficiency of the technology of the information producer. But the endowment can always be too low. Hence, this market-imposed barrier to entry might prevent that the information producer with the most efficient technology runs the bank. In this case an inefficient equilibrium is reached in which the information producer with the technology with the highest efficiency of those information producers with an endowment large enough to signal credibility sells financial claims. The main learning with respect to the reasoning by Leland and Pyle (1977) is, that the requirement of some level of equity might entail reduced efficiency of the equilibrium solution.

Boyd and Prescott (1986) accommodate all three components, though with some twists. The larger the number of projects addressed by a bank, the larger the probability that post evaluation sufficient resources remain to fund at least all projects of the best type. This is required for the stability of the bank. And in this way there are economies of scale. The mechanism governing a bank's flow of funds is designed in such a way as to ensure the revelation of types of the bank's borrowers, lenders, and members which is the type of the individual project they have access to. As a part of this mechanism the endowment is handed over to the bank. And in this way equity is involved for signalling and credibility is established. In return for their endowments, borrowers, lenders, and members receive financial claims. While borrowers and members receive state dependent claims, lenders are promised a fixed return. In any case, the bank sells financial claims to ensure appropriability. A general lesson for any reasoning along the lines of Leland

---

[33] Gorton and Winton (2003) and Freixas and Rochet (2008) include presentations of the specific contribution by Leland and Pyle (1977). But both offer questionable classifications. Gorton and Winton (2003) take banks to be explained as "information producers", a term borrowed from Campbel and Kracaw (1980). Freixas and Rochet (2008) take banks to be explained as "coalitions of borrowers", a term borrowed from Boyd and Prescott (1986). Now the former classification seems too generic. Some production of some information is a feature of many otherwise quite different contributions to the microeconomics of banking with asymmetric information. And the latter classification seems to point to the wrong specific. Leland and Pyle (1977) repeatedly stress that they explain a sort of intermediation.

and Pyle (1977) is, that the claims of equity and debt holders may differ with the former being residual claims and the latter fixed.

Coexistence with financial markets

For Leland and Pyle (1977) whether and how banks and financial markets coexist as alternative routes for investment depends on the degree of sorting in the equilibrium. Given some sorting occurs, worse investment opportunities remain on the financial market only, if any.

Campbel and Kracaw (1980) find that of two types of projects with different risk return characteristics the bank only invests in the better type. These are undervalued in a market equilibrium without the production of information. And this difference between real and attributed value minus the costs for the production of information is the profit potential of the bank. Hence, the reasoning by Leland and Pyle (1977) is confirmed in a basic binary setting.

Boyd and Prescott (1986) find that of three types of projects with different risk return characteristics a bank invests in all of the best type and some of the medium type. But the remaining medium type and all the worst type remain unfunded as resources are spent on project evaluation instead.[34] The capital market is substituted completely without the realization of all investment opportunities. Thus, the reasoning by Leland and Pyle (1977) is confirmed in a slightly more complex setting.

Competition among banks

The topic of competition among banks is not addressed by Leland and Pyle (1977) explicitly. But the precise form of the economies of scale in producing information suggests itself as one of the key determinants of the market structure.

Campbel and Kracaw (1980) claim to remain open to different forms of market structure but their reasoning points toward a natural monopoly. The level of investment necessary to signal credibility is independent of market size and market share. And the technology for producing information covers all projects for a fixed cost that varies only between information producers. Thus, the same result is immanent as one might expect of Leland and Pyle (1977) with some standard economies of scale.

Boyd and Prescott (1986) model a bank as heaving a countable infinity of borrowers, lenders, and members but at the same time zero market share and no market power. This mathematical possibility allows for every bank to realize economies of scale without diminishing overall competitive efficiency. This result suggests, that with a similar market sizing, Leland and Pyle (1977) might just as well be able to have their cake and eat it too.

3.2.2 Delegated monitoring

In a ground-breaking model Diamond (1984) explains a bank as facilitating delegated monitoring. Given that investors can learn the returns of a risky technology, operated by entrepreneurs, through costly monitoring only, delegating this task to a bank is preferable to direct monitoring, and to no monitoring, provided that the bank is sufficiently diversified. Diversification turns out to be key, even though all agents are risk neutral, for solving what is known as the "monitoring

---

[34] The definition of how the risk return characteristics depend on types and noisy signals by Boyd and Prescott (1986) allows to distinguish the following three types for exposition purposes (with the features in the original paper in parenthesis): best (good type and good signal), medium (bad type, no signal), and worst (good type, bad signal).

the monitor"[35] problem. The following treatment focusses on the fundamental mechanics leading to this result.[36]

Existence of banks

Diamond (1984) constructs a model with the following basic specifications. There are three types of risk neutral agents, investors, entrepreneurs, and a bank. Each of the N entrepreneur has access to a production technology that requires an investment of 1 and yields a stochastic non-negative return of $\tilde{y}$ that is independent and identically distributed across entrepreneurs. Each investor has an endowment of $1/m$ that is smaller than 1 as $m > 1$ but there are mN of them such that total funds provided equal total funds required. The bank enables indirect investments but direct investments are also possible. Now, the informational setup is such that no agent observes any payment received by any other agent. In particular, each entrepreneur privately observes his realization of $\tilde{y}$. In the case of a direct investment, the investor only observes the payment he receives from the entrepreneur. In the case of an indirect investment, the bank only observes the payments it receives from the entrepreneurs and the investor only observes the payment he receives from the bank. Given that payments made cannot exceed payments received, zero payments have to be permitted in order to account for the case of a realization of $y = 0$. But given this informational setup and without special arrangements in place, the entrepreneurs and the bank are always induced to make zero payments independent of the payments they actually receive. This is anticipated by the investors who therefore do not invest in the first place. And this is obviously suboptimal, if $E(\tilde{y})$ exceeds some risk-free return R.

As for special arrangements to improve this situation, Diamond (1984) presents three alternatives that involve no monitoring, individual monitoring, and delegated monitoring, respectively. Alternative one of no monitoring makes direct investments incentive-compatible through non-pecuniary penalties.[37] If the payment received by investors is below a certain threshold, a non-pecuniary penalty of the size of the difference d is imposed on the entrepreneur. And the threshold is set at a level h high enough such that the entrepreneur is induced to make payments large enough such that the expected return for the investors matches R. Alternative two makes direct investments incentive-compatible through individual monitoring. At the cost of K each investor becomes able to observe the relevant entrepreneur's realization of $\tilde{y}$. And thus enabled to write a contingent contract, all involved agents can be made at least indifferent, if $mK + R \leq E(\tilde{y})$. Alternative three makes indirect investments incentive-compatible through delegated monitoring. Parallel to alternative two, at a cost of NK the bank becomes able to observe all investors' realizations of $\tilde{y}$. Additionally and parallel to alternative one, if the payment received by investors is below a certain threshold H, a non-pecuniary penalty of the size of the difference D is imposed on the bank. Crucially, the non-pecuniary penalty induces the monitoring as the profit of the bank increases in the payments it receives from the entrepreneurs. The social costs of the three alternatives are given by

$$C_1 = NE(d) \tag{3.1}$$

$$C_2 = mNK \tag{3.2}$$

---

[35] Given the result of Diamond (1984) the term is misleading as it turns out that the monitor is not monitored but incentivized.

[36] Gorton and Winton (2003) and Freixas and Rochet (2008) include complementary treatments of Diamond (1984).

[37] A non-pecuniary penalty is not subject to the constraint that payments made cannot exceed payments received. Diamond (1984) suggests an interpretation as bankruptcy costs.

3 Microeconomics of banking

$$C_3 = NK + E(D) \qquad\qquad (3.3)$$

and the individual monitoring costs need to be assumed to be below the expected value of the non-pecuniary penalty to be imposed on an entrepreneur, that is $K < E(d)$, if alternative one is not to dominate alternatives two and three trivially.

The existence of banks is rationalized by Diamond (1984) by showing that $E(D)$ is monotonically decreasing toward 0 in N. Because this implies that C_3 approaches NK which is less than C_2 provided $m > 1$ and less than C_1 provided $K < E(d)$. The contingent contracts enabled through monitoring ensure, that the bank receives a payment from each entrepreneur, that has an expected value of at least $(1/N)H$, and that depends on the individual entrepreneur's realization of $\tilde{y}$ only. Hence, these payments are independent and identically distributed, provided this holds for $\tilde{y}$ across entrepreneurs. Thus, the law of large numbers implies that the probability of the sum of payments from all N entrepreneurs to the bank being below H monotonically approaches zero as N increases. Finally, this implies that the expected value of the non-pecuniary penalty $E(D)$ is monotonically decreasing toward 0 in N as the bank accepts zero profits in lack of an outside option. Therefore, if the bank is sufficiently diversified meaning N is large enough, alternative three dominates the other two.

Debt contract

As Diamond (1984) points out, the contract with a non-pecuniary penalty is a debt contract with the threshold as its face value. The return of this debt contract cannot exceed its face value but may be lower. Whenever the return is lower, the non-pecuniary penalty is imposed and harms the borrower without benefiting the lender. In order for an investor to be at least indifferent, the expected return of the debt contract has to match the risk-free return. For this to be the case, the face value of the debt contract has to exceed the risk-free return. But the required difference between the face value of the debt contract and the risk-free return decreases with the probability of a lower return of the debt contract. Therefore, the face value of the debt contracts between investors and the bank approaches the risk-free return as the number of entrepreneurs increases. Williamson (1987) derives a debt contract as the optimal arrangement that does not feature a non-pecuniary penalty.

Coexistence with financial markets

Diamond (1984) explicitly compares direct investment and indirect investment and shows that indirect investment can under certain conditions be facilitated in an incentive-compatible and socially preferable way. As an alternative route for investment, the bank substitutes financial markets in this case. Instead of substitutability, the models by Gorton and Haubrich (1987) and Seward (1990) accommodate complementarity with banks and financial markets coexisting as complementary routes for investment. The first model features a pay-off structure for entrepreneurs that can be designed in a more incentive-compatible way through some level of bank debt and where this bank debt hence enables the selling of shares. The second model includes monitoring as a non-binary tool where monitoring the return of a larger part of the activities of an entrepreneur comes at higher costs.

Dependence on observables

Diamond (1984) argues that the assumption of independence of the return of the production technology across entrepreneurs can be weakened. Specifically, dependence on observables could be permitted, if contingent claims were traded that made it possible for the bank to hedge systematic risks. Diamond (1984) can show that such hedging does not reduce the incentive of the bank to monitor the entrepreneurs. But the financial markets this result presupposes are not built into the model in any way and accordingly coexistence is not systematically analyzed. Instead Diamond (1984) suggests that in the absence of hedging markets, the bank can simply condition its contracts with investors on observables.

Interest rate risk

Diamond (1984) explicitly refers to interest rates as observables the exposure to which the bank is to hedge on hedging markets or through an appropriate conditioning of its contracts with investors. Interest rate risk belongs to the systematic risks which do not have to be borne by the bank to ensure adequate incentives but instead are to be shared in an optimal way. Hence, the bearing of interest rate risk by actual banks cannot be explained with this model.

Competition among banks

Diamond (1984) prominently features economies of scale. An increase of diversification is always beneficial. Therefore the model has a single bank occupying a natural monopoly. Krasa and Villamil (1992) introduce increasing costs of monitoring and non-diversifiable risk to derive some optimal bank size. Cerasi and Daltung (2000), too, point to diseconomies of scale of monitoring as an explanation for the limited size of banks. Still, even with frictions of some sort, the model by Diamond (1984) can be taken to justify the claim that larger banks are preferable to smaller banks at least on some interval of size. Yanelle (1997) stages competition between two banks in a setup borrowed from Diamond (1984) and finds that there are multiple equilibria and that many of them are inefficient. Stiglitz (1985), however, suggests that competition helps in inducing banks to exercise effective monitoring.

Demand deposits

As an alternative to a non-pecuniary penalty as a tool for incentivizing a bank with some private knowledge on investment opportunities Calomiris and Kahn (1991) point to demand deposits. The option to withdraw induces depositors to invest in monitoring and sequential servicing allows to overcome the free-rider problem. Among others, Flannery (1994) elaborates on this line of thinking. The developed model features noisy information.

3.2.3 Liquidity insurance

The seminal model of Diamond and Dybvig (1983) depicts a bank as providing liquidity insurance. In the face of a privately observed and as such uninsurable risk of a liquidity shock, the competitive solution falls short of, but a deposit contract enables optimal risk sharing between risk averse consumers. In what follows, this model is presented and analyzed.[38]

Existence of banks

Diamond and Dybvig (1983) build a model with the following components. There are three periods (periods zero, one, and two), two types of risk averse consumers (type one and two), and one risk-free production technology with constant returns to scale. The time structure is as follows. In period zero all consumers are identical. In period one each consumer privately

---

[38] Standard expositions of the model of Diamond and Dybvig (1983) can be found in Gorton and Winton (2003), Tirole (2006), and Freixas and Rochet (2008).

learns his type. Type one and type two consumers only derive utility from consumption in period one and period two, respectively. All consumers start with an initial endowment of one unit (1) in period zero, storage is possible and future consumption is discounted (φ). The return of the production technology for one unit of investment (-1) in period zero depends on a decision to be made in period one. If liquidated, it returns as much as the initial investment (1) in period one and nothing (0) in period two. If untouched, it returns nothing (0) in period one but more than the initial investment ($R > 1$) in period two.

Optimal risk sharing avoids as much liquidation as possible, aligns marginal utility and marginal productivity, and satisfies the intertemporal budget constraint. With $t \in (0;1)$ being the share of type one consumers and c_k^i denoting the consumption of type i in period k, Diamond and Dybvig (1983) state

$$c_1^{2*} = c_2^{1*} = 0 \tag{3.4}$$

$$u'(c_1^{1*}) = \varphi R u'(c_2^{2*}) \tag{3.5}$$

$$t c_1^{1*} + (1-t)\frac{1}{R}c_2^{2*} = 1. \tag{3.6}$$

Given that $u(c)$ satisfies some standard assumptions[39], Diamond and Dybvig (1983) show that assuming $1 \geq \varphi > R^{-1}$ and $-cu''(c)/u'(c) > 1$, implies that $1 < c_1^{1*} < c_2^{2*} < R$. Hence, the optimal insurance narrows the gap between the consumption levels against the purely technology induced distribution. Furthermore, it is incentive compatible in the sense that it satisfies the self-selection constraints as no type envies the other type.

Now optimal risk sharing cannot be achieved by a competitive market. Here the crucial assumption is, that the type of a consumer is private information. Because without the possibility of conditioning on the type of the consumer, there cannot be a market in contingent claims, that provides optimal insurance in the face of individual uncertainty. Since all consumers are identical in period zero, no trade takes place and each consumer arrives at the autarchy solution which implies the purely technology induced distribution. Thus, type one consumers liquidate their investment in period one and consume 1 while type two consumers leave their investment untouched till period two and then consume R.

But optimal risk sharing can be achieved by a deposit contract. Here the crucial assumption is, that there is no aggregate uncertainty. Because with the share of type 1 consumers t known ex ante, the deposit contract can be tailored to provide optimal risk sharing. In general, a deposit contract gives each consumer who deposits his endowment in period zero the claim to either withdraw a certain fixed amount r_1 in period one or a pro rata share of the bank's remaining assets in period two. Specifically, the deposit contract with $r_1 = c_1^{1*}$ can achieve optimal risk sharing. Because with the bank investing all deposits in period zero and avoiding as much liquidation as possible, it can pay out c_2^{2*} in period two.

---

[39] By assumption $u(c)$ is a real valued function, twice continuously differentiable, increasing, strictly concave, and $u'(0) = \infty$ and $u'(\infty) = 0$.

Bank run

Diamond and Dybvig (1983) demonstrate that optimal risk sharing is not the only pure strategy Nash equilibrium of the deposit contract with $r_1 > 1$. The other is a bank run. In this case, all consumers want to withdraw their deposits in period one.

Given $r_1 > 1$, in period one the claims of all consumers exceed the liquidation value of the total investment. If too many consumers want to withdraw their deposits, the bank cannot honour every claim. As a way of the bank to cope with this, Diamond and Dybvig (1983) introduce sequential servicing. Consumers who want to withdraw in period one are served sequentially and receive r_1 until the entire investment has been liquidated and 0 thereafter. Hence with the placement in line being random, each consumer faces a random payoff with mean 1 and variance larger than 0.

This scenario is a pure strategy Nash equilibrium, if wanting to withdraw in period one is the best response, given this is what all the others want. This is obviously the case, if the investment is liquidated completely, independent of the decision of each individual consumer about whether he wants to withdraw or not.[40] Because in this case, waiting till period two yields a secure return of 0. Implicitly, Diamond and Dybvig (1983) assume that the number of consumers is large enough for this to be the case. In this case, a deposit contract that improves the competitive solution with $r_1 > 1$ features a bank run equilibrium.[41]

As a countermeasure against a bank run as a pure strategy Nash equilibrium, Diamond and Dybvig (1983) introduce a policy of suspension of withdrawals. In general, with such a policy in place, the bank in period one only pays out r_1 to a certain fraction of depositors. Specifically, setting this threshold equal to t ensures that with $r_1 = c_1^{1*}$ the bank pays out c_2^{2*} in period two. Thus, no consumer of type two has an incentive to withdraw in period one. Hence, this policy of suspension of withdrawals ensures that the optimal deposit contract achieves optimal risk sharing as its unique pure strategy Nash equilibrium.

Insolvency

In period one, the bank in the model of Diamond and Dybvig (1983) may not only be illiquid but may also be insolvent in a present value sense. More precisely, the bank may be insolvent without being illiquid. The bank is illiquid, if it is unable to meet its obligations as they come due. This is the case if the share of depositors f who want to withdraw exceeds the critical value given by r_1^{-1}. Because in this case the face value of deposits to be withdrawn fr_1 exceeds the liquidation value of the total investment of 1. Thus the bank is illiquid in the bank run equilibrium. And the bank cannot be illiquid without being insolvent in the model by Diamond and Dybvig (1983). In the bank run equilibrium the entire investment is liquidated. And the bank ends up without assets while obligations remain. However, the bank can be insolvent without being illiquid. The bank is insolvent, if the value of its liabilities exceeds the value of its assets. And in a present value sense this is the case if the face value of total deposits r_1 exceeds the present value of the total investment of φR. Now this is obviously independent of which equilibrium prevails. And for this reason the bank may be insolvent without being illiquid.

---

[40] To be precise, the critical value is actually larger than zero. Even if the deviation of an individual consumer would allow for a small part of the investment to remain untouched. The secure return in period two might still not compensate for the random return in period one in terms of utility. For an exposition of this reasoning see Tirole (2006, p. 456).

[41] Note that the model of Bryant (1980), which is commonly cited as an ancestor of the model of Diamond and Dybvig (1983), relies on risky assets in order to rationalize bank runs.

The rationale for the possibility of the bank being insolvent in a present value sense starts from the general conditions (3.5) and (3.6) for optimal risk sharing derived by Diamond and Dybvig (1983), with the latter rearranged in order to express c_1^1 as in terms of c_2^2

$$u'(c_1^1) = \varphi R u'(c_2^2) \tag{3.7}$$

$$c_1^1 = \frac{1}{t} - \frac{1-t}{t}\frac{1}{R}c_2^2. \tag{3.8}$$

Visualizing these two equations in a diagram with c_2^2 on the abscissa and c_1^1 on the ordinate allows an easy to follow reasoning (see Figure 3.1). In this diagram, Equation (3.8) describes a straight and downward sloping line with the axis intersect $1/t$ and going through the point $(R,1)$. Note that if t decreases towards zero, the intersect increases and the slope of the line becomes arbitrary negative. Now consider the intersection of this line with the horizontal line $c_1^1 = \varphi R$, call it I_1. Obviously I_1 can be moved towards the point $(R,\varphi R)$ from the left by decreasing t. Actually, the distance between these points can be made arbitrarily small by selecting a t arbitrarily close to 0. In the same diagram, Equation (3.7) describes a curve going through the point $(0,0)$[42] that is upward sloping. Because if c_2^2 increases, $u'(c_2^2)$ decreases. And since $\varphi R > 0$, this requires a matching decrease of $u'(c_1^1)$ which in turn requires an increase of c_1^1. Now consider the intersection of this curve with the horizontal line $c_1^1 = \varphi R$, call it I_2. Whenever I_2 is to the left of the point $(R,\varphi R)$, there is a t such that I_1 lies between I_2 and $(R,\varphi R)$. In this case the straight line described by Equation (3.8) and the curve described by Equation (3.7) intersect above the horizontal line $c_1^1 = \varphi R$. And since this intersection identifies the volumes of optimal consumption, c_1^{1*} turns out to be above φR. The last thing one has to note is that I_2 is to the left of the point $(R,\varphi R)$, if and only if the curve described by Equation (3.7) intersects with the vertical line $c_2^2 = R$ above the horizontal line $c_1^1 = \varphi R$. Formally,[43]

$$\text{if } u'^{-1}(\varphi R u'(R)) > \varphi R, \text{ a } t^- \text{ exists such that, if } t < t^-, \text{ then } c_1^{1*} = r_1 > \varphi R. \tag{3.9}$$

The implication of this result is, that if the additional non-insolvency constraint $r_1 \leq \varphi R$ is introduced, it may be binding. For this to be the case, the share of impatient consumers t has to be sufficiently small. And if the additional non-insolvency constraint is binding, the bank cannot provide optimal risk sharing even given the share of impatient consumers t is known ex ante.

Coexistence with financial markets

Jacklin (1987) points out that the bank in the model by Diamond and Dybvig (1983) cannot coexist with complete financial markets, if the deposit contract it offers is to achieve optimal risk sharing as a pure strategy Nash equilibrium. This is due to the fact that complete financial markets enable the following arbitrage. A consumer deviates in period zero such that he does not deposit his endowment but invests it directly. If he turns out to be of type two, he leaves his investment untouched in period one and consumes R in period two. Since $R > c_2^{2*}$ this is an improvement. If he turns out to be of type one, he conducts the following trades in period one. First, the deviant sells a claim of R' in period two in exchange for c_1^{1*} in period one. Setting $R' \geq c_2^{2*}$ makes any consumer of type two with deposits at the bank a possible trading partner. This trading partner simply withdraws all his deposits and buys the claim. Second, the deviant

---

[42] Because $u'(0) = \infty$.
[43] Note that u'^{-1} is the inverse of u'.

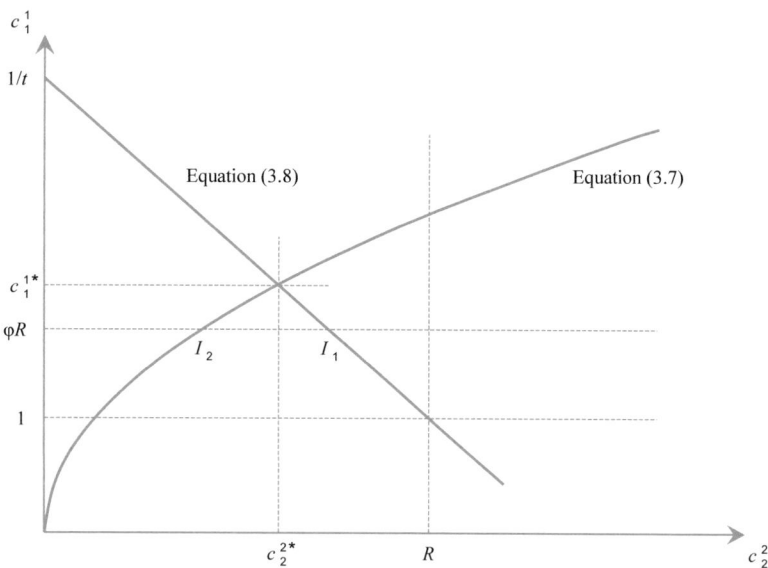

Figure 3.1: Insolvency in the model by Diamond and Dybvig (1983).

sells a claim of the remaining period two return of his investment $R - R'$, that he can ensure to be positive by setting $R' < R$, for a payment of P in period one. Setting $P \leq (R - R')/c_2^{2*}$ again makes any remaining consumer of type two with deposits at the bank a possible trading partner.[44] This trading partner withdraws the necessary share of his deposits to buy the claim. And since the deviant is already indifferent after the first trade, setting $P > 0$ makes this an improvement, too. Hence, independent of his type, a consumer can improve his situation by deviating in this way. Haubrich and King (1990) make the same point. Diamond (1997) responds to this critique with a model with limited participation in financial markets that features the results of Diamond and Dybvig (1983) and Jacklin (1987) as polar cases. Yet, von Thadden (1998) establishes instability in a continuous time setting. Analyzing the liquidity needs of entrepreneurs instead of depositors, Holmstrom and Tirole (1998) draw back to simply ruling out a redirection of funds to realize possible gains from arbitrage via financial markets. Gorton and Pennacchi (1990) focus on liquidity provision by banks on financial markets and rationalize it as a protection of uninformed agents from exploitation by informed agents.

Interest rate risk

Hellwig (1994) extends the model by Diamond and Dybvig (1983) to include technology-induced interest rate risk. The return of a newly introduced short-term production technology available in period 1 equals the realization of the random variable $\tilde{R}'$ for one unit of investment. In period 0, when the decision about investment in the still available long-term production technology is taken, only the distribution of this random variable is known. Its actual value becomes known in period 1 when the decision about investment in the newly introduced short-run production technology is taken. Hence, interest rate risk derives from the uncertainty about short-term interest rates between period 1 and 2 in period 0.

Hellwig (1994) shows that all of this interest rate risk is optimally borne by the depositors. Conducting maturity transformation a bank can have a market-making function or a risk-shifting function. Whereas the former involves the securitization of long-term claims only the latter

---

[44] This immediately follows from the condition that the trading partner cannot be made worse off through the trade and therefore it has to hold that $c_2^{2*}(1 - P) + (R - R') \geq c_2^{2*}$.

includes the taking of interest rate risk. And finding the modeled bank to limit itself to the market-making function leads to the interest rate risk being allocated to its depositors or some hedging markets if there are any.

Overlapping generations

Qi (1994) extends the model by Diamond and Dybvig (1983) to an overlapping generations model. The inflow of new deposits in every period enables the bank to leave a larger share of the investment in the productive technology untouched. Hence it can afford to pay out more than 1 for withdrawals after one period as well as more than R for withdrawals after two periods.[45] And paying out more than R for withdrawals after two periods makes deviation through trading as described by Jacklin (1987) impossible. But this dependence on continuous inflows of deposits makes the bank vulnerable to a new sort of bank run. Because even a policy of suspension of withdrawals cannot force a new generation of consumers to deposit their endowments at the bank in the first place. Allen and Gale (1997) introduce an alternative production technology with stochastic returns in a similar overlapping generations model and show that the coexistence with financial markets prevents a bank from facilitating optimal risk sharing.

Competition among banks

The model by Diamond and Dybvig (1983) does not lend itself naturally to the analysis of competition among banks. Offering the optimal deposit contract, the bank makes zero profit. But interpreting this as the outcome of perfect competition seems implausible. Since for a bank run to be a pure strategy Nash equilibrium on the individual bank level, each bank needs to attract a total amount of deposits sufficiently larger than the endowment of each consumer. And this minimum size of a bank might be associated with some market power. Yet, in a model with Bertrand competition between two banks, Adao and Temzelides (1998) derive optimal risk sharing and hence zero bank profits as the unique pure strategy Nash equilibrium.

Aggregate uncertainty

Besides the case in which the share of type one consumers t is known ex ante, Diamond and Dybvig (1983) analyse the case of aggregate uncertainty with a stochastic t. In this case a deposit contract cannot achieve optimal risk sharing. And this does not change, if the deposit contract is complemented by a policy of suspension of withdrawals. But if the government provides complementary deposit insurance, optimal risk sharing can be achieved as the only pure strategy Nash equilibrium, even in dominant strategies. The key difference between the deposit contract and the deposit insurance is that the bank services the consumers sequentially while the government can condition on the total share of withdrawals in period one. Hence, the after tax proceeds of the governmental deposit insurance can be designed in such a way that, if only type one consumers withdraw in period one, the optimal risk sharing is achieved, and that type two consumers always prefer withdrawal in period two.

3.3 Paradigm of risk

The microeconomics of banking under the paradigm of risk produces explanations of banks as quintessentially conducting risk management or risk-taking. Allen and Santomero (1998) are the first to suggest a shift to the paradigm of risk and they specifically highlight the importance of risk

---

[45] Note that this is not possible in the single generation model by Diamond and Dybvig (1983) as it violates the intertemporal budget constraint (3.6).

management. Hakenes (2004) develops a model that explains banks as offering risk management. Scholtens and van Wensveen (2000, 2003) go further and argue for risk-taking also of systematic risks as the characterising activity of banks. A model to capture this idea is still missing. In what follows the advances that shape these two strands of emerging research are presented in brief.

3.3.1 Risk management

In their evocative contribution, Allen and Santomero (1998) introduce the paradigm of risk into the microeconomics of banking. They find that the existing literature overemphasises the reduction of market frictions in the form of transaction costs or asymmetric information as the characterising function of banks. Instead, they suggest to focus on risk and more specifically on risk management as the essential activity of banks, which includes the facilitation of participation in financial markets. They claim that the risk management function of financial intermediaries in general and of banks in particular has gained paramount importance recently and in effect demand for economic research to account for this development. They base their claim on data that shows that the trading of derivatives and the securitization of loans have increased significantly in the US since the 1970s.

In their empirical study, Schmidt et al. (1999) find evidence for the increasing specialisation of banks in lending operations that crucially include borrower monitoring as a form of risk management. They make use of national account statistics from the U.K., France, and Germany that cover the years 1982 to 1995 and calculate intermediation ratios as shares of financial means channeled through financial intermediaries. They find that the funding of banks has changed in that deposits from households have to a significant extent been replaced by debt from non-bank financial intermediaries such as pension funds. And they also find that the empirical evidence does not point to a general decrease in bank lending. They draw the conclusion that banks are cutting back on the mobilizing of savings and focus on lending operations including the monitoring of borrowers or risk managers, instead.

Investigating further data from the US, Allen and Santomero (2001) find empirical evidence for a decrease of both deposit taking and loan making of banks and for a shift from these classical activities to the facilitation of participation in financial markets as their signature activity. And they reason that risk management is at the heart of this activity. Facilitating participation in financial markets involves the reduction of participation costs. And the largest part of this reduction can be achieved through specialized and hence sophisticated risk management. Because it is the risk associated with the participation in financial markets the management of which presents the biggest challenge to the individual investor and the highest cost at least in terms of opportunity cost of time if conducted individually. Therefore banks can add value at the interface between individual investors and financial markets.

In his pioneering contribution, Hakenes (2004) presents a model of a bank that features risk management as its pivotal activity. He models a classical bank in the sense that its main business is to grant loans. In so far one might argue that he accounts for the findings of Schmidt et al. (1999) but not of Allen and Santomero (2001). The model is briefly introduced in what follows. Again, the focus is on essentials and the three aspects of existence, coexistence, and competition provide the structure.

Existence of banks

Hakenes (2004) distinguishes between risk analysis and risk controlling as elements of risk management. Risk analysis is the collection of information about risk, that is not only about distribution of but also of correlations between relevant random variables. Risk controlling is the provision of instruments for the hedging of risk, that is for the intentional reduction of the risk of an investment portfolio. Naturally, risk analysis is an essential prerequisite for effective risk controlling.

Hakenes (2004) develops a model populated by an entrepreneur and a risk analyst. The entrepreneur faces bankruptcy risk which he wants to hedge. But he does not know the correlations between the return of his project and the instruments available to him on the financial market and is incapable of conducting the risk analysis required for learning them. This is where the risk analyst comes in because he is capable of learning the correlations of interest at the price of some fixed effort.

Hakenes (2004) identifies a principal agent problem which prevents the entrepreneur from simply paying the risk analyst for the production and provision of the required information. The necessary alignment of interest can be achieved by the risk analyst offering not only risk analysis but also risk controlling which makes his payoff dependent on the hedging of the bankruptcy risk of the entrepreneur. Crucially, the associated costs of delegation can be reduced by the risk analyst offering a loan which adds to the harmonization of interest between him and the entrepreneur. Hence, risk analyst that also engages in risk controlling and in making loans emerges as enabling the hedging of the bankruptcy risk of the entrepreneur at the lowest possible delegation costs. And this economic agent may be interpreted as being a bank. Its funding may include deposits but is not modeled.

Coexistence with financial markets

Hakenes (2004) does not effectively model the coexistence of banks and financial markets. The entrepreneur cannot hedge his bankruptcy risk by participating in financial markets directly as he is incapable of risk analysis. The bank is capable of risk analysis but it turns out that it cannot simply facilitate the entrepreneur's participation in financial markets by providing him with the required information. Instead, the bank engages in a risk management relationship with the entrepreneur that includes risk controlling through the provision of hedging instruments. And the bank in turn is assumed not to have any funding restrictions or need to hedge its risk on the financial markets itself.

Competition among banks

Hakenes (2004) attributes all bargaining power to the entrepreneur who can make a take-it-or-leave-it offer for the entire contractual relationship between him and the risk analyst. The rationale provided consists in the assumption that there are many identical risk analysts for each entrepreneur to choose from. In this way, competition among banks that implies the absence of bargaining power on their side is an important driver of the results of this model.

3.3.2 Risk-taking

Hellwig (1998) identifies the risk-taking of banks and more specifically their taking of non-diversifiable risk as the major empirical phenomenon for which the microeconomics of banking has not yet provided an appropriate theoretical explanation. And he explicitly highlights the taking of interest rate risk by banks as a striking empirical fact which still awaits adequate reproduction in a theoretical model. In this way he formulates a challenge for future research.

Scholtens and van Wensveen (2000, 2003) elaborate on this challenge for future research. They call the taking of diversifiable plus non-diversifiable risk "the absorption of risk" and identify it as "the central function" of banks (Scholtens and van Wensveen 2003, p. 35). They propose an understanding of banks as adding value through risk-taking in the form of running a mismatch between the instruments provided to borrowers on one side and to lenders on the other side.

A canonical model that captures the idea of risk-taking as the characterising activity of banks has not yet emerged. But the expositions of Scholtens and van Wensveen (2000, 2003) at least informally address all three main questions and provides explanations not only of the existence of banks but also of the coexistence of banks and financial markets and of the competition among banks. These explanations, which are yet to be modeled formally, are presented here in brief.

Existence of banks

As already set forth, Scholtens and van Wensveen (2000, 2003) explain the existence of banks with adding value through risk-taking. Banks are active economic agents that provide financial services partly embodied in financial instruments that meet the diverging needs of borrowers and lenders. Banks build up a reputation in order to be trusted with more complex affairs than their customers might understand and optimize their entire balance sheet plus off-balance sheet items trading off risk and return.

Coexistence with financial markets

Scholtens and van Wensveen (2000, 2003) agree with Hellwig (1998) in that banks and financial markets are not to be understood primarily as alternatives but as complementing one another since banks not only make use of but also run financial markets and even create new sub-markets. Banks make use of financial markets as they reallocate some of their risk. Banks run financial markets by ensuring availability. And banks create new sub-markets through fragmentation by means of offering new products.

Competition among banks

Scholtens and van Wensveen (2000, 2003) describe the competition among banks as a process of creative destruction as famously introduced by Schumpeter (1912). Through offering a new products a bank can redirect demand to a new sub-market in which it can secure monopolistic profits for a limited period of time. Because as the success of the new product becomes apparent, other banks enter the new sub-market and competitive profits are again driven down to zero.

3.4 Conclusion

Banks take interest rate risk, but this simple fact turns out to be hard to explain on the basis of transaction costs or asymmetric information. The reason for this is that interest rate risk is a systematic or non-diversifiable risk the realization of which depends on publicly observable parameter values. The discussion below presents how these specific characteristics of interest rate risk make standard explanation patterns inapplicable. But the discussion below also discovers somewhat more innovative explanatory approaches on the basis of transaction costs or asymmetric information. It turns out that in both cases a revision of one of the more or less implicit predominant assumptions about interest rate risk is required. In fact, what is required is a richer and more realistic understanding than the one taken as a basis most commonly at least in economics. It is debatable, whether this improves or harms the persuasiveness of the explanatory approaches identified.

In contrast to the understandings of banks as mainly reducing transaction costs or mitigating problems arising from asymmetric information, the understanding of banks as quintessential risk-takers is predestined to be an appropriate basis for an explanation why banks take interest rate risk. The discussion below investigates in how far this most recent paradigm lives up to that promise. It turns out that the persuasiveness of the explanation identified can be increased significantly with a switch from the traditional to the modern understanding of banking. Understanding banking not as intermediation of loanable funds but as financing through money creation gives a new meaning to the established idea that availability is key. Finally, it turns out that taking interest rate risk may best not be seen as some optional addition but rather as an essential part of the core business of banks which only larger and more sophisticated banks might be able to get rid of in a profitable way.

Recapitulating specific characteristics of interest rate risk

The aforementioned specific characteristics of interest rate risk have important implications or aspects which are introduced below. In the form presented here, these characteristics effectively prevent an explanation why banks take interest rate risk based on transaction costs or asymmetric information. As pointed out above, the more innovative explanatory approaches presented later only work if these characteristics are qualified in certain ways. In so far, the following presentation is to be read with reservations. However, it captures the still predominant understanding of interest rate risk in economic research. This already makes it worthwhile. And it is the starting point for what follows.

Interest rate risk is a systematic or non-diversifiable risk. In lack of uncorrelated exposures, it cannot be diversified as the law of large numbers cannot be applied. This has two important implications. First, interest rate risk cannot be reduced but only reallocated and therefore the question is not why interest rate risk is taken at all but only who takes it.[46] Second, there are no scale economies inherent in the taking of this risk and consequently there is no classical insurance business case.

Furthermore, interest rate risk is a risk the realization of which depends on the development of publicly observable parameter values, namely of market interest rates. It is important to note both distinct aspects of this characterization. First, the development of market interest rates can be followed at virtually zero costs, at least in so far as it is relevant for traditional banking activities.[47] Second, the development of market interest rates can hardly be influenced by any single market participant individually.

Examining possible explanations: transaction costs

The first of the three paradigms of the microeconomics of banking explains what banks are and do mainly with reference to the reduction of transaction costs. The competitive advantage of banks in doing so is traditionally traced to size advantages or economies of scale in the intermediation of loanable funds. Benston and Smith (1976) point to increases in specialization and to reductions of search costs. Baltensperger (1972) highlights the diversification of idiosyncratic risks. An examination of these three explanation patterns reveals two things. First, none of them is a basis for a plausible explanation why banks take interest rate risk as it is predominantly understood. Second, each of them, and not only the third, is a basis for a plausible explanation for banks' taking of any idiosyncratic or diversifiable risk. This second point motivates a further investigation into whether the interest rate risk banks take does not at least have some idiosyncratic or diversifiable part. And indeed the part steaming from possible exercising of behavioural options such as from the risk of withdrawals of retail demand deposits may be regarded as being of this type. This is the suggested qualification of the predominant understanding of the specific characteristics of interest rate risk.

A bank which increases its specialization can benefit from what one may call classical economies of scale. If the volume of a specific type of business increases, a finer division of

---

[46] This point is prominently emphasized by Hellwig (1998).
[47] In contrast, in trading on interest rates, the speed required may be costly.

the associated tasks becomes profitable and larger one-time investments pay off. For example, handling a sufficiently large amount of mortgage business may allow to hire sales people dedicated to a specific region and to develop a set of standardized application forms. However, classical size advantages in the taking of interest rate risk are hard to imagine. To be sure, economies of scale of this type may well be realized in the taking of idiosyncratic risks. For example, as a bank's experience increases with the number of cases handled, its ex ante assessment of the credit risk of a new potential borrower may become more efficient and so may the ongoing monitoring of its loan portfolio and any collection in cases of default. But a bank's experience in the development of market interest rates does not increase with the number of cases handled. The development of interest rates is a common factor and it is precisely the dependence on such a common factor that makes interest rate risk a systematic risk.

A bank reduces search costs by making the individual matching of potential depositors and borrowers superfluous. The basic idea is that there is a dispersed surplus of funds on one side and an also dispersed deficit on the other. Then a central intermediary can reduce the number of bilateral contracts required to achieve an efficient allocation of funds. Channelling funds through a bank not only overcomes the problem of different lot sizes but also reaches maximum diversification. And this only requires one bilateral contract between the bank and every potential depositor and borrower. Without the bank, achieving an equivalent outcome would require one bilateral contract between each potential depositor and each potential borrower, instead.[48] However, a reduction of the mere number of contracts is no plausible source of scale economies in banks' taking of interest rate risk because each contract may simply be conditioned on the development of market interest rates. Hellwig (1998) further investigates whether a reduction of the number of contingencies in the contracts may be a source of these scale economies. For idiosyncratic risks this is indeed the case. Malinvaud (1972) proves that with a central intermediary it is unnecessary to condition on the realizations of the idiosyncratic risks of others because the bank can diversify them away. But for systematic risks this is, in contrast, not the case. The bank cannot spare its customers a conditioning on the development of market interest rates at zero costs.

Finally, a bank diversifies idiosyncratic risks in reducing the overall risk of its portfolio to a certain level by composing it of a sufficiently large number of sufficiently uncorrelated exposures. Hence, if the number of exposures matters diversification is subject to economies of scale. But for a systematic risk the number of exposures does not matter because the exposures are not uncorrelated in the first place. The law of large numbers cannot be applied and therefore it does not matter how large the number of exposures is. Since systematic risks cannot be diversified there are no scale economies of this specific type in taking them. And in so far as it is a systematic risk, this also applies to interest rate risk.

Two insights inform the discovery of a more innovative approach to explaining why banks take interest rate risk. First, each of the three economies of scale discussed above could be the basis for that part of an explanation why banks take interest rate risk that concerns this risk's idiosyncratic part, provided there is such a part. Second, Baltensperger (1972) already points out that it is possible for banks to diversify the risk of withdrawal by depositors and in doing so he effectively highlights one source of interest rate risk as the source of an idiosyncratic part of this risk. The underlying reasoning builds on a richer understanding of the actual interest rate risk of banks. This is introduced first.

At the risk of oversimplification, one might say that in the microeconomics of banking, interest rate risk is predominantly understood as just another type of market risk. In particular, theoretical contributions usually do not distinguish between interest rate risk resulting from a bank's business

---

[48] In more formal terms, what would be required is an implementation of a Arrow-Debreu system of contingent claims.

with professional counterparts and with retail customers. But there is an important difference. Whereas professional counterparts usually act in predictable ways, e.g. always exercise an option which is in the money before it expires, predicting retail customers' behavior is not as straightforward. In particular, the behavioral maturity of demand deposits is generally understood to diverge significantly from the contractual maturity. Whereas demand deposits come with no contractual maturity at all, their behavioral maturity is commonly estimated to amount to several years. In its most recent regulatory standards the BCBS (2016) again confirms the need to estimate the behavioral maturity of demand deposits instead of simply taking the contractual maturity of zero for quantifying a bank's exposure to changes in interest rates. Taking the contractual maturity would lead to a higher estimates of this exposure and hence would be more conservative from a regulator's view point. But these estimates are rejected as unrealistically high. Besides demand deposits there are other bank products that also come with options the exercising of which is difficult to predict if retail customers are involved. The most prominent examples include the prepayment of loans and the drawing down on lines of credit. Collectively, these types of options are commonly referred to behavioral options.

Taking up on this, that part of the interest rate risk of a bank may be considered idiosyncratic that results from behavioral options. Because, for example, if demand deposits are withdrawn, other sources of funds need to be tapped that possibly charge higher interest rates.[49] Taking the risk of withdrawal of demand deposits can plausible be thought of as exhibiting all three economies of scale discussed above. First, accepting demand deposits from a larger number of customers may make a more sophisticated assessment of the individual withdrawal behavior possible. Second, if the withdrawal risk can be diversified, this would explain why deposit contracts are commonly not conditioned on the withdrawals of others. Third, withdrawal risk may indeed be diversifiable as the individual withdrawal probabilities appear not to be perfectly correlated and bank runs are rare events. For other bank products with behavioral options, similar conclusions may be drawn.

However, this explanation why banks take interest rate risk merits critical comment. To begin with, this explanation only addresses one specific source of the interest rate risk of banks. And it hinges on the empirical assumption of the exercising of the relevant behavioral options not being perfectly correlated. Put differently, it is only applicable, if the understanding of banks' interest rate risk is enriched in a certain way which may make it more realistic but at the same time makes it less general. More importantly, this explanation does not explain why banks retain interest rate risk on the level of the individual bank. The interest rate risk remaining after diversification could in principle be hedged completely on financial markets. But the explanation for why banks take interest rate risk presented here does not explain why this is not observed.

Examining possible explanations: asymmetric information

The second of the three paradigms of the microeconomics of banking explains what banks are and do mainly with reference to the mitigation of problems arising from asymmetric information. The question why banks take interest rate risk is explicitly addressed in the belonging literature. And interestingly, the focus is on demand deposits. In particular, Hellwig (1998) investigates whether explanations based on asymmetric information provided for why banks take demand deposits also explain why banks take interest rate risk. Dwyer and Samartin (2009) find that these explanations for why banks take demand deposits seem applicable to various historical episodes of banking.

---

[49]   Frequently, the risk of withdrawal of demand deposits is thought of as a liquidity risk. But as long as other sources of funds are accessible it is rather a solvency risk, if the interest rates to be paid for funds from these sources are higher.

Hellwig (1998) looks at the two defining characteristics of demand deposits and how they can be explained with reference to asymmetric information in turn. The first of these defining characteristics is that demand deposits are a form of debt. As opposed to equity, debt gives rise to payment obligations independent of the financial condition of the originator, unless the originator goes bankrupt. Depending on the precise problem of asymmetric information, debt can be preferable to equity for different reasons. If the effort level of the bank cannot be observed, debt might reduce moral hazard provided that the bank benefits from the residual surplus. And if the profit of the bank cannot be observed, debt spares costly state verification which would otherwise be necessary in order to avoid misrepresentation. The second defining characteristic of demand deposits is that they are payable on demand. As opposed to claims with a fixed term or maturity, claims payable on demand can be presented any time and then have to be met immediately. And again depending on the precise problem of asymmetric information, on demand can be preferable to fixed term for various reasons. If the random liquidity needs of depositors cannot be observed, on demand is a possibility whereas, for example, conditioning a fixed term on the unobservable liquidity needs of depositors is not. If a possible harmful action of the bank can only be observed afterwards, on demand comes with the threat of punishment in the form of liquidation. And if gathering information about the actions of a bank is costly, on demand discourages free riding provided a sequential servicing constraint is in place.

Now Hellwig (1998) is quick to point out that neither of these explanations also explains banks' taking of interest rate risk. According to him, this follows directly from the fact that the development of interest rates is publicly observable. He even notes that inducing the bank to select a more beneficial effort level is subject to less disturbances if macro developments are controlled for. However, this argument implicitly also rests on another aspect of interest rate risk as predominantly understood, namely that market interest rates can hardly be influenced by any market participant individually. Because otherwise there may is a potential for moral hazard.

It is generally agreed that the central bank is able to change market interest rates at least at the short end. Short-term interest rates are targeted with standard refinancing operations and long-term rates additionally through forward guidance and quantitative easing or tightening. This has also long been recognized by economists. The central bank's steering of interest rates features in many theoretical models and empirical studies. Furthermore, it has also long been recognized that treating the central bank's interventions as external shocks is a significant simplification. Instead, policy reaction functions have been analyzed and estimated. But the strategic interaction between the central bank's interest rate decisions and normal banks' taking of interest rate risk only recently became the subject of mainstream economic research. Borio and Zhu (2012) fire the starting gun on a new strand of research investigating how monetary policy influences the risk-taking of banks in general. Farhi and Tirole (2012) model how in turn monetary policy is influenced by banks' risk-taking, more specifically by banks' taking of interest rate risk. They find that banks have an incentive to take this systematic risk. Because the more correlated an individual banks risk is with the risks of other banks, the higher is the probability that it is bailed out if necessary. The basic rationale is that the central bank cannot commit itself to letting a significant number of banks fail. The idea that a central bank may be hesitant to increase short-term interest rates, if many banks have a large exposure toward such a change, is one dimension of what has become known as the "Greenspan put", named after the former Chairman of the Federal Reserve.

The assessment of this explanation why banks take interest rate risk is more positive. It is true that, whereas the explanation based on transaction costs presented earlier only concerns an idiosyncratic part of banks' interest rate risk, the explanation based on asymmetric information presented here only concerns its systematic part. But in contrast to the earlier explanation this explanation also explains why banks retain interest rate risk on the level of the individual bank. Due to the more or less implicit guarantee of the central bank, normal banks have a cost advantage in retaining this risk compared with market participant without this guarantee.

Examining possible explanations: quintessential risk-taking

The third of the three paradigms of the microeconomics of banking explains what banks are and do mainly with reference to risk management or risk-taking. Advancing the strand which focuses on quintessential risk-taking, Scholtens and van Wensveen (2000, 2003) explicitly address banks' taking of interest rate risk. According to them, interest rate risk is one of the idiosyncratic or systematic risks the "absorbtion" of which constitutes the value adding service of banks to the economy or, put differently, their business model. In so far the interest rate risk is a systematic or non-diversifiable risk, absorbtion cannot mean elimination. The idea is rather that a bank is particularly adept in managing the risk it takes itself.

In its Financial Stability Review the BBK (2014a) reports that savings banks and credit cooperatives take significantly more interest rate risk in their non-trading business[50] and are significantly more dependent on net interest income than other credit institution such as the rather larger commercial banks. As a case in point, the Deutsche Bank (2015, p. 197) assesses its previous year interest rate risk from non-trading business[51] to be "immaterial". For one thing, this suggests that the taking of interest rate risk should not be seen as an essential part of banking but rather as a business decision. In the same vain, this observation raises the question what the reason for the difference in taking of interest rate risk may be. Two potential reasons immediately come to mind. First, larger and more sophisticated banks may be able to hedge interest rate risk on more favorable terms. Second, the same banks may also be able to realize more cross-selling opportunities and earn fees for services rather than returns from risk-taking. Both potential reasons effectively draw on some economies of scale. Along these lines, the taking of interest rate risk by some banks can be traced to insufficient scale in some critical area such as capital market activities. Note that the scale economies in question are such that smaller banks take more interest rate risk. This is the other direction than scale economies discussed earlier. For example, a bank with more depositors may have better economies of scale in predicting the individual depositor's exercising of the behavioral option involved, namely the potential withdrawal of his deposits.

But of course the scale economies at issue here could also readily feature in an explanation focusing on transaction costs. Now there is another potential reason for why the smaller banks take interest rate risk. The benefit from an exposure that is more correlated with the exposure of other banks may be larger for smaller banks. Because with correlated exposures smaller banks may increase their probability of being bailed out if required, or of influencing monetary policy in their interest. In contrast, a larger bank may count on being bailed out even if it is the only one in trouble and on being considered by policy makers individually. This sort of reasoning obviously ties in with the rationale presented as an explanation focusing on asymmetric information. Here it becomes apparent that understanding banks as quintessential risk-takers does not imply that one has to reject explanations of risk-taking that are based on transactions costs or asymmetric information. On the contrary, what is required is to understand these explanations as explanations of an essential part of what banks do.

The question remains where the interest rate risk that banks take originally comes from. Unsurprisingly, the answer depends on the understanding of banking that is employed. But crucially, between the two answers the degree to which taking interest rate risk belongs to the core business of banks varies significantly. The understanding of banking as the intermediation of

---

[50]   To be precise, here interest rate risk in the banks' banking books is referred to.
[51]   Again, interest rate risk in the banking book is referred to here.

loanable funds implies that a bank's interest rate risk results from a per se non-essential mismatch between claims and obligations of ultimate lenders and ultimate borrowers. If the core of what a bank does is to channel funds, a mismatch in repricing terms is possible but not necessary. On the contrary, the understanding of banking as financing through money creation entails that a bank's interest rate risk is a much more natural result from the signature service provided to its customers. If a bank primarily grants loans by creating deposits, a mismatch in repricing terms is still not strictly necessary but indeed very natural. It could even be argued that this mismatch is an elementary part of the overall mismatch which makes financing as offered by banks attractive in the first place. Consider, for example, a customer who intends to purchase real estate and to finance this with a bank loan. In order to purchase the real estate the customer has to transfer the new deposits created in his account to the account of the current owner. Hence, these deposits have to be immediately transferable, that is have to have zero maturity. But it is implausible that the customer is in turn willing to take a loan that is immediately due. If he had the money at hand to pay back the loan, there would be no point in taking it out in the first place. Consequently, financing through money creations naturally goes along with accepting a maturity mismatch on the side of the bank. And a maturity mismatch may very well come with a mismatch in repricing terms which then implies interest rate risk, again as a result of risk-aversion of the of the counterparties involved.

In the model of Hellwig (1994) interest rate risk is induced by technology. It is non-essential in the sense described ealier because the modelled bank acts as an intermediary of loanable funds. With the same traditional understanding in mind, Hellwig (1998) points to the availability of a bank as one possible source of its interest rate risk. As he understands it, a bank that is always available for ultimate lenders and ultimate borrowers may end up taking some interest rate risk, if the tools it has for shifting risk are clumsy for whatever reason.[52] With the modern understanding of banking as financing through money creation, the availability of a bank is mainly to be understood as being available for providing finance. And if providing finance goes along with taking interest rate risk as discussed above, then banks can be seen as also essentially being available to take interest rate risk.

---

[52] Hellwig (1998) considers a bon issue to private households.

Chapter 4 Monetary economics of the transmission channels

One of the primary topics of monetary economics is how monetary policy affects the economy. There is a consensus that the transmission mechanism in operation may feature a variety of transmission channels. Three transmission channels that receive particular attention in economic research are the interest rate channel, the credit channel, and the risk-taking channel. These transmission channels are compatible in the sense that they can in principle all operate simultaneously.

Friedman and Schwartz (1963) and subsequent empirical studies are generally seen as having established that monetary policy has real effects. And these real effects are commonly understood as what makes the analysis of the transmission mechanism worthwhile. The interest rate channel, the credit channel, and the risk-taking channel are specific chains of effects that start with a monetary policy shock and lead to some real effects. The most fundamental real effect is of course a change in real output.

The interest rate channel, the credit channel, and the risk-taking channel each feature a different characterising key effect of monetary policy. Through the interest rate channel monetary policy affects general market interest rates. Through the credit channel monetary policy affects the individual risk premium of borrowers.[53] And through the risk-taking channel monetary policy affects the individual risk-taking of lenders. Of course, some of the remaining parts of these three chains of effects overlap.[54]

The interest rate channel can be traced back to the work of Keynes (1936). And the credit channel's identification is part of the research of Bernanke (1983). But by now a huge literature on these two transmission channels exists. The following review confines itself to presenting them in their prototypical forms. It contrasts the traditional version with the modern version where there are the two. And it presents empirical findings where the existence or quantitative importance has been subject to debate.

The risk-taking channel is first referred to with this designation by Borio and Zhu (2012). The literature on this transmission channel is still by far the smallest but it is growing rapidly. The following review covers the most important models but focusses on the empirical evidence for the existence and quantitative importance of the risk-taking channel. One important take-away is that the research on the taking of interest rate risk as induced by monetary policy is still underdeveloped. One comment is in order concerning the organization of what follows. As to be expected of a body of literature of this size, other ways to delimit the transmission channels can also be found. The most frequently identified alternative fault line separates the balance-sheet channel and the bank lending channel and thereby divides the credit channel as it is delimited here. For example, Hubbard (1995) sees the balance-sheet channel only as a part of a broad but not of the narrow credit channel which is confined to the bank lending channel. Bofinger (2001) applies the distinction between the money and the credit view, the latter of which corresponds to the bank lending channel. And Kashyap and Stein (1997) isolate the bank lending channel as bank-centric, a categorization that can plausibly be seen to extend to the risk-taking channel. The delimitation applied here follows Bernanke and Gertler (1995), Mishkin (1996), and Borio and Zhu (2012) among many others. It is seen as best accommodating the modern versions of both the interest rate channel and the bank lending channel. The modern version of the bank lending channel is similar to the balance-sheet channel. This is the main reason for keeping them

---

[53] As is explained below, this is an adequate description at least of the modern version of the credit channel according to which the bank lending channel is similar to the balance-sheet channel for borrowers that are themselves lenders.

[54] For example, both the interest rate channel and the credit channel feature unambiguous effects on real output.

under one roof. Another reason is that the modern version of the credit channel also features bank lending and the modern version of the bank lending channel extends to non-banks. Hence, being bank-centric is not an unambiguous defining characteristic any more.

4.1 Interest rate channel

Through the interest rate channel monetary policy affects general market interest rates. The idea of the interest rate channel is the most traditional and a still widely accepted explanation of the transmission of monetary policy. The groundbreaking innovation of this idea is to counter the notion of the neutrality of money with repricing frictions, commonly called sticky prices. Whereas real effects of monetary policy cannot be explained under the assumption of the neutrality of money, they can with reference to the interest rate channel. The interest rate channel has been subject to intense scrutiny and other transmission channels of monetary policy have been suggested to improve on supposed shortcomings. But it is a consensus that the interest rate channel exists and is of quantitative importance. Other suggested transmission channels are commonly presented as amendments rather than alternatives. Hence, the interest rate channel is of particular relevance on its own and as a reference and starting point.

4.1.1 Neutrality of money

In his canonical definition, Patinkin (2008) identifies the neutrality of money as the notion that changes in the quantity of money only affect the level of prices but not actual outputs.[55] Put differently, the notion of the neutrality of money asserts the dichotomy between nominal and real variables and claims that changes in the quantity of money only affect the former but not the latter. The notion of the neutrality of money originates from the quantity theory of money which is an integral part of classical economics.[56] According to this theory, at least in its most basic form, a change in the volume of money only leads to a proportionate change of all prices, and hence nominal values, but leaves all real values unaffected.

The neutrality of money holds under three assumptions. First, money cannot be consumed in a way that yields utility. Second, only relative prices determine production and allocation. Third, prices adjust without frictions. Whereas the first assumption is generally accepted, the second and the third assumption are commonly contested. More precisely, the second assumption is frequently opposed with reference to the money illusion[57] and the third assumption is often rejected in favour of sticky prices. Whereas the money illusion conflicts with the standard assumption of rationality, sticky prices can be the result of frictions integrable into the standard framework. However, sticky prices can also be the result of the money illusion, for example in the form of nominal rigidities imposed through contracts. But before turning to alternative theories of money, two differentiations and two clarifications are in order.

The following two differentiations are important. First, long-run neutrality is distinguished from short-run neutrality. Theories with long-run neutrality and short-run non-neutrality feature real disturbances but only during some limited period of adjustment to the changed quantity of

---

[55] The "neutrality of money" is the most common term used to designate this notion. An alternative term is the "veil of money". For an investigation into the origin of both terms see Patinkin and Steiger (1989) who ascribe the introduction of the former term into the debate among English-speaking economists to von Hayek (1931) and of the latter to Hicks (1935).

[56] However, this is not to say that all proponents of the quantity theory denied the existence of any real effects of changes in the quantity of money. For a detailed presentation of the individual positions adopted see Patinkin (1972) who pays particular attention to the differentiation between short-run and long-run effects in the thinking of Fisher (1922).

[57] The money illusion consists in people rather thinking in nominal than in real terms. Fisher (1928) and Patinkin (1965) provide the standard expositions of this phenomenon. Shafir et al. (1997) marshal empirical evidence.

money.[58] The most prominent advocate of a theory of this kind is Friedman (1970). He presents long-run neutrality and short-run non-neutrality as the seventh of his eleven key-propositions of monetarism. Second, neutrality is distinguished from superneutrality. Whereas neutrality concerns the quantity of money, superneutrality concerns its growth rate. Superneutrality consists in the lack of effects on actual output of a shift of the growth rate of the amount of money. One of the best-known models featuring superneutrality is the one developed by Sidrauski (1967).

The following two clarifications are helpful. First, neutrality is not the same as irrelevance. The neutrality of money is consistent with the view that the introduction of money improves on the barter economy and hence that money is relevant. Money can still be assumed to increase efficiency by functioning as a medium of exchange, a store of value, and as a unit of account. Second, neutrality also extends to distribution. The neutrality of money does not only say that a change in the quantity of money leaves the aggregate of actual outputs unaffected but also their allocation. The standard rationale for the possibility of short-run neutrality features a proportionate change of the money holding of every agent.

The notion of the neutrality of money has a long and influential history in economics. And at least the idea of long-run neutrality remains influential. But the claim of short-run neutrality is hardly championed any more.[59] And distributional effects have received particular attention.[60] Monetary economics has abandoned the assumption that prices adjust without frictions. Instead, prices are assumed to be sticky. The money illusion, however, does not feature explicitly in the most influential models.

4.1.2 Sticky prices

The interest rate channel is a chain of effects in which sticky prices feature critically. Due to sticky prices monetary policy affects not only nominal interest rates but also real interest rates. Real interest rates in turn determine the real cost of capital for firms and households. And the real cost of capital govern real investment which pays into real output. Hence, according to the interest rate channel, expansionary monetary policy decreases real interest rates, thereby decreases the real cost of capital, therefore increases real investment, and thus increases real output. And the effects of contractionary monetary policy simply have the opposite sign. In so far as the cost of capital depend on long-term interest rates monetary policy that directly only affects a certain short-term interest rate has an indirect effect through expectations. With the interest rate channel, sticky prices and expectations enable the central bank to influence real long-term interest rates by setting a nominal short-term interest rate or policy rate.

The introduction of the interest rate channel into economic research is commonly traced back to Keynes (1936).[61] Paying tribute to this time, some of the traditional expositions of the interest rate channel still readily referred to today center around monetary aggregates. For example, Hubbard (1995) describes the central bank as controlling the quantity of money.[62] Households hold money for transaction purposes and bonds because they yield interest. An increase in the quantity of money leads to a balancing effect in the form of an increase in the nominal price of bonds and thereby to a decrease in the nominal interest rate. Provided prices are sticky, this entails a decrease in the real interest rate. And this leads to a decrease in the cost of capital

---

[58] The standard reference for an explanation of short-run non-neutrality is Lucas (1972).

[59] This observation is already made by Bernanke and Gertler (1995) among others.

[60] As will be shown below, one of the characterizing features of the credit channel is that it features distributional effects. With a different twist, Piketty (2014) fired the starting gun on the current public debate. For a recent discussion of the bearing of monetary policy on inequality from the perspective of a central banker see Mersch (2014).

[61] As for many other matters, the presentation by Hicks (1937) is particularly illustrative in this respect.

[62] In particular, Hubbard (1995) here argues along the lines of the money multiplier theory.

and in turn to an increase in interest-sensitive spending and in particular in investment. A more modern understanding of the interest rate channel accommodates the fact that monetary policy in advanced economies is nowadays interest rate focused.[63] This understanding underlies current research. In so far as it conducts conventional monetary policy, the central bank is seen as determining a certain nominal short-term interest rate referred to as the policy rate, influencing the rest of the nominal term structure via expectations and again the real term structure via sticky prices.

The traditional and the modern version of the interest rate channel differ in more than just semantics. This becomes particularly apparent in the different roles they assign to banks. According to the traditional version, banks are relevant only in so far as monetary policy can influence the volume of deposits through determining the quantity of reserves. Bank loans do not matter as in Modigliani and Miller (1958). According to the modern version, bank loans do matter because the interest rates charged on them depend on the interest rate set by the central bank and affect the non-bank economy. Interest rates on bank loans influence the cost of capital.

Two further chains of effects are worth a closer look. First, in an open economy a change in the real interest rate affects the exchange rate. If the real interest rate of investments denominated in one currency increases, these investments become relatively more attractive. Thus, the demand for these investments increases and with it the demand for the respective currency and so does the exchange rate. Hence, net exports decrease and with them total output. The canonic expositions of this chain of effects is provided by Fleming (1962). Second, the prices of other assets are affected in the same direction as real bond prices. If the real price of bonds decreases, they become relatively more attractive compared to other assets such as equities. Thus, the demand for these other assets decreases and and so do their prices. Hence, the value of firms and the wealth of households decrease and with them investment and consumption and ultimately total output. Most prominently, Tobin (1969) analyzes the role of changes in equity prices and Modigliani (1971) emphasises the relevance of changes in wealth through their impact on consumers' expenditure. Mishkin (1996) presents these two chains of effects as the exchange rate channel and the equity-price channel, respectively. He distinguishes them from the interest rate channel and collectively introduces them as other asset price channels. However, it is important to note the close link of these two chains of effects to the interest rate channel. Both also build on sticky prices. And both tie in with the change in real interest rates. The first one does so directly, the second one indirectly via the change in the real price of bonds. After all, this is nothing but the flipside of the real interest rate. These observations suggest at least to treat both chains of effect in conjunction with the interest rate channel or even to include them in a broad interest rate channel. A final observation is that both chains of effects have final effects with the same sign as the final effect of what may be seen as the narrow interest rate channel. However that they are amplifying is not straight forward since they source from arbitrage and hence in so far also reduce the original effect.

4.2 Credit channel

Through the credit channel monetary policy affects the individual risk premium of borrowers. The idea of the credit view or credit channel is not that of an alternative transmission channel of monetary policy but that of a collection of chains of effects that amplify the interest rate channel. The credit channel amends the interest rate channel with two chains of effects that source from the problem of asymmetric information between borrowers and lenders about the utilization of

---

[63] For a brief presentation of the shift of focus from money aggregates to interest rates in economic research and monetary policy see Bofinger (2001, p. 80).

funds. These two chains of effects are known as the balance-sheet channel and the bank lending channel.

The defining characteristic of the credit channel and the connecting element of the balance-sheet channel and the bank lending channel is the underlying hypothesis that asymmetric information makes uncollateralized external finance more expensive than internal finance. This underlying hypothesis is elaborated on in two different ways. The balance-sheet channel functions through a change in borrowers' financial situation. The bank lending channel works via a change in the supply of bank loans.

Two motives for the development of the credit channel can be identified. First, to account for the magnitude of the effects of changes in interest rates, which are perceived as larger than can plausibly be explained with the interest rate channel alone. Second, to account for the problem of asymmetric information, which is not featured in the interest rate channel as such.[64] Whereas the first is clearly due to empirical observations, the second steams at least in part from methodological and theoretical considerations.

The credit channel is the subject of a large body of literature. Bernanke (1983) points the way. Gertler and Hubbard (1988) develop an early model featuring the balance-sheet channel and Bernanke and Blinder (1988) introduce the bank lending channel. Bernanke and Gertler (1995), Hubbard (1995), Cecchetti (1995) and Mishkin (1996) provide the canonical reviews.[65] The balance-sheet channel and the bank lending channel are presented in turn.

4.2.1 Balance-sheet channel

The balance-sheet channel functions through a change in borrowers' financial situation, that is his net worth, liquidity and cash flows, but in a different way than the equity-price channel as delimited by Mishkin (1996). As Mishkin (2001) emphasizes, only the former rests on asymmetric information while the latter does not. The distinguishing feature of the balance-sheet channel is that a change in a borrower's financial situation has an effect through the accompanying change of the severity of problems arising from asymmetric information between him and his lender. More specifically, the worse the financial situation of a borrower, the more severe are the agency problems between him and his lender. Put differently, the less the incentives of a borrower and his lender are aligned, the more expensive is external finance under asymmetric information. In the extreme case, there can even occur credit rationing as described by Stiglitz and Weiss (1981).[66]

Gertler and Hubbard (1988) develop an early model that includes the balance-sheet channel. The classical references are the models by Bernanke and Gertler (1989, 1990). Of the reviews on the credit channel mentioned above, the one by Mishkin (1996) focusses on the balance-sheet channel in particular. Furthermore, Bernanke et al. (1996) provide a dedicated analysis of the balance-sheet channel which they are the first to address as the financial accelerator.[67] The essential rationale is as follows. Monetary policy affects the financial situations of borrowers. And the financial situation of a borrower determines not only his need for external finance but

---

[64] These two motives are extracted from the literature by Hubbard (1995), Bernanke and Gertler (1995), and Mishkin (1996). Besides the magnitude of the effects, Bernanke and Gertler (1995) point to the timing and the composition of the effects of changes of interest rates as unexplainable with the interest rate channel. Besides, Bernanke and Gertler (1995) points out that it is also possible to provide a rationale for the credit channel which does not feature asymmetric information but certain other frictions such as costly enforcement of contracts.

[65] Hubbard (1995) points to Bernanke (1983) as one of the earliest contributions to the modern literature on the credit channel but also identifies a number of historical predecessors.

[66] Remember that credit rationing is the situation in which the lending market ceases to clear due to the classical lemons problem in screening as introduced by Akerlof (1970).

[67] Referring to the balance-sheet channel as the financial accelerator emphasises that it amends the interest rate channel.

in particular the price he has to pay for external finance and whether he has access to external finance at all. Therefore monetary policy affects the overall costs and availability of finance for borrowers and thereby their expenditure including especially their investment and thus ultimately total output.

Monetary policy affects the financial situation of a borrower directly as well as indirectly.[68] The direct effects most importantly include changes in the interest to be paid on debt and in the value of assets. The indirect effects are direct effects on the financial situations of other agents in the economy which affect markets the borrower is active in. For a given investment, a borrower's financial situation determines his need for external finance. The less finance can be raised internally, the more finance has to be raised externally from lenders.[69] The borrower's need for external finance therefore increases if his financial situation deteriorates. Furthermore, a borrower's financial situation determines the price he has to pay for external finance. If a borrower's financial situation deteriorates, he becomes less creditworthy. Because if the value of his assets decrease, he can pledge less collateral. And if his liquidity or cash-flows decrease sufficiently, he cannot meet payment obligations as they come due. Hence a deterioration of the financial situation of the borrower leads to a decrease in alignment of his incentives with the incentives of his lender. Put differently, with less skin in the game the borrower might be induced to gamble for resurrection, and the lender increases the risk premium and may in the extreme case deny any funding.

There is a large number of empirical studies that investigate the existence and quantitative importance of the balance-sheet channel. By and large Bernanke (2007) summarizes the main results as follows. For firms both the existence as well as the quantitative importance of the balance sheet channel is generally accepted. For households the existence is widely agreed upon but the quantitative importance of the balance-sheet channel is still subject to debate.

4.2.2 Bank lending channel

As the name suggests, the bank lending channel assigns a special role to banks and the lending they provide in the transmission of monetary policy. It is built on the premise that banks have a comparative advantage over the securities market in addressing the problem of asymmetric information in the market for funds. Diamond (1984) famously kicks off the development of a theoretical rationale for this assumption with his explanation of banks as delegated monitors. James (1987), Lummer and McConnell (1989), and Slovin et al. (1993) provide some of the earliest and still widely cited empirical evidence on what is known as the uniqueness of bank loans.[70] The bank lending channel draws on this research in that it critically features bank-dependent borrowers. The crucial assumption here is that for these bank-dependent borrowers

---

[68] Mishkin (1996) proposes to distinguish between effects of changes in real and nominal interest rates, instead. He points out that changes in real interest rates change asset values but that the interest payments in particular on short-term debt depend on nominal interest rates. Implicitly he makes the point that the net worth of a borrower or its solvency, may be of secondary importance for a lender, in particular if the credit is short-term, as long as the borrower has sufficient liquidity and does not declare bankruptcy.

[69] Note that in most expositions of the balance-sheet channel externally raised finance includes not only debt but equity also and the terms "borrower" and "lender" are used in an inclusive way, accordingly. For a discussion about the distinction between finance raised internally and externally see Bernanke et al. (1996). Among other things they address the question in how far retained earnings, which usually serve as the prime example for finance raised internally, can plausibly be treated as such for publicly owned firms.

[70] More specifically, James (1987) finds that an announcement of the granting of a bank loan has a positive effect on the stock value of the borrower while an announcement of the issuing of a bond does not have this effect. Lummer and McConnell (1989) find that it is not the granting of the first loan of any one lender to a certain borrower but rather the renewal of a loan that fuels the positive effects on the stock value of the borrower. And Slovin et al. (1993) find that the bankruptcy of a bank affects the stock value of firms adversely that have borrowed from that bank.

there exists no perfect substitute for bank loans, neither provided by a non-bank intermediary nor raised directly.

Bernanke and Blinder (1988) develop the reference model of the bank lending channel. Of the reviews on the credit channel mentioned above, the ones by Bernanke and Gertler (1995) and Hubbard (1995) contain particularly insightful discussions of the bank lending channel. The traditional story is as follows. Monetary policy influences the volume of loans banks can grant. And the volume of bank loans influences the expenditures of firms and households that pay into total output. Therefore monetary policy influences total output.

The traditional rationale for how monetary policy affects the volume of loans banks can grant goes like this. Through its open market operations the central bank determines the volume of reserves as it pays and charges reserves when it buys and sells securities. And given a reserve requirement for loanable funds this implies that the central bank determines the maximum volume of loanable funds and thereby of loans. Hence, through its open market operations the central bank not only determines the short-term interest rate but also the volume of loans. For example, if the central bank aims at implementing a contractionary monetary policy, it sells securities and charges reserves. Thereby reserves are drained from the system. As a consequence, the possible volume of loans is decreased. Obviously, the crucial assumption here is that there are no perfect substitutes for loanable funds for which there is a reserve requirement.

Two standard lines of attack against the bank lending channel can be identified. First, the influence of monetary policy on the volume of bank loans is contested. This line of attack aims at the assumed non-existence of a perfect substitute for loanable funds for which there is a reserve requirement for banks. Second, the lack of substitutability of bank loans for firms is questioned. This line of attack targets at the assumed non-existence of a perfect substitute for bank loans for some borrowers, that is the existence of bank-dependent borrowers.

The standard reference for the first line of attack is the objection by Romer and Romer (1990). Their rationale is inspired by the finding of Fama (1985) that debt issued by banks and debt issued by non-banks behave similarly. In effect, they reason that banks should be able to substitute loanable funds for which there are high reserve requirements such as deposits easily with other forms of debt for which there are lower or no reserve requirements.[71] However, there is an equally well-known response to this objection by Stein (1998). His basic point is that deposits on the one hand come with particularly high reserve requirements but on the other hand are insured. And given asymmetric information between the bank and the providers of its loanable funds, uninsured sources of funds turn out not to be a perfect substitute for deposits as they come with agency problems.[72]

Even though the response by Stein (1998) is widely seen as saving the bank lending channel at least in principle, it marks an important turning point toward a modern version of the bank lending channel. The traditional version of the bank lending channel features monetary policy as determining the quantity of loans directly and not only indirectly as a market outcome. As Bernanke (2007) points out, this version of the bank lending channel was identified under policy arrangements and market conditions that held in the US during the 1960s and 1970s but do not hold any more. In particular, banks' access to loanable funds without reserve requirements has improved markedly. And even though they are not perfect substitutes because they are not ensured and hence come with agency problems, these agency problems simply lead to higher funding costs. As higher funding costs for the bank lead to higher interest rates charged for loans

---

[71] Romer and Romer (1990) also provide an empirical analysis which uses changes in monetary policy identified to be independent of real economic development by Romer and Romer (1989). They analyze the relation between lending and output and find no sign of the transmission of monetary policy. This empirical analysis is more related to the second line of attack on the bank lending channel.

[72] Lucas and McDonald (1992) also highlight to the significance of deposit insurance for the capital structure of banks.

from the bank the quantity of loans is also affected but only indirectly as a market outcome. The modern version of the bank lending channel, the development of which started with the response by Stein (1998), hence resembles the balance-sheet channel with banks as borrowers. And this version of the bank lending channel naturally extends to non-banks that not only lend but also borrow. What remains of the price-quantity-dichotomy of the balance-sheet channel and the bank lending channel is that when a bank lends to a firm or household the balance-sheet channel works through changes on the side of the firm or household and the bank lending channel works through changes on the side of the bank. In this sense, the balance-sheet channel is regarded as working through the demand side and the bank lending channel as working through the supply-side. But at the heart of both channels is that monetary policy affects the individual risk premium of borrowers.

There is a large number of contributions that follow the second line of attack and question the supposed lack of substitutability of bank loans for firms. These contributions bring forward at least three types of observations that are seen as conflicting with this idea of the bank lending channel. First, the timing of events after a change of monetary policy. Second, the development of bank-loans relative to the development of non-bank lending after a change of monetary policy. Third, the development of bank-loans relative to the development of non-bank lending through time. However, all three types of evidence are also challenged.

Ramey (1993) investigates timing of events after a change of monetary policy. The main result of her empirical analysis is that changes in monetary aggregates have a much higher explanatory power for changes in output than changes in the volume of bank loans. And she concludes that apart from possible reinforcing effects in later periods the transmission of monetary policy through changes in the volume of bank loans is not of quantitative importance.[73] This type of critique is generally dismissed as mistaken. Because, as for example Mishkin (1996) and Cecchetti (1995) point out, the bank lending channel is not committed to a certain timing of events. Instead, events that are earlier in the chain of effects may be later in time.[74] Meltzer (1995) investigates the development of bank-loans relative to the development of non-bank lending after a change of monetary policy. He hypothesizes that only if the volumes of bank loans and non-bank lending are affected differently this is evidence for a bank lending channel of quantitative importance. However, he does not find any evidence for significantly different developments of the volume of bank loans and the volume of non-bank lending. Among many others, Edwards and Mishkin (1995) investigate the development of bank-loans relative to the development of non-bank lending through time. They find that in the US bank lending is decreasing as a share of total lending. And they conclude that if the bank lending channel exists, its quantitative importance must also be decreasing.

Answers to the second and third type of critique usually involve a switch from time series to cross sections. Put differently and on the edge of oversimplification, the two main lessens to be drawn can be stated as follows. First, the overall quantitative importance of the bank lending channel indeed seems to be rather limited. Second, the effects are however distributed unequally and some agents are affected significantly. This second lesson actually has two aspects. First, some borrowers' investment changes with the supply of bank loans. Second, some banks' supply of loans changes with the amount of deposits.[75] In effect, both crucial assumptions of the bank

---

[73] Ramey (1993) aims at the bank lending channel, but cannot distinguish between supply and demand effects for lack of data. Hence her attack actually concerns the credit channel as a whole.

[74] The point here is that causality in an economic sense is seen not to require that the cause occurs before the effect but that expectations can do the trick.

[75] A related point emphasised by Cecchetti (1995) is that distributional effects bear on the efficiency of the outcome of monetary policy. Because the dependence on which agents, banks and firms, are affected is not in any unambiguous way related to the social advantageousness of a firm's intended utilization of funds that is the efficient allocation of resources.

lending channel are confirmed empirically. They hold in the sense that the assumed mechanism exists and is quantitatively relevant for some agents, if hardly in the aggregate. The distinction between borrowers that depend on bank loans and borrowers that do not has always been a part of the idea of the bank lending channel. The distinction between banks that are affected and banks that are not is however however a somewhat newer part of the story. Hence, even though neither of the two lines of attack is seen as fatal, both weigh on the quantitative importance of the bank lending channel.

Most prominently, Kashyap and Stein (2000) study cross-sectional differences between the lending of banks. They find that a tightening of monetary policy leads to a reduction of lending by small banks. And further they find that this reduction is more pronounced for less liquid banks. They reason that for small banks it is costly to take on uninsured debt. And further they reason that less liquid banks have to take more pronounced measures that reduce lending in case of a tightening of monetary policy. Less liquid banks have a smaller buffer of assets that can be sold in case of a reduction of insured liabilities. Adjustment needs exceeding this buffer can be met in two ways. Either lending is reduced directly. Or uninsured debt is increased which leads to an increase in the price that needs to be charged for lending and in effect lending is reduced indirectly. Now, they conclude to have produced results that are not only consistent with the bank lending channel but are sufficiently difficult to explain in any other way. Nevertheless, they admit that their results shed no light on the quantitative importance of the lending channel.

Two more recent empirical studies provide cross sectional evidence for the bank lending channel in relationship lending. Black et al. (2007) examine lending to small businesses. Black et al. (2010) investigate lending in subprime communities. Both studies test the same hypothesis which is based on the same rationale, apply the same identification strategy, and produce similar results. The hypothesis has two main parts. First, a tightening of monetary policy leads to an increase in the marginal loan rate charged by banks with an insured-liabilities-to-loan ratio of or just below one. Second, the increase in the marginal loan rate is more pronounced if the bank is more engaged in relationship lending. The rationale is straight forward. With an insured-liabilities-to-loan-ratio of or just below one a tightening of monetary policy forces the bank to take on uninsured debt which is more expensive. For a bank that is more engaged in relationship banking uninsured debt is particularly expensive due to less transparency and hence a more severe agency problem. The identification strategy is adapted from the literature. Only increases of the spread over the risk-free rate count as increases of the loan rate in line with the bank lending channel.[76] The results support the hypothesis for lending to small businesses and lending in subprime communities, respectively. Hence, these studies marshal empirical evidence for the existence of the bank lending channel, though only for banks with a certain balance sheet structure and depending on their engagement in a certain business.

4.3 Risk-taking channel

Through the risk-taking channel monetary policy affects the individual risk-taking of lenders. Banks are at the center of attention of the emerging research. The idea of the risk-taking channel as presented by Borio and Zhu (2012) associates lower interest rates with more risk-taking and in turn higher interest rates with less risk-taking. Two rationales of this link have emerged as canonical. First, banks may aim at a target rate of return. A decrease in interest rates leads to a decrease in the expected return of a portfolio with a given level of risk. But keeping the expected return of the portfolio equal to some target rate can be achieved through an increase of the level of risk. This way of reasoning is usually attributed to Rajan (2005). Second, banks may aim at

---

[76] Black et al. (2007) adapt the measure by Kashyap and Stein (1995) and account for loan default. The basic idea is that with standard supply and demand curves a decrease in supply entails an increase in price.

a target leverage ratio.[77] A decrease in interest rates leads to an increase in asset values and thereby to a disproportionate increase in the value of leveraged equity. But keeping the leverage ratio equal to some target ratio can be achieved by a debt financed balance sheet extension. The standard references for this line of thinking is Adrian and Shin (2008).[78] Both canonical rationales explain why banks react to a decrease of interest rates with additional risk-taking. But in a strict sense, only the first implies an overall increase of the risk of a bank. In its basic form, the second is reconcilable with overall constant risk of a bank before and after the interest rate decrease. Borio and Zhu (2012) grant this point for what they identify as perceived or measured risk. Empirical evidence supportive of a link between lower policy rates and higher overall risk of banks is most prominently marshalled by Altunbas et al. (2014).[79]

In general, the risk-taking channel extends to all types of risk. But actually, the related research has hitherto focused on credit risk. More precisely, the link between lower interest rates and more taking of credit risk by banks has until now received most attention. Notably, Adrian and Shin (2011), and Drees et al. (2013) develop theoretical models. They formalize different rationales for how and under which conditions looser monetary policy leads to more pronounced taking of credit risk by banks. Prominently, De Nicolo et al. (2010), Maddaloni and Peydró (2011), Paligorova and Santos (2013), Buch et al. (2014), Jimenez et al. (2014), and Ioannidou et al. (2015) marshal empirical evidence. The main result supported consistently is that that lower short-term interest rates induce banks to grant riskier new loans. Allen and Rogoff (2011) provide one of the first reviews of the literature. In so far as credit risk is concerned, the risk-taking channel is particularly related to the credit channel and the bank lending channel therein.

Research on the risk-taking channel that goes beyond credit risk is still at an early stage. Deviating from the canonical rationale, some results suggest that banks may not aim at a target leverage ratio but that leverage may be inversely related to some risk-free rate. A decrease in this interest rate may induce banks to increase their leverage. Links of this nature are investigated by Dell'Ariccia et al. (2014) and Angeloni et al. (2015). Besides leverage, interest rate risk receives growing attention. A disproportionate reduction of short-term rates may induce banks to increase their interest rate risk through a larger maturity mismatch. This is one of the lessons drawn by Farhi and Tirole (2012). Another dimension of the relationship between monetary policy and interest rate risk is investigated by Landier et al. (2013), namely interest rate risk in so far as it constitutes the exposure to monetary policy.

Two further observations about the development of the research on the risk-taking channel are noteworthy. First, with the extension to interest rate risk the research on the risk-taking channel advances to a systematic risk, or a risk with a prominent systematic part.[80] Second, interactions between the different aspects of risk become apparent. For example, increases in leverage hardly leave the interest rate risk unaffected. In the following the state of the research on the taking of credit risk, leverage, and interest rate risk as induced by monetary policy is presented and discussed in greater detail.

---

[77] Borio and Zhu (2012) refer to a certain risk budget instead. In terms of content, they make the same point.

[78] Note that as Adrian and Shin (2008) point out, an active balance sheet management of this kind implies an upward sloping demand curve and a downward sloping supply curve for financial assets.

[79] Dell'Ariccia et al. (2014) identify opposing effects through which a decrease in interest rates induces a decrease in risk-taking. They establish theoretically that the net effect of a decrease in interest rates could also be a decrease of the overall risk of a bank.

[80] Note that as such interest rate risk is also a prime candidate for a systemic risk, that is a risk to the overall stability of the financial system. Because it is a frequently cited stylized fact that banks tend to be exposed to a given change in interest rates in a similar way.

4.3.1 Credit risk

The strand of literature on the risk-taking channel that addresses credit risk is by far the largest and most advanced. Two demarcations are important to keep in mind in the assessment of contributions to this topic. First, the risk-taking channel is a transmission channel of monetary policy. Therefore it only concerns the impact of monetary policy but is not necessarily limited to extreme events. Nevertheless, some theoretical models occasionally cited focus on extreme events or do not feature monetary policy as a driving force. Second, credit risk is not the same as risk from lending. Credit risk may result from other activities than lending and other risks may also be understood as risks from lending. The latter fact is the reason why some pivotal empirical studies also report results which touch on leverage and interest rate risk. In what follows both theoretical models and empirical studies are reviewed with these two demarcations in mind.

Not all theoretical models that are occasionally referred to as capturing the risk-taking channel of monetary policy in so far as it concerns credit risk are similarly enlightening. Some models feature monetary policy as inducing the taking of credit risk by banks only in the context of bubbles or bailouts. The model by Allen and Gale (2000, 2004, 2007) explains asset price bubbles as the result of loose monetary policy and its effect on the lending of banks. With agency problems due to limited liability, credit expansion facilitates risk-shifting and asset prices rise above non-leveraged levels. In the model by Diamond and Rajan (2009) a general bailout through a reduction of policy rates is preferable to a bailout of individual banks but is still distortionary. The disciplinary force of demand deposits suffers. Other models do not feature monetary policy as inducing the taking of credit risk by banks at all. The model by Dell'Ariccia and Marquez (2006) explains a lending boom as a result of banks seizing to screen potential borrowers as the share of unknown borrowers becomes too large. But monetary policy does not play a role in this. In the model of Acharya and Naqvi (2012) excess liquidity resulting from increased deposit holdings in times of heightened macroeconomic uncertainty distorts banks' lending decisions. But monetary policy is only discussed in so far its optimal response is concerned which turns out to be contractionary.

In contrast, the two theoretical models presented below are each enlightening to the highest degree but in different ways. None of two these models focusses on bubbles or bailouts. And both models concentrate on the effect of monetary policy on banks' taking of credit risk. The first model features a transparent version of the unambiguous link between lower interest rates and higher risk-taking. The second model presets a natural way to accommodate ambiguity.

Adrian and Shin (2011) present a model which features a decrease in short-term interest rates as the cause for an increase in the volume of risky loans granted and a decrease in the risk premium earned. To begin with, they make three crucial assumptions. First, a decrease in short-term interest rates leads to an increase in the term spread. They present US data from 1987 to 2008 to justify this assumption. Second, banks in general borrow short and lend long. They call this the business of banking. Third, banks are constrained in their granting of risky loans by their risk-bearing capacity. They in effect associate the risk bearing capacity of a bank with its equity.[81] Based on this, they reason in three steps. First, an increase in the term spread increases the profitability of banks. Because the net interest margin increases as the funding costs decrease disproportionately. Second, an increase in the profitability of banks increases their risk-bearing capacity and thereby the volume of granted risky loans. Any arising slack in the risk-bearing constraint is eliminated, provided granting risky loans is profitable. Third, a supply-side driven increase in the volume of granted risky loans decreases the risk premium earned. Because with demand unchanged an increase in supply decreases the market price.

---

[81] The mechanics of the model by Adrian and Shin (2011) basically require a bank to hold its leverage ratio constant. Because the equilibrium leverage ratio is constant this model is featured in this section that concerns credit risk and not in the next section on leverage.

Drees et al. (2013) develop a model which does not only feature random project returns but also noisy signals and in which the overall effect of a low interest rate is ambiguous. They distinguish between the randomness of a project's actual return as its fundamental risk and the noisiness of the signal about a project's return as its opacity risk. The overall risk of the investment in a project is the aggregate of these two risks. They find that, given a low interest rate, such projects are relatively more invested in that have a lower fundamental risk but a higher opacity risk. A case in point is the popularity of senior tranches of collateralized debt obligations during the low interest rate period after the dot-com bust. They receive this result since in their model both a lower fundamental risk and a higher opacity risk imply that signals have less influence on beliefs. And given low interest rates, only those projects are not invested in the beliefs about the returns of which sufficiently deteriorate as a result of the signal perception. They conclude that the overall effect of a low interest rate is ambiguous and depends on the population of available projects. Only if the available projects are more similar in their fundamental risk than in their opacity risk, a low interest rate entails higher overall risk.

There already exists a fair number of empirical studies that investigate the influence of monetary policy on banks' taking of risk through lending. The most prominent of these studies are presented below.[82] The data investigated comes from diverse sources such as lending surveys and credit registers and covers the US, the Eurosystem, Spain, and Bolivia. The identification strategies used to isolate changes in the loan supply of banks vary but are commonly based on answers to survey questions on banks' motives or on pricing information. The consistent main result found is that lower short-term interest rates induce banks to grant riskier new loans. Furthermore, the following complementary results are supported by evidence discovered by at least one of the presented empirical studies. If short-term rates are lower, existing loans are less risky. If short-term rates remain low for longer, the effects are more pronounced. If long-term rates are lower, the loan supply of banks remains unchanged. Interestingly, three of the presented empirical studies come to the following conflicting conclusions on the influence of the leverage of a bank. One study reports that a lower capital-to-asset ratio weakens or even inverts the influence of low short-term rates on the risk-taking of banks through lending. Two other studies reports a more pronounced influence, instead. As mentioned earlier, the taking of risk through lending is not the same as the taking of credit risk and three of the presented empirical studies find evidence for an influence on the taking of interest rate risk, though this evidence is conflicting. In accordance with the risk-taking channel for interest rate risk, one study finds that lower short-term rates induce banks to grant loans with longer maturity. In contrast, two other studies finds that the maturity becomes shorter.[83] Where these studies produce findings about the interest rate risk of banks, these findings are also presented in what follows.

De Nicolo et al. (2010) analyse data from US corporate lending surveys. Their identification strategy is to control for overall economic performance in order to isolate the deliberate changes in banks' risk-taking. They perceive the range of new loans for which there is a demand shifted toward more risk in a weaker economy. And they aim at controlling for this demand effect in order to isolate the supply effect which is the subject of the risk-taking channel. Their main result is that the real federal funds rate is negatively correlated with the ex ante risk of new bank loans measured as the average internal rating. With respect to the influence of banks' leverage they find that this correlation is much weaker or even inverted for banks with a particularly low capital-to-asset ratio.[84]

---

[82] An alternative presentation of some of these empirical studies can be found in Abbassi (2015).

[83] Obviously an increased maturity of loans does not necessarily lead to increased interest rate risk. For example, the repricing dates and the maturity can differ or the funding can have similar terms. Nevertheless, increased maturity can plausibly be assumed to point to higher interest rate risk.

[84] Using call report data De Nicolo et al. (2010) also assess the influence of low short-term rates on the overall riskiness of the bank measured as the risk-weighted-assets-to-asset ratio. They find a strong negative correlation.

Maddaloni and Peydró (2011) use data from lending surveys in the Eurosystem.[85] Their identification strategy is to take advantage of detailed information on why lending standards are adjusted contained in their data.[86] Their main result is that a lower EONIA interest rate leads to a higher appetite of banks for risk from new loans as indicated by lending standards.[87] They also present two particularly noteworthy complementary findings. If the EONIA interest rate remains low for longer, lending standards are softened further. If a long-term rate such as the 10-year government bond rate is lower, this does not affect lending standards. As a result that points to increased taking of interest rate risk they report that the average maturity of loans increases in case of a decrease in the EONIA interest rate.

Paligorova and Santos (2013) combine data from the US from various sources including a corporate loan pricing database and a loan officer opinion survey. Their identification strategy involves making use of answers to the explicit survey question whether changes in loan terms are due to increased tolerance for risk.[88] Their main result is that a lower federal funds rate entails a higher risk banks are willing to take by granting new corporate loans as conveyed by loan pricing policies. More specifically, they investigate the difference between loan spreads banks charge investment grade and below-investment grade borrowers. And they show that a lower federal funds rate leads to this difference being lower. Hence, they find that a lower short-term interest rate results in lower price charged by banks for additional default risk.[89]

Buch et al. (2014) also investigate data from US corporate lending surveys. Their identification strategy is build on joint data on loan prices and volumes. They assume that the loan supply curve is upwards sloping and the loan demand curve is downward sloping. Accordingly, they can identify changes in market outcome that are supply side driven as those with changes of prices and volumes with opposite sign. And their data is granular enough to enable the application of this technique separately to loans with different levels of risk.[90] Their main result is that a decrease of the federal funds rate leads to an increase in the risk-taking of smaller banks as a consequence of an increased share of new riskier loans. They also present the complementary finding that if the federal funds rate remains low for longer, foreign banks also start to increase the share of new loans to riskier borrowers. As a result that speaks against an increased taking of interest rate risk they report average maturity of loans by small banks to riskier borrowers to decrease with a decrease in the federal funds rate.

Jimenez et al. (2014) use data from the Spanish credit register on corporate loans and on loan applications. Their identification strategy involves the saturation of their loan application model with fixed effects.[91] Their benchmark model focusses on changes in the granting of loan applications of the same potential borrower in the same period between banks. Concerning the

---

But since assets do not only include loans this finding does not constitute evidence on the influence of interest rates on the riskiness of existing loans in a strict sense. Nevertheless one should note that this finding points in a different direction than other findings in the literature which associate lower interest rates with existing loans becoming less risky.

[85] A very similar analysis is provided by Maddaloni and Peydró (2013). Their focus is on bank lending in the euro area during the recent financial crises.

[86] The most important influencing factors that are assumed by Maddaloni and Peydró (2011) to present pure supply side effects are the influence of capital and liquidity constraints.

[87] The lending standards Maddaloni and Peydró (2011) have data on are margin, size, collateral requirements, loan-to-value ratio, covenants, and maturity.

[88] The identification strategy applied by Paligorova and Santos (2013) also involves various other techniques including an analysis of how loan volumes change with prices.

[89] Furthermore, Paligorova and Santos (2013) find that this correlation is exclusive to banks' loan pricing and cannot be found in the pricing of bonds.

[90] Note that this technique but without the differentiation by level of risk is also one of the various other techniques applied by Paligorova and Santos (2013).

[91] Jimenez et al. (2014) explicitly aim at controlling for any effects through the interest rate channel or credit channel by controlling for the time-varying heterogeneity of borrowers and banks.

exogeneity of monetary policy, they benefit from the fact that economies in the euro area are not fully synchronized.[92] Their main result is that a lower EONIA interest rate induces banks to grant a larger number of loan applications of ex-ante riskier firms with a higher average loan amount. They also present the complementary finding that if a long-term rate such as the 10-year Spanish government bond rate is lower, this does not affect the granting of loan applications. With respect to the influence of banks' leverage they find that the link between a lower EONIA interest rate and more and larger riskier loans granted is more pronounced for banks with a particularly low capital-to-asset ratio.

Ioannidou et al. (2015) analyse date from the credit register of Bolivia. Their identification strategy again rests on the insight that a change in market outcome that consists in a positive change in volume accompanied by a negative change in price is supply side driven, given the supply curve slopes upward and the demand curve slopes downward.[93] Concerning the the exogeneity of monetary policy, they benefit from the fact that the banking system of Bolivia is almost fully dollarized in the period of interest.[94] Their main result is that a lower the federal funds rate entails a higher ex-post default frequency but also a higher ex-ante risk of loans granted by banks.[95] The various risk measures they apply include the time to default as an ex-post measure as well as internal ratings and borrowers' credit history as ex-ante measures. They also present the complementary finding that if the federal funds rate is lower, the default risk of existing loans is lower. With respect to the influence of banks' leverage they find that the link between a lower federal funds rate and higher risk of granted loans is stronger for banks with a particularly low capital-to-asset ratio. As a result at odds with an increased taking of interest rate risk they report that average maturity of loans decreases in case of a decrease in the federal funds rate.

4.3.2 Leverage

On the first level of disaggregation liabilities split into debt and equity. Debt is used to lever equity in order to acquire excess amounts of assets. The more debt is used relative to equity, the higher is the leverage.[96] Leverage is important because equity makes up the loss absorbing part of liabilities. A loss that exceeds equity brings about bankruptcy. Other things being equal, a higher leverage thus implies a higher solvency risk. This is true for all kinds of firms, including banks.

Being a measure of a bank's resilience to losses, leverage differs from credit risk on a systematic level. The same holds true with respect to interest rate risk and in general all risks that are measures of some probability-weighted losses. An increase in a bank's taking of such a risk is reflected in a worsening of the probability distribution of its losses. Deviating from that, an increase in a bank's leverage reduces the amount of losses it can bear. Nevertheless, both an

---

[92] In a methodological note directed to authors of empirical analyses on the credit channel that only consider granted loan amounts, Jimenez et al. (2014) point out that not controlling for the sample selection that results from the granting or not granting of loan applications leads to biased results.

[93] This is the same strategy as the one applied by Buch et al. (2014) but again without access to data that differentiates by level of risk.

[94] Ioannidou et al. (2015) note that they are therefore provided with a quasi-natural experiment because even though US monetary policy might be endogenous with respect to the business cycles of the US economy, the business cycles of the US economy and of the economy of Bolivia are not synchronized.

[95] Buch et al. (2014) point out that relying on ex-post measures only is not appropriate for an investigation of the risk-taking channel because this channel concerns banks' risk appetite. Accordingly, Ioannidou et al. (2015) complement their ex-post measures by ex-ante measures such as internal bank ratings.

[96] Note that the leverage ratio, which is calculated as the ratio between equity and total assets or total liabilities, expresses the leverage in a reverse way such that a high (low) leverage ratio indicates a low (high) leverage.

increase in probability weighted losses and an increase in leverage constitute increases in the risk-taking of the bank.

The reduction of the amount of losses a bank can bear is the first order effect of an increase in leverage. This leads to a higher solvency risk, other things being equal. But an increase in a bank's leverage may also have second order effects. Other things may change as a result of the increase in leverage. In particular, a reduction of the amount of losses a bank can bear may induce further risk-taking, for example if the bank gambles for resurrection, which leads to a worsening of the probability distribution of the bank's losses, especially given limited liability.

Dell'Ariccia et al. (2014) develop a partial equilibrium model in which a decrease in the real risk-free interest rate leads to an increase in a bank's leverage which in turn leads to an increase in the credit risk the bank takes. In this model, the optimal leverage of the bank is determined through a trade-off along the following lines. On the one hand, equity is more expensive than debt. In this respect, less equity is beneficial. On the other hand, more equity makes a given amount of debt less expensive. In this regard, more equity is beneficial. Consequently, that level of leverage is optimal at which total costs of equity and debt is minimal. More specifically, in the model at hand equity is more expensive than debt due to an equity premium charged and more equity makes a given amount of debt less expensive because it is the only commitment device available to counter a problem of asymmetric information that entails a moral hazard. This problem of asymmetric information results from the fact that the bank's investment in the monitoring of its loan portfolio determines the credit risk it takes but is unobservable to its debtors who however require to be compensated for the risk they take, or cannot rule out to be taking. And equity is the only commitment device available because the bank operates under limited liability. This second order effect of the bank's leverage on its taking of credit risk drives the model. Now, for any leverage, a decrease in the risk-free interest rate makes debt less expensive because it decreases opportunity costs. And this has two important implications. First, the repayment of less expensive debt can be ensured in expectation through a smaller investment by the bank in the monitoring of its loan portfolio. Second, for the commitment of the bank to a smaller investment in the monitoring of its loan portfolio a lower share of equity suffices, that is a higher leverage. For these reasons, a lower risk-free rate implies a that the bank runs a higher leverage and takes more credit risk, accordingly.[97] Angeloni et al. (2015) construct a general equilibrium model with nominal rigidities in which a moderately persistent monetary policy shock that reduces the nominal policy rate leads to an increase in a bank's leverage which in turn leads to an increase in the risk of a bank run. The trade-off that determines the optimal leverage of the bank in this model is of the following sort. Again, equity is more expensive than dept. Accordingly, less equity is beneficial. But now, more equity makes a bank run less likely. In view of this, more equity is beneficial. All in all, that level of leverage is optimal at which the marginal benefits of cheaper funding and of less risk of a bank run are equal. The bank invests all its funds, that is debt and equity, in risky projects. The credit risk it takes by doing so remains unaffected by the banks leverage, as this model features no second order effects.[98] Nevertheless, this credit risk lies at the heart of the mechanism that links a higher leverage to a higher risk of a bank run, that is a higher debt roll-over risk. A bank run, which inflicts project liquidation

---

[97] Dell'Ariccia et al. (2014) call this effect the "leverage effect". They identify two further effects of a change in the risk-free interest rate on the bank's investment in the monitoring of its loan portfolio which do not function through a change in leverage and which they call the "pass-through effect" and the "risk-shifting effect". They show that the net impact of the 'pass-through effect' and the "risk-shifting effect" is ambiguous, but that the "leverage effect" tilts the balance.

[98] Angeloni et al. (2015) acknowledge that the effect of a change of the nominal short-term interest rate on the bank's leverage and the associated roll-over risk of its funding is only one of at least three aspects of the risk-taking channel. As other aspects they mention the direct as well as the indirect effect on the credit risk the bank takes, the latter of which resulting from changes in the bank's leverage. They justify their decision not to model these other two aspects particularly with regard to model complexity.

costs, occurs, if it turns out that total project returns are insufficient to meet the claims of all debt holders. Because debt holders that withdraw their funds are served sequentially, that is one after the other and in full but only as long as the bank has sufficient resources available.[99] And given some total amount of funds invested in risky projects, the critical value of the realization of total project returns under which not all claims of the debt holders can be met is higher, the higher the share of debt, or put differently, the leverage. The present model has two further noteworthy features. First, the model also features the balance-sheet channel. A monetary policy shock that reduces the nominal policy rate leads to an increase asset prices, investment, and loan demand. Second, the model features negative external effects of bank's risk-taking. Social costs associated with the liquidation of project required in case of a bank run are not internalized.

The two models by Dell'Ariccia et al. (2014) and Angeloni et al. (2015) both establish a link between a decrease in interest rates and an increase in the leverage of banks. And both models associate an increase in the leverage of banks with an increase in banks' risk-taking. as noted earlier, the term spread is of particular relevance for banks' earnings from traditional banking activities. Unfortunately, none of these models features the term spread. Instead, both models limit their attention to some single reference rate. Nevertheless, Angeloni et al. (2015) provide a rationale for their model that sheds some light on which role they would have assigned to the term spread, if they had modeled it. For them the crucial consequence of a decrease in the policy rate is that it reduces the cost of short-term funding relative to long-term funding. And this implies that they associate a decrease in the policy rate with an increase in the term spread. Hence, they implicitly suggest a link between an increase in the term spread and an increase in the leverage of banks and consequently in bank's risk-taking.

Dell'Ariccia et al. (2014) and Angeloni et al. (2015) also provide some of the first empirical evidence on the link between interest rates and banks' leverage. Dell'Ariccia et al. (2014) make use of a natural experiment. They hypothesize that with the start of the recent financial crisis it became much more difficult for banks to adjust their leverage ratio. And they can show that while prior to the crises the relationship between the real US federal funds rate and the average rating of loans by US banks was strongly negative, during the crisis it was ambiguous. As such, this evidence suggests that for interest rate changes to have an effect on the taking of credit risk by banks the change of the banks' leverage is crucial.[100] Angeloni et al. (2015) provide time serial evidence based on US data. They focus on non-core liabilities with particularly high roll-over risk for the measurement of banks' funding risk And they find that the share of this type of liabilities is indeed inversely related to the level of policy rates.

4.3.3 Interest rate risk

On the one hand, interest rate risk is similar to credit risk and even leverage. Just like credit risk, it is a measure of some possible losses. And like both credit risk and leverage, increasing it is a lever the pulling of which is possible in a search for yield. Accordingly, it appears natural that a bank's taking of interest rate risk is influenced by monetary policy. Farhi and Tirole (2012) provide the first model featuring this link and thereby extend the theory of the risk-taking channel to interest rate risk.

---

[99] With respect to this feature of their model it becomes particularly apparent how Angeloni et al. (2015) build on Diamond and Dybvig (1983).

[100] Dell'Ariccia et al. (2014) admit that the size of their sample is rather limited as it only includes data for eight crisis quarters. Another possible objection concerns the choice of natural experiment as other symptoms of the recent financial crisis possibly affect the results. Further empirical evidence supportive in particular of other implications of the model by Dell'Ariccia et al. (2014) not focused on here is provided in an accompanying paper by Dell'Ariccia et al. (2013).

On the other hand, interest rate risk differs from credit risk and leverage. Its relationship to monetary policy has a further, exclusive dimension. Interest rate risk is defined as the exposure to changes in interest rates and this includes changes in policy rates. In so far, the interest rate risk of a bank is also a measure of the bank's exposure and responsiveness to monetary policy. Landier et al. (2013) investigate this link empirically with a particular focus on the bank's lending capacity.

Landier et al. (2013) present empirical evidence which suggests that the sensitivity of a bank's lending capacity to changes in the policy rate depends on the interest rate risk of the bank. More precisely, this study finds that the size of the short-run exposure of a bank's net interest income to changes in short-term interest rates critically determines the strength of the inverse relationship between the policy rate and the bank's lending volume. The supportive rationale runs as follows. In the short-run, the typical bank that borrows short and lends long has to roll over and therefore reprice more liabilities than assets. This difference in volumes already implies that given a sufficiently limited time horizon, a uniform change in interest rates has a stronger effect on interest expenses than on interest income. Furthermore, to the extend that short-term interest rates are more responsive to changes in the policy rate than long-term interest rates, this difference in responsiveness entrenches the asymmetry of the impact of changes of policy rates on interest expenses and interest income.[101] In effect, an increase in the policy rate leads to a decrease of the bank's net interest income and a decrease of the policy rate leads to an increase of its net interest income. Finally, given that the other sources of funding are constrained at least in the short-run, a reduction of the net interest income and hence of earnings available for retainment leads to a reduction of the possible lending volume, that is of the bank's lending capacity.

On the face of it, this empirical analysis does not concern the risk-taking channel because it does not address the claim that monetary policy influences a bank's risk-taking. Instead, the evidence provided sheds further light on how monetary policy influences a bank's lending and hence concerns the bank lending channel which is a sub-channel of the credit channel. But on a higher level, there is an important lesson to be drawn with particular relevance for the risk-taking channel end especially for how policy rates influences a bank's taking of interest rate risk. It becomes clear that the relationship between interest rate risk and monetary policy has at least two dimensions that need to be accounted for. Not only may the bank's interest rate risk be influenced by monetary policy. But the influence of monetary policy may also be determined by the bank's interest rate risk.

Ultimately, the influence of monetary policy on a bank's taking of interest rate risk may be determined by the bank's interest rate risk. As already laid out, the maturity mismatch of a bank is one of the input factors that determine the size of the decrease in the bank's net interest income that results from an increase in the policy rate. But furthermore, the maturity mismatch of a bank is also one of the action parameters the bank is empowered to change in order to counter the decrease in its net interest income in a search for yield. Similar rationales can be developed for determinants of interest rate risk other than the maturity mismatch. Until now, however, no theoretical model has emerged that explicitly addresses this dual role of interest rate risk. Hence, the challenge implicitly set by Landier et al. (2013) remains unanswered. But by modeling how monetary policy affect a bank's taking of interest rate risk, Farhi and Tirole (2012) initiate the theoretical treatment of at least one of the two roles.

---

[101] Landier et al. (2013) do not explicitly distinguish between the difference in volumes and the difference in responsiveness. Instead, they simply establish the inverse relationship between short-term interest rates and banks' earnings empirically.

Farhi and Tirole (2012) develop the first theoretical model which accommodates a taking of interest rate risk by banks as induced by some past and present development of policy rates.[102] In this model, a decrease in the policy rates has two important effects. First, a decrease in policy rates reduces the costs of short-term refinancing. Thus, running a maturity mismatch becomes more profitable for banks. Second, a decrease in policy rates to counter one crisis signals the central bank's willingness to do the same in the next crisis. Hence, running a maturity mismatch becomes less risky for banks. Both the immediate reduction of the costs of short-term refinancing and the signaling that the central bank is willing to decrease policy rates again in the next crisis encourage banks to run a larger maturity mismatch.[103] In this way, monetary policy influences banks' taking of interest rate risk.

Of these two effects, the immediate reduction of the costs of short-term refinancing and its effect on banks' taking of interest rate risk receives particular attention in the emerging literature. In greater detail the standard supportive reasoning may be outlined as follows. If policy rates are lower, yield curves are steeper, because shorter-term rates align more closely to policy rates than longer-term rates. If yield curves are steeper, maturity transformation is more profitable, because for any given setup of borrowing short and lending long the interest rate margin is higher. If maturity transformation is more profitable, banks run a larger maturity mismatch, because higher expected return compensates for higher risk. Hence, a decrease in policy rates leads to an increase in banks' taking of interest rate risk. This reasoning strongly influences the existing research dedicated to the interest rate risk of banks.

4.4 Conclusion

A striking observation that can be made about the existing research on the risk-taking channel in so far as it concerns interest rate risk is that this research is still one-dimensional in an important respect. In this research, a decrease in the short-term interest rate is commonly associated with an increase in the profitability of running a maturity mismatch and this in turn with an increase in the taking of interest rate risk. Along these lines, a decrease of the policy rate, or indeed any monetary policy intervention that increases the term spread, is associated with an increase in banks' interest rate risk. However, this rationale is not only diametrically opposed to the canonical search-for-yield-rationale provided by Rajan (2005). But there also exists a much older and very prominent rationale that features a link between profitability and risk-taking of opposite sign. Stiglitz and Weiss (1981) argue that an increase in profitability reduces agency problems and implies that with more skin in the game a bank's risk-taking decreases. Furthermore Kane (1989) adds that a decrease in profitability that aggravates agency problems induces a bank to gamble for resurrection, that is to increase risk-taking. Indeed, this sort of reasoning is at the heart of the idea of the credit channel. To say the least, the link between an increase in profitability and an increase in risk-taking is nowhere close to self-evident. On the contrary, a possible search for yield is an important dimension of banks' taking of interest rate risk that needs to be investigated and potentially accounted for. De Nicolo et al. (2010) and Maddaloni and Peydró (2011) are among the few that do not overlook this. Chapter 8 below addresses this research gap on the theoretical as well as on the empirical level. This chapter provides a theoretical rationale for banks' search for yield in interest rate risk and also produces some empirical evidence.

---

[102] Diamond and Rajan (2009) develop a related model. Their focus is on the effect of a bank bail out on the disciplinary role of deposits.

[103] Farhi and Tirole (2012) also pay particular attention to strategic complementarities in the banking sector. They condense their theoretical findings in the slogan that "it is unwise to play safely while everyone else gambles". More precisely, they find that banks maximize the positive correlation of their risk with the risks of other banks in order to maximize the probability being bailed out if needed. And a bailout is the rational policy response only if large parts of the financial sector are in trouble and not merely a single bank.

Another interesting dimension that can be identified and which is already on its way to become a prominent research topic is the reverse link of the two-way link between monetary policy and banks' interest rate risk. Through the risk-taking channel, monetary policy influences banks' taking of interest rate risk. But through a reverse link banks' taking of interest rate risk may also influence monetary policy. Interest rate risk is, at least to a large part, a systematic risk the realization of which depends on a common risk factor, namely the development of market interest rates. Hence, by taking interest rate risk, banks can correlate their exposures. And as a result of correlating their exposures, the involved banks may collectively become too many to fail. By this, they may induce the government to bail them out in the case of default. And this threat may already be sufficient to induce the central bank to prevent the case of default in the first place. To this end, the central bank would then need to take actions to influence interest rates in a way beneficial for banks.

The idea of "too many to fail" goes back to Acharya and Yorulmazer (2007). It says that authorities are bound to bail out failed banks, if their number is large, because in a situation of widespread bank failure market solutions are not viable. Anticipating this, each bank has an incentive to herd, that is to take risks in a way that maximizes the probability of failing only when the other banks also fail. In their model, which was already referred to earlier, Farhi and Tirole (2012) study the strategic complementarity on which the idea of "too many to fail" rests in greater detail. However, there are hardly any empirical investigations of this topic. Dam and Koetter (2012) analyze how the risk-taking of German banks changes with the probability of being bailed out in case of failure. They find that an external increase of the probability of being bailed out does not induce banks to take more interest rate risk. However, the measures for interest rate risk they employ are rather crude. Furthermore, they do not address the hypothesized strategic complementarity in banks' taking of interest rate risk. To sum up, the existence of the two-way link between monetary policy and banks' taking of interest rate risk that features too-many-to-fail appears plausible. There is already a theoretical model that accommodates this. But there is a research gap as far as empirical studies are concerned.

Both topics, that of banks' search for yield in interest rate risk as well as that of banks' taking of interest rate risk in order to become too many to fail, add rather complex dimensions to the research on optimal monetary policy.[104] Large parts of the literature frame the discussion as the search for the optimal interest rate reaction function. The most prominent example of such an interest rate reaction function is the one identified by Taylor (1993).[105] The Taylor rule relates the monetary policy target for the short-term interest rate to the rate of inflation and to the growth rate of real output.[106] It is frequently argued that rules as simple as the Taylor rule are deficient because they do not account for all relevant information available and are insensitive to differences in the types of shocks. And indeed, accounting for a search for yield in interest rate

---

[104] Naturally, this topic is discussed under the precondition that the neutrality of money is rejected. Because the neutrality of money implies that monetary policy only drives inflation. And it consistently implies further that inflation does not have any real effects. But the discussion about optimal monetary policy centers around two sorts of real effects. First, the increase and decrease of actual real output relative to potential real output. Second, the real benefits and real costs of inflation. Besides, compared to these two topics distributional effects of monetary policy are still a side topic in the debate.

[105] For a recent discussion of the Taylor rule with a focus on its prescriptive use by its inventor see Bernanke (n.d.).

[106] To be precise, Taylor (1993) suggests, focussing on the FED's interest rate policy, $r = p + 0.5 * y + 0.5 * (p - 2) + 2$ with r the federal funds rate in per annum terms, which is the overnight lending rate between banks targeted by the Federal Reserve or its Federal Open Market Committee, p the annual rate of inflation, and y the percent deviation of real GDP from a target which is originally set equal to trend real GDP and is nowadays identified as potential real GDP with the deviation simply being the output gap. Two properties of the Taylor rule are noteworthy. First, the formula already features a target rate of inflation of 2%. Second, if the inflation rate and real GDP equal their respective targets, a target for the federal funds rate of 4% results. Last but not least, the ECB (2001) notes that a prescriptive use of a forward looking Taylor rule would assume a mandate of the central bank that covers not only price stability but also output growth. And this is the case for the FED but not for the ECB.

risk and hence for a negative link between profitability and risk-taking as well as accounting for the banks taking interest rate risk in order to become too many to fail and hence to influence monetary policy, comes with extra complexity.

On the side, it can be observed that a shift from the traditional to the modern understanding of banking is already in progress in the research on the bank lending channel as well as in the research on the risk-taking channel. The development of the modern version of the bank lending channel as initiated by Stein (1998) goes in this direction. And the understanding of banks as essential risk takers which shapes the risk-taking channel as identified by Borio and Zhu (2012) is also an expression of this development.

Chapter 5 Specifics of interest rate risk in economic research

The treatment of interest rate risk of banks as a topic of economic research goes back to Samuelson (1945) and Hicks (1946). Their early contributions establish the fundamental result that a maturity mismatch between assets and liabilities exposes a bank's income and value to changes in interest rates. This result is still one of the cornerstones of the nowadays existing large body of economic research on the interest rate risk of banks. In what follows this research is reviewed selectively with focuses on two aspects. First, the existing findings on the interdependence of the taking of interest rate risk and the term spread are presented. The term spread is again focused on here as it is the most prominent measure of the profitability of maturity or term transformation and hence of the signature dimension of asset transformation classical banking, that is borrowing short and lending long, comes with. Second, the established methods for the measurement of interest rate risk are introduced. In preparation of the following extensions of the research, these methods are presented and evaluated.

5.1   Taking of interest rate risk and the term spread

The empirical analyses of the impact of changes of the term spread are of two types. Studies of the first type investigate the interest rate risk of banks in so far as it concerns potential changes of the term spread. Hence, these studies quantify banks' exposure to term spread changes. Studies of the second type investigate how the interest rate risk of banks changes with the term spread. Thus, these studies quantify banks' changes in risk-taking as induced by by term spread changes. Studies of both types are presented successively below.

In reality banks' earnings from the classical banking business of borrowing short and lending long do not, of course, only consist in the monetization of the term spread. Banks earnings also come from mark-downs on the interest rates they pay for what they borrow and mark-ups on the interest rates they charge for what they lend. There are contributions to the economic research on banks' interest rate risk that account for this fact. The one by Entrop et al. (2015) presented below establishes a link between the earnings coming mark-downs and mark-ups and the term spread. What is more, this contribution establishes a positive link between the term spread and banks' taking of interest rate risk.

5.1.1   Exposure to term spread changes

The empirical evidence on banks' exposure to changes in the term spread is mixed. More precisely, the exposure is found to differ between banks of different sizes as well as across time periods and economic regions. The following two empirical studies illustrate this point.

Faff and Howard (1999) explore the relationship between the return on shares of financial institutions and changes in interest rates. They extend the study by Madura and Zarruk (1995) geographically by analyzing Australian financial institutions and systematically by also testing for sensitivity to changes in the term spread, which they measure as the difference between ten-year and 90-day reference interest rates. Their regression results suggest a significant sensitivity of the return on shares to changes in the term spread but only for some sub-groups of financial institutions during some sub-periods confined by regulatory changes. Overall, they find the sensitivity to term spread changes to be insignificant. For large banks, they uncover significant sensitivity to changes in long-term interest rates but not to changes in short-term interest rates. For small banks they find no significant sensitivity at all. However, they admit that their results for small banks may be due to lack of sufficiently rich data.

Viale et al. (2009) assess various established asset-pricing models with respect to their explanatory power for bank stock returns. In particular, they assess the capital asset pricing model (CAPM) by Sharpe (1964) and Lintner (1965), its intertemporal version (ICAPM) by Merton (1973), and the Fama-French three-factor model by Fama and French (1992, 1993) using US data. They find that a two-factor ICAPM model featuring a measure of market return and a measure of the term spread has the highest explanatory power for bank stock returns. They measure the term spread as the difference in return between a portfolio of government bonds with more than 25 years to maturity and the 1-month treasury bill. They find that the impact of an increase in the term spread varies across banks depending on their size, namely that small banks benefit from an increase in the term spread while large banks lose. They hypothesize that this difference in effect may be due to a difference in interest rate risk management techniques employed at banks of different sizes.

The fact that these studies produce different and partly conflicting results suggests two conclusions. First, banks' taking of interest rate risk may indeed differ depending on bank size and market conditions. Second, using measurement approaches and different reference values may also lead to different results.

5.1.2 Changes in risk-taking as induced by term spread changes

The empirical evidence on changes in banks' interest rate risk-taking induced by term spread changes appears to be clear. From Germany alone three studies find evidence for an increase in the term spread inducing banks to increase their interest rate risk.

Memmel (2011) studies the risk and the earnings resulting from maturity transformation. He has the results of internal interest rate risk calculations of German banks at his disposal covering the period from 2005 to 2009. He finds that an increase in possible earnings from maturity transformation goes along with an increase in interest rate risk. Moreover, earnings from maturity transformations make up a significant share of interest income, in particular for savings and cooperative banks. This varies significantly through time. Yet, he find no evidence for a correlation of interest rate risk and the net interest margin.

Memmel and Schertler (2013) analyze how banks' net interest margin changes with interest rates and balance sheet composition. They use detailed bank report data on German banks from 1999 to 2010. They find that changes in interest rates explain three times as much of the change in the net interest margin as changes in balance sheet composition. And they find that banks adjust their balance sheet composition to take advantage of changes in interest rates in such a way that an increase of the net interest margin due to a change in interest rates is amplified through a change in balance sheet positions. Their empirical findings suggest that an increase in term spreads induces banks to conduct more maturity transformation.

Ruprecht et al. (2013) investigate banks' interest rate risk management with a focus on maturity transformation. They base their analysis on detailed bank report data on German banks from 2000 to 2011. They find that when yield curves become steeper, banks' duration gaps become larger and they associate this with the higher profitability of maturity transformation. Furthermore, they point to the finding that the slope of the yield curves is highly negatively correlated with the level of short-term rates. Put differently, lower short-term rates lead to steeper yield curves which in turn induce larger duration gaps and hence higher interest rate risk.

5.1.3 Mark-downs and mark-downs and the term spread

A microeconomic rationale for how an increase in term spread may lead to an increase in the taking of interest rate risk by a bank has been provided implicitly by a recent contribution to what is called the intermediation or dealership literature on a bank's margin. This literature kicks-off with the work by Ho and Saunders (1981). The recent advance is the merit of Entrop et al. (2015).

Ho and Saunders (1981) develop a model of the determination of a bank's net interest rate margin that serves as a framework for a large strand of literature on the taking of interest rate risk by banks. In this model a bank takes time deposits and makes risk-less loans of identical maturity. The supply of deposits and the demand for loans are stochastic and the bank uses short-term money market funds to close any gap resulting from a mismatch of inflows and outflows. As this short-term funding needs to be rolled over, the bank is exposed to changes of the interest rate on the money market. And it turns out that, the interest rate margin charged by the bank increases in the volatility of this short-term interest rate. But it also depends on market structure, transaction sizes, and the degree of managerial risk aversion.

As of today, several extensions of the model by Ho and Saunders (1981) exist which include further factors in the explanation of a bank's net interest rate margin. Allen (1988) introduces different loan types. She shows that diversification benefits may induce the bank to decrease its margin. Angbazo (1997) includes credit risk. He finds that higher credit risk is compensated for by a bank through a higher margin. Maudos and de Guevara (2004) account for operating costs and introduce the Lerner index as a measure of market power. They conclude that both higher operating costs and more market power lead to a higher margin charged by the bank. Carbó and Rodríguez (2007) accommodate non-interest activities. They figure that non-interest activities change the market power of a bank.

Entrop et al. (2015) extend the model by Ho and Saunders (1981) to accommodate maturity transformation between deposits and loans. They feature the term spread as the difference between the risk-free rate of bonds with the maturities of the deposits and loans. And they introduce the net intermediation margin as the net fees that a bank charges as a mark-down on deposits and a mark-up on loans. They predict an increase in the term spread to induce a bank to adjust its fees such that its net intermediation margin falls. Their economic rationale is that a higher term spread compensates for a larger part of the interest rate risk from maturity transformation.

In their model the bank also has access to the money market, which offers instruments with a shorter maturity than both deposits and loans. And they derive the result that how a bank adjusts its fees on deposits and loans depends on how the respective default-free rates change in relation to the money market rate. They find that if the spread between the money market rate and the default-free rates for deposits and loans increases, a bank increases its fees on deposits and decreases its fees on loans. Their economic rationale for the increase in fees on deposits is that they present a liability position and higher interest payments have to be compensated for.

Finally, their model links lower fees to a higher probability of new business and higher fees to a lower probability and has a bank closing any gap in volumes of deposits and loans on the money market. Hence, they accommodate two effects of an increase in the slope of the yield curve which increases the spreads between the money market rate and the default-free deposit rate and at the same time between the default-free deposit rate and the default-free loan rate. First, as the bank decreases its loan fees, the likelihood of new loan business increases. This implies that the volume of business employed in maturity transformation increases. Second, as the bank increases its deposit fees, the likelihood of new deposits decreases and more funding has to be provided via the money market. This implies that the overall maturity mismatch of the bank increases. Hence, both effects link an increase in term spreads to an increase in a bank's taking of interest rate risk by some plausible measure.

5.2 Measuring interest rate risk

Three approaches to the measurement of a bank's interest rate risk can be found in the empirical literature. First, some studies make use of estimates provided by banks themselves. Second, other studies make their own estimations based on bank report data. Third, the remaining studies also make their own estimations but base them on stock market data instead. The following provides a closer view on each of these three established measurement approaches.

5.2.1 Estimates provided by banks themselves

It is in the self interest of banks as well as required of them by regulation to manage and to this end to measure their interest rate risk. Banks measure their interest rate risk through estimations utilizing internal data and calculated with internal models.

Since the implementation of Basel II banks are required to report own estimates of their banking book's exposure to certain term structure changes to the supervisory authorities. The precise requirements currently to be fulfilled by German banks have been defined by the Bundesanstalt für Finanzdienstleistungsaufsicht, the BaFin (2011). According to these requirements each bank has to report the exposure of its banking book to a standard interest rate shock on a regular basis. The standard interest rate shock is an immediate parallel shift of the yield curve by 200 basis points upward (scenario one) and downward (scenario two). The exposure of the banking book is the induced change in the net present value of the expected future cash flows given the current portfolio. Each bank has to report the absolute exposure of its banking book as well as the ratio between this exposure and its regulatory capital for each scenario every quarter. The ratio between the exposure of a bank's banking book according to the more harmful scenario and its regulatory capital is the Basel interest rate coefficient of the bank. Each bank with a Basel interest rate coefficient that exceeds 20%, that is with more than 20% of its regulatory capital reported to be at risk, is considered to require extra supervisory attention. Studies that make use of the estimates of exposure to interest rate changes provided by banks themselves include the ones by Memmel (2011) and Entrop et al. (2011).[107]

The regulatory requirements that have to be met by the internal methods used by German banks to estimate the exposure to interest rate changes of their banking book are defined by the BaFin (2012). These requirements leave significant leeway particularly in the treatment of non-maturity positions, defined as positions with an indeterminate lock-in period. Even though supervisory practice may have established more restrictive de facto requirements the exact wording of the regulation only indeterminately obliges to "appropriate assumption" in the treatment of non-maturity positions.

Making use of the estimates of exposure to certain interest rate changes provided by banks themselves has one major advantage. The estimates are based on data more granular than the data available to external parties and this is particularly true for data on off balance sheet positions. But there are also three noteworthy disadvantages. First, the estimates provided by the banks themselves only quantify the potential impact of a given shock and hardly allow any conclusions on the impacts of other possible shocks. Second, the estimates only quantify the impact on the net present value but do not convey information on the net interest income over time. Third, the estimates depend on individual assumptions that may differ between banks, for

---

[107] The estimates used by Memmel (2011) were reported under slightly different requirements than the current ones. Two differences are noteworthy. First, the standard interest rate shock featured an upward shift by 130 basis points (scenario 1) and a downward shift by 190 basis points (scenario 2) - today the shifts are 200 basis points upwards and downward. Second, a bank was only required to report its estimate, whenever its Basel coefficient was above 20% - today every bank has to report its estimates every quarter. The estimates used by Entrop et al. (2011) are the results of an interest rate risk survey that already featured the shift of 200 basis points.

example on the maturity of demand deposits, as banks make different use of the leeway in the estimation requirements.

The first of the mentioned disadvantages deserves extra attention because it points to a more fundamental issue. As should be clear from the presentation above, the Basel interest rate coefficient is a measure of exposure and not of risk. It measures the greater of the two exposures to an immediate parallel shift of the term structure up or down by 200 basis points. But it does not account for the probability that this term structure change actually comes about. And risk is to be measured as probability weighted exposure.

Of course, even a measure that results from multiplying the Basel interest rate coefficient of a bank with the probability that the more adverse of the two shock scenarios materializes, would not be a comprehensive measure of the banks interest rate risk. Because any actual bank also has negative exposures toward other term structure changes. Hence, a comprehensive measure of a bank's interest rate risk would have to account for all these exposures and the probabilities that the respective term structure changes materialize.

5.2.2 Estimations based on bank report data

Various regulations require banks to report information on their portfolio to the public or the supervisory authorities. For the estimation of banks' interest rate risk, the most relevant data that is made available to bank outsiders through reports is the portfolio breakdown into brackets of original or remaining maturity or, occasionally, into brackets of initial or residual interest rate fixation period.

Two standard measures of the interest rate risk of banks that make use of this sort of data are the maturity gap and the modified duration gap. The maturity gap quantifies the difference in volumes of assets and liabilities that are repriced over a given time horizon. For example, Angbazo (1997) uses the one year maturity gap, that is the excess amount of assets over liabilities that are repriced within one year. The modified duration gap quantifies the impact of a marginal change in interest rates on the net present value of assets minus liabilities per maturity bracket and then aggregates across maturity brackets. For example, Entrop et al. (2015) use the volume weighted average of modified duration gaps across maturity brackets which is equivalent to the impact of a marginal parallel shift of the yield curve. Both the maturity gap and the modified duration gap are measures of interest rate sensitivity. The maturity gap allows conclusions to be drawn about the sensitivity of the net interest income. The modified duration gap conveys information on the sensitivity of the net present value. For an analysis of the impact of some proposed interest rate shock the informative value of both standard measures is limited. The maturity gap measures the exposure to a change in interest rates as the net position in business volumes affected but it does not actually measure the net impact of the change. The modified duration gap measures the net impact of a marginal change in interest rates but is silent on the impacts of non-marginal changes because the size of the impact does not necessarily depend linearly or in any other expectable way on the size of the change. The impact of some proposed interest rate shock has to be calculated through scenario analysis. A scenario analysis starts from a granular view on the portfolio and then calculates the impact of the shock directly, that is without building on some measure that already condenses information, at least in so far as the data available permits this. Hence, in comparison to the standard measures, scenario analysis provides a more conditional measure of interest rate risk. The maturity gap and the modified duration gap depend on the time horizon and the mode of aggregation across maturity bracket, respectively. The interest rate measure calculated in a scenario analysis, however, is conditional on the precise shock applied. And this raises the question which shock or set of shocks is adequate.

For US banks the central bank, more precisely the Board of Governors of the Federal Reserve, and the Office of Thrift Supervision, an agency under the Department of the Treasury, developed models to estimate the interest rate risk from report data. These official models are presented, examined, and compared by Houpt and Embersit (1991), Wright and Houpt (1996), and Sierra and Yeager (2004). For German banks the Deutsche Bundesbank collects all microdata in a prudential information system, its Bankaufsichtliches Informationssystem (BAKIS). An introduction to this system is provided by Memmel and Stein (2008). It includes data on volumes and interest rates per maturity bracket. Yet, the Deutsche Bundesbank does not report any official interest rate risk measure based on this data.

Estimating the interest rate risk by banks based on reporting data has three noteworthy advantages. First, the estimations can build on a direct view on the current portfolio of the bank. Second, the estimations can then calculate standard sensitivity measures or conduct a scenario analysis applying whatever interest rate shock seems appropriate. Third, the estimations can finally regard the net interest income as well as the net present value. But there is also one major disadvantage. The bank report data available to base estimations on is not very detailed for on-balance sheet positions and nearly non-existent for off-balance sheet positions. Regarding on-balance sheet positions, Entrop et al. (2009) show that the estimate of the interest rate risk of a bank is very sensitive to the assumption about the maturity distribution within maturity brackets. They find that this sensitivity is negligible only if data for much more granular maturity brackets is available than currently featured in the relevant reporting requirements. Entrop et al. (2011) introduce the use of time series bank report data to derive insights about the maturity distribution within maturity brackets. They use not only the latest but also earlier bank report data and derive insights from the migration between maturity brackets as the remaining maturity decreases. By applying this estimation technique they claim to be able to increase the share of explained cross-sectional variation of interest rate risk estimates provided by banks themselves from 19% to 27%.[108] Memmel (2008), however, objects that this estimation technique is difficult and time-consuming and that structural breaks in the data are particularly problematic. The very limited availability of data on off-balance sheet positions is handled differently in the empirical literature. Some studies exclude off balance sheet positions altogether, e.g. Entrop et al. (2015). Other studies include comparably rough measures such as the nominal amount of interest rate swaps outstanding, e.g. Ruprecht et al. (2013). For banks in Europe, the collection of data on derivatives is currently significantly increased by the implementation of the European Market Infrastructure Regulation (EMIR).[109]

5.2.3 Estimations based on stock market data

The interest rate risk of listed banks can be estimated as the sensitivity of their stock market returns to changes in yield curves. To this end, the banks' stock market excess returns are regressed on parameters from a term structure model.

The basic idea for this estimation approach goes back to Stone (1974). He proposes not to use a single-factor asset-pricing model, featuring only the overall market return, but a two-factor asset-pricing model, featuring separately the equity market return and the debt market return.[110] And he identifies the responsiveness of the return of an asset to the equity market return and the debt market return as the asset's systematic equity risk and systematic interest rate risk,

---

[108] Note, however, that this evaluation is based on a measure for the interest rate risk similar to the Basel interest rate coefficient.

[109] It is worthwhile to note that the empirical evidence on the effect of derivative usage is mixed. Among others, Purnanandam (2007) marshals evidence suggesting that banks use derivatives to hedge their interest rate risk such that their overall interest rate risk is lower than their on balance sheet interest rate risk. In contrast, Begenau et al. (2013) identifies a number of banks that seem to increase their interest rate risk through the use of derivatives, that is use derivatives not for hedging but for speculative purposes.

[110] Of course, the most famous and still widely used asset-pricing model is the single-factor CAPM by Sharpe (1964) and Lintner (1965). Fama and French (2004) provide a critical review.

respectively. The first empirical applications of this two-factor asset-pricing model are provided by Lloyd and Shick (1977), Chance and Lane (1980), and Flannery and James (1984). They regress the changes of financial institutions' stock market returns on the changes of some index of market returns and of some index of interest rates. An early extension of the two-factor asset-pricing model to a three-factor asset-pricing model, featuring short-term and long-term interest rates, is provided by Lynge and Zumwalt (1980). They include the changes of both an index of short-term interest rates and an index of long-term interest rates as explanatory variables in the same regression. A more recent application of the two-factor asset-pricing model is provided by Faff and Howard (1999). Successively, they include indices of interest rates for different maturities but also an index of the term spread. Furthermore, they also provide a review of the three main design issues for the application of an asset-pricing model of the kind suggested by Stone (1974). First, the interest rates used for measuring debt market return can be either yields to maturity or holding-period returns. Akella and Chen (1990) suggest to use holding-period returns as interest rates if the other variables included in the analysis are holding-period returns. Second, the changes of interest rates included in the regression analysis can be either all actual changes or only unanticipated changes. Choi et al. (1992) report different results for the two specifications but even though the efficient market hypothesis has it that only unanticipated changes should have an effect, the overall empirical evidence is mixed. Third, the interdependency of market returns and interest rates results in multicollinearity that needs to be addressed appropriately. Giliberto (1985) finds that simple orthogonalization as used in some early contributions leads to biased coefficients. Current contribution still tie in with Stone (1974) in featuring separately equity and debt market variables even in applying models of different kinds. For example Viale et al. (2009) suggests to use an ICAPM with measures for changes in market return and changes in the term spread as input factors.

Estimating the interest rate risk by banks based on stock market data has two main advantages. First, the estimations make use of market prices that can plausible be assumed to reflect all available information. Second, the estimations in principle allow to accommodate any changes in the term structure, for instance, they are not limited to assessing parallel shifts. But there are also two main disadvantages. First, estimations using stock market data are possible for listed banks only. Second, the estimations are based on historic data and thus offer a limited amount of information on the current risk of banks. With respect to an estimation of the interest rate risk of German banks the first disadvantage is particularly serious because in Germany only a very small fraction of the existing banks is listed on a stock exchange. Czaja et al. (2009, 2010) estimate the interest rate risk of German banks on the basis of stock market data. But of the 2,592 banks that existed in Germany at the end of 2002 according to the BBK (2002), they find stock market data for 28 only, that is for just over 1%.

5.3 Conclusion

The two possible explanations for the mixed results for banks' exposure to changes of the term spread have different implications for the extensions that follow. The first possible explanation is that banks significantly differ in their taking of interest rate risk depending on their own characteristics as well as on those of the market they are active in. This suggests that a dedicated treatment of German banks' taking of interest rate risk is a valuable research contribution. Chapter 6 is motivated by this insight. The second possible explanation is that the reference value matters on which the measurement of the interest rate risk of banks is based. The two fundamental types of reference values are, of course, net present value measures such as the current portfolio value or the economic value of equity on the one hand and net income measures such as next year's net interest income on the other hand. Chapter 7 picks up on these different ways of measurement.

The obvious reason why the empirical evidence on changes in banks' taking of interest rate risk as induced by the term spread appears to be clear is that all of the existing studies are designed in a one-dimensional way. The research gap identified in Chapter 4 presents itself here again. The empirical setup of the existing studies does not permit the additional identification and independent quantification of a possible search for yield in interest rate risk. The research effort in Chapter 8 fills this gap.

The three established approaches to the measurement of banks' interest rate risk all come with advantages and disadvantages. Estimations based on stock market data are impossible for the vast majority of German banks because only a tiny fraction of them is listed. In contrast, the other two approaches, namely using estimates provided by banks themselves and conducting own estimations based on bank report data, are generally feasible for German banks. Both, however, also come with limitations that must not be overlooked.

The Basel interest rate coefficient that German banks report, only measures the exposure to a very specific term structure change, or the more harmful of two very specific term structure changes. Chapter 7 is motivated by this insight and analyzes the empirical adequacy of these as well as of other possible and proposed shock scenarios. In practice, however, the Basel interest rate coefficient is the German supervisor's standard yardstick for banks' interest rate risk. Chapter 8 follows this lead and effectively uses an exposure measure closely related to the Basel interest rate coefficient as if it was a comprehensive risk measure.

The bank report data available is limited in scope, granularity, and relevance for an investigation of banks' interest rate risk.[111] Nevertheless, the amount of available data of this sort makes its analysis potentially rewarding, in particular given that most of this data is publicly accessible for everyone at least on some level of aggregation. Chapter 6 makes an attempt to extract as much information as possible about German banks' taking of interest rate risk. The most important advantage of this data is that it can be used for scenario analysis. Chapter 7 features such an impact assessment.

---

[111] The relevance of the data is limited for an investigation of banks' interest rate risk as breakdowns are mostly provided by original maturity and not by residual interest rate fixation period.

II Extensions

Chapter 6 The interest rate risk of banks in Germany: an investigation based on publicly available statistics

6.1 Abstract

Taking interest rate risk is a natural part of traditional banking. Nevertheless, there are hardly any specific statistics available on the interest rate risk of banks in Germany. As a result, the current level and recent development of these banks' interest rate risk is far from clear. Addressing this important lack of information, the present chapter marshals a comprehensive set of available statistics which do not specifically cover banks interest rate risk, but from which specific conclusions can be drawn with the help of tailored methods of analysis. Two main insights are produced. First, banks in Germany have a higher interest rate risk than banks in the euro area and it is bound to increase in particular as a result of a persistent shift toward shorter-term funding. Second, of the types of banks in Germany, savings banks and cooperative banks are particularly engaged.

6.2 Introduction

Interest rate risk naturally comes with the traditional banking activities of borrowing short and lending long. Accordingly, it is generally regarded as an important risk in quantitative terms for many banks. And since its realization depends on the development of a common risk factor, namely market interest rates, interest rate risk has a particular potential to endanger financial stability overall. Despite its importance, the current regulation of interest rate risk is still far from comprehensive. In particular, there are no capital requirements for interest rate risk in the banking book.[112] This makes transparency crucial. Without a stringent regulatory requirement in place to back interest rate risk in the banking book with an appropriate amount of risk bearing capacity in the form of capital, it is imperative to monitor this risk closely. The present chapter aims to make a contribution to this end, focussing on Germany.

In Germany, the supervisor's standard yardstick for banks' interest rate risk in the banking book is the Basel interest rate coefficient. This coefficient measures the more severe present value reduction a bank would be subject to, if an overnight parallel shift of the term structure by 200 basis points upward or downward occurred, normalized with regulatory capital. Every bank has to calculate its Basel interest rate coefficient using its internal models, in particular for determining the duration of non-maturity positions such as overnight deposits, and taking account of on- as well as off-balance sheet items.[113] Any bank for which the coefficient exceeds 20% is classified as a bank with elevated interest rate risk. Independent of this classification, the supervisor may require a bank to hold additional capital on a discretionary basis.[114]

Information on the Basel interest rate coefficient of German banks is not published as part of any regular statistics. However, the Financial Stability Review 2015 of the Deutsche Bundesbank

---

[112] In June 2015 the Basel Committee on Banking Supervision (BCBS) published a consultative document including the introduction of capital requirements as one of two options for future regulatory treatment (see BCBS (2015)). However, in the final standards of April 2016, the BCBS opts for the second option, namely no capital requirements but increased supervision and transparency only (see BCBS (2016)).

[113] Details on the requirements can be found in the Circular 11/2011 of the Bundesanstalt für Finanzdienstleistungsaufsicht (BaFin (2011)) to all credit institutions in Germany.

[114] Chapter 7 scrutinizes the Basel interest rate coefficient in much greater detail.

(BBK) contains a graph at least of the average coefficients of savings banks, cooperative banks, and all other banks combined (see BBK (2015)). It starts in Q4 2011, the beginning of obligatory reporting for all German banks on a quarterly basis (see Figure 6.1).

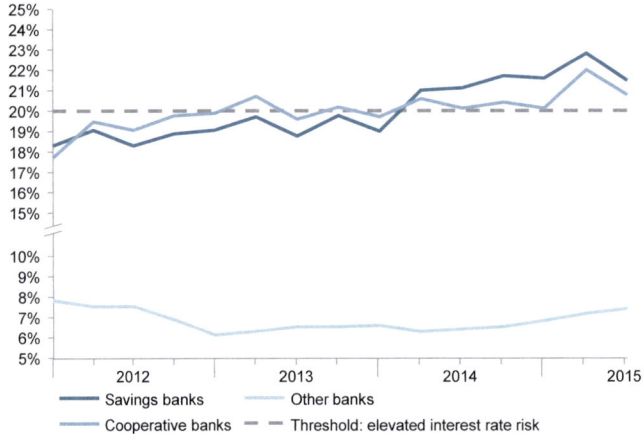

Figure 6.1: The development of the average Basel interest rate coefficient of German banks as reported by the BBK (2015) (Q4 2011 to Q2 2015) and the threshold value for elevated interest rate risk according to the BaFin (2011).

The information contained in this graph may be summarized in two statements. First, the average Basel interest rate risk coefficients of savings banks and cooperative banks have developed rather parallel, apparently following a long-term upward trend and continuously exceeding the regulatory threshold of 20% since Q1 2014. Second, although the average Basel interest rate risk coefficient of all other banks combined is much lower and does not seem to follow any long-term trend, it has continuously increased since Q1 2014. All in all, these findings create a sense of urgency to make any effort to increase the transparency of the interest rate risk of German banks.

The present chapter aims at increasing the transparency on the interest rate risk of German banks by analyzing information contained in official statistics that are publicly available. In effect, this limits the information base, compared to the one the Basel interest rate risk coefficient rests on, in two important ways. First, no information generated by internal models can be used. The official and publicly available statistics do not include any results from internal models with any relevance for an assessment of banks' interest rate risk.[115] Second, only information on on-balance sheet items is of any use. Even though official and publicly available statistics do include a few numbers on off-balance sheet items, these are generally not meaningful for any assessment of banks' interest rate risk as relevant details and breakdowns are missing.[116]

In light of these informational limitations it cannot be the purpose of the present chapter to quantify the interest rate risk of banks in Germany in an absolute and comprehensive way. Rather, the focus is on cross-sectional and time-series comparisons. Furthermore, the focus is on on-balance sheet term transformation. Information on on-balance sheet term transformation is what can most reliably be extracted from the official statistics publicly available. And comparisons can produce insights about the relative sizes of interest rate risk implied across banks and over time. Put differently, the present chapter investigates the potential sources of the interest rate risk from on-balance sheet term transformation. And it does so by applying a mostly comparative approach.

---

[115] Note that an assessment of banks' credit risk would be able to use results generated by internal models at least for those banks using the internal ratings based approach for the calculation of risk weighted assets.

[116] The most prominent example is the nominal amount of interest rate derivatives without any further details on the specifics of the derivatives in question.

The comparisons most of the analyses below feature are conducted on two different levels. One set of analyses features comparisons of all banks in Germany to all banks in the euro area, all banks in other individual member countries of the euro area, and all banks in the European Union (EU). Another set of analyses features comparisons of different types of banks in Germany. Wherever possible, the comparisons are conducted on both levels of aggregation in order to provide an integrated picture. However, data availability is a natural limiting factor.

The following investigation only makes use of statics that are publicly available but the statistics used are publicly available to different extents. Most analyses build on information contained in statistics published by the European Central Bank (ECB) or the BBK and which are accessible online for the general public. Some analyses, however, make use of information from statistics only accessible for external researchers on the premises of the BBK. Compared to the statistics available online the statistics exclusively held ready on the premises of the BBK have two main advantages. First, they feature data on the individual bank level. Second, they feature additional data fields. Hence, these statistics enable additional and more detailed analyses.

The chapter starts with overviews of available statistics, key methods and main results (Section 6.3). It then presents the analyses of the information contained in official and publicly available statistics on banks' balance sheets (Section 6.4), income statements (Section 6.5), interest rates (Section 6.6) and from the bank lending survey (Section 6.7). The chapter concludes with a short evaluation (Section 6.8).

6.3 Available statistics, key methods, and main results

There are no official statistics publicly available that were designed to provide information about the interest rate risk of banks in Germany. Accordingly, an important part of the present investigation is the extraction of relevant information from statistics that were designed for a different purpose. This process involves making appropriate selections and decisions, that is developing and applying sensible methods. And the results produced always have to be seen in the context of these methods. The statistics available, key methods, and main results are briefly presented below.

6.3.1 Available statistics

The information base of the present chapter consist of four types of statistics, namely balance sheet statistics, income statement statistics, interest rate statistics, and the bank lending survey results. Balance sheet statistics here also include statistics on issues and holdings of debt securities. These statistics contain different pieces of information that can be exploited to generate insights on banks' interest rate risk. The statistics that are built on in what follows are introduced in turn.

Balance sheet statistics

Statistics on the balance sheets of banks and other monetary financial institutions (MFIs) are an important source of information for monetary policy. For this reason, national central banks in the euro area collect data in a full census on a large number of balance sheet items and supply this data to the ECB. The current legal basis for this collection of balance sheet data are Regulation (EU) No 1071/2013 and ECB/2014/15. Technical guidance is provided by the ECB (2012) and, with a focus on Germany, by the BBK (2014b). Under the designation "MFI balance sheet statistics", the ECB publishes data reported by monetary financial institutions in the euro area. This data is available on two levels of aggregation, namely for the euro area as a whole and for each member state individually.[117] For Germany and under the designation "monthly balance sheet statistics", the BBK publishes corresponding balance sheet data. This data is also available on different levels of aggregation, that is to say on the national level and on the level of types of banks in Germany.

There are, however, discrepancies between the numbers published for MFIs in Germany by the ECB on the one hand and by the BBK on the other hand. Apart from very few high-level time-series, the data published by the BBK differs from that published by the ECB in two systematic ways. First, the scope of institutions covered differs. While the ECB reports numbers for all MFIs, the BBK reports numbers for MFIs excluding money market funds. The BBK hence only covers credit institutions and building societies and simply refers to these MFIs as banks. Second, the accounting rules are not identical. More precisely, the deducting items differ. These differences impair the comparability of the data from the ECB and the BBK.[118]

The reporting requirements of the "MFI balance sheet statistics" include breakdowns of the balance sheet or parts of it by, among other things, instrument, maturity, and counterparty. Thirteen main types of instruments on the asset and the liability side of the balance sheet are distinguished, some of which feature further subtypes. Maturity is generally recorded as original maturity at the time the facility is first drawn. The original maturity has to be reported in maturity brackets with limits of one year or two or five or ten years. For deposits redeemable at notice, the threshold period length is three month. Counterparties are distinguished by country of residence and economic sector, on the first level into MFIs and non-MFIs.

Concerning the counterparties covered, the ECB publishes suitable data on deposits for households including non-profit institutions servicing households, non-financial corporations, insurance corporations and pension funds, and other financial corporations[119], and it publishes suitable data on loans for non-financial corporations only.[120] The BBK publishes suitable data on deposits and loans for all non-MFIs, mostly in an aggregated format. However, the precise data fields published by ECB and BBK are not all identical.

The securities issues and holdings statistics complement the narrowly defined balance sheet statistics in a way that is very relevant for the investigation at hand. The securities issues statistics provide information on debt and equity securities issued and outstanding by issuing sector. Hence, they shed further light on the liabilities side of MFIs' balance sheets. The security holdings statistics contain data on the outstanding debt and equity securities held by holding sector. Therefore, they can be scanned for insights about the asset side of the balance sheets of MFIs and banks.

Standardizations need to be applied to the amounts of interest in order to ensure comparability. For most analyses the absolute amounts are normalized with total assets. But for some analyses the absolute amounts are normalized with the total amounts for which a relevant breakdown is provided for, instead. Which standardization is used depends on the specific question under investigation.

In order to avoid misinterpretation of the results produced, it should be mentioned that due to the modernization of accounting standards through the adoption of the Act Modernising Accounting Law in Germany, the Bilanzmodernisierungsgesetz (BilMoG), there is a statistical break in the numbers displayed between November and December 2010. As the BBK (2011a)

---

[117] Note that for member countries of the European Union that are not members of the euro area the ECB also collects and reports data. However, the published data for non-members of the euro area is much less detailed.

[118] Detailed guidance to the statistics the comparison of which reveals accordances as well as discrepancies are provided, as mentioned earlier, by the ECB (2012) and the BBK (2014b).

[119] That is, financial institutions other than monetary financial institutions, insurance corporations, and pension funds.

[120] Even though the ECB publishes data for all types of counterparties for the euro area as a whole, for individual member states the maturity breakdowns are missing for any counterparty except for non-financial corporations till the end of 2014. Starting in 2015 they are, however, provided.

points out in its financial stability review for the period in question, the new requirement to report derivatives held for trading at fair value led to a significant increase of total assets reported in particular by large banks. Furthermore, the BBK (2011b) points out in its monthly report featuring a review of the income of German banks in 2010, the construction of several positions in the profit and loss account changed fundamentally as for example the rules were revised that govern the allocation of interest income earned in proprietary trading to either net interest income or net trading result. Hence, this statistical break can also be found in the income statement statistics which are introduced next.

Income statement statistics

Statistics on the incomes and expenses of banks are an important source of information about banks' business models and performance, and in turn about the state of the financial industry. Therefore, it is only natural that the collection of data from banks' income statements is a standard element of the information gathering of central banks and other financial authorities. The legal foundation for the collection of data on revenues and costs is currently Regulation (EU) No 575/2013 accompanied by the Implementing Technical Standard EBA/ITS/2013/02 for the euro area plus, specifically for Germany, the German Banking Act[121]. The ECB publishes data for the euro area as a whole and for each member state individually as a part of its "consolidated banking data". The BBK makes data available for Germany in total as well as disaggregated by type of bank in its "statistics of the banks' profit and loss accounts". Both data sets are based on a full census of banks in the respective economic region.

The income statement statistics provided by the ECB and the BBK largely contain annual data. The ECB provides data going back to 2007 for the euro area and to 2008 for Germany. The BBK provides data starting in 1968 and since 1999 for all major items reported on today. There is a difference in scope with respect to the institutions covered. While the ECB includes all banks in Germany, the BBK includes all German banks. Hence, additionally to the domestic branches of German banks, the ECB includes branches of foreign banks in Germany whereas the BBK includes branches of German banks in foreign countries.[122] It should also be noted that the income statement data provided does not differentiate between banks and non-banks as counterparties. In what way an assessment of banks' interest rate risk benefits from differentiating between counterparties in this way is elaborated on in detail below.

Interest rate statistics

Statistics on interest rates paid and charged by MFIs when doing business with non-financial counterparties as well as on the corresponding business volumes are an important source of information on the transmission of monetary policy. Since 2003 and on a monthly basis the ECB and associated national central banks publish harmonized interest rate statistics called "MFI interest rate statistics" for the euro area as a whole as well as for the individual member states. These statistics cover interest rates for outstanding amounts and new business, and for new business also business volumes. They cover deposits from and loans to euro area households and non-financial corporations. They feature breakdowns by original maturity for outstanding and new deposits, by original and remaining maturity and by residual interest rate fixation period for outstanding loans, and by initial interest rate fixation period for new loans. Besides, they feature

---

[121] Disclosure is regulated in §26 of the Kreditwesengesetz (KWG).

[122] The distinction between banks in Germany and German banks is important in order to understand why the numbers reported in the balance sheet statistics by the ECB and the BBK do not match exactly. The title of this chapter, however, is intended to refer to both groups of banks. When the results of this chapter are referred to in other parts of this dissertation in general terms, only the designation "banks in Germany" from the title of this chapter is used.

breakdowns by purpose of loan for households and by size of loan for non-financial corporations. More importantly, they disclose interest rates and business volumes of fully collateralized new loans separately for most subtypes. These statistics are generated not from a full census but from a sample of MFI's. This sample covers far more than half of total business volume and is dominated by credit institutions (see ECB (2003b) and Keuning (2003)).[123]

Since the interest rate statistics are not based on a full census, their representativeness might be questioned. The large share of total business volume covered may be referred to as a point in favour of representativeness. However, an important objection can be raised. One might reasonably suspect that the sampling approach aims at a large share of total business volume covered with a small number of MFIs questioned, and hence produces a sample which is biased toward larger MFIs.[124] Hence, if large MFIs behave differently from smaller MFIs the results may not be representative on the MFI level. The underlying reason for this is, of course, that the statistics were not designed to provide information on the average MFI but on the prevailing market conditions for non-financial customers of MFIs. And for representativeness in this respect, total business volume covered might indeed be regarded a sensible metric, independent of which banks are sampled.

Last but not least, note that the MFI interest rate statistics only cover business with euro area counterparties. Interest rates are annualized and volume-weighted. And new business includes business based on new financial contracts as well as business resulting from renegotiations.

Bank lending survey results

The bank lending survey conducted by the ECB and the associated national central banks consists of a set of qualitative questions. It is directed at senior loan officers from a small sample of banks[125] and is designed to generate an informational basis for taking a broader view of bank lending to households and non-financial corporations in the euro area. It addresses the supply side and the demand side. And it covers past developments as well as expectations for the future. In greater detail, the survey differentiates between lending to households for house purchase, consumer credit and other lending to households, and loans and credit lines to non-financial corporations. Thus, the product scope of the survey is broader than loans only. With respect to the supply side, the survey investigates the tightening or easing of credit standards, that is general guidelines for lending, and the contribution to any tightening or easing by changes of some specific terms and conditions, that is actual contractual arrangements. With respect to the demand side, the survey examines increases or decreases in demand. And for past changes in credit standards and in demand it also inspects the underlying reasons. Finally, the survey is conducted on a quarterly basis since the end of 2002, and it asks for developments in the last quarter and expectations for the next (see ECB (2003a) and Berg et al. (2005)).

Since the bank lending survey is directed at a small sample of banks only, the representativeness of the results may again be questioned. Because as with the interest rate statistics, sample selection possibly leads to biased results. Deviating from how the interest rates are calculated for the interest rate statistics, the individual banks' answers to the questions of the bank lending survey are not volume weighted in any way when aggregated to produce the results. In a sense,

---

[123] According to Keuning (2003) the share of total business volume covered in the euro area as a whole was above 80% at the time of the first release of the MFI interest rate statistics in 2003.

[124] Keuning (2003) highlights the reduced burden from reporting requirements as a positive feature of the sampling approach. The sampling approach results from the focus on borrowing and lending conditions for households an non-financial corporations and not on the interest rate risk of banks.

[125] The number of banks included increased from 86 surveyed initially to 137 surveyed at the beginning of 2015 on Q4 2014. In Germany, the number of banks surveyed increased from 17 initially to 34 currently as reported by the BBK (2016).

however, this even makes the results more meaningful for an assessment of the average banks' interest rate risk.

For the study of banks' interest rate risk, the following three sets of questions included in the ECB's bank lending survey are of interest. First, in its investigation of tightening or easing of credit standards for loans and credit lines to non-financial corporations the survey distinguishes between short-term and long-term loans. If there was less tightening or more easing of the credit standards for long-term loans observed, this could be interpreted as evidence for a bank-driven promotion of long-term loans relative to short-term loans. And if it was assumed that such a promotion was reflected in the market outcome, that is in actual lending, one could infer that banks are taking more interest rate risk. Second, among the specific terms and conditions the changes of which the survey investigates with respect to their contribution to any tightening or easing, is the maturity. If there was a contribution to easing observed in changes of the maturity, this would suggest that banks are willing to accept more interest rate risk. And if it was assumed that the counterparties of banks in lending prefer longer maturities to shorter maturities, one could infer that banks are indeed taking more interest rate risk. In principle, a change in terms and conditions concerning the maturity could also lead to less interest rate risk, but this seems rather unlikely and runs against the common understanding.[126] Third, in its examination of increases or decreases of the demand for loans and credit lines to non-financial corporations the survey again distinguishes between short-term and long-term loans. If the demand for long-term loans increased more than the demand for short-term loans, this would imply an increase in the pressure on banks to take interest rate risk. And such an increase in pressure entails an increase in actual interest rate risk of banks, if the additional demands for long-term and short-term loans are met to extends sufficiently similar. As will be elaborated on below, for each question there are five possible answers, one indicating no change and the others indicating a weaker or a stronger change in either direction.

6.3.2 Key methods

As a matter of research design, the present investigation follows a small number of guiding principles. Setting these principles charts the general course. Aiming at the greatest possible consistency, this investigation is based on set of general assumptions. Making these assumptions allows to address the research question at hand with the statistics available. In order to take full advantage of the specific data provided, some specific techniques are introduced to this investigation. Applying these techniques allows to extract deeper insights. These guiding principles, general assumptions, and specific techniques are presented below.

Guiding principles

The investigation in this chapter addresses the interest rate risk of banks. However, it is based on statistics some of which do not differentiate between credit institutions and other types of institution with a comparable business model such as money market funds. Instead, these statistics report numbers collectively for these MFIs.[127] At least, the numbers for central banks are usually reported separately. In what follows, statistics that report numbers for MFIs excluding central banks are built on to learn something about the interest rate risk of banks. More precisely, the numbers reported are treated as if they were reported for banks only. In support of proceeding

---

[126] In a bilateral email exchange with the responsible unit of the BBK it was confirmed that a reported change of the terms and conditions regarding maturity that contributes to an easing is standardly interpreted as being a lengthening of the maturity.

[127] For a precise definition see the "Explanatory notes on statistics on the Monetary Financial Institutions sector" made available online by the ECB (1998).

in this way, one might point to the quantitative dominance of credit institutions which in terms of total assets make up 97% of all MFIs in the euro area by the end of 2014.[128]

The investigation is framed in such a way as to concern the risk of an increase in interest rates. This is the risk commonly associated with the traditional banking activities of borrowing short and lending long expose a bank to. For example, empirical findings suggests that for the vast majority of German banks the negative exposure to a parallel upward shift of the term structure is more material than the negative exposure to a parallel downward shift.[129] Hence, this framing is more than a well motivated convention. But of course, the same results could have also been reported with a different sign and then as concerning a decrease in interest rates. The question which changes of the term structure are how harmful for banks in Germany is investigated in detail in the impact assessment in Chapter 7. The investigation does not produce an absolute quantification of banks interest rate risk but instead is comparative in nature. All comparisons rest on the following idea: The higher the reliance on short-term liabilities or the higher the fraction of long-term assets, the higher is the interest rate risk, everything else equal. It is important to note that the individual comparisons are only meaningful ceteris paribus. But even more importantly, the same is true also for all comparisons taken together, as they only cover on-balance sheet items systematically. As a final point on the comparative approach, it is important to note that the following analyses diagnose more or less interest rate risk or risk potential always against the background of the normalization applied, for example in terms of more interest rate risk per asset.

The investigation focusses on interest rate risk and not on the capacity to bear this risk. In practical terms this implies that no attention is paid to the amount of equity banks have and that the balance-sheet positions studied are also never normalized with any measure of equity. To avoid confusion, it is important to remember that the German supervisor's standard yardstick for the measurement of interest rate risk, namely the Basel interest rate coefficient, does feature the amount of own funds in the denominator. This coefficient may hence be understood as a ratio of a measure of bank's interest rate risk and a measure of its risk bearing capacity. Putting the focus on interest rate risk only may be seen as a particular instance of applying the ceteris-paribus assumption with respect to the capacity of bearing this risk. One might also argue that if one wanted to take the risk bearing capacity into account, one should not refer to the total amount of own funds or a comparable measure but rather to that amount that is not already budgeted for other types of risk such as credit risk, an effort that is not taken for the calculation of the Basel interest rate coefficient.[130] Anyway, in what follows, the balance-sheet positions of interest are in most cases normalized with total assets and in some specific cases with the total amount for which the maturity breakdown is provided which is exploited in the analysis at hand.

Strictly speaking, the following investigation does not focus on banks' interest rate risk but on Banks' exposure to changes of the term structure. That this difference is important is an essential part of the motivation for the investigation undertaken in Chapter 7. Here changes in the probability of the materialization of certain possible term structure changes is not addressed. Nevertheless, the results are presented in terms of risk and not in terms of exposure. This reflects the common ways results are presented on this topic. And it may be seen as the application of yet another ceteris-paribus assumption, namely that the probabilities of the materialization of the relevant changes of the term structure do not change. Chapter 7 picks up on this in detail.

---

[128] In greater detail, the aggregated balance sheet of euro area credit institutions features about 30 EUR trillion in total assets for 2014. The corresponding number for euro area money market funds is about 950 EUR billion.

[129] Memmel et al. (2016) report that for 95% of their observations of German banks a parallel upward shift of the term structure by 200 basis points would have more negative effects than a downward shift of the same magnitude.

[130] This may be regarded as one of the major deficits of the Basel interest rate coefficient. In particular as the realization of interest rate risk may well be correlated with the realization of other types of risk such as credit risk.

When investigating the development of interest rate risk, the period after the financial crisis is of particular interest for at least two interconnected reasons. First, during the financial crisis strong extraordinary influences possibly mask underlying developments in banks' interest rate risk. And second, at the end of the financial crisis the new policy rate regime emerged which is lasting until the current edge of the data investigated here. For these two reasons the analysis that follows mostly focusses on the period after the financial crisis. Prior data is plotted mainly to provide background information only.[131] However, dating the end of the financial crisis precisely is not straightforward. By and large, 2010 is commonly seen as the first post-crisis year. Coincidentally, annual data for 2010 and monthly data for December 2010 are the first to be reported under BilMoG in Germany. To ensure consistency, the following investigation focusses on data reported under BilMoG, at least as far as this data comes from balance sheet statistics or income statement statistics. The period covered may be seen as a subperiod of the post-crisis period or alternatively as the post-crisis period delimited rather conservatively.

Using the statistics made available by the ECB, the development in Germany is compared to the development in the euro area as a whole. An alternative approach would be to compare the development in Germany to the one of the euro area without Germany. In the investigation that follows the euro area including Germany is looked at as its development is considered interesting also in its own right. Using the statistics made available by the BBK, only selected banking groups are compared. The selection procedure, which is detailed below, aims at ensuring traceability and relevance.

General assumptions

All three general assumptions that are made in the analyses that follow concern the question how to identify and quantify short-term and long-term positions in the sense relevant for an investigation of banks' interest rate risk. The first general assumption is that the relevant metric on which the answer to this question should be based is the residual interest rate fixation period of the position at issue. And the time till the next interest rate reset date is understood to be capped by the time to maturity.

The assumption that the residual interest rate fixation period is the relevant metric for distinguishing short-term and long-term positions is arguably more plausible in a static setting than in a dynamic setting. Because in a dynamic setting, possible changes in business volumes as reactions by banks and their counterparties to changes in interest rates have to be factored in, additionally. And accounting for this sensitivity requires a richer metric, closer to some form of elasticity measure. By contrast, the present investigation is conducted in a static setting, that is it puts aside possible accompanying changes in business volumes and instead focusses on possible changes in interest rates, only. The main reason for proceeding in this way is to avoid a host of additional assumptions the analyses would otherwise additionally have to be based on.

A second noteworthy implication of this first general assumption is that no distinctions are made according to the degree of interest rate pass-through. That is, positions with the same residual interest rate fixation period are treated similarly independent of the size of expectable interest rate adjustments as a consequence of a change in reference rates. Again, this is considered reasonable in order to keep the assumptions that govern how the analyses generate results from the data provided easily comprehensible.

The majority of the statistics available only feature breakdowns by original maturity. The second general assumption is that original maturity corresponds to residual interest rate fixation period, that is that a longer original time to maturity comes with longer residual interest rate fixation period at any point in time. This is not only simple but also a particularly natural

---

[131] In order to present ten full years of data, the plots go back to 2005 where possible.

assumption as it would be true in a number of scenarios, most notably, if the initial interest rate fixation equals the original time to maturity and if business runs out and is renewed evenly. Obviously, this assumption may also misrepresent reality. However, without an assumption or a set of assumptions that links original maturity and residual interest rate fixation period, the amount of data available to base an investigation into banks' interest rate risk on would be much more limited. Because only very few publicly available statistics report actual numbers on the residual interest rate fixation period. Note that, for deposits redeemable at notice the distinction between short-term and long-term is naturally based on the length of the period of notice.

Of course, there are alternative ways to make use of the publicly available data than to make the simple assumption that original maturity directly corresponds to residual interest rate fixation period. In particular, from the available breakdowns by original maturity one might in a first step try to infer the portfolio profile by remaining maturity and then in a second step make the arguably more natural assumption that remaining maturity corresponds to residual interest rate fixation period. The downside is that the first of these two steps requires a set of additional assumptions. In Appendix 1 one possible version of these assumptions is introduced and all standard analyses are reproduced based on them. However, in the main part the second general assumption is maintained, that is original maturity is used as an indicator for residual interest rate fixation period. The two main interconnected reasons for proceeding in this way are that the link to the original data is closer and that, as is shown in the appendix, the results produced in the other way with a natural set of assumptions turn out to be extremely similar in terms of rankings and trends if, of course, not in levels.

As a feature that facilitates a summarized presentation, the statistics available feature break-downs into a handful of maturity ranges. The third general assumption is that uniformly the positions in the maturity ranges up to one year are to be treated as short-term and the positions in the maturity ranges above one year are to be treated as long-term. This assumption has two important parts. First, it defines one year as the threshold value for the delimitation of short-term and long-term positions and puts all other threshold values provided aside. In most analyses that follow, all positions above and below the threshold value of one year are treated equally, even if there is further information available. For example, loans with five and up to ten years original maturity are not treated differently from loans with more than ten years. Second, this assumption ignores any possible differences of the distributions of positions within maturity ranges across entities or over time. How sensitive estimates of the interest rate risks of banks are to this assumption has been highlighted by Entrop et al. (2009). In particular, the loans within one of the wider maturity ranges provided might be distributed in very different ways, with quantitatively important implications. Both parts of this assumption are consciously made to keep the overall number of assumptions at bay and the results traceable.

An important issue to be raised concerns non-maturity positions. In accordance with the assumptions made, overnight deposits are considered short-term, independent of the respective counterparty. Alternatively, overnight deposits from households could be treated differently. This is indeed common practice in internal models where overnight deposits from households are treated as more stable than overnight deposits of more professional counterparties. Banks are understood to regard the precision of their internal models in this respect as an important determinant of their competitiveness because it directly feeds into their liquidity management and pricing. And even in the standard approach for the interest rate risk measurement which had been envisaged by the BCBS (2015) calculations regarding non-maturity deposits were planed to be left to internal models. However, since the present investigation does not aim at a precise quantification of banks' interest rate risk, treating overnight deposits consistently as short-term liabilities is favoured over making additional assumptions which would be required for making further distinctions. The simple alternative of regarding overnight deposits of households as long-term instead of as short-term liabilities is rejected as not conservative enough.

Three further points need to be mentioned. First, sometimes the delimitation of long-term positions in this investigation is not congruent with the official designations in so far as occasionally a medium-term category is included in the statistics available. As the lower bound for medium-term always is one year, it is subsumed here under long-term. Second, money market papers are considered to be short-term. Because by definition, their original maturity does not exceed one year. Third, for deposits redeemable at notice the threshold between short-term and long-term is determined differently. It is determined to be three month. This mirrors the traditional distinction between that part of deposits redeemable at notice included in monetary aggregates and that part which is considered non-monetary.

Specific techniques

The statistics that make up the data basis for this investigation all have certain peculiarities which make tailored approaches necessary. In general, all these approaches have in common the guiding principles and general assumptions introduced above. Only very few exceptions are made. For example, at one point the focus is on loans with an original maturity of more than five years and on overnight deposits only.

Besides exceptions or adaption of this sort, some specific techniques are applied in order to derive more interesting insights from some of the statistics provided. To be precise, in the investigation below, one specific technique is applied in the analysis of the interest rate statistics and another in the analysis of the bank lending survey results. These techniques are introduced in turn.

With data on MFIs' interest rates and business volumes for new deposits and loans broken down by original maturity and initial interest rate fixation period, respectively, it is possible to distinguish not only between changes that increase and changes that decrease the interest rate risk of MFIs, everything else equal. But it is also possible to distinguish between MFI-driven changes and counterparty-driven changes. The procedure for this distinction applied in the analysis below builds on a very simple market model for deposits and for loans, each. These models are based on the following two propositions. First, the higher the interest rate on loans, the higher the volume of loans supplied by MFIs but the lower the volume of loans demanded by counterparties. Second, the higher the interest rate on deposit, the higher the volume of deposits supplied by counterparties but the lower the volume of deposits demanded by MFIs. Hence, both models feature a downward sloping demand curve and an upward sloping supply curve with the market equilibrium where these two curves intersect. And the two models differ in so far as in the model for loans the MFIs are on the supply side and the counterparties are on the demand side whereas in the model for deposits it is the other way round and the counterparties are on the supply side while the MFIs are on the demand side.

Remember that this identification strategy of distinguishing changes in the market outcome that are supply-side driven and those that are demand-side driven based on the signs of the price or interest rate change in combination with the sign of the volume change is prominently applied by Paligorova and Santos (2013), Buch et al. (2014), and Ioannidou et al. (2015) as presented in Section 4.3.1.

Putting the two market models to use, MFI-driven changes and counterparty-driven changes can be distinguished as shifts of the supply curve or of the demand curve. According to the model for loans, an MFI-driven change is equivalent to a shift in the supply curve while a counterparty-driven change is equivalent to a shift in the demand curve. Therefore, if the volume and the interest rate change in opposite directions, the change is MFI-driven (see Figure 6.2a), whereas if they change in the same direction, the change is counterparty-driven (see Figure 6.2b). And according to the model for deposits, an MFI-driven change is equivalent to a shift in the demand curve and a counterparty-driven change is equivalent to a shift in the supply curve. Hence, if the volume and the interest rate change in the same direction, here the change is MFI-driven (see Figure 6.2c), and if they change in opposite directions, now the change is counterparty-driven (see Figure 6.2d).

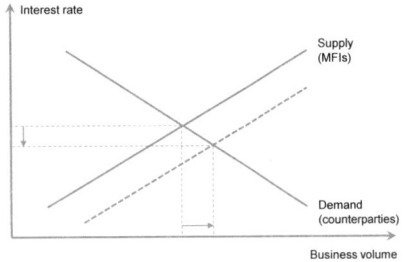

a: MFI-driven loan expansion

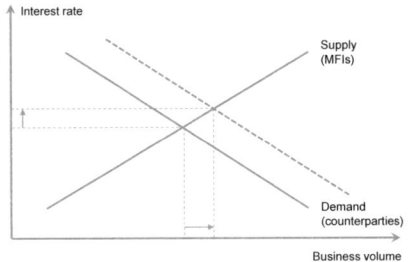

b: Counterparty-driven loan expansion

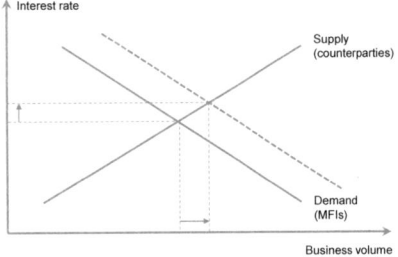

c: MFI-driven deposit expansion

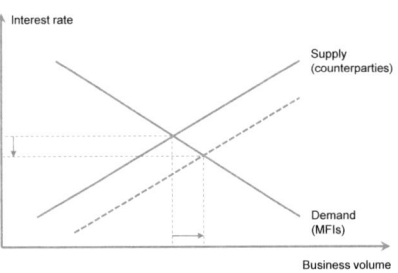

d: Counterparty-driven deposit expansion

Figure 6.2: Basic market model allows to identify and distinguish (a) bank-driven loan expansions and (b) counterparty-driven loan expansions as well as (c) bank-driven deposit expansions and (d) counterparty-driven deposit expansions (and also the corresponding contractions, not displayed). Source: own illustration.

Using these models requires data not only on interest rates but also on new business volumes. With respect to the information on business volumes available, a specific deficit now needs to be addressed. For most items or subtypes the volumes of gross new business are reported. For some subtypes, however, the volume of outstanding business at the end of the reporting period is reported instead. The relevant subtypes for which this is the case are overnight deposits and deposits redeemable at notice.[132] In the analysis below, the data on outstanding business volumes for these subtypes is, nevertheless, used in the same way as the data on gross new business volumes supplied for the other subtypes. This is considered reasonable as for these subtypes it is plausible to assume that the entire outstanding amount is subject to the establishment of a new market equilibrium every month in the sense relevant here. Deposits redeemable at notice are the obvious exception here because the notice is commonly longer than one month. With respect to these it needs to be assumed that an increase (decrease) of the total outstanding amount comes with a larger (smaller) volume of gross new business. In the discussion below, it will be particularly important to remember that the values used as new business volumes of overnight deposits are the outstanding amounts at the end of the reference period.

Furthermore, using these models requires to control for external changes of interest rates, that is reference rates need to be factored in. Factoring in reference rates is the most straightforward

---

[132] Concerning loans, only the volume of outstanding business is reported for revolving loans and overdrafts and for extended credit card credit. In what follows, however, these are irrelevant as the focus is on collateralized loans for reasons explained below.

way to control for changes in time preferences and opportunity costs. Each subtype of deposits and loans is assigned an average maturity and then for each reporting period the interest rate for this maturity from the risk free yield curve of the economic region in question is subtracted from the bank interest rate reported as paid to or charged to the counterparty. What remains is the margin.

With the help of these models it is possible to identify MFI-driven and counterparty-driven changes of expansionary and contractionary nature for every deposit or loan subtype. Here, expansionary and contractionary always refer to an increase and decrease in business volume, respectively. However, for the production of a digestible output, these changes need to be aggregated in one of a number of possible ways. In the analysis below the aggregation uses business volumes as weights. When a change of a certain type is found to have occurred at a certain deposit or loan subtype, it is weighted with the respective change in business volume. And then the changes are aggregated across all deposit and loan subtypes, respectively, to quantify what part of the overall change in business volume is due to which type of change. It is important to note that this way of aggregation is based on a simplification. Naturally, any change in the market equilibrium for a certain deposit or loan subtype may be the result of different types of changes. For example, there may be a strong counterparty-driven expansion counteracted partly by a small MFI-driven contraction. Here, however, the net-change in business volume is completely attributed to the dominating type of change.

Taking a step back, two of the assumptions these models are based on require additional consideration as they appear to conflict with fundamental insights. First, the explicit assumption of an upward sloping loan supply curve appears to conflict with the idea of a backward bending loan supply curve which gives rise to the phenomenon of credit rationing. Second, the implicit assumption that the market for loans and the market for deposits can be modelled separately appears to conflict with both the traditional understanding of banking as intermediation of loanable funds and with the modern understanding of banking as financing through money creation. The justifiability of the assumptions that appear to conflict with fundamental insights is investigated in turn.

The idea of a backward bending loan supply curve as prominently advanced by Stiglitz and Weiss (1981) builds on the basic insight that the expected return of a loan made by a bank may be non-monotonic in the interest rate charged to the counterparty. As the interest rate increases, so may the severity of the adverse selection problem in a loan market with asymmetric information. And above a certain threshold, a further increase in the interest rate may then deteriorate the average credit worthiness of potential borrowers by so much that the overall expected return of a loan falls. However, for fully collateralized loans credit rationing is arguably a much more special case.[133] Because under normal circumstances, the collateral eliminates or at least substantially reduces the downside risk for the bank.[134] Luckily, the interest rate statistics at hand report interest rates as well as business volumes for fully collateralized loans separately. And these loans are explicitly defined as those with a collateral of at least the same value as the nominal value of the loan. Thus, in order to make the assumption of an upward sloping loan supply curve plausible, the following analysis focusses on fully collateralized loans.

As presented in Chapter 2, the traditional understanding of banking as the intermediation of loanable funds features the market for deposits and the market for loans as an upstream market

---

[133] Even fully collateralized loans may lead to a loss for the bank if the counterparty defaults. Because as the counterparty defaults it may not be possible to sell the collateral at the price originally assigned to it. This is the most obvious reason for which a credit rationing equilibrium is still a possibility even for fully collateralized loans.

[134] Of course, the proper valuation of the collateral is key. Common risk factors may lead to a default of the borrower and to a decrease in the value of the collateral. Or the default of the borrower may lead to a decrease of the value of the collateral. To take these possible interactions into account is one of the challenges for banks' credit risk management.

and a downstream market, respectively, just like in a standard industrial setting. Accordingly, they are seen as interdependent in a way similar to the market for crude oil and the market for gasoline. In contrast, the modern understanding of banking as financing through money creation is based on the idea that when a bank makes a loan to a certain counterparty it credits this counterparty's account with deposits which it creates in this process. As a result, the market for deposits and the market for loans are seen as interdependent in that deposits and loans are jointly brought into existence. At first sight, this seems to prevent the use of the independent market models introduced above. But two things are important to note. First, the interest rate statistics' coverage of the markets for deposits and loans is not comprehensive. Only business with euro area counterparties and therein only business with households and non-financial corporations is covered. For example, business with insurance companies and pension funds is not covered at all. This means that the markets for deposits and loans as they present themselves in the interest rate statistics at hand are at least not as tightly connected as they are according to the traditional understanding of banking. Because not all possible sources of deposits and targets for loans feed into the data. With respect to the modern understanding of banking, the same reasoning does not apply, though. Because according to this modern understanding a new loan always comes with a new deposit of the same counterparty. And this means that a simple lack of comprehensiveness of the coverage of counterparties does not entail a disconnect between the covered markets for deposits and loans. However, with the data at hand, this disconnect does indeed exist but for a different reason. As discussed above, what is reported as the business volume for new overnight deposits actually is the outstanding amount at the end of the reporting period. This means that when a loan is made and, according to the modern understanding of banking, overnight deposits are created in the process, it is not the case that the business volumes of new loans and new overnight deposits necessarily increase by the same amount. This is only the case if the overnight deposits are not transferred beyond the coverage of the interest rate statistics, for example to a household in the UK, or used or transformed in any way, for example to pay off a loan or into deposits with an agreed maturity. The last point suggests a restriction of the following analysis to make the assumption of separated markets most easily acceptable. The analysis that follows will primarily focus on how loans and deposits are each distributed between short-term and long-term. And as far as it is only at issue how the sum of loans is distributed between short-term and long-term loans, and the same for deposits, the interdependence of the deposit and the loan market is considered a negligible problem also given the modern understanding of banking.

That the analysis proposed is compatible with the modern understanding of banking is best appreciated when one understands the different subtypes of deposits as essentially similar to different sorts of bank bonds. As they are featured here, they can be seen as investment options offered by a bank and are in so far similar to bank bonds. Depositing one's money in a bank account is in this view equivalent to buying a financial claim from the bank. Yet, the money is not destroyed in this process as it would be if an actual asset was bought from the bank as explained in Chapter 2.

Next, the special technique applied to process the data from the bank lending survey is introduced. The bank lending survey only concerns changes over time. That is, the questions ask how certain aspects of bank lending have changed since the last time the question was asked or how these aspects are expected to change in the future. Hence, the results have to be seen as concerning marginal changes. The special technique applied to make these results digestible is comparable to constructing the antiderivative. Starting from an arbitrary initial value, the marginal changes are aggregated cumulatively. Below, the initial value is set to zero for the first reporting date of interest. But as this initial value is set arbitrarily, it has to be abstained from level comparisons across entities, of course.

Going into greater details on the bank lending survey, for the questions of interest, there are the following five possible answers each. The questions on tightening and easing of credit standards can be answered with "tightened (eased) considerably", "tightened (eased) somewhat", and "remained basically unchanged". The questions on the contribution to tightening or easing of changes of terms and conditions concerning maturity can be answered with "contributed considerably to tightening (easing)", "contributed somewhat to tightening (easing)", and "contributed to basically unchanged credit standards". Finally, the questions on increases or decreases of demand can be answered with "increased (decreased) considerably", "increased (decreased) somewhat", and "remained basically unchanged". Two results measures are consistently made available by the ECB and the BBK. Both are calculated as means and both assign a positive sign to tightening, contribution to tightening, and increase in demand, and a negative sign to the respective opposite answers. But whereas the so called "diffusion index" is calculated as a weighted mean with the weights for answers including "considerably" of 1 and -1 and for answers including "somewhat" of 0.5 and -0.5, respectively, the so called "net percentage" is calculated as a simple mean with the weights of 1 and -1 for both types of directed answers. In what follows, only the net percentage is used. The reason for this more conservative procedure is the lack of calibration of the answers. The assumption that the loan officers can distinguish changes in one direction from changes in the other direction is arguably less strong than the assumption that all loan officers distinguish between the sizes of the changes captured by the attributes "considerably" and "somewhat" in a consistent way.

6.3.3 Main results

As a final step before embarking on the actual investigation the main results are previewed here. To begin with, a brief summary is given, which presents the overarching lessons that can be learnt. All main findings are then listed together in an overview with derived conclusions. This list refers to all analyses of the following investigation. Of the many findings and conclusions, the list only contains the most important ones for every analysis. And the results it contains are always to be understood as implicitly being framed in a everything-else-equal way.

Summary

Analyzing the available statistics in depth produces the following general findings. MFIs in Germany run a larger on-balance sheet term mismatch than MFIs in the euro area as a whole and have been driving up this mismatch in recent years, mostly by shifting to shorter-term funding. MFIs in Germany also earn a larger part of their operating income in the form of net interest income and hence with direct dependence on market interest rates. MFIs in Germany particularly actively increase the amount of new short-term deposits. And MFIs in Germany do comparatively little in the form of adjusting credit standards or terms and conditions in face of a relatively high increase in demand for long-term loans.

Of the types of banks in Germany, savings banks and cooperative banks clearly run the largest on-balance sheet term mismatches, but for all types of banks it has increased recently. And savings and cooperative banks also earn the largest parts of their operating income in the form of net interest income with the relative sizes of interest income and interest expenses pointing to a particular engagement in term transformation. Many further more specific findings point into the same direction and only very few into another. In view of these findings, the following principal conclusions can be drawn. Banks in Germany already exceed the euro area average interest rate risk from traditional term transformation and they are bound to increase it further. Of the various types of banks in Germany, savings banks and cooperative banks stand out.

Overview

Next, an overview of the main results is presented in a list.

#	Statistic	Scope	Subject	Main finding	Derived conclusion	Figures (6.X)
1	Balance sheet statistics	Germany and the euro area	Identification of relevant balance sheet positions	MFIs in Germany have higher shares of assets and liabilities with non-reference MFIs as counterparties	Banks in Germany currently have a higher potential for interest rate risk	4, 5, 6, 7
2	Balance sheet statistics	Germany and the euro area	Determination of maturity structure at current edge	MFIs in Germany have higher shares of long-term assets or of short-term liabilities	Banks in Germany currently have more interest rate risk	8
3	Balance sheet statistics	Germany and the euro area	Assessment of the recent development of the maturity structure	MFIs in Germany have more strongly increased short-term liabilities and have also increased long-term assets	Banks in Germany are in the process of particularly increasing their interest rate risk	9, 10, 11, 12
4	Balance sheet statistics	Germany and euro area member countries	International comparison (additional analysis)	MFIs in Germany have one of the highest shares of long-term loans and show the biggest increase of the share of short-term deposits between 2010 and 2014	Banks in Germany have a particular high and increasing interest rate risk	13, 14
5	Balance sheet statistics	Germany and the euro area	Long-term fixed-rate debt securities issued (additional analysis)	MFIs in Germany have a higher share of long-term fixed-rate debt securities issued	Banks in Germany have a lower interest rate risk from long-term fixed-rate debt securities issued	15
6	Balance sheet statistics	Germany and the euro area	Remaining maturity of debt securities issued (additional analysis)	MFIs in Germany have higher shares of shorter-term and lower shares of longer-term debt securities outstanding	Banks in Germany have a higher interest rate risk from debt securities outstanding according to their remaining maturity	16
7	Balance sheet statistics	Types of banks in Germany	Identification of relevant balance sheet positions	Savings banks and cooperative banks have the highest shares of assets and liabilities with non-MFIs as counterparties	Savings banks and cooperative banks have the highest potential for interest rate risk	18
8	Balance sheet statistics	Types of banks in Germany	Determination of maturity structure at current edge	Savings banks and cooperative banks currently have the highest shares of long-term assets and of short-term liabilities	Savings banks and cooperative banks currently have the highest interest rate risks	19
9	Balance sheet statistics	Types of banks in Germany	Assessment of the recent development of the maturity structure	All types of banks have clearly increased short-term liabilitites and/or long-term assets	Most types of banks are in the process of increasing their interest rate risk	20
10	Balance sheet statistics	Banks in Germany	Cross-border positions (additional analysis)	Banks in Germany borrow short from and lend long to foreign banks	Banks in Germany have cross-border positions with foreign banks that add to their interest rate risk	23

#	Statistic	Scope	Subject	Main finding	Derived conclusion	Figures (6.X)
11	Balance sheet statistics	Savings and cooperative banks in Germany	Synthetic swaps (additional analysis)	Cooperative banks borrow long from and lend short to cooperative central institutions	Cooperative banks receive hedging against rising interest rates through bidirectional interbank lending with their head institutions	24
12	Balance sheet statistics	Banks and types of banks in Germany	Concentration in interbank lending (additional analysis)	Particularly many savings banks have above median shares of long-term receivables and short-term liabilities from domestic interbank lending	Interest rate risk from domestic interbank lending is particularly concentrated in savings banks	25, 26
13	Income statement statistics	Germany and the euro area	Quantification of the directly interest rate related part of the operating income	Banks in Germany have a slightly higher net interest income as a share of total operating income	Banks in Germany have a larger share of operating income directly dependent on interest rates and hence a higher interest rate risk	27
14	Income statement statistics	Germany and the euro area	Decomposition of net interest income into interest income and interest expenses at current edge	Banks in Germany have a lower interest income and higher interest expenses relative to total assets	Banks in Germany have a smaller exposure to changes in interest rates	28
15	Income statement statistics	Germany and the euro area	Review of the recent development of net interest income and components	Banks in Germany have recently narrowed the gap in interest income and just surpassed banks in the euro area in interest expenses	Banks in Germany have increased their exposure to interest rates	29, 30
16	Income statement statistics	Types of banks in Germany	Quantification of the directly interest rate related part of the operating income	Landesbanks, savings banks, and cooperative banks have the highest net interest incomes as a share of total operating income	Landesbanks, savings banks, and cooperative banks have the highest interest rate risk	31
17	Income statement statistics	Types of banks in Germany	Decomposition of net interest income into interest income and interest expenses at current edge	Savings banks and cooperative banks have comparably high interest incomes given their interest expenses relative to total assets	Savings banks and cooperative banks are particularly engaged in term transformation and hence have particularly high interest rate risk	32
18	Income statement statistics	Types of banks in Germany	Review of the recent development of net interest income and components	For all types of banks interest income and interest expenses have decreased slowly	Change in the interest rate environment leaves its mark on all types of banks	33
19	Interest rate statistics	Germany and the euro area	Development of new short-term and long-term loans	German MFIs show weaker decreases of both new short-term loans and new long-term loans	German MFIs may experience a change in their lending mix but the direction remains unclear	34

#	Statistic	Scope	Subject	Main finding	Derived conclusion	Figures (6.X)
20	Interest rate statistics	Germany and the euro area	Development of new short-term and long-term deposits	German MFIs show stronger increases of new short-term deposits and stronger decreases of new long-term deposits	German MFIs experience a change in their funding mix that goes along with an increase in their interest rate risk	35
21	Interest rate statistics	Germany and the euro area	Identification of those parts of changes of short-term and long-term deposits which are MFI-driven and of those which are counterparty-driven	MFIs in Germany contribute more to the increase in new short-term deposits than MFIs in the euro area and in both regions MFIs drive the reduction of new long-term deposits	German MFIs are particularly active in taking interest rate risk through increasing short-term deposits	36
22	Bank lending survey	Germany and the euro area	Development of tightness of credit standards by loan maturity	Banks in Germany have tightened credit standards for long-term loans more than for short-term loans but the gap is much smaller than that of banks in the euro area as a whole	Banks in Germany have done less to shift the maturity structure of the loans they grant toward less long-term and more short-term and hence toward less interest rate risk	37
23	Bank lending survey	Germany and the euro area	Development of tightness of terms and conditions relating to maturity	Banks in Germany have tightened terms and conditions relating to maturity to a lesser extend	Banks in Germany have done less to adjust the maturity structure of the loans they grant and hence to reduce their interest rate risk	38
24	Bank lending survey	Germany and the euro area	Development of loan demand by maturity	Banks in Germany have experienced a particularly strong increase in demand for long-term loans	Banks in Germany have faced a demand that as far as met by supply leads to higher interest rate risk	39

6.4   Balance sheet statistics

The investigation of what can be learned about the interest rate risk of banks in Germany from balance sheet statistics has two parts. In the first part, the aggregated balance sheet of MFIs in Germany is analyzed and compared to that of MFIs in the euro area as a whole. In the second part, the aggregated balance sheets of the most relevant types of banks in Germany are analyzed and compared to one another. Each of these parts has two subparts. The first subpart is the standard subpart. Besides a definition of the scope in terms of entities covered, it contains three analyses, namely the identification of relevant balance sheet positions, the determination of the maturity structure at the current edge, and the assessment of the recent development of the maturity structure. These three standard analyses are conducted in the first as well as in the second part. They are based on data made available by the ECB and the BBK on the internet, only. The second subpart is the additional subpart. It contains three additional analyses which make use of additional data available to address more specific questions. Hence, these three additional analyses differ between the first and the second part. Some of them are based on data only available on the premises of the BBK.

A few preparatory remarks on possible uses of the available data are in order. The balance sheet statistics made available by the ECB are detailed enough to distinguish between reference

MFIs and non-reference MFIs as counterparties. This distinction is important for the following reason. The overall interest rate risk of a certain group of MFIs only depends on the business these MFIs do with counterparties that do not belong to the same group. Because as to business among MFIs inside a certain group, the downside risk of one MFI is the upside risk of another MFI and these risks net out. Put differently, the net interest rate risk of a group of MFIs is independent of the business these MFIs do with one another. The counterparties that do not belong to the group of MFIs of interest fall into two categories, namely non-MFIs and non-reference MFIs. Obviously, all business with non-MFIs is relevant for the interest rate risk of the group of MFIs under investigation. But of the business with other MFIs, only the business with non-reference MFIs is relevant, too. In tangible terms, for the interest rate risk of all MFIs in the euro area, all business with MFIs in the euro area is irrelevant. And accordingly, for the interest rate risk of all MFIs in Germany, the business with MFIs in Germany does not matter. One may argue that particularly high concentrations of interest rate risk resulting from business between MFIs is a potential problem despite the fact that this interest rate risk cancels out for the aggregate of MFIs. This point is addressed in an additional analysis for types of banks in Germany.

Unfortunately, the balance sheet statistics provided by the BBK are not detailed enough to distinguish between reference MFIs and non-reference MFIs on the level of types of banks. There are two possible ways to deal with this deficiency. First, one might assess business with non-MFIs only. Second, one might also assess business with reference-MFIs. The investigation below proceeds in the second way. The business with MFIs is also assessed, even though it includes business with reference MFIs. The reason for proceeding in this way is that being of different types is not considered an important barrier for business between MFIs. Moreover the market shares of the individual types are not particularly large, at least when measured in terms of total assets. Hence, the share of business with banks of the same type can be expected to be sufficiently small and thus the results can be anticipated to be sufficiently undistorted.

6.4.1 Germany and the euro area

Scoping

In terms of aggregated balance sheets, MFIs in Germany account for one fourth of the total assets of MFIs in the euro area as a whole as of year-end 2014 (see Figure 6.3). In the euro area, MFIs in Germany take second place only to MFIs in France. As advertised above, the following investigation compares MFIs in Germany to MFIs in the euro area as a whole. As already mentioned, the main reason for proceeding in this way is that the insights produced about MFIs in the euro area in the course of the investigation are considered interesting in their own right. The obvious alternative, namely to compare MFIs in Germany to MFIs in all other member countries of the euro area only, would not produce similarly interesting insights as a by-product. However, the downside of proceeding in this way is easy to identify. Any comparison of MFIs in Germany to MFIs in the euro area as a whole necessarily produces smaller differences than a comparison of MFIs in Germany to MFIs in all other member countries of the euro area would, because to a considerable extend MFIs in Germany are compared to themselves. But since the bias is consistently toward smaller differences, it can easily be accounted for. It just has to be remembered that any difference discovered in what follows is even larger between MFIs in Germany and MFIs in all other member countries of the euro area.

Identification of relevant balance sheet positions

The balance sheets as of December 2014 can be analyzed in order to quantify potentially interest rate risk inducing balance sheet positions. As laid out above, these are the balance sheet positions with other counterparties than reference MFIs, that is with non-MFIs or with non-reference MFIs as counterparties. The breakdowns by counterparty provided by the ECB cover the asset side and the liabilities side of the balance sheet to different extends. On the asset side, the distinction between reference MFIs and other counterparties is made for loans as well as for debt securities held. On the liabilities side, however, the distinction is only made for deposits but not for debt securities issued.[135]

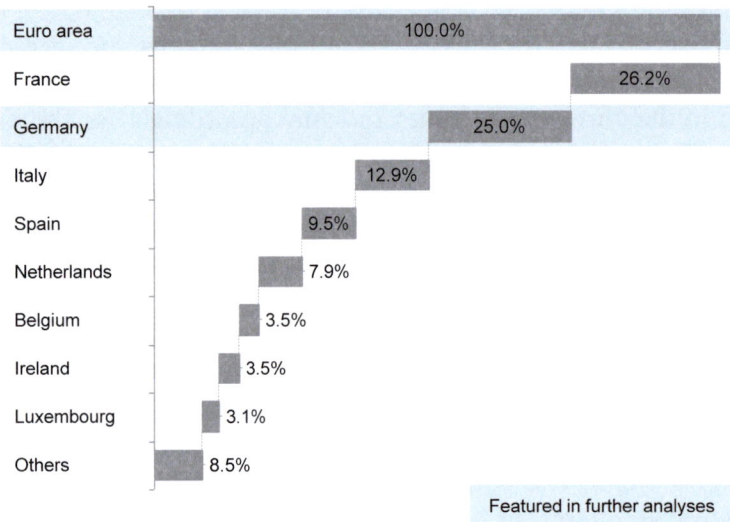

Figure 6.3: MFIs' total assets by member country as a share of the euro area aggregate from largest to smallest (December 2014). Source: ECB, MFI balance sheet statistics; own calculations.

As far as the balance sheets with the breakdowns by counterparty as provided by the ECB are concerned, the following two things stand out (see Figure 6.4). On the asset side, loans not to reference MFIs and debt securities not from reference MFIs account for 47.6% (37.7% + 10.0%) for MFIs in the euro area and for 49.6% (41.3% + 8.3%) for MFIs in Germany. The delta of 2.0 percentage points is a first indication that MFIs in Germany possibly have a higher interest rate risk than MFIs in the euro area. On the liabilities side, deposits not from reference MFIs make up 36.5% for MFIs in the euro area and 43.7% for MFIs in Germany. The even larger delta of 7.3 percentage points again indicates a potentially higher interest rate risk for MFIs in Germany than for MFIs in the euro area.

One special feature of the data provided by the ECB remains to be exploited, though. Namely, that the ECB publishes data on business with euro area residents only. This implies that for the euro area as a whole, the amount of debt securities from reference MFIs on the asset side of the balance sheet necessarily equals that part of the amount of debt securities issued by MFIs and on the liabilities side of the balance sheet which is held by reference MFIs. Put differently, even though debt securities issued by MFIs are not assigned to one specific counterparty one can easily infer the amount that is held not by reference MFIs and which is thus a potential source for interest rate risk of MFIs in the euro area overall. In numerical terms, the amount of debt securities issued by MFIs but not held by reference MFIs amounts to 8.4% of MFIs' total assets in the euro area (see Figure 6.5a).[136] The same technique can be applied with a focus on Germany because the ECB provides a breakdown of the amount of debt securities issued by MFIs in the

---

[135] It is, of course, easy to understand where this lack of coverage comes from, because bearer debt securities can be traded on the secondary market without involvement of the issuing bank.

[136] One simply subtracts the amount of debt securities issued and held by MFIs, that is 4.6%, from the amount of debt securities issued by MFIs, that is 13.0%.

euro area and held by MFIs in Germany into a part issued by MFIs in Germany and another part issued by MFIs in other member countries of the monetary union. This breakdown was already exploited in the construction of the asset side of the balance sheet of MFIs in Germany. From the numbers displayed one can directly calculate that the amount of debt securities issued by but not held by MFIs in Germany amounts to 9.2% of the total assets of MFIs in Germany (see Figure 6.5b).[137] Overall, this delta of 0.8 percentage points adds to the findings that show that compared to MFIs in the euro area, MFIs in Germany do more business with counterparties that are not reference MFIs. And as this business is the potential source for interest rate risk of MFIs in the respective economic region overall, these findings suggest that the interest rate risk of MFIs in Germany may be higher than that of MFIs in the euro area.

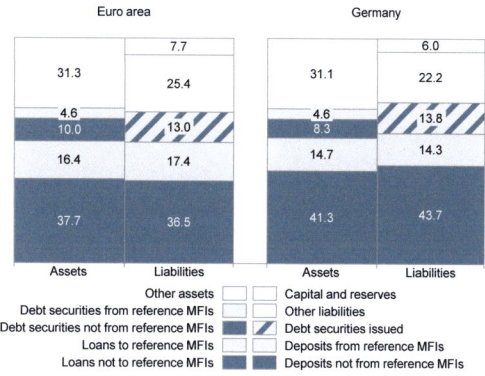

Figure 6.4: Balance sheets of MFIs in the euro area and in Germany with positions clustered by type of instrument and counterparty, in percent of total assets (December 2014). Source: ECB, MFI balance sheet statistics; own calculations.

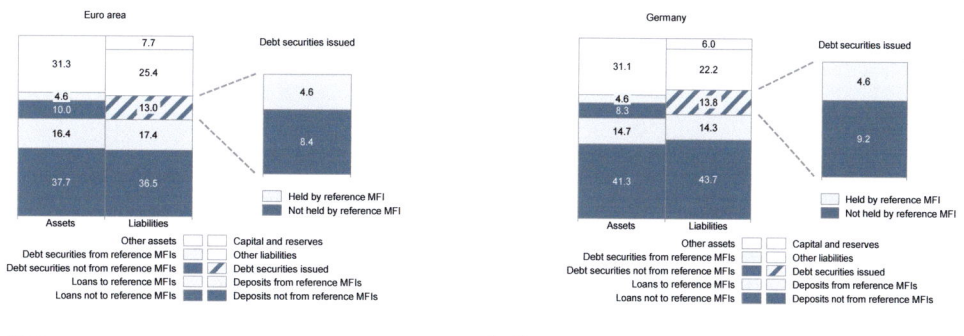

a: Euro area   b: Germany

Figure 6.5: Debt securities issued by type of counterparty holding the security for (a) MFIs in the euro area and for (b) MFIs in Germany, in percent of total assets (December 2014). Source: ECB, MFI balance sheet statistics; own calculations.

Of course, the amount of business not with reference MFIs constitutes only a potential for interest rate risk. One promising way forward to learn something about the actual interest rate risk of MFIs in the euro area and in Germany is to investigate the maturity structures of their assets and liabilities. However, before turning to these maturity structures, two other aspects are looked at in order to shed more light on the balance sheets. First, the amounts of total external assets and liabilities is disclosed. These are the result of business with counterparties not resident in the euro area. Second, the composition of types of counterparties of MFIs in Germany is analyzed in greater detail. In particular, the business with non-reference MFIs is quantified.

---

[137] The calculation is parallel to the one described in the previous footnote. The amount of debt securities issued and held by MFIs in Germany, that is 4.6%, is subtracted from the amount of debt securities issued by MFIs in Germany, that is 13.8%.

As mentioned above, the ECB only provides detailed information, that is, among other things, breakdowns by counterparty and by type of instrument for balance sheet positions resulting from business with counterparties that are resident in the euro area. For the balance sheet positions resulting from business with counterparties not resident in the euro area the ECB only reports total amounts. In the balance sheets presented earlier, these amounts are included in the other assets and other liabilities. Here, these amounts are now disclosed separately (see Figure 6.6). Two points are noteworthy. First, the balance sheet shares of total external assets are very similar between MFIs in the euro area and in Germany. Second, however, the balance sheet shares of total external liabilities differ markedly. At 7.8% the share of MFIs in Germany is three percentage points below that of MFIs in the euro area. Now, of course, the business with counterparties not resident in the euro area is also a potential source of interest rate risk, because these counterparties cannot be reference MFIs. Contrary to previous findings, the difference in the shares of total external liabilities uncovered here suggests that the potential for interest rate risk of MFIs in the euro area is higher than that of MFIs in Germany. However, with respect to the liabilities side of the balance sheet overall, this finding does not tip the scales. The sum of the shares of deposits not from reference MFIs, debt securities issued which are held not by reference MFIs, and, finally, total external liabilities equals 55,7% (36.5% + 8.4% + 10.8%) for MFIs in the euro area but 60.7% (43.7% + 9.2% + 7.8%) for MFIs in Germany.

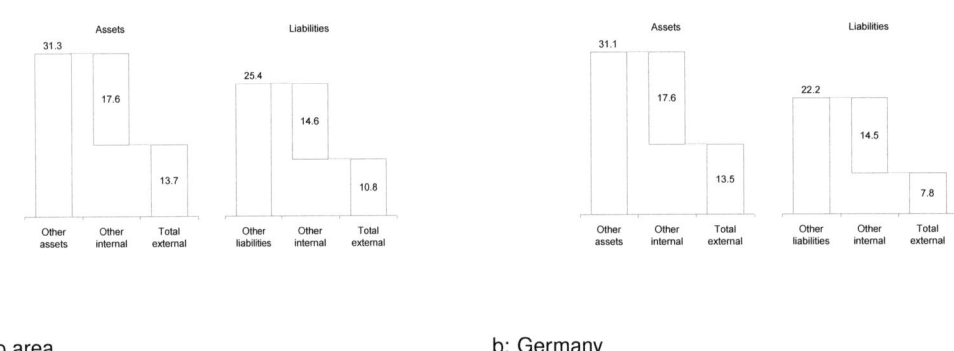

a: Euro area   b: Germany

Figure 6.6: Other assets and liabilities of (a) MFIs in the euro area and (b) MFIs in Germany by location of the counterparty, i.e. internal and external, in percent of total assets (December 2014). Source: ECB, MFI balance sheet statistics; own calculations.

One last thing to look at before turning to the maturity structure is the breakdown by counterparties of balance sheet positions of MFIs in Germany. For MFIs in the euro area as a whole, the statistics provided by the ECB do not make it possible to quantify the shares of assets and liabilities resulting from business with non-reference MFIs. Because with respect to the euro area as a whole, non-reference MFIs are necessarily counterparties not resident in the euro area and the respective balance sheet positions are therefore included in the total external assets and liabilities. For MFIs in Germany, the statistics made available at least make it possible to quantify the shares of assets and liabilities resulting from business with non-reference MFIs which are resident in the euro area. Hence, it is possible to compare the share of assets from business that MFIs in Germany do with MFIs in other member countries of the euro area to the corresponding share of liabilities. The main result of this comparison is that the share of assets is much larger than the share of liabilities, namely 6.1% versus 3.6% (see Figure 6.7). This result points to a net capital transfer from MFIs in Germany to MFIs in other member countries of the euro area. And this net capital transfer exposes MFIs in Germany to the risk of insolvency of MFIs in other member states in the euro area. Thereby, the net capital transfer also makes the interest rate risk of MFIs in other member states of the euro area relevant for MFIs in Germany. This is of course also true for other types of risk.

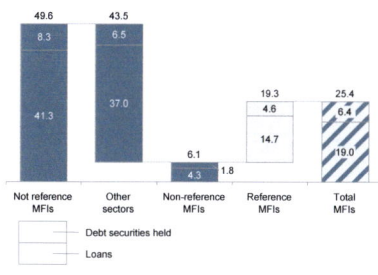
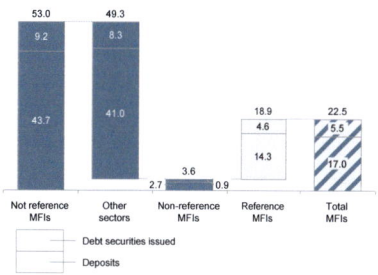

a: Assets   b: Liabilities

Figure 6.7: (a) Assets and (b) liabilities of MFIs in Germany by type of instrument and counterparty, quantifying positions with MFIs as counterparty, in percent of total assets (December 2014). Source: ECB, MFI balance sheet statistics; own calculations.

Determination of the maturity structure at the current edge

So far the focus has been on the potential for interest rate risk of MFIs in the euro area and in Germany. From here on, the focus is on their actual interest rate risk. This second section of the present investigation builds on the first section in an important way. The first section has identified the relevant balance sheet positions, namely those balance sheet positions which result from business not with reference MFIs and which therefore are the potential sources for interest rate risk. The second section now assesses the maturity structures of these balance sheet positions in order to uncover any mismatches between assets and liabilities which are then regarded as evidence for actual interest rate risk. Of course, as detailed earlier, it is not really the maturity structure that determines interest rate risk but rather, at least in a static setting, the residual interest rate fixation period. However, the analyses that follow are all based on data on the original maturity. The analyses hence rest on the assumption introduced above that there is a direct correspondence between original maturity and residual interest rate fixation period. This correspondence is assumed to be direct enough to at least permit meaningful comparisons, if not a reliable absolute quantification of interest rate risk.[138]

An important issues in this context is data availability. Unfortunately, the ECB does not provide the required maturity breakdowns for all relevant balance sheet positions for both MFIs in the euro area as a whole and MFIs in Germany. Most importantly, the ECB does not publish a maturity breakdown for lending to households by MFIs in Germany. Hence, this part of relevant assets is not analyzed further in what follows. Accordingly, even for MFIs in the euro area, for which the ECB does make the required numbers available, the maturity breakdown is not reported below.

It might be objected that instead the data provided by the ECB could be complemented by data provided by the BBK. After all, the BBK does publish maturity breakdowns that look similar, at least at first sight. However, taking a closer look reveals that the numbers do not match. The totals published by the ECB do not equal the totals published by the BBK, which are then broken down by maturity. As detailed above, the main reasons for this discrepancy are differences in the institutions covered and differences in accounting rules applied. In order to avoid distortion, the data provided by the ECB is therefore not complemented with data provided by the BBK for the analyses here. Only in one of the additional analyses, data from both sources is analyzed together but this analysis also uses different data from the ECB.

Concerning the availability of data, also the availability over time is an important issue. As will be detailed below, some of the maturity breakdowns provided by the ECB for loans and for

---

[138] It is again pointed to Appendix 1 for a procedure to derive a portfolio profile in terms of remaining maturity from data in terms of original maturity and to Appendices 2 and 3 for the belonging results of the standard analyses.

debt securities held only go back to June or December 2014. As a consequence, the part of the relevant assets for which the development of the maturity structure can be analyzed over time is more limited.

To begin with, the focus is on the maturity structures of the relevant positions of the balance sheets as of December 2014. Maturity breakdowns are provided by the ECB for loans and debt securities held as well as for deposits and debt securities issued. More precisely, the ECB provides maturity breakdowns for MFIs in the euro area and for MFIs in Germany for the following relevant balance sheet items: for loans to non-financial corporations, to the general government, and to financial vehicle corporations engaged in securitisation, for securities held which were issued by the general government, and for deposits from households, from non-financial corporations, from the general government, from insurance companies and pension funds, and from other financial corporations. Furthermore, the ECB publishes the data necessary to derive the maturity breakdown of debt securities issued which are not held by reference area MFIs.

Additionally, with the data made available by the ECB it is possible to determine the maturity breakdown of debt securities held by MFIs in Germany which were issued by non-domestic MFIs, that is non-reference MFIs resident in other member countries of the euro area. As far as only the balance sheets as of December 2014 are concerned, this additional maturity breakdown in not featured in the analyses. Here, priority is given to comparability between MFIs in the euro area and MFIs in Germany. Only when the developments of the maturity structures over time are concerned, the additional maturity breakdown is featured in order to get a fuller picture. Here, priority is given to maximum information on MFIs in Germany. But it is always ensured that the comparison with MFIs in the euro area is not unnecessarily distorted. That is, the results excluding the additional maturity breakdown available only for MFIs in Germany are also reported.

Investigating the maturity structures of the relevant positions of the balance sheets as of December 2014 produces three main findings. First, for both MFIs in the euro area and MFIs in Germany the share of identifiable long-term assets is higher than that of identifiable short-term assets while the share of identifiable long-term liabilities is smaller than that of identifiable short-term liabilities (see Figure 6.8a and b). In numerical terms, for MFIs in the euro area the numbers are 18.5% and 4.9% on the asset side, but 17.1% and 26.3% on the liabilities side and for MFIs in Germany the numbers are 18.5% and 2.4% on the asset side, but 19.6% and 30.4% on the liabilities side. This points to positive term transformation of MFIs in both economic regions. Second, the identifiable share of long-term assets is of the same absolute size for MFIs in the euro area and MFIs Germany, while the absolute size of the identifiable share of short-term liabilities is smaller for MFIs in the euro area than for MFIs in Germany (see Figure 6.8c). In numerical terms, for MFIs in the euro area as well as in Germany 18.5% of the relevant assets can be identified as long-term. But of the relevant liabilities only 26.4% can be identified as short-term for MFIs in the euro area whereas the corresponding number is as high as 30.4% for MFIs in Germany. This points to a more pronounced term-transformation of MFIs in Germany. Third, expressed as fractions of all assets or liabilities that can be identified as either long-term or short-term, the identifiable share of long-term assets is smaller for MFIs in the euro area than for MFIs in Germany, while the identifiable share of short-term assets is roughly similar (see again Figure 6.8c). In numerical terms, the fraction of identifiable long-term asset is only 78.9% for MFIs in the euro area but as high as 88.4% for MFIs in Germany. At the same time, the fraction of identifiable short-term liabilities is 60.7% for MFIs in the euro area and with 60.8% nearly the same for MFIs in Germany.[139] Again, this points to a more pronounced term-transformation of MFIs in Germany. Hence, finding two and finding three show that two very natural ways to

---

[139] How these fractions are calculated is best shown by an example. The 78.9% reported as the fraction of identifiable long-term assets for MFIs in the euro area simply results from dividing the respective absolute share of long-term

analyse the numbers suggest that MFIs in Germany are more engaged in term transformation. And this in turn suggests that they take a higher interest rate risk than MFIs in the euro area.

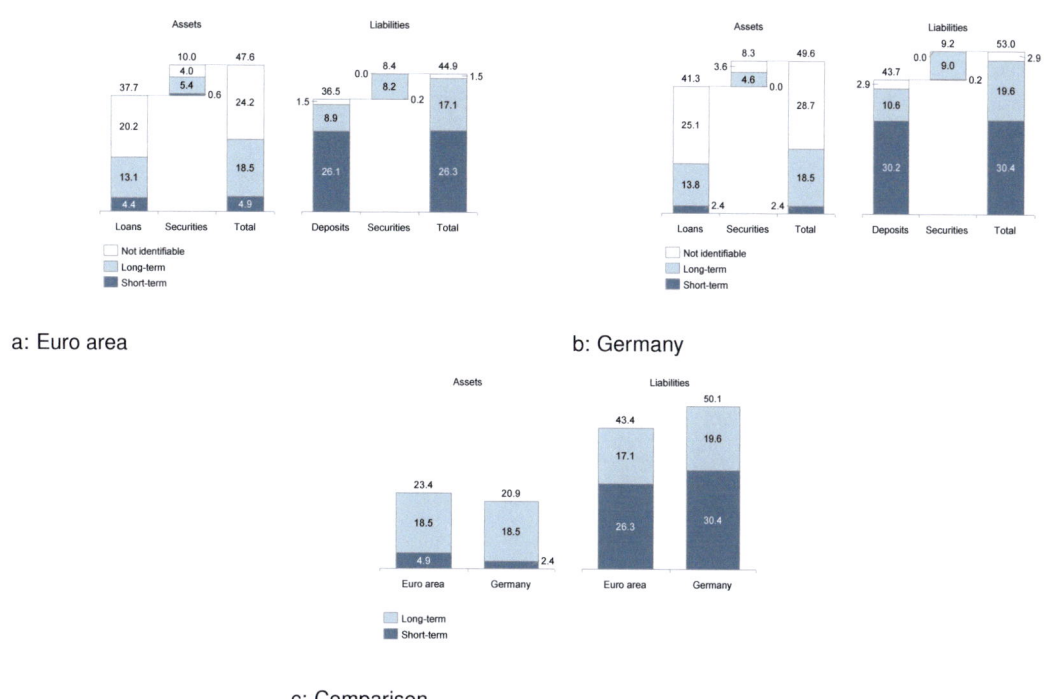

a: Euro area   b: Germany

c: Comparison

Figure 6.8: Long-term and short-term assets and liabilities of (a) MFIs in the euro area and (b) MFIs in Germany, plus (c) direct comparison, in percent of total assets (December 2014). Source: ECB, MFI balance sheet statistics; own calculations.

Assessment of the recent development of the maturity structure

As announced previously, not all maturity breakdowns that are available for the balance sheets as of December 2014 are also available for earlier dates. On the asset side some maturity breakdowns are not available before June or December 2014. More precisely, of the maturity breakdowns for loans, only the maturity breakdown for loans to non-financial corporations is available for earlier dates. And concerning debt securities held, the only maturity breakdown exploited above, namely that for debt securities issued by the general government, is not available for earlier dates. As also announced previously, for MFIs in Germany only, there is another maturity breakdown available, namely for debt securities held which were issued by non-reference MFIs resident in other member countries of the euro area. And this maturity breakdown is also available for earlier dates. It is featured in the analyses that follow.

In order to establish the connection to the previous analysis it is helpful to look at the maturity breakdown of the asset sides of the balance sheets as of December 2014, as they present themselves with precisely those maturity breakdowns exploited that are also exploited in the following analyses of the developments over time (see Figure 6.9). Two things are noteworthy. First, the fractions of loans identifiable as long-term loans divided by all loans identifiable as either long-term or short-term loans are very similar to those in the previous analysis. For MFIs in the euro area the 74.8% here are only twelve basis points below the corresponding 74.9% above. For MFIs in Germany the 84.6% here are just more than half a percentage point below the corresponding 85.2% above. Even though this is just a snapshot it suggests that the maturity

---

assets of 18.5% by the sum of this absolute share of long-term assets and the respective absolute share of short-term assets, that is 18.5% + 4.9%.

structure of loans to non-financial corporations rather accurately resembles the maturity structure of loans to non-financial corporations, the general government, and financial vehicle corporations engaged in securitisation combined. Second, additionally exploiting the maturity breakdown for debt securities held which were issued by non-reference MFIs resident in other member countries of the euro area, makes it possible to assign an extra 1.8% of total assets of MFIs in Germany. Of these, 1.7% are long-term and 0.1% are short-term. Of course, these two numbers could simply be added to the numbers in the previous analysis to produce a fuller picture at least for MFIs in Germany.

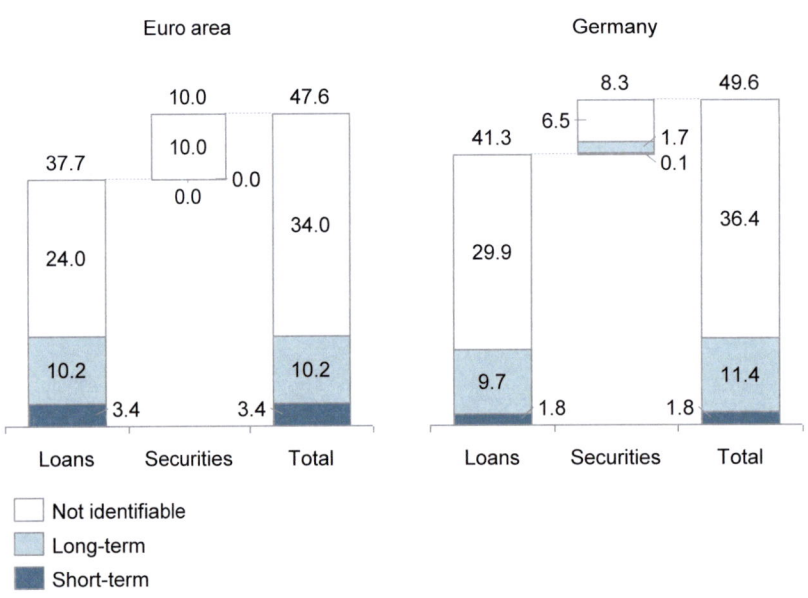

Figure 6.9: Long-term and short-term assets of MFIs in the euro area and in Germany for which historic data is available, in percent of total assets (December 2014). Source: ECB, MFI balance sheet statistics; own calculations.

Next, the investigation turns to the development of maturity structures over time. Tracking the relevant shares that can be identified as either short-term or long-term leads to five important observations (see Figure 6.10). First, the maturity structures of the assets of MFIs in the euro area and in Germany have been much more stable than those of their liabilities. Second, the share of short-term loans has remained rather stable but experienced a level shift downward during the financial crisis for MFIs in the euro area and for MFIs in Germany. Between 2008 and 2010 the share of short-term loans dropped from about 4.5% to about 3.5% for MFIs in the euro area and from about 2.5% to about 1.8% for MFIs in Germany. But apart from this drop the shares remained very stable, particularly in the years after the financial crisis. Third, the share of long-term loans has hardly changed for MFIs in the euro area but has increased somewhat for MFIs in Germany since 2012. In May 2012 and in December 2014 the share of long-term loans equaled 10.2% for MFIs in the euro area.[140] In the same time period, the share of long-term loans has increased from 8.6% to 9.7% for MFIs in Germany. Fourth, the sum of shares of long-term deposits and long-term debt securities issued has slightly increased for MFIs in the euro area, but considerably decreased for MFIs in Germany since the beginning of the financial crisis. For MFIs in the euro area the sum of shares increased from around 16% to just over 17% but for MFIs in Germany it decreased from over 25% to below 20%. For MFIs in Germany about half of the

---

[140] The selection of May 2012 as the beginning of the period referred to here simply suggests itself in view of the plotted data. Selecting a nearby, but different starting date does not materially affect the conclusions to be drawn.

decrease appears to be attributable to the introduction of BilMoG but the other half is mostly due to a notable decrease in the share of long-term debt securities issued. Fifth, the share of short-term deposits has increased considerably for MFIs in the euro area since 2012 but more so for MFIs in Germany. Between May 2012 and December 2014, the share of short-term deposits increased from 21.4% to 26.1% for MFIs in the euro area and from 23.5% to 30.2% for MFIs in Germany. And note that the latter increase is larger both in absolute and in relative terms.

Concerning the lessons to be learnt with respect to interest rate risk, observation three, four, and five strongly suggest that the interest rate risk of MFIs in Germany has increased more than that of MFIs in the euro area as a whole. It should also be remembered that MFIs in Germany account for about one fourth of MFIs in the euro area as a whole in terms of total assets and that differences observed here therefore correspond to considerably larger differences between MFIs in Germany and MFIs in all other member countries of the euro area. Hence, the third, the fourth, and the fifth observation just made can be regarded as very serious indications for an increase in interest rate risk specific for MFIs in Germany.

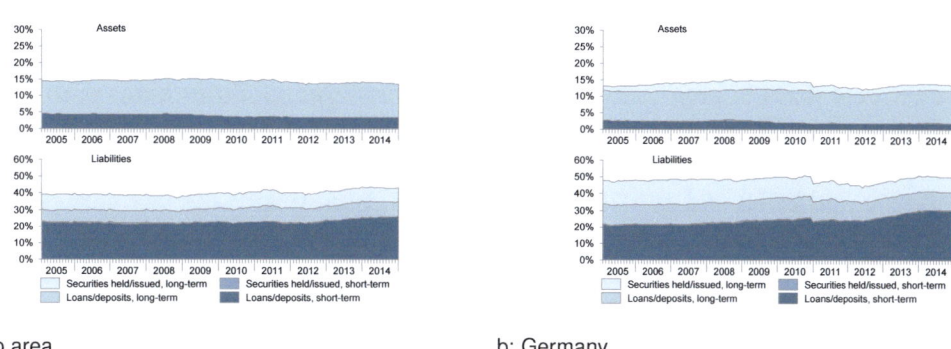

a: Euro area   b: Germany

Figure 6.10: Development of long-term and short-term assets and liabilities of (a) MFIs in the euro area and (b) MFIs in Germany, in percent of total assets (January 2005 to December 2014). Source: ECB, MFI balance sheet statistics; own calculations.

Two more directly comparative approaches are taken next. The first approach compares surpluses of long-term assets and of short-term liabilities. The second compares the most extreme parts of long-term assets and of short-term liabilities.

The surplus of long-term assets is calculated simply as the sum of identifiable shares of long-term loans and long-term debt securities held minus the sum of identifiable shares of short-term loans and short-term debt securities held. The surplus of short-term liabilities is calculated accordingly as the sum of identifiable shares of short-term deposits and short-term debt securities issued minus the sum of identifiable shares of long-term deposits and long-term debt securities issued. As the additional maturity breakdown for debt securities held which is only available for MFIs in Germany might distort the comparison, an extra measure for the surplus of long-term assets of MFIs in Germany is calculated that does not use this additional maturity breakdown.

The surpluses of long-term assets of MFIs in the euro area and in Germany developed rather similarly until 2012 (see Figure 6.11a). But then a gap opened up and at the current edge even the extra measure that builds only on maturity breakdowns also available for MFIs in the euro area takes a higher value for MFIs in Germany. The surpluses of short-term liabilities of MFIs in the euro area and in Germany developed in a roughly parallel way until the beginning of the financial crisis (see Figure 6.11b). Back then, the value for MFIs in Germany was negative and clearly below that of MFIs in the euro area. But since the end of 2007 the surplus of short-term liabilities of MFIs in Germany has increased considerably. And in Q1 2013 it overtook the surplus of short-term liabilities of MFIs in the euro area. This second finding shows that, when considering short-term and long-term liabilities together in this way, a long-term trend becomes particularly visible that can be associated with an increase of interest rate risk of MFIs in Germany.

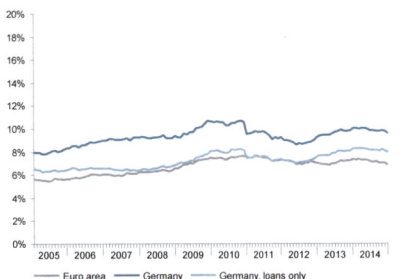 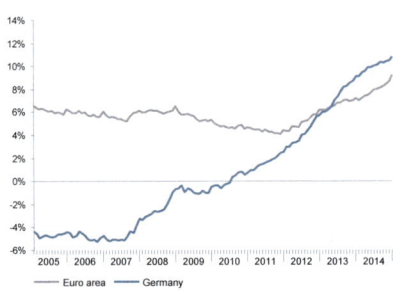

a: Surplus of long-term assets   b: Surplus of short-term liabilities

Figure 6.11: Development of the surplus of (a) long-term assets (b) short-term liabilities of MFIs in the euro area and MFIs in Germany, in percent of total assets (January 2005 to December 2014). Source: ECB, MFI balance sheet statistics; own calculations.

As most extreme parts of long-term assets and of short-term liabilities loans with an original maturity of more than five years and overnight deposits are focused on next. For the share of loans with an original maturity of more than five years one can observe a particularly long increase between mid 2012 and end 2013 for MFIs in Germany only, the last part of which can also be observed for MFIs in the euro area (see Figure 6.12a). But at the current edge the shares are very similar. For the share of overnight deposits one can observe strong increases during 2009 and again between mid 2012 and end 2013 for MFIs in Germany and during the same periods only notably weaker increases for MFIs in the euro area (see Figure 6.12b). Both findings point to relative increases of the interest rate risk of MFIs in Germany compared to MFIs in the euro area as a whole.

 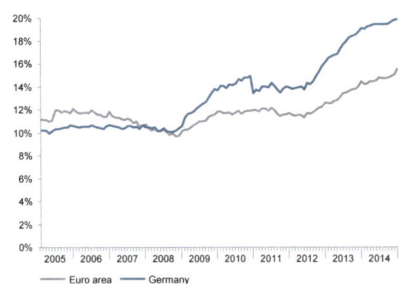

a: Loans   b: Deposits

Figure 6.12: Development of (a) loans with more than 5 years original maturity and (b) overnight deposits of MFIs in the euro area and in Germany, in percent of total assets (January 2005 to December 2014). Source: ECB, MFI balance sheet statistics; own calculations.

At this point the standard subpart of the investigation of balance sheet statistics for MFIs in the euro area as a whole and MFIs in Germany terminates. Most of the methodology is applied again in the investigation of balance sheet statistics for types of banks in Germany in the next part of this investigation. Now follows the additional part of the comparison of MFIs in the euro area to those in Germany. This part includes additional analyses that exploit particular features of the data available and address specific questions. Accordingly, the analyses that follow directly differ with respect to the methodology applied from those that make up the additional part in the next part.

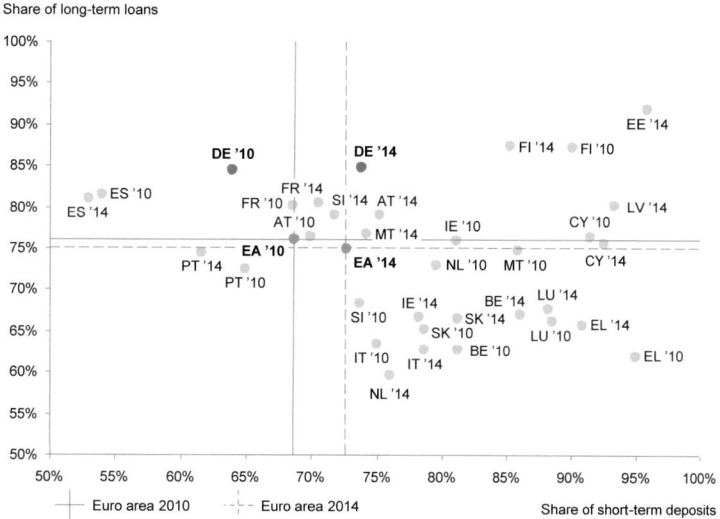

Figure 6.13: Shares of short-term deposits and of long-term loans of MFIs of euro area member countries, in percent of totals of deposits and loans for which a maturity breakdown is provided (December 2010 and December 2014). Source: ECB, MFI balance sheet statistics; own calculations.

First additional analysis: International comparison

The balance sheet data provided by the ECB can be used for an international comparison between euro area member countries. Because, naturally, the ECB does not only publish country-level data for Germany but for all other member countries of the euro area, too. This international comparison focusses on short-term deposits from and long-term loans to non-MFIs at two points in time, namely December 2010 and December 2014. Securities held and issued are not analyzed because, as discussed above, the only available historic data on the maturity structure of debt securities held concerns debt securities issued by non-reference MFIs. And the focus here is on non-MFIs in order to make the observations as independent as possible across countries.[141]

For this international comparison, it is considered reasonable to normalize the absolute amounts of interest not with total assets, but with the total amounts for which maturity break-downs are provided. The key feature of this alternative normalization is that it produces results independent of differences in the higher-level balance sheet structure. This is a caveat as well as a benefit. It is a caveat in so far as the results have informative value only for the respective parts of the balance sheet. But it is a benefit in so far as it makes cross-sectional comparisons more straightforward. Here the alternative standardization is applied in order to promote the international comparison. Put differently, here comparability is given priority over scope.

During the time period under consideration Estonia and Latvia joined the euro area. In 2015 Lithuania followed. Of these three countries, for Estonia and Latvia the figures for December 2014 enter the analysis only and Lithuania is excluded altogether.

Visualizing the data in a scatter plot with the share of short-term deposits on the horizontal axis and the share of long-term loans on the vertical axis generates five noteworthy findings (see Figure 6.13).[142] First, for every single member country of the euro area and at both points in time featured, both the share of short-term deposits and the share of long-term loans exceed

---

[141] Note that non-reference MFIs in this context are all MFIs from other euro area member countries. Hence, including debt securities issued by non-reference MFIs would entail dependence between the observations.

[142] The following standard abbreviations are used: AT (Austria), BE (Belgium), CY (Cyprus), DE (Germany), EE (Estonia), ES (Spain), FI (Finland), FR (France), EL (Greece), IE (Ireland), IT (Italy), LU (Luxembourg), LV (Latvia), MT (Malta), NL (Netherlands), PT (Portugal), SI (Slovenia), SK (Slovakia), and, of course, EA (euro area).

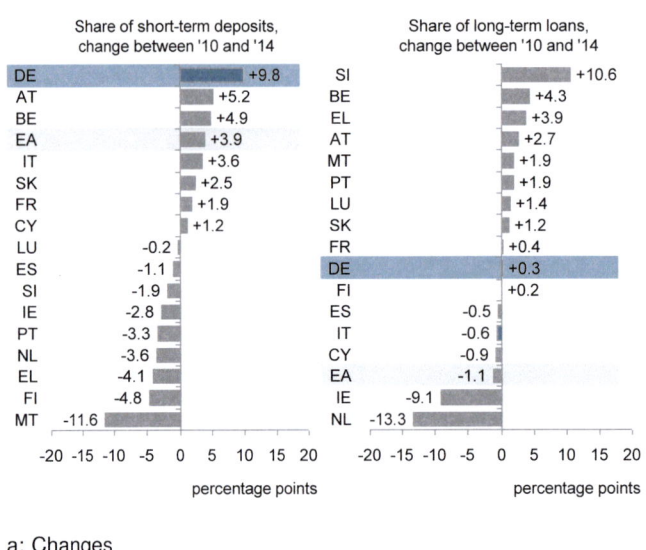

a: Changes

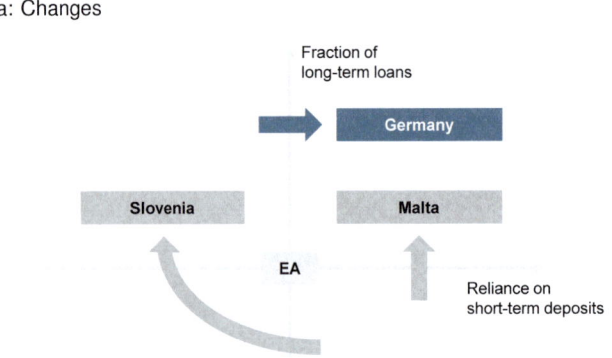

b: Moves

Figure 6.14: (a) changes of MFIs' shares of short-term deposits and of long-term loans by euro area member country, in percent of totals of deposits and loans for which a maturity breakdown is provided, plus (b) moves (December 2010 and December 2014). Source: ECB, MFI balance sheet statistics; own calculations.

50%. This means that consistently more than half of the deposits from households, non-financial corporates, other financial institutions including insurance companies and pension funds, and from the government are overnight deposits or deposits with an agreed maturity of up to one year or deposits redeemable at a notice of up to three month. And it also means that consistently more than half of the loans to non-financial corporations are loans with an original maturity of more than one year. Second, MFIs in Germany consistently have one of the highest shares of long-term loans and show the biggest increase of the share of short-term deposits (see also Figure 6.14a). Third, even though being at a very high level already, MFIs in Germany show an increase in the share of long-term loans below the median, this increase is still above the euro area average which is negative. Fourth, at the current edge, Germany is one of seven countries in the area to the upper right of the euro area as a whole, that is where the reliance on short-term deposits as well as the fraction of long-term loans are both above average. Only Finland and Estonia are further up and right. Fifth, what is more, Germany is besides Malta one of only two countries that have newly entered this area between December 2010 and December 2014 (see also Figure 6.14b). Note that the measures for the euro area as a whole also change between December 2010 and December 2014. To sum up, these findings suggest that the potential interest rate risk of MFIs in Germany is comparably high and that it has recently increased mainly due to an increase of the share of short-term deposits.

Second additional analysis: Long-term fixed-rate debt securities issued

The ECB does not only provide a breakdown of the outstanding amounts of debt securities issued by MFIs by original maturity. Additionally, the ECB separately quantifies the outstanding amounts of long-term debt securities with a floating rate and of those with a fixed rate. This additional information enables a more direct assessment of the potential interest rate risk resulting from MFIs' refinancing by means of debt securities issuance. Because for an MFI with negative exposure to rising interest rates, the issuance of long-term debt securities with a fixed rate has a hedging effect, which the issuance of long-term debt securities with a floating rate does not have. That is, the higher the share of long-term fixed-rate debt securities, the smaller the interest rate risk of the issuing MFI, everything else equal. An inspection of the amount of long-term fixed-rate debt securities issued by MFIs in the euro area and in Germany over the ten years ending with 2014 leads to three main observations (see Figure 6.15). First, the amount of outstanding long-term fixed-rate debt securities normalized with total assets is consistently higher for the MFIs in Germany than for the MFIs in the euro area as a whole. Second, between 2008 and 2012 the gap narrowed notably as the measure in the euro area increased while it decreased in Germany. Third, until 2008 and since 2012 the measures have developed in a parallel way. These observations suggest that as to long-term fixed-rate debt securities, MFIs in Germany still facilitate a higher hedging against rising interest rate but the difference to MFIs in the euro area as a whole is much smaller at the current edge than it was before the financial crisis.

Figure 6.15: Outstanding amounts of long-term fixed rate debt securities issued by MFIs in the euro area and Germany, in percent of total assets (January 2005 to December 2014). Source: ECB, MFI balance sheet statistics, securities issues statistics; own calculations.

Third additional analysis: Remaining maturity of debt securities issued

As further complementary information, the BBK publishes a breakdown by remaining instead of original maturity of the outstanding amounts of fixed-rate debt securities issued by German MFIs. Even though the match is not perfect, the breakdown provided by the BBK can be compared to the breakdown by remaining instead of original maturity the ECB publishes for the outstanding amounts of all debt securities issued by banks only in the entire European Union.[143] The two data sets notably differ in that the amounts provided by the BBK cover fixed-rate debt securities only while the numbers reported by the ECB cover fixed-rate as well as variable-rate debt securities. The analysis that follows focusses on the amounts in individual maturity buckets relative to the total amounts the maturity breakdown is provided for.[144]

Comparing the data from the BBK to the data provided by the ECB, three lessons can be learnt (see Figure 6.16).

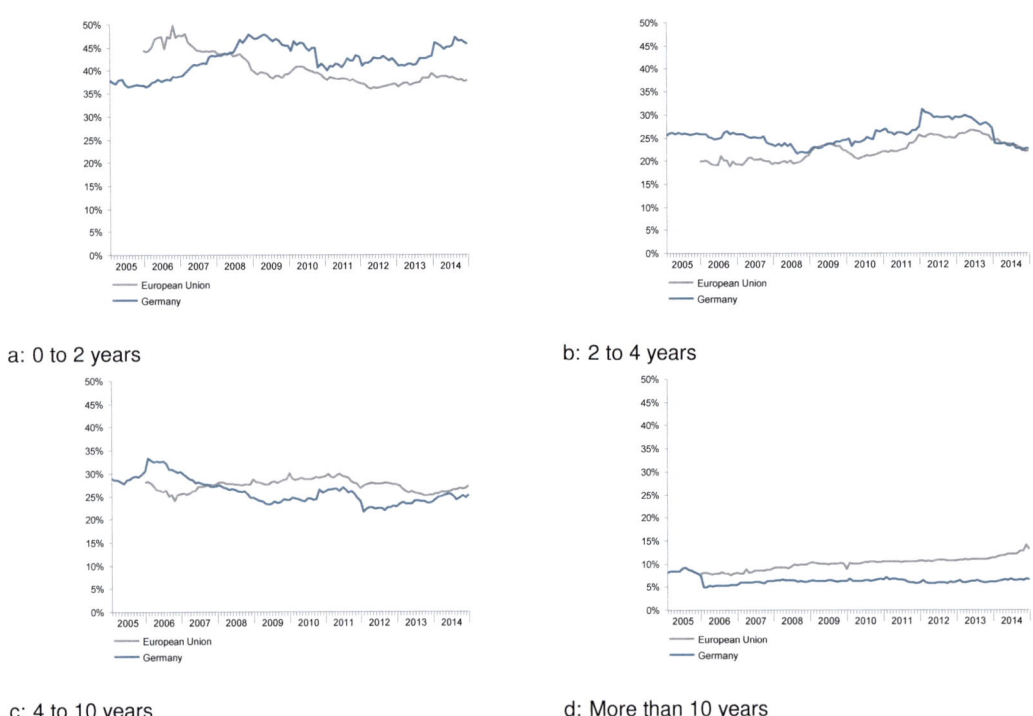

a: 0 to 2 years

b: 2 to 4 years

c: 4 to 10 years

d: More than 10 years

Figure 6.16: Share of outstanding debt securities issued by MFIs with a remaining maturity of (a) 0 to 2 years, (b) 2 to 4 years, (c) 4 to 10 years, and (d) more than 10 years in the euro area and Germany, in percent of totals of debt securities outstanding for which a maturity breakdown is provided (January 2005 and December 2014). Source: ECB, securities statistics; BBK, securities statistics (Monthly Report, Statistical Section, Capital market); own calculations.

First, for recent years and in particular at the current edge it can be observed that the longer the remaining maturity, the lower the share of the outstanding amount of debt securities of German MFIs compared to that of EU banks. Whereas for maturities between zero and two years the share is higher for German MFIs at the current edge, it is roughly equal to that of EU banks for maturities between two and four years and below for longer maturities. Second, with respect to very short maturities, the gap between German MFIs and EU banks has widened recently. Third, with respect to very long maturities, the gap between German MFIs and EU banks has already been widening for many years. What can be learnt from this for the potential interest rate risk of German MFIs compared to EU banks depends on what assumption one is willing to make on whether and if so how the difference in types of debt securities covered influences the comparison. The simplest assumption would be that including or excluding variable-rate securities does not

---

[143] A technical note is in order. Making a reasonable comparison possible requires to identify common maturity brackets. However, some blurriness at the boundaries has to be dealt with as the BBK defines the limits of the maturity brackets in terms of "...to less than..." while the ECB reports in terms of "over...and up to...".

[144] Note that, in the comparison, the difference in the types of debt securities covered features in the numerator as well as in the denominator of the measures analyzed.

materially change the results. Given this assumption the results clearly suggest a higher and relatively increasing interest rate risk of MFIs in Germany compared to banks in the EU.

Recap

Compared to MFIs in the euro area as a whole, and as of year-end 2014, MFIs in Germany have a higher potential for interest rate risk in the form of larger identifiable balance sheet positions that potentially induce interest rate risk. The available maturity breakdowns suggest that currently MFIs in both economic regions conduct positive term transformation but that MFIs in Germany are particularly engaged and therefore have more interest rate risk than MFIs in the euro area as a whole. Furthermore, the recent developments of the relevant balance sheet positions suggest that the interest rate risk of MFIs in Germany has increased compared to that of MFIs in the euro area as a whole mainly due to shifts toward more short-term funding and more long-term lending.

Compared to MFIs in other member countries of the euro area, MFIs in Germany stand out clearly due to the particularly high level of their share of long-term loans and due to the particularly strong increase of their share of short-term deposits. In sum, the evidence suggests a comparatively high and increasing interest rate risk of MFIs in Germany. Even though MFIs in Germany still have a larger outstanding amount of long-term fixed-rate debt securities normalized with total assets, the gap to MFIs in the euro area as a whole has narrowed since the beginning of the financial crisis. Put differently, this extra hedging against interest rate risk of MFIs in Germany is decreasing. Last but not least, it turns out that the outstanding debt securities of MFIs in Germany have a shorter remaining maturity than those of MFIs in the euro area as a whole. Ceteris paribus, this naturally comes with a higher interest rate risk of MFIs in Germany.

6.4.2 Types of banks in Germany

Scoping

The analyses that follow feature only those types of banks in Germany that account for at least 10% of total assets at the end of 2014 (see Figure 6.17). Two exceptions are made. First, cooperative central institutions are included even though they account only for 3.6% of total assets because of their strong ties with cooperative banks. Second, special purpose banks are excluded even though they account for 12.0% of total assets because of their exceptional business models. Proceeding in this way aims at ensuring traceability and relevance. In effect, the analyses that follow cover large banks, regional banks, Landesbanks, savings banks, cooperative central institutions, and cooperative banks. Note that the type of banks referred to as regional banks includes all other credit banks which are neither large banks nor branches of foreign banks.

Identification of relevant balance sheet positions

The quantification of potentially interest rate risk inducing balance sheet positions of types of banks in Germany suffers from an important lack of data. As discussed at length above, the relevant balance sheet positions are those resulting from business with counterparties other than those referred to. For any type of bank in Germany this translates to all balance sheet positions resulting from business with counterparties other than banks of this very type. However, as stated previously, the data required to make the necessary delimitation is not available. Hence, it is not possible to distinguish between balance sheet positions with non-reference MFIs and with reference MFIs as counterparties. Deviating from the investigation of the balance sheets of MFIs in the euro area and in Germany, the main distinction of counterparties made in what follows is the distinction between non-MFIs and MFIs. The investigation above distinguishes between counterparties that are not reference MFIs and those that are reference MFIs, instead. The difference between these two distinctions is that in what follows, non-reference MFIs are analyzed together with reference MFIs, collectively simply called MFIs, while in the investigation above, non-reference MFIs are analyzed together with non-MFIs, collectively referred to as counterparties which are not reference MFIs.

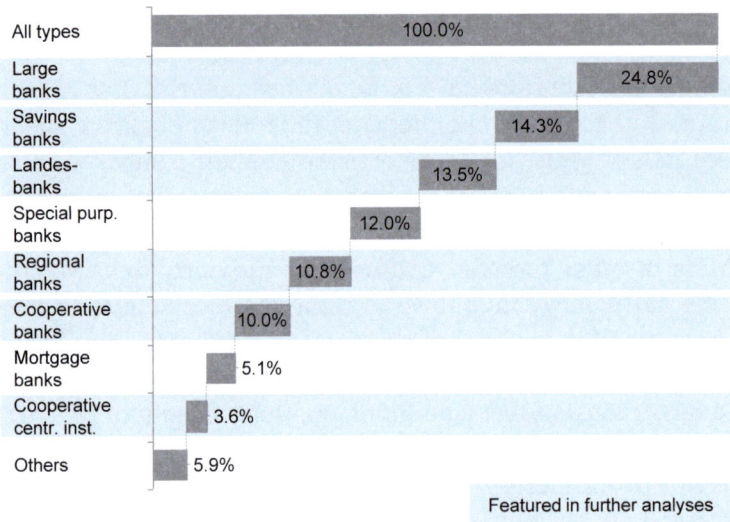

Figure 6.17: Total assets by type of bank in Germany as a share of the German aggregate from largest to smallest (December 2014). Source: BBK, banking statistics (Statistical Supplement 1); own calculations.

Another important data issue remains to be addressed. The balance sheet statistics published by the BBK do not contain the data necessary to assign the debt securities issued to any specific type of counterparty. In the investigation of the balance sheets of MFIs in the euro area and in Germany, it was discovered to be possible to distinguish between debt securities issued which are held by reference MFIs and those which are not held by reference MFIs. In the current investigation of the balance sheets of types of banks in Germany, it is not even possible to distinguish between debt securities issued which are held by MFIs and those which are held by non-MFIs. The data provided by the BBK is simply not comprehensive enough.

Turning to the actual balance sheets of types of banks in Germany as of December 2014 five interesting observations can be made (see Figure 6.18). First, there are large differences between the different types of banks. These differences are much larger than those identified previously between MFIs in the euro area and MFIs in Germany. Second, savings banks and cooperative banks, and to a lesser extend regional banks have much larger shares of assets and liabilities that result from business with non-MFIs than Landesbanks, large banks, and cooperative central institutions. As mentioned before, it remains unclear what part of the debt securities issued is held by non-MFIs. But even extreme variation across types of banks would not lead to a different observation. Because the shares of debt securities held which were issued by non-MFIs, of loans to non-MFIs, and of deposits from non-MFIs dominate. Third, large banks have the largest shares of other assets and liabilities which are mostly made up of derivatives. Fourth, cooperative central institutions have by far the largest shares of inter-bank positions on the asset as well as on the liabilities side. Fifth, Landesbanks have sizeable shares of assets and liabilities with non-MFIs as counterparties, but also seizable inter-bank positions on both sides of the balance sheet. As to interest rate risk, the second observation suggests that savings banks and cooperative banks have particularly high potentials and that the potential of regional banks comes close.

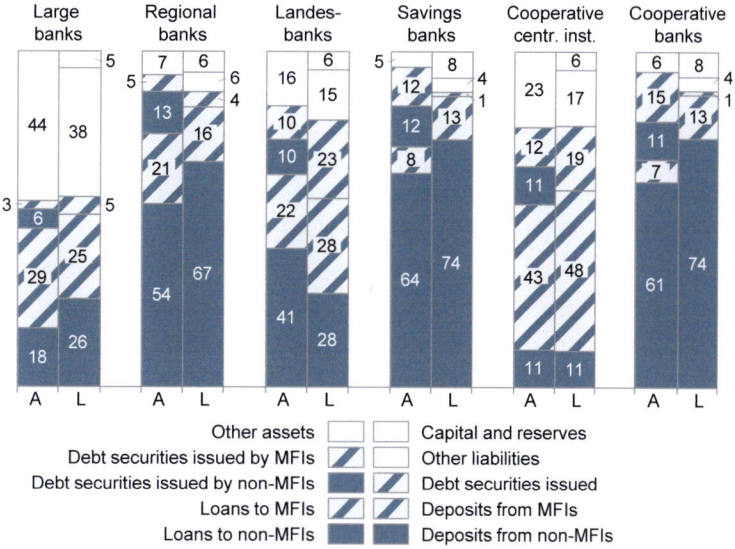

Figure 6.18: Balance sheets of banks in Germany with positions clustered by type of instrument and counterparty, in percent of total assets (December 2014). Source: BBK, banking statistics (Statistical Supplement 1); own calculations.

These balance sheet structures, of course, reflect the different business models. Large banks are particularly active on derivative markets. Landesbanks supply non-banks with loans but refinance themselves significantly through savings banks for which they are the head institutions. And cooperative central institutions mainly fulfill supportive functions for cooperative banks such as the provision of liquidity. Returning to savings banks and cooperative banks, their particular engagement in business with non-banks makes them the prime candidates for the highest interest rate risk resulting from this sort of business.

Determination of the maturity structure at the current edge

As announced previously, the following investigation covers balance sheet positions with non-MFIs but also with MFIs as counterparties. Like the ECB, the BBK provides maturity breakdowns for loans and debt securities held as well as for deposits and debt securities issued. And just like the maturity breakdowns provided by the ECB, the ones provided by the BBK are also incomplete in that they do not identify all relevant positions as either long-term or short-term. While the ECB does not provide maturity breakdowns for all counterparty sectors, the BBK does not do so for all instrument categories. In particular, the BBK does not provide a maturity breakdown for the largest part of debt securities held which were issued by MFIs. Additionally, for lending to and borrowing from MFIs in the form of balances and loans, the BBK only provides a maturity breakdown for business with domestic MFIs but not for business with foreign MFIs as counterparties. The only exception are overnight deposits from MFIs for which also the aggregate is reported for domestic and foreign MFIs as counterparties together. On the positive side of things, where MFIs and non-MFIs as counterparties are distinguished, the maturity breakdowns for balance sheet positions with non-MFIs as counterparties are complete. And where MFIs and non-MFIs as counterparties cannot be distinguished, that is for debt securities issued, the maturity breakdown is also complete.

In a strict sense, the foregoing is only correct for savings banks and cooperative banks. For each of the other four types of banks one of two specific maturity breakdowns is missing. For large banks and regional banks, no maturity breakdown is provided for bearer debt securities held which were issued by MFIs. For Landesbanks and cooperative central institutions, no maturity breakdown is provided for savings deposits from non-MFIs. In each case, however, the maturity breakdown in question is provided for a collection of types of banks that includes the types of banks for which the specific maturity breakdown is not provided individually. For what follows, the provided maturity breakdowns are then used consistently for the individual types of banks in question, scaled appropriately.[145] Last but not least, it should be noted that for all six types of banks, the minimum of the outstanding amount of variable-rate bearer debt securities issued and of the outstanding amount of bearer debt securities with a maturity of up to one year is referred to as the outstanding amount of short-term bearer debt securities.

Assessing the maturity structures of the relevant balance sheet positions of the featured types of banks in Germany leads to three main observations (see Figure 6.19). First, for all types of banks, the share of identifiable long-term assets is higher than that if identifiable short-term assets and for four out of six types of banks the share of identifiable long-term liabilities is smaller than that of identifiable short-term liabilities. The two exceptions are Landesbanks and cooperative central institutions. For all other types of banks, this observation clearly points to positive term transformation and hence negative exposure to an increase in interest rates. Second, savings banks and cooperative banks have the largest shares of identifiable long-term assets and of identifiable short-term liabilities in absolute terms as well as expressed as fractions of all assets or liabilities that can be identified as either long-term or short-term. Savings banks are in first place in the ranking of shares of identifiable long-term assets in absolute terms and cooperative banks are in first place in the three other rankings. For both savings banks and cooperative banks, this observation points to a comparably high engagement in positive term transformation and hence to a relatively large negative exposure to rising interest rates. Third, regional banks come close to savings banks and cooperative banks but only in absolute terms. Expressed as fractions of all assets or liabilities that can be identified as either long-term or short-term, Landesbanks and cooperative central institutions have larger shares of long-term assets and large banks have a higher share of short-term liabilities. Hence, the evidence for a relatively high interest rate risk of regional banks is considerably weaker than that for savings banks and cooperative banks.

The numbers for savings banks and cooperative banks are indeed noteworthy. While 74.9% and 71.3% of total assets are long-term, 67.3% and 69.1% of total liabilities are short-term, respectively. In terms of the afore mentioned fractions the numbers are as high as 89.7%, and 90.2% and 77.2% and 79.3%, respectively.[146] The maturity structures reported allow to further conclusions to be drawn. That the coverages of the maturity breakdowns for loans and deposits are nearly complete shows that savings banks and cooperative banks do very little business with foreign MFIs. And that the shares of debt securities held which cannot be identified as either long-term or short-term are relatively large shows that they hold comparatively large shares of debt securities issued by MFIs. Both conclusions can be drawn in face of the data availability described earlier.

Assessment of the recent development of the maturity structure

Luckily, data availability over time is of no concern here. All maturity breakdowns built on for the identification of the maturity structure at the current edge are also available going back 10 years and more. Hence, there is a direct connection from the previous analysis to the next analyses of the development of the maturity structure over time.

---

[145] It should be noted that by using bank-level data only available on the premises of the BBK, this approximation would not be necessary. Instead, the precise values could be calculated. However, in this standard part of the investigation exploiting balance sheet statistics, comprehensive traceability is given priority over that last bit of extra precision.

[146] It must be remembered though, that these numbers refer to original maturity. In terms of remaining maturity the levels of long-term volumes are naturally lower. This is shown in Appendices 2 and 3.

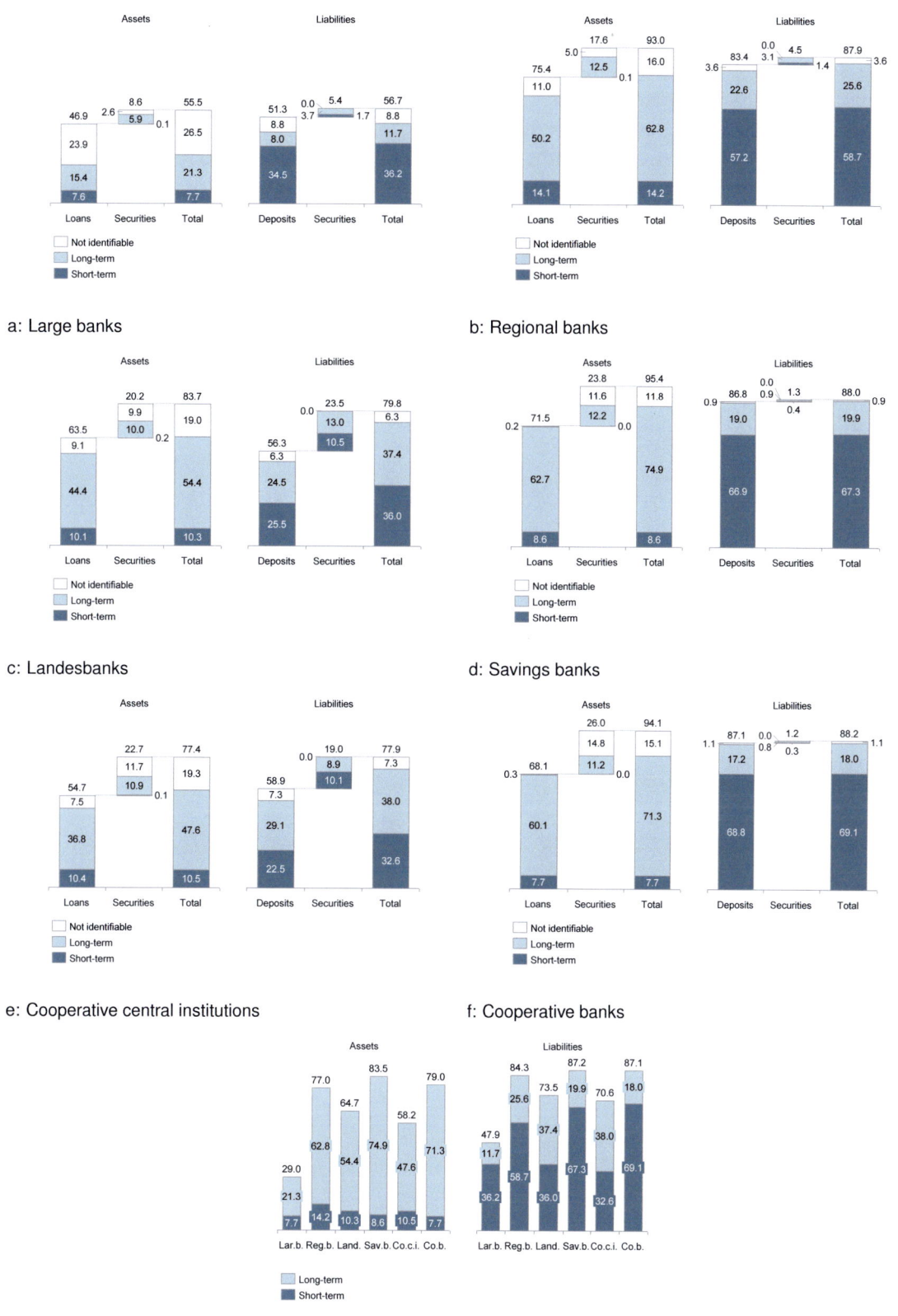

Figure 6.19: Long-term and short-term assets and liabilities of (a) large banks, (b) regional banks, (c) Landesbanks, (d) savings banks, (e) cooperative central institutions, and (f) cooperative banks in Germany, plus (g) comparison, in percent of total assets (December 2014). Source: BBK, banking statistics (Statistical Supplement 1); own calculations.

Taking a close look at the development of the shares of relevant balance sheet positions that are identifiable as long-term or short-term leads to three important observations (see Figure 6.20). First, the long-term trends for savings banks and cooperative banks are clearly toward higher shares of long-term assets and lower shares of short-term assets as well as toward lower shares of long-term liabilities and higher shares of short-term liabilities. For long-term assets and short-term liabilities, the increases amount to 5.5 and 5.7 percentage points for savings banks and to 4.2 and 5.5 percentage points for cooperative banks since December 2010, respectively. And for short-term assets and long-term liabilities, the decreases amount to 1.0 and 7.3 percentage points for savings banks and to 1.9 and 6.5 percentage points for cooperative banks over the same period of time, respectively. Second, for large banks, regional banks, and Landesbanks, there are long-term trends toward higher shares of short-term deposits as well as toward higher shares of long-term securities held or of long-term loans. And all other bank-type specific upward or downward trends work in the same direction, that is higher shares of short-term or lower shares of long-term liabilities and higher shares of long-term or lower shares of short-term assets.

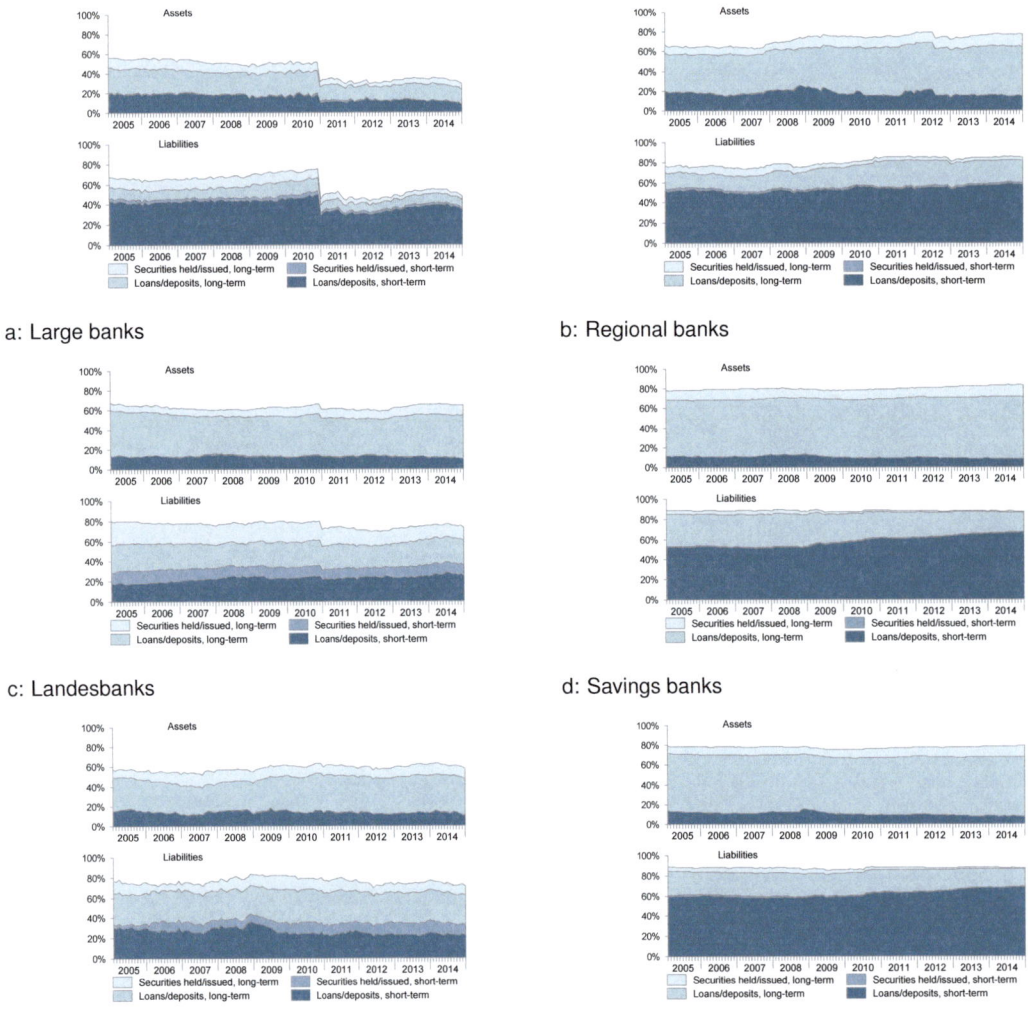

a: Large banks

b: Regional banks

c: Landesbanks

d: Savings banks

e: Cooperative central institutions

f: Cooperative banks

Figure 6.20: Development of long-term and short-term assets and liabilities of (a) large banks, (b) regional banks, (c) Landesbanks, (d) savings banks, (e) cooperative central institutions, and (f) cooperative banks in Germany, in percent of total assets (January 2005 to December 2014). Source: BBK, banking statistics (Statistical Supplement 1); own calculations.

Many shares, however, only move sideways. Third, for cooperative central institutions not a single clear long-term trend attracts attention. To a small extend short-term deposits have decreased while long-term loans have increased. Note that the introduction of BilMoG again clearly left its mark.[147]

The first observation clearly suggests a sizeable increase of the term transformation conducted by savings banks and cooperative banks. And in turn it points to a remarkable increase of the negative exposure to a rise in interest rates, that is of interest rate risk as it is generally referred to in the chapter at hand. The second finding also suggest an increase of the term transformation conducted by large banks, regional banks, and Landesbanks, and therefore also of the related interest rate risk. Even though the trends are not as pronounced as those observable for savings banks and cooperative banks, they clearly point into the same direction. Before drawing a conclusion for cooperative central institutions, the results of the next two analyses should be waited for.

Next, the two more comparative approaches are taken, which have already been introduced at the end of the standard part of the investigation of the balance sheets of MFIs in the euro area and of MFIs in Germany. To start with, the developments of the surpluses of long-term assets as well as of the surpluses of short-term liabilities are compared across types of banks. A type's of banks surplus of long-term assets is simply calculated as the total share of long-term assets minus the total share of short-term assets. And its surplus of short-term liabilities is calculated accordingly. Thereafter, the developments of the shares of the most extreme parts of long-term assets as well as of short-term liabilities are compared across types of banks. As the most extreme part of long-term assets the share of loans with an original maturity of more than five years is looked at. And for short-term liabilities overnight deposits play this role.

Concerning the surpluses, three main lessons can be drawn (see Figure 6.21). First, the surpluses of long-term assets as well as of short-term liabilities for savings banks and for cooperative banks follow long-term upward trends and have left behind the respective surpluses of all other types of banks. Second, the surpluses of long-term assets observed for regional banks, Landesbanks, and cooperative central institutions develop in a rather similar fashion with particularly strong recent upward trends observed for regional banks and Landesbanks. The surplus of long-term assets observed for large banks is much below that for the other types of banks, but there is also a recent upward trend to be observed. Third, the surplus of short-term assets observed for large banks and regional banks develop rather similarly as do the ones observed for Landesbanks and cooperative central institutions but on a lower level. For all four types of banks one can observe rather long-term upward trends for the surpluses of short-term liabilities.

The first lesson of this analysis again suggests that the positive term transformation and hence the related interest rate risk of savings banks and cooperative banks has been increasing for a long time and has reached a comparably high level at the current edge. But lesson two and three suggest that also the other types' of banks involvement in term transformation and with it the related interest rate risk has been increasing over the last few years. This also holds for cooperative central institutions, for which at least an increase of the surplus of short-term liabilities can be observed.

Concerning the extreme parts of long-term assets and short-term liabilities, three observations are particularly interesting (see Figure 6.22). First, the shares of long-term loans with an original maturity of more than five years are much more constant than the shares of overnight deposits. Over the last ten years the shares of overnight deposits observed for savings banks and cooperative banks have roughly doubled. For the shares of loans with an original maturity of more than five years no change of a comparable magnitude can be observed for any type of bank. The only

---

[147] This is clearly visible for large banks and less so for Landesbanks. The sudden increase of the amount of total assets leads to a sudden decrease of the ratios in focus.

exception are large banks. But that their share of loans with an original maturity of more than five years has roughly been cut in halve can mostly be attributed to the introduction of BilMoG. Second, the shares of long-term loans with an original maturity of more than five years can be observed to have followed a strong upward trend for savings banks and cooperative banks. The respective shares have increased by 3.6 or 4.0 percentage points since December 2010. The increases observable for Landesbanks and cooperative central institutions have been somewhat weaker at 3.4 and 2.6 percentage points. Yet, for large banks and regional banks the increases are even smaller and the trends are not as clear. Third, the shares of overnight deposits can be observed to have followed a much stronger upward trend for savings banks and cooperative banks. The increases during the same period of time amount to 8.3 and 9.4 percentage points, respectively. Here, Landesbanks and regional banks show similar upward movements even if only by 5.9 and 5.8 percentage points, respectively. Again, large banks are among those types with the smallest increase but this time together with cooperative central institutions and with still rather sizeable 3.1 and 2.9 percentage points, respectively.

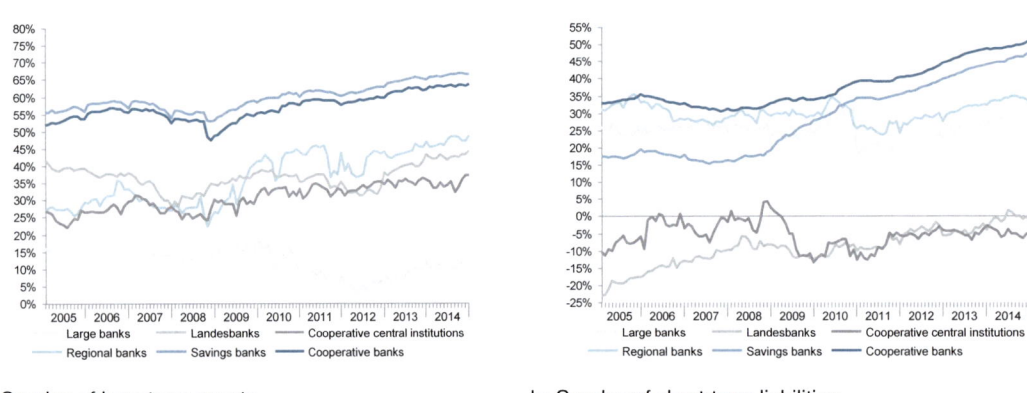

a: Surplus of long-term assets   b: Surplus of short-term liabilities

Figure 6.21: Development of the surplus of (a) long-term assets (b) short-term liabilities of types of banks in Germany, in percent of total assets (January 2005 to December 2014). Source: BBK, banking statistics (Statistical Supplement 1); own calculations.

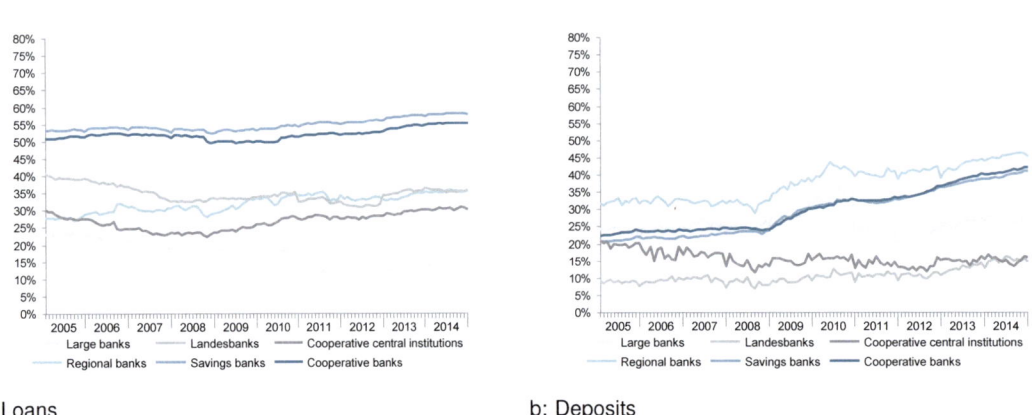

a: Loans   b: Deposits

Figure 6.22: Development of (a) loans with more than 5 years original maturity and (b) overnight deposits of types of banks in Germany, in percent of total assets (January 2005 to December 2014). Source: BBK, banking statistics (Statistical Supplement 1); own calculations.

First additional analysis: Cross-border positions

The balance sheet statistics published by the BBK contain information on the maturity profile of German banks' lending to and borrowing from foreign banks. And as foreign banks cannot be reference banks, this cross-border business is a potential source for net interest rate risk of banks in Germany. In this first additional analysis, different types of banks are not distinguished.[148]

The data provided by the BBK permits to include the amount of money market papers in the short-term lending to foreign banks. However, the amount of other debt securities cannot be included in the same straightforward way in the long-term lending to foreign banks as only the aggregate of long-term securities is provided which includes equity securities. As to borrowing from foreign banks, the data provided does not permit to include bearer debt securities.

An important point to consider before embarking on an analysis of the interest rate risk resulting from cross-border lending to and borrowing from banks is that reference interest rates may differ between countries. Most prominently, the zero-coupon government bond yield curve is essentially country-specific. However, the interest rates in interbank lending are usually regarded as being based on international indices such as the Euribor and the Libor. In any case, since the BBK does not publish a breakdown by country of the foreign banks involved, no more detailed analysis is possible.[149] Put differently, the following analysis rests on the implicit assumption of a general co-movement of the relevant reference interest rates across countries.

One finds that German banks' short-term and long-term lending to and borrowing from foreign banks normalized with total assets can be characterized as follows (see figure 6.23a). The volume of short-term borrowing is the largest (historically mostly between 6% and 9%). It is followed by the volume of long-term lending which is about half the size (3% to 5%). The volumes of long-term borrowing and of short-term lending are much lower (below or just above 1%). These findings suggests that cross-border interbank positions indeed add to the interest rate risk of German banks. To see this more clearly, two simple transformations are helpful.

The first transformation consists in simply calculating the net-exposure to changes in short-term rates on the one hand and to long-term rates on the other hand (see Figure 6.23b). As a matter of convention only affecting the sign of the result, here the calculation is conducted as lending minus borrowing. A negative result hence implies a negative net-exposure to an increase of the relevant reference interest rates. The main takeaway here is the striking difference between the two net-exposures with the one to changes in short-term rates being considerably negative and the one to changes long-term rates being clearly positive even if only half the size in absolute terms. This shows that there clearly is term transformation involved.

The second transformation isolates the hedging through bidirectional interbank lending deviating in terms (see Figure 6.23c). How this hedging technique works in principle can be illustrated with a stylized example. Bank A lends an amount of money M to bank B with an interest rate fixation period of length X. At the same time, bank B lends an amount of money N to bank A with an interest rate fixation period of length Y. If now the money amounts are equal, that is $M = N$, but the interest rate fixation periods differ, that is $X \neq Y$, this bidirectional interbank lending is comparable to an interest rate swap in the hedging it brings about. Obviously, if $X < Y$ ($X > Y$), then bank A's interest income is fixed for a shorter (longer) period of time than its interest expenses. And for a bank with a negative exposure to an increase of interest rates it contributes to hedging this risk to have one's interest income fixed for a shorter period of time. A more in-depth discussion of this hedging technique is provided later.

The analysis focusses on the residual part of interbank lending which cannot be explained as a capital transfer. Two measures are constructed and tracked over time. Both measure the amount of hedging against rising interest rates. And both measures are normalized by total assets.

---

[148] Here the focus is on the position of all banks in Germany vis-à-vis foreign banks.

[149] Such an analysis might, for example, account for historical correlations between interest rates across countries.

The first measure is the minimum of long-term claims and short-term liabilities. This measure is employed to quantify the volume of hedging provided by German banks to foreign banks. The second measure is the minimum of short-term claims and long-term liabilities. This measure is employed to quantify the hedging received by German banks from foreign banks.[150]

It becomes very transparent that the hedging provided by German banks is much larger than the hedging they receive. Hence, the net position of German banks is that they provide hedging against rising interest rates to foreign banks. This obviously adds to the interest rate risk of German banks. Interestingly, however nterbank lending has been decreasing. With short-term borrowing and long-term lending going down and long-term borrowing and short-term lending going up, the negative exposure to an increase in interest rates decreases.

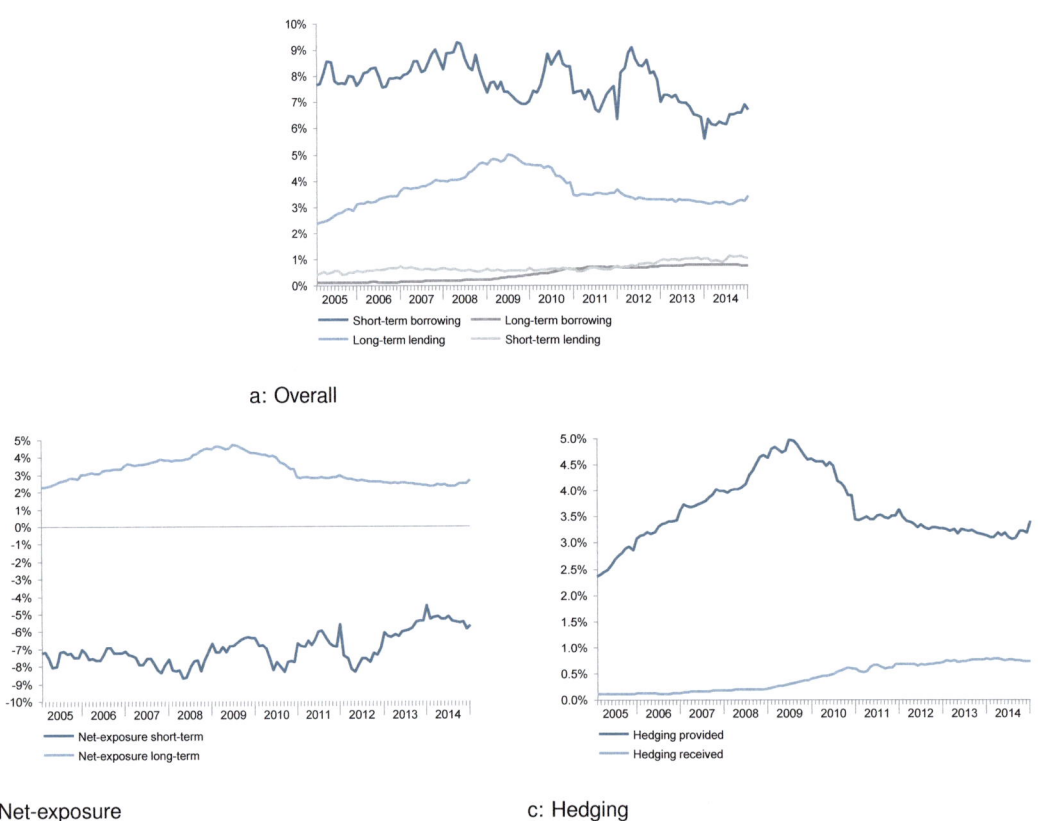

a: Overall

b: Net-exposure   c: Hedging

Figure 6.23: Development of cross-border positions of banks in Germany (a) overall as well as (b) implied net-exposures and (c) hedging, in percent of total assets (January 2005 to December 2014). Source: BBK, banking statistics (Statistical Supplement 1); own calculations.

Second additional analysis: Synthetic swaps

Within Germany, there are prime candidates for applying the technique of hedging through bidirectional interbank lending deviating in terms. These are the savings banks and the cooperative banks together with their respective head institutions, the Landesbanks and the cooperative central institutions. There are two interrelated reasons for this. First, a fair share of savings banks and credit cooperatives does not access the derivatives market directly. Rather, the respective head institutions do this for them. And the bidirectional lending at issue here may then be used to pass on the position taken on the derivative market. Second, within these banking groups,

---

[150] Note that both measures refer to a minimum in order to capture the residual part of interbank lending, that is the part that cannot be explained as a capital transfer.

interbank loans receive a preferred regulatory treatment. They do not have to be backed with regulatory capital. And this reduces the costs attached to this hedging technique.

Bidirectional lending is very common, not only among banks but also between banks and other types of counterparties. For example, every retail customer who has a mortgage but at the same time some money in his current account engages in it with his bank. Only that part of the money borrowed (lent) in excess of the money lent (borrowed) makes up the net capital transfer. The remaining part can only be explained as serving some other purpose. The most readily thought of possible purpose besides hedging of interest rate risk is, of course, ensuring liquidity for transactions. The relative importance of these two purposes, or indeed any other possible purposes, for the positions taken cannot be assessed with the data at hand, though. The analysis here rests on the assumptions that for the banks under consideration, the importance of hedging one's interest rate risk is sufficiently large and the movements due to other reasons are sufficiently small.

In the analysis, the focus is again on the residual part of interbank lending which cannot be explained as capital transfer. The same two measures constructed above for the hedging provided and received are tracked over time, normalized with total assets of savings banks and cooperative banks, respectively. For this analysis data is used that is accessible on the premises of the BBK only as the BBK does not make the numbers from the relevant data fields available online.

The analysis produces three principal findings (see Figure 6.24). First, the amounts of hedging received by both savings banks and cooperative banks from the respective head institutions have historically been clearly larger than the amounts of hedging provided in the opposite direction. Second, the amounts of hedging received have decreased significantly since 2008 and with respect to savings banks, the gap between hedging received and hedging provided has disappeared, but as for cooperative banks, the gap between hedging received and hedging provided has narrowed but not disappeared. Third, generally savings banks have a clearly lower level of hedging received and a somewhat higher level of hedging provided than cooperative banks. These findings suggest that bidirectional interbank lending with the respective head institutions has historically had and, not so much for savings banks, but indeed for cooperative banks, still has a sizeable net hedging effect against rising interest rates.

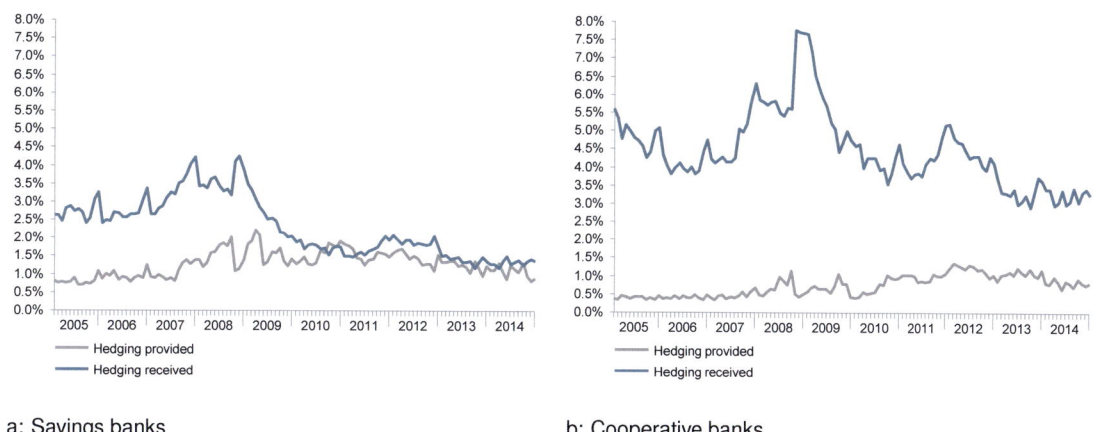

a: Savings banks   b: Cooperative banks

Figure 6.24: Development of hedging provided to and received from respective head institutions against rising interest rates by (a) savings banks and (b) cooperative banks, in percent of total assets (January 2005 to December 2014). Source: Research Data and Service Centre (RDSC) of the Deutsche Bundesbank, monthly balance sheet statistics (BISTA), January 2005 to December 2014; own calculations.

Third additional analysis: Concentration in interbank lending

The balance sheet statistics the BBK grants access to on its premises can be used to investigate the distribution of interest rate risk from lending among German banks. Even though the overall net interest rate risk from interbank lending in Germany must be zero, individual banks may be particularly exposed due to a particularly high level of long-term receivables from and short-term liabilities to domestic banks. Deviating from other analyses, here a more restrictive delimitation is applied of what constitutes long-term receivables. Namely, only receivables with an original maturity of more than five years are considered long-term. The resulting gap of four years between the threshold values for the original maturities of long-term receivables and short-term liabilities ensures that a more pronounced maturity transformation is in focus.

Any individual bank may have a substantial negative exposure to certain changes in interest rates resulting from its borrowing from and lending to other domestic banks. And if this risk materializes, possibly leading to failures of particularly engaged banks, this may lead to severe disruptions. Hence, even though net interest rate risk resulting from domestic interbank lending necessarily is zero in the aggregate, because one bank's downside risk must be another one's upside risk, the distribution among banks is of concern. This distribution is focused on here.

The following analysis is not limited to the national level, but is also conducted on the bank-type level. However, for confidentiality reasons, any reported value has to be based on inputs from at least three different banks. On bank-type level, this effectively prevents any meaningful analysis of the distribution of interest rate risk among large banks, Landesbanks and cooperative central institutions. The numbers of institutions of these types are simply too small. Accordingly, where the following analysis is conducted on the bank-type level it is limited to regional banks, savings banks, and cooperative banks.

On the national level, no clear upward or downward trends of the concentrations of long-term receivables or short-term liabilities can currently be observed (see Figure 6.25). The respective concentration ratios, namely 90th percentile divided by the median, have mostly moved sideways in recent years. For long-term receivables the concentration ratio has obviously increased between mid 2009 and Q1 2012 when it reached its post-crisis high (see Figure 6.25a). But since then the ratio has not only gone down but also back up again. For short-term liabilities the concentration ratio is much more volatile, mostly due to the high volatility of the median (see Figure 6.25b). And while the peaks are getting higher, the lows remain on roughly the same level in recent years.

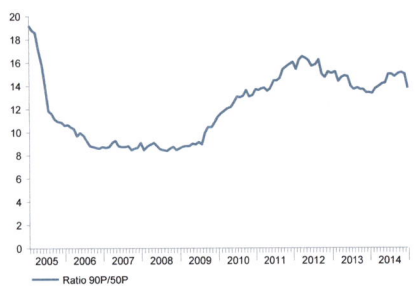

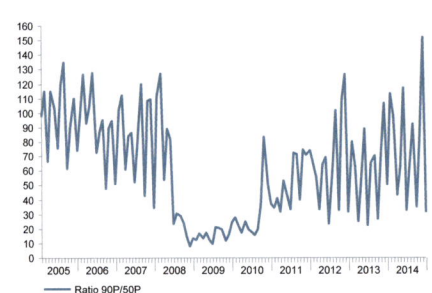

a: Long-term receivables

b: Short-term liabilities

Figure 6.25: Development of the ratios of the 90th percentile divided by the median (50th percentile) for balance sheet share of (a) interbank receivables with more than 5 years original maturity and (b) interbank overnight liabilities and liabilities with an original maturity of up to one year (January 2005 to December 2014). Source: Research Data and Service Centre (RDSC) of the Deutsche Bundesbank, monthly balance sheet statistics (BISTA), January 2005 to December 2014; own calculations.

A straightforward way to investigate the concentrations on the bank-type level is to analyze the fraction of banks of a given type for which the measure of interest is above the median value on the national level. If the share of banks of a certain type above the national median exceeds 50%, this provides evidence for particular involvement of the respective type of banks. As a matter of definition, overall only 50% of the banks exceed the national median. Here the focus is on regional banks, savings banks, and credit cooperatives only due to confidentiality requirements.

The share of regional banks above the national median with respect to long-term receivables is measured to be below 20%, but for short-term liabilities above 60% (see Figure 6.26a). Both shares do not follow a clear trend but rather move sideways. This makes for mixed evidence with respect to the concentration of interest rate risk of regional banks from domestic interbank lending. The share of savings banks above the national median with respect to long-term receivables is measured to exceed 60% and for short-term liabilities is even higher (see Figure 6.26b). Concerning trends, the share for long-term receivables appears to be very stable while the share for short-term liabilities might be going down. The current levels, however, clearly constitute evidence for interest rate risk from domestic interbank lending being particularly high among savings banks. This observation is strongly supported by the finding that more than 40% of the savings banks have exceeded both medians.[151] Because note that, across all banks and provided the measures are independent, the expected value would be 25%. The share of cooperative banks above the national median with respect to long-term receivables is measured to be above 50% but for short-term liabilities below or just above 40% (see Figure 6.26c). For long-term receivables, there does not seem to be a trend, but for short-term liabilities, there is some indication of a rise at the current edge. In sum, this suggest a rather average interest rate risk from domestic interbank lending for cooperative banks. It fits in this picture that the share of cooperative banks that exceed both national medians is around but recently mostly just above 20%.

Recap

Among the types of banks in Germany, savings banks and cooperative banks, and to a lesser extend regional banks, attract attention because particularly large parts of their assets and liabilities result from business with non-MFIs, a prime source for interest rate risk. Including balance sheet position which result from business with MFIs, and investigating the available maturity breakdowns as of year-end 2014, positive term transformation turns out to be wide-spread with savings banks and cooperative banks being particularly engaged and hence most likely to have the highest interest rate risk. The long-term developments of the relevant balance sheet positions are characterized by shifts toward more short-term funding and, to a slightly lesser extend, toward more long-term lending which suggests an increase in interest rate risk, again in particular for savings banks and cooperative banks.

The cross-border interbank positions of all banks in Germany taken together are characterized by a clearly positive term transformation. This adds to their interest rate risk. Within Germany, the interbank positions of cooperative banks with their head institutions, namely cooperative central institutions, turn out to still have a net hedging effect against rising interest rates. For savings banks the same was true about their interbank positions toward Landesbanks, but only until the financial crisis. With respect to the concentration of term transformation resulting from domestic interbank positions, savings banks are discovered to be particularly vulnerable. The realization of interest rate risk from interbank lending would affect a large number of savings banks disproportionately.

---

[151] This type of analysis cannot be conducted for regional banks, again for confidentiality reasons.

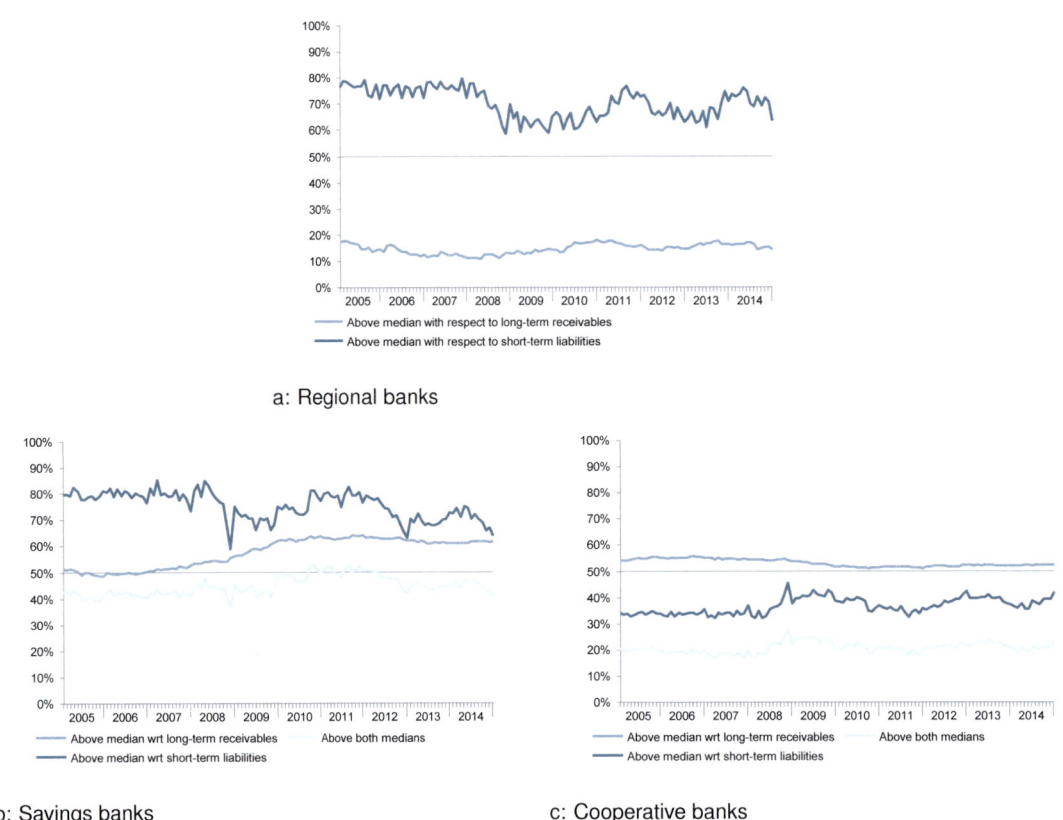

a: Regional banks

b: Savings banks   c: Cooperative banks

Figure 6.26: Development of shares of (a) regional banks, (b) savings banks, and (c) cooperative banks above overall medians of balance sheet shares of long-term receivables from and short-term liabilities to other domestic banks, plus for (b) savings banks and (c) cooperative banks the share of banks above both overall medians (January 2005 to December 2014). Source: Research Data and Service Centre (RDSC) of the Deutsche Bundesbank, monthly balance sheet statistics (BISTA), January 2005 to December 2014; own calculations.

6.5 Income statement statistics

Just like the balance sheet statistics, the income statement statistics available permit comparisons of Germany to the euro area as a whole as well as between different types of banks in Germany. Accordingly, the following investigation is again organized in two parts. Both parts consists of the same three standard analyses.

6.5.1 Germany and the euro area

Most prominently, the statistics published by the ECB on banks' income statements quantify the main components of operating income. These main components are the net interest income, the net fees and commissions and the net trading result.[152]

Banks generate their net interest income through a variety of activities. Besides term transformation, Busch and Memmel (2016) identify two more quantitatively important sources of banks' net interest income, namely the bearing of credit risk on the one hand and payment and liquidity management on the other hand. In exchange for these services, the customers of banks accept lower interest rates on their deposits and higher interest rates for their loans.

---

[152] Here, the net trading result also includes the foreign exchange result.

Comparing the euro area to Germany reveals a pronounced similarity (see Figure 6.27).[153] As of 2014, net interest income accounts for around 60%, net fees and commissions for just below 30%, and the net trading result for less than 10% of total operating income. For this initial comparison of the relative sizes of the components of operating income of banks in the euro area and in Germany the levels from 2014 are complemented by the five year average since 2010, because the net trading result is sometimes considered to be rather volatile. However, the numbers are not materially different.

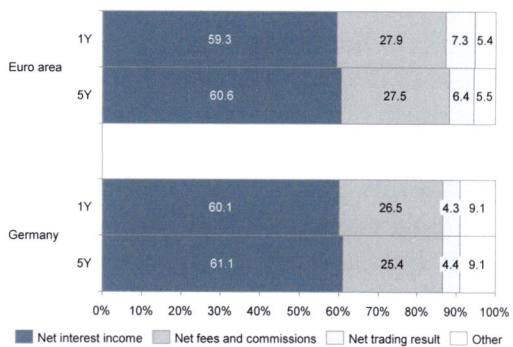

Figure 6.27: Banks' operative income by type of income in the euro area and Germany, in percent of total operative income (2014 and average across five years up to and including 2014). Source: ECB, consolidated banking data; own calculations.

The statistics on banks' income statements provided by the ECB also include information not only on net interest income but also on interest income and interest expenses individually. Analyzing this information reveals that, normalized with total assets, banks in Germany earn less interest income than banks in the euro area (see Figure 6.28). And since the interest expenses are of about the same size, the net interest income of banks in Germany is also smaller than that of banks in the euro area.

The lower net interest income relative to total assets might be a sign for lower dependence and hence lower interest rate risk of banks in Germany. And the lower interest income could be due to less long-term lending compared to banks in the euro area, at least given a normal term-structure. But due to the high degree of similarity, the evidence for differences in interest rate risk has to be regarded as rather weak.

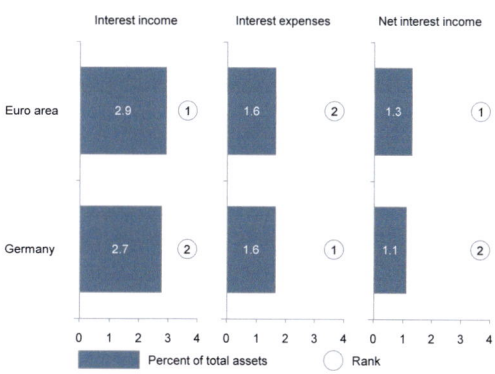

Figure 6.28: Banks' interest income, interest expenses and net interest income in the euro area and Germany, in percent of total assets (2014). Source: ECB, consolidated banking data; own calculations.

---

[153] It should not be forgotten that this similarity partly results from the simple fact that Germany is a large member country of the euro area. However, the net operating income generated by banks in Germany only accounts for about one fourth of what is generated in the euro area as a whole.

Interestingly, however, this very high degree of similarity seems to be a recent phenomenon (see Figure 6.29a). Assessing earlier data reveals that interest incomes as well as interest expenses of banks in the euro area and in Germany developed very much in parallel from 2009 to 2013. But during this period, banks in Germany earned an interest income normalized with total assets consistently between 102 and 114 basis points below that of banks in the euro area. And they paid interest expenses which were between 31 and 48 basis points lower. Only in 2014 these gaps narrowed notably. The interest income of banks in Germany increased more than that of banks in the euro area such that the gap narrowed to 17 basis points. And the interest expenses of banks in Germany even grew by so much that they just passed the also slightly growing interest expenses of banks in the euro area. That both gaps narrow at the current edge suggests that the interest rate related positions of banks in Germany have become more similar to those of banks in the euro area. And this might also be seen as evidence suggesting that the interest rate risk becomes more similar. It is natural to associate lower levels of interest income and interest expenses, normalized with total assets or as a fraction of total operating income, with lower interest rate risk. Because one would expect that these lower levels result from smaller interest rate related positions. Along these lines, the recent increases observed for banks in Germany also point to an increase of the interest rate risk of German banks, approaching the level of interest rate risk of banks in the euro area from below.

Of course, this is not the only possible explanation. Thinking of a normal upward sloping term structure, lower levels of interest income and interest expenses might also result from the interest related positions being further to the earlier end of the term structure. And as the earlier end is usually more volatile, one might then associate lower levels of interest income and interest expenses with higher interest rate risk. However, in particular with respect to interest income, the previous analyses of banks' balance sheets do not suggest that this is indeed the case here.

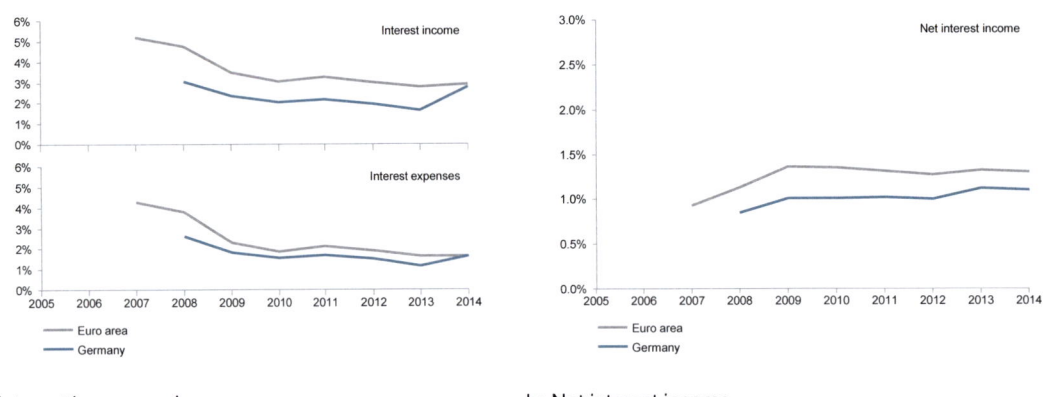

a: Interest income and expenses b: Net interest income

Figure 6.29: Development of banks' (a) interest income and interest expenses and (b) net interest income in the euro area and Germany, in percent of total assets (2007/08 to 2014). Source: ECB, consolidated banking data; own calculations.

Banks' net interest income normalized with total assets has remained close to 1% in both economic regions (see Figure 6.29b). The gap between the net interest income of banks in the euro area and the net interest income of banks in Germany has been narrowing slowly since 2009. This trend has continued in 2014. But the sudden increases of the interest income and the interest expenses of banks in Germany have hardly left a mark. They have nearly balanced out.

As a further step, one might contrast the developments of interest income, interest expenses, and net interest income with the development of reference interest rates and reference earnings from term transformation. An established way to calculate reference earnings from term transformation is from lending with a term of ten years and borrowing with a term of one year at the respective reference rates. One further makes the assumption that both the financing portfolio and the refinancing portfolio are rolled over steadily. As a result, the reference earnings from term transformation simply take the value of the average of the reference 10-year interest rate over the last ten years minus the average of the reference 1-year interest rate over the last year (see Figure 6.30b).[154] Accordingly, the ten-year average of the 10-year reference rate is referred to as the reference interest income and the one year average of the 1-year interest rate as the reference interest expenses (see Figure 6.30a).

Comparing the developments of the actual values to the developments of the reference values suggests that the recent increases in interest income and interest expenses of banks in Germany are not the result of changes in the reference rates. This only leaves changes in volumes and movements along the term structure as potential explanations of which at least the former would clearly imply an increase in interest rate risk. With respect to the reference income from term transformation it is interesting to note that it has been clearly lower in the euro area than in Germany between 2008 and 2013, while the actual net interest income of banks in the euro area exceeded that of banks in Germany. That the reference net interest income in Germany then fell behind that in the euro area in 2014 is, however, not reflected in the actual net interest income of banks in Germany. Again, changes in volumes as well as movements along the term structure might have compensated for this change in interest rates.

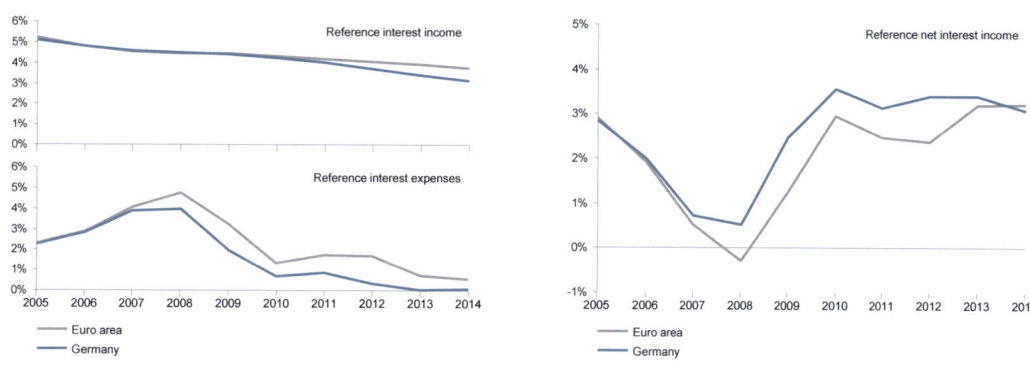

a: Interest income and expenses   b: Net interest income

Figure 6.30: Development of reference (a) interest income and interest expenses and (b) net interest income in the euro area and Germany (2005 to 2014). Source: ECB, term-structure data; BBK, term-structure data (Statistical Supplement 2); own calculations.

6.5.2 Types of banks in Germany

Next, income statement data from types of banks in Germany is investigated. Here other operating income is not included as the BBK only publishes other operating income net other operating expenses and deducts positions so large, that the result is sometimes negative. Instead the focus is on the percentages of the net interest income, the net fees and commissions, and the net trading result on the aggregate of these three items. Comparing different types of German banks brings to light pronounced differences (see Figure 6.31). The net interest income accounts for about 90% for Landesbanks, just below 80% for savings banks and cooperative banks, about 70% for regional banks, and close to 60% for large banks and cooperative central institutions.[155] In order to make sense of these numbers, one might again make the assumption that the larger the

---

[154] Further details on the construction of these reference earnings from term transformation are presented by Memmel (2008) and Memmel (2011). Note that the selection of the terms ten years and one year also originates from these sources.

[155] The difference in levels between Landesbanks and cooperative central institutions is particularly striking. It suggests that even though these types of banks have similar functions for savings banks and credit cooperatives, respectively, their business models differ significantly nevertheless.

share of the net interest income, the higher the exposure to interest rate risk. Accordingly, these statistics suggest that of the German banks Landesbanks, savings banks and cooperative banks are more exposed than regional banks, large banks, and cooperative central institutions.

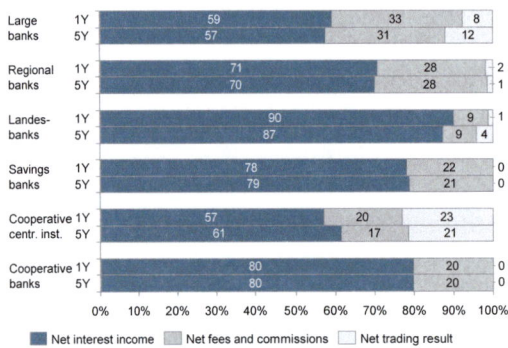

Figure 6.31: Banks' operative income by type of income for types of banks in Germany, in percent of total operative income (2014 and average across five years up to 2014). Source: BBK, the performance of German credit institutions (Monthly Report, September); own calculations.

Just like the statics provided by the ECB, the statistics published by the BBK on banks' income statements include information on how the net interest income is comprised of interest income and interest expenses. Analyzing this information produces three main results (see Figure 6.32). Again like in the comparison of the euro area and Germany above, the values are normalized with total assets. First, savings banks and cooperative banks have particularly high interest incomes in view of their interest expenses. These two types of banks are the only ones that have a higher rank in the interest-income ranking than in the interest-expenses ranking. While they earn the second and third highest interest incomes, they only pay the fourth and fifth highest interest expenses, respectively. This results in the second highest interest income for savings banks and the highest net interest income for cooperative banks. Second, for regional banks and cooperative central institutions it is the other way round. That is, their interest incomes are comparably small given their interest expenses. But while regional banks generate the third highest net interest income, cooperative central institutions end up with the lowest. Third, large banks and Landesbanks take extreme positions with respect to the components of net interest income. Large banks earn the lowest interest income and also pay the lowest interest expenses while Landesbanks earn the highest and also pay the highest. In terms of net interest income they end up in the lower half.

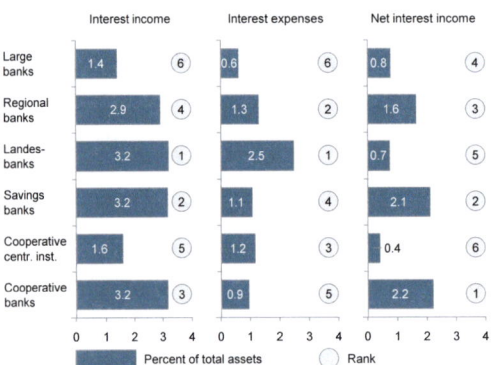

Figure 6.32: Banks' interest income, interest expenses and net interest income for types of banks in Germany, in percent of total assets (2014). Source: BBK, the performance of German credit institutions (Monthly Report, September); own calculations.

Concerning interest rate risk, a high interest income in combination with low interest expenses might result from particular engagement in term transformation. Along these lines, savings banks and cooperative banks can be identified as prime candidates for particularly high interest rate risk. This conclusion must, however, not only be based on the rankings of interest income and interest expenses but must also take into account the net interest income generated. For this reason, it is not similarly straightforward to conclude that regional banks and cooperative central institutions are likely to have a particularly low interest rate risk. Because even though their ranking profile for interest income and interest expenses is a mirror image of that of savings banks and cooperative banks, the interest incomes they generate are not both as extreme. Only for cooperative central institutions one might reason along the same lines as above and expect a particularly low interest rate risk because they also generate the lowest net interest income. For regional banks this reasoning does not apply. Concerning large banks, the low levels of interest income and interest expenses are most likely due to low levels of interest related positions relative to total assets. This would point to a particularly low interest rate risk. The opposite holds for Landesbanks.

The direct comparison of the different types of German banks evinces that between 2005 and 2014 the ranking of types of banks according to their net interest income normalized with total assets remained unchanged over long periods of time (see Figure 6.33b). Two groups can be identified, namely cooperative banks, savings banks, and regional banks with higher values and large banks, Landesbanks, and cooperative central institutions with lower values. Regional banks and large banks are the only two types that have experienced notable level shifts, in both cases downward.

The developments of the components of net interest income, that is interest income and interest expenses, have been rather similar for all types of German banks (see Figure 6.33a). The only exception are Landesbanks for which a change in accounting practices resulted in a sudden increase of reported interest income and interest expenses in 2011.[156] Apart from that, one can observe decreases of both interest income and interest expenses since 2008 that are largely parallel across all types of banks. Only large banks show somewhat stronger decreases, in particular between 2008 and 2011. This may be due to a reduction in the size of interest rate related positions and may then go along with a decrease of interest rate risk. But of course, it should not be forgotten, that the introduction of BilMoG particularly affected the amount of total assets of large banks. Last but not least, besides for large banks, also for cooperative central institutions a notable decrease in net interest income can be observed.

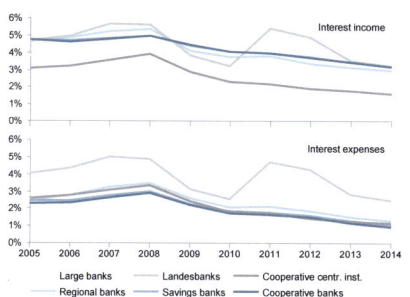
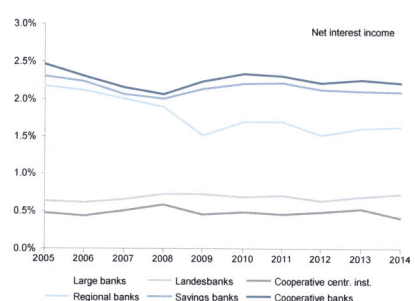

a: Interest income and expenses   b: Net interest income

Figure 6.33: Development of banks' (a) interest income and interest expenses and (b) net interest income for types of banks in Germany, in percent of total assets (2005 to 2014). Source: BBK, the performance of German credit institutions (Monthly Report, September); own calculations.

---

[156] For further details see BBK (2012a).

6.6 Interest rate statistics

Unlike suggested by the name, but as mentioned before, the interest rate statistics published by the ECB and associated central banks do not only contain information on interest rates but also on business volumes. To begin with, this information on business volumes is analyzed in isolation in order to identify developments relevant for the interest rate risk of MFIs which therefore warrant further investigation. Thereafter, the information on interest rates is called in additionally and the specific technique introduced earlier is applied in order find out to what extend the relevant developments are MFI-driven or counterparty-driven. Note that the information used here is available for the euro area and for Germany, but not for individual types of banks in Germany.

In the analysis of the information on business volumes the focus naturally is on new business. Wherever business volumes of outstanding amounts are reported in publications on the interest rate statistics, these business volumes are taken from the balance sheet statistics. Hence, business volumes of outstanding amounts are no genuine part of the interest rate statistics. But the material reason for the focus on new business is not the source of the data, but rather that specific technique to be applied targets new business. This is also the reason why the information on interest rates called in below is on new business only. As explained earlier, overnight deposits and deposits redeemable at notice are the exceptions.

The analysis of the information on new business becomes much more manageable if the data is processed in two ways. First, one calculates the rolling twelve-month average. This smoothes the otherwise very volatile developments and therefore makes comparisons over time easier. Second, one calculates indices and sets the initial values to some standard value such as 100. This makes comparisons between the euro area and Germany easier as the absolute numbers reported naturally differ greatly. As June 2010 is the first month for which the required data is available, May 2011 is the first month for which a twelve-month average can be calculated. And this value is set to 100 for short-term and long-term loans and deposits in the euro area and in Germany.

The developments of the volumes of new short-term and long-term loans do not point into a clear direction in so far as interest rate risk is concerned (see Figure 6.34a and b). The volume of new short-term loans has decreased in the euro area and in Germany in recent years but a little more so in the euro area. The volume of new long-term loans has decreased till mid 2012 in the euro area and in Germany but much more so in the euro area which still has not caught up again. The fact that both the volumes of new short-term and of new long-term loans are higher in Germany than in the euro area does not indicate whether the overall term structure of loans granted by banks in Germany shifts toward short-term or long-term. Hence, no conclusion about the development of the related interest rate risk can be drawn directly.

The developments of the volumes of new deposits, however, consistently point to one conclusion. While the amount of new short-term deposits increases more in Germany than in the euro area, the amount of new long-term deposits decreases more in Germany than in the euro area, at least over a large share of the period covered (see Figures 6.35a and b). Both findings point to the same conclusion, namely that the interest rate risk of MFIs in Germany is growing faster than that of MFIs in the euro area. The developments of new short-term and long-term deposits therefore warrant further investigation. Hence, in the following the developments of the amounts of new deposits are in focus. Also note that lending is the natural subject of the the bank lending survey results to be analyzed below.

In order to find out to what extent the developments of the amounts of new deposits are MFI-driven or counterparty-driven the information on interest rates of new deposits are called in on top of the information on business volumes. As introduced above, for deposits the special technique to be applied identifies the underlying driver based on a simple market model with the

MFIs on the demand side and the counterparties on the supply side. That is, if interest rates and business volumes change in the same direction, the change is characterized as MFI-driven, and if interest rates and business volumes change in opposite directions, the change is considered counterparty-driven. Furthermore, if the business volume increases, the change is regarded as expansionary, and if the business volume decreases, the change is seen as contractionary. If the interest rate does not change, a change in business volume cannot be assigned to either the MFIs or the counterparties and falls into a separate category, referred to simply as "other". And if the business volume does not change, a change in interest rates is simply ignored. As already mentioned, the interest rates referred to here are the reported rates net of corresponding reference rates. Furthermore, here individual month-on-month changes are considered. No rolling twelve-month averages are employed in the analysis because here the month-on-month changes in market equilibrium are in focus. It should also be recalled that in the aggregation across all the relevant deposit subtypes, the business volumes are used as weights. Last but not least, the comparisons between the euro area and Germany as well as between short-term and long-term deposits are more comprehensible when the total changes are all normalized to a standard value such as 100 with the appropriate sign.

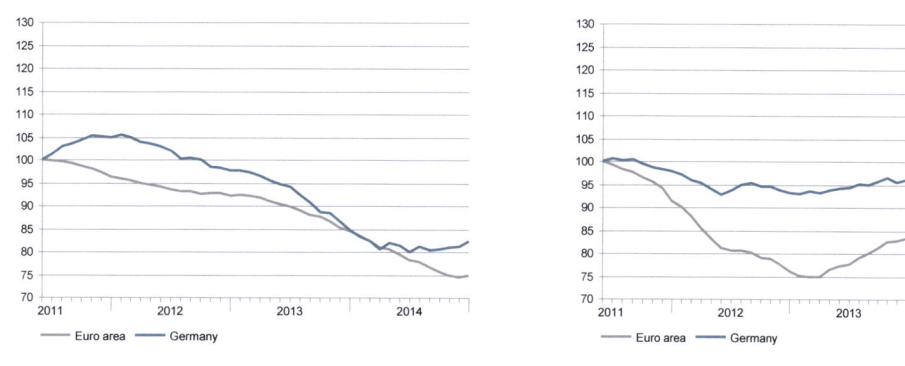

a: New short-term loans   b: New long-term loans

Figure 6.34: Development of volumes of (a) new short-term collateralized loans and (b) long-term collateralized loans in the euro area and Germany measured as indices of the one year rolling average with May 2011 set to 100 (May 2011 to December 2014). Source: ECB, MFI interest rate statistics; own calculations.

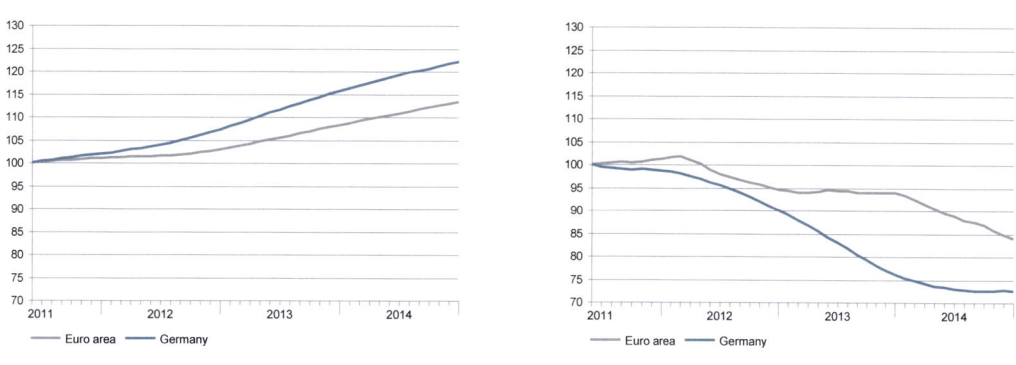

a: New short-term deposits   b: New long-term deposits

Figure 6.35: Development of volumes of (a) new short-term deposits and (b) new long-term deposits in the euro area and Germany measured as indices of the one year rolling average with May 2011 set to 100 (May 2011 to December 2014). Source: ECB, MFI interest rate statistics; own calculations.

To begin with, the focus is on short-term deposits. Three results stand out (see Figures 6.36a and b).[157] First, in the euro area and in Germany the net effects of both the MFI-driven changes and the counterparty-driven changes are expansionary. That is, expansions are larger than contractions in absolute terms. Hence, both MFIs and counterparties contribute to the increase in business volume of new short-term deposits. Second, of the total increase, in the euro area 25% are MFI-driven and 61% are counterparty-driven while in Germany the corresponding numbers are 31% and 63%. As the total increase is normalized to 100 for the euro area and Germany, these numbers can simply be read from the net effects. The remaining parts are due to changes in business volumes without changes of interest rates, at least on the level of detail reported. Third, with respect to gross changes, in absolute terms both MFI-driven expansions and contractions are clearly larger in the euro area than in Germany. In the euro area the absolute size of MFI-driven contractions is 76% of that of MFI-driven expansions while in Germany the corresponding number is 51%.[158] A similar observation can be made for counterparty-driven expansions and contractions.

As to the implications for the taking of interest rate risk, the second result suggests that in the euro area as well as in Germany a larger part of the increase in short-term deposits is due to counterparty-driven changes than to MFI-driven changes. Comparing the euro area and Germany, the second and the third result suggest a greater contribution to the increase of their interest rate risk by MFIs in Germany than by MFIs in the euro area. Because the second result shows that a larger part of the total increase is MFI-driven in Germany than in the euro area. And the third result may be evidence of a higher degree of determination as MFIs only counteract a smaller part of their expansions with contractions.

Next, the focus is on long-term deposits. Again, three results are particularly noteworthy (see Figures 6.36c and d) First, in the euro area the net effect of MFI-driven changes is contractionary while the net effect of counterparty-driven changes is expansionary but in Germany both net effects are contractionary. Second, with the total decrease as the base, in the euro area the MFI-driven changes amount to 127% and the counterparty-driven changes to -27% while in Germany the corresponding numbers are 69% and 32%. Third, as to gross changes, in absolute terms again both the MFI-driven and the counterparty-driven changes are notably larger in the euro area than in Germany. And the absolute size of MFI-driven expansions is 67% of that of MFI-driven contractions in the euro area while only 41% in Germany.

With respect to the taking of interest rate risk, the second result suggests that the decrease in long-term deposits was to a larger part due to MFI-driven changes than to counterparty-driven changes in the euro area and in Germany. Put differently, deviating from what is found for short-term deposits, the decrease of the business volume of new long-term deposits is mostly due to MFIs. Comparing the euro area and Germany, the third result may again suggest a greater determination of MFIs in Germany than of MFIs in the euro area. But the first and the second result point into the opposite directions. In the euro area the decrease of long-term deposits would have been even larger if the net counterparty-driven expansion had not reduced the MFI-driven contraction by about a fifth. Finally, for short-term and long-term deposits seen together, the analysis therefore produces mixed evidence as to whether the increase in interest rate risk has been more MFI-driven in the euro area or in Germany.

---

[157] The following abbreviations are used: MFI-Exp (MFI-driven expansion), MFI-Con (MFI-driven contraction, Cpt-Exp (counterparty-driven expansion), and Cpt-Con (counterparty-driven contraction).

[158] In order to avoid confusion: These numbers are calculated by dividing the absolute size of the MFI-driven contraction (78 in the euro area or 32 in Germany) by the absolute size of the MFI-driven expansion (103 in the euro area or 63 in Germany).

a: Euro area, short-term   b: Germany, short-term

c: Euro area, long-term   d: Germany, long-term

Figure 6.36: Contributions of market participants in (a and c) the euro area and (b and d) Germany to changes of volumes of new (a and b) short-term and (c and d) long-term deposits with the respective total change set to 100 with the appropriate sign (June 2010 to December 2014). Source: ECB, MFI interest rate statistics; own calculations.

6.7 Bank lending survey results

As described previously in detail, the bank lending survey includes three sets of questions that are of interest for the study of banks' interest rate risk. The answers to these three sets of questions are analyzed in turn. Note that, like the interest rate statistics analyzed previously, the bank lending survey results to be analyzed next are available for the euro area and for Germany, but not for individual types of banks in Germany.

The bank lending survey results generated from the answers to the first interesting set of questions make it possible to compare the tightening or easing of "credit standards as applied in the approval of loans and credit lines to enterprises" (ECB (2015a), question one) for long-term and short-term lending. Long-term and short-term lending are distinguished based on original maturity and with a threshold value of one year.

Evaluating the cumulated net percentages since Q1 2005 produces three main insights. First, in the euro area the credit standards for long-term lending were tightened[159] considerably between 2007 and 2009 as well as between 2011 and 2013 and in both periods much more so for long-term than for short-term lending (see Figure 6.37a). Second, in Germany the credit standards were also tightened between 2007 and 2009, but rather similarly for long-term lending an short-term lending (see Figure 6.37b). Third, as a result, the excess tightness[160] of long-term lending has increased markedly more in the euro area than in Germany (see Figure 6.37c).

---

[159] Note that an increase of the cumulated net percentages signals a tightening and a decrease an easing.

[160] The excess tightness of long-term lending is calculated simply as the net percentage for long-term lending minus the net percentage for short-term lending. Again, of course, only changes can be interpreted in a meaningful way.

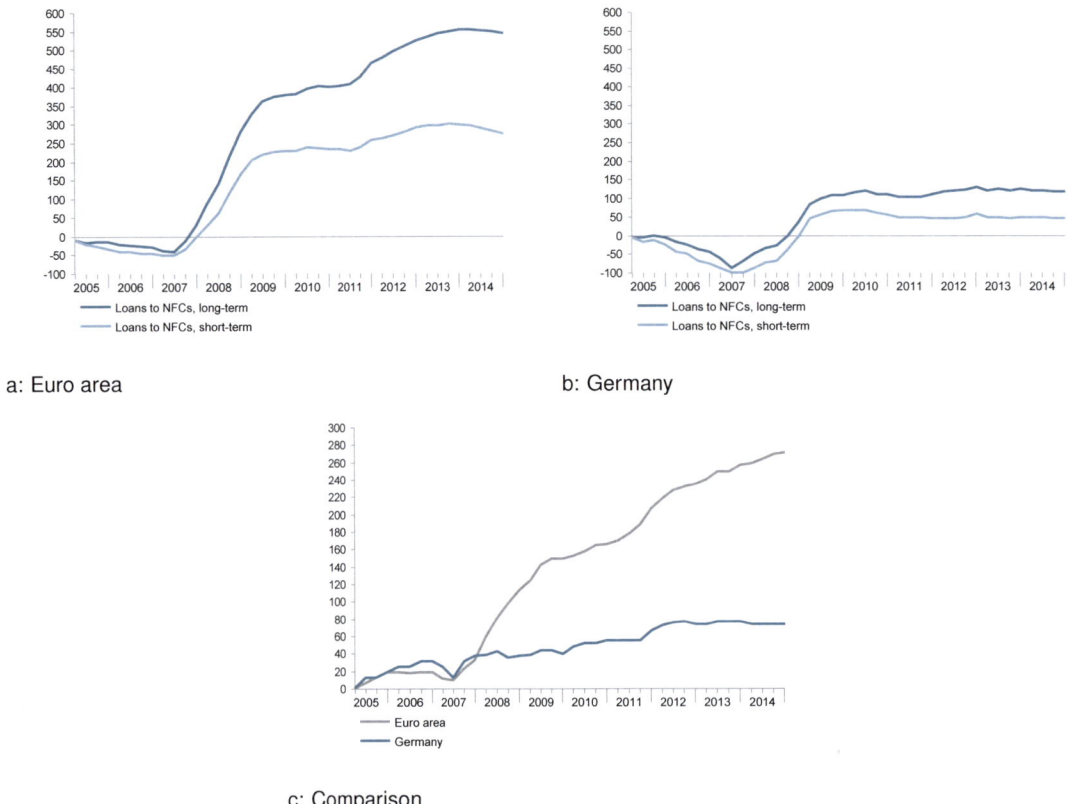

a: Euro area   b: Germany

c: Comparison

Figure 6.37: Development of the tightness of credit standards for long-term and short-term loans to non-financial corporations in (a) the euro area and (b) Germany, plus (c) a comparison of the excess tightness of long-term lending, all measured as cumulative net percentages starting in Q1 2005 (Q1 2005 to Q4 2014). Source: ECB, bank lending survey; own calculations.

As to the interest rate risk of banks, a tightening of the credit standards for long-term lending in excess of the tightening of the credit standards for short-term lending points to a reduction of interest rate risk. Because it is only natural to expect that this excess tightening changes the composition of actual lending toward more short-term and less long-term lending. And such a portfolio change comes with less interest rate risk in the form of exposure to an increase of interest rates. Accordingly, these bank lending survey results suggest that the interest rate risk of banks in the euro area as well as in Germany has decreased but that the interest rate risk of banks in the euro area has decreased more than that of banks in Germany. Put differently, one finds that relative to the interest rate risk of banks in the euro area the interest rate risk of banks in Germany has decreased less. Or put differently, it has increased in relative terms.

The bank lending survey results generated from the answers to the second interesting set of questions make it possible to assess in what way changes with respect to maturity contributed to the tightening or easing of "terms and conditions for new loans and credit lines to enterprises / new loans to households for house purchase / new consumer credit and other lending to households" (ECB (2015a), question three / twelve / fifteen). As terms and conditions refer to actual contractual arrangements, these questions directly address the realized marked outcome.

Examining the cumulated net percentages the following three principal lessons can be learnt. First, as to lending to non-financial corporations, maturity changes clearly contributed to the tightening of terms and conditions between 2007 and 2009 in the euro area and in Germany and between 2011 and 2013 in the euro area, but hardly in Germany (see Figure 6.38a). Second, concerning lending to households for house purchase, the developments in the euro area and in Germany are in principle rather similar to the developments observed for lending to non-financial

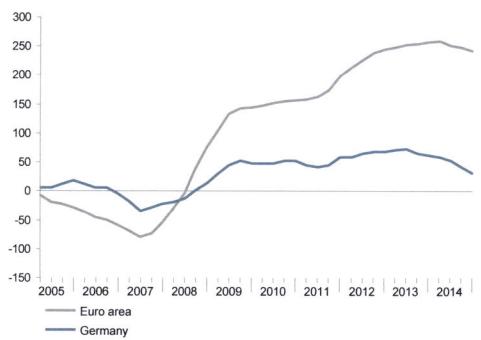

a: Non-financial corporations

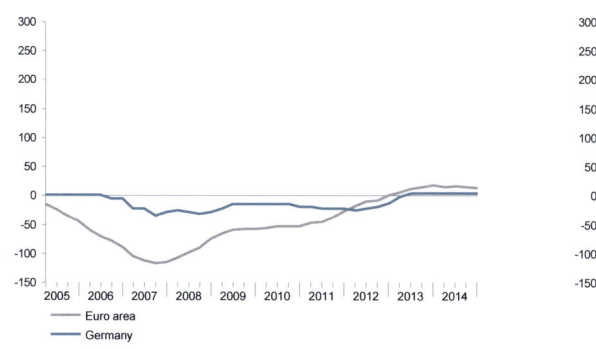

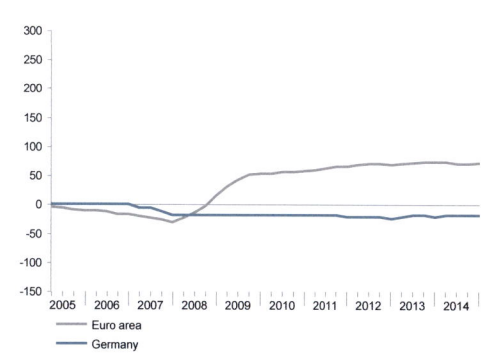

b: Households for house purchase

c: Households for other purposes

Figure 6.38: Development of the tightness of terms and conditions relating to maturity for loans to (a) non-financial corporations, to (b) households for house purchase, and to (c) households as consumer credit and other lending, measured as cumulative net percentages starting in the Q1 of 2005 (Q1 2005 to Q4 2014). Source: ECB, bank lending survey; own calculations.

corporations but much less pronounced (see Figure 6.38b). Third, with respect to lending to households for other purposes, only a tightening between 2007 and 2009 in the euro area is visible (see Figure 6.38c). It is also interesting to note that at the current edge, changes regarding maturity seem to contribute to an easing of the terms and conditions in particular of the loans and credit lines to non-financial corporations in the euro area and even more so in Germany.

Changes regarding maturity that contribute to the tightening of terms and conditions can be associated with a reduction of interest rate risk for the reasons outlined earlier, namely that this tightening usually results in a shortening of the maturity. Hence, the findings suggest that the interest rate risk has decreased in the euro area and in Germany, but more so in the euro area. And at the current edge it is increasing in the euro area and in Germany, but more so in Germany. Again, compared to the interest rate risk of banks in the euro area, the interest rate risk of banks in Germany is found to have increased.

Other regular as well as further ad-hoc questions in the bank lending survey investigate what leads the banks to adjust their credit standards as well as terms and conditions. The answers suggest that for the euro area three driving forces were most important, namely funding difficulties, equity shortages, and credit deterioration of the actual and potential borrowers. For Germany, after the funding difficulties in the wake of the financial crisis were overcome, only equity shortages have played a role comparable to the role they have played in the euro area. These equity shortages can partly be traced back to the introduction of more restrictive capital requirements. That funding difficulties are still an important factor in the euro area but not so much in Germany shows itself in the demand for the targeted long-term refinancing operations

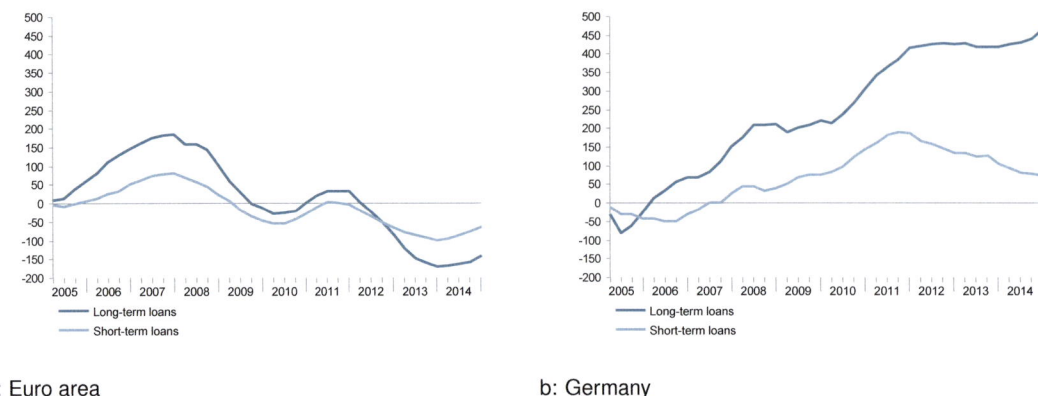

a: Euro area   b: Germany

Figure 6.39: Development of the demand for long-term and short-term loans in (a) the euro area and (b) Germany, measured as cumulative net percentages starting in the Q1 of 2005 (Q1 2005 to Q4 2014). Source: ECB, bank lending survey; own calculations.

of the ECB in September and December 2014, which was sizeable in the euro area, but negligible in Germany.

The bank lending survey results generated from the answers to the third interesting set of questions shed light on the development of "the demand for loans or credit lines to enterprises" and also separately for long-term and short-term lending (ECB (2015a), question six). As changes in demand potentially lead to a new market outcome, banks' interest rate risk may be affected.

A study of the cumulated net percentages reveals noteworthy differences between changes in demand faced by banks in the euro area and in Germany. In the euro area the demand of non-financial corporations for both long-term and short-term lending has been decreasing since 2007 with small increases in late 2010 and early 2011 and at the current edge. And during 2012 and 2013 the demand for long-term lending decreased much more than the demand for short-term lending (see Figure 6.39a). In Germany, however, the demand for both long-term and short-term lending increased till 2011. And since then, the demand for long-term lending has remained rather stable while the demand for short-term lending decreased (see Figure 6.39b).

Changes in demand can be directly associated with market pressure on banks to change their lending offerings. And in so far as banks change their lending offerings in the way demanded, changes in demand lead to changes in banks' interest rate risk. Along these lines, the major changes in demand since 2012 suggest that there was pressure on banks in the euro area to reduce their average interest rate risk and pressure on banks in Germany to increase their average interest rate risk. Here, average interest rate risk refers to interest rate risk per unit of loan volume. This concept may be helpful as here no standardization through normalization with total assets ore some comparable measure is applied. While in the euro area demand changes built up pressure to change the composition of lending offered toward more short-term lending and less long-term lending, in Germany demand changes built up pressure in the opposite direction. Hence, again the evidence points to a possible increase of the interest rate risk of banks in Germany at least compared to banks in the euro area.

Answers to other questions in the bank lending survey shed light on the underlying causes of changes in demand for lending. According to these answers, the increase in demand for long-term lending in Germany can be traced back to increased capital investments, but also to low long-term interest rates. The latter point is of particular interest for the current investigation, because it is only natural to expect that non-financial corporations that want to benefit from low long-term interest rates are interested in long-term fixed rate lending. And the amount of lending of this sort is directly related to the interest rate risk of the banks involved.

6.8 Conclusion

Taken together, the analyses carried out strongly suggest that the interest rate risk from on-balance sheet term transformation of banks in Germany exceeds the euro area average and is bound to increase even further. Within Germany, savings banks and cooperative banks turn out to be particularly engaged. A strong shift toward shorter-term funding but also a notable shift toward longer-term lending can be observed for German banks. Net interest income makes up close to two thirds of their operating income. Banks in Germany clearly push for more short-term and less long-term deposits by adjusting interest rates. And they do comparatively little to counteract the relatively high increase in the demand for long-term loans by adjusting credit standards or terms and conditions.

On a meta-level, one possible conclusion to be drawn from the investigation conducted is that the amount of information available on German bank's interest rate risk from traditional term transformation is rather limited. Of course, the analyses carried out were designed to make the best use of the statistics available, aiming at producing the most comprehensive set of insights about the interest rate risk of banks possible. But an honest evaluation has to admit that it is not particularly hard to think of more compelling insights than the ones produced. In light of this evaluation, a very natural policy recommendation is the expansion of the transparency requirements relating to interest rate risk from term transformation, or more generally in the banking book. This links in with the ongoing revision of the relevant regulatory framework. And the present investigation makes a clear case for the importance of such undertakings.

6.9 Appendices

Balance sheet data that features portfolio breakdowns by original maturity can be used to infer a portfolio profile by remaining maturity. The following appendices initially introduce one particular way of doing so and thereafter present the results in the format of the standard analyses. It turns out that several additional assumptions are needed and that data-related problems become a more important issue. The results do not materially differ from those based simply on original maturity as far as rankings and trends are concerned, but levels differ in an expectable manner.

Appendix 1: Method for inferring remaining from original maturity

Inferring a portfolio profile by remaining maturity from data that features portfolio breakdowns by original maturity involves three basic steps that need to be taken for every maturity bracket (see Figure 6.40). In step one the amount reported for the original maturity bracket of interest in the first period that one decides to include in the analysis needs to be distributed across the range of possible remaining maturities. A uniform distribution between a remaining maturity of zero and of the upper bound of the original maturity bracket is a particularly natural choice. As one moves to the second time period, in step two the remaining maturity of all amounts needs to be reduced by one time period. All amounts that reach a maturity of zero are to be erased. And still in the second time period, in step three the additional amount reported for the original maturity bracket of interest needs to be distributed across the range of possible remaining maturities. The additional amount is calculated as the reported amount for the second period minus all amounts from the previous period that have not yet matured. Hence, the additional amount is a proxy for new business. And as such it is natural to distribute it uniformly across the remaining maturities between the lower and the upper bound of the original maturity bracket of interest. Moving to the next period, steps two and three are then to be repeated. Note that the selection of the first

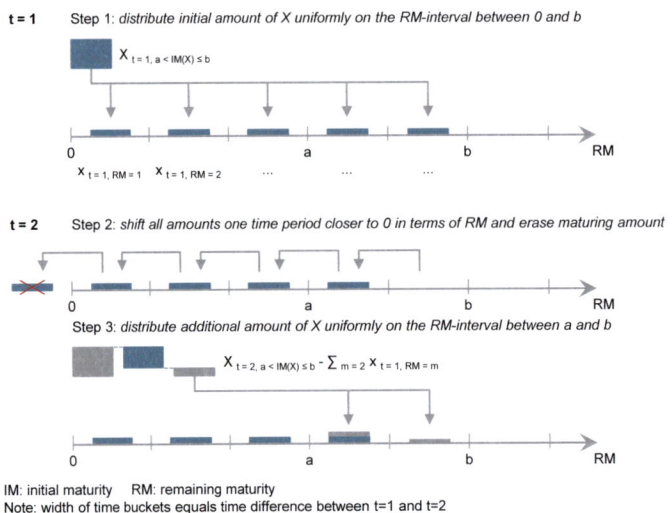

IM: initial maturity   RM: remaining maturity
Note: width of time buckets equals time difference between t=1 and t=2

Figure 6.40: Approximation of remaining maturity from data on original maturity, basic steps with steps steps two and three to be iterated.

period matters. Because step one produces a different portfolio profile in terms of remaining maturity than an iteration of steps two and three even for a constant amount reported in the original maturity bracket. Furthermore, additional assumptions are necessary. Some original maturity brackets do not have an upper bound which therefore needs to be assumed. The results presented below are produced assuming that the width of the last maturity bracket is effectively the same as that of the second last. An exception is only made for government securities for which the upper bound of the original maturity is assumed to be effectively 10 years. Structural breaks in the data such as that resulting from the implementation of BilMoG have potentially disturbing effects for more than one period. For the following analyses, the amounts across all remaining maturities are reduced pro rate in order to avoid heavily negative new business volumes. Changes in the number of reporting institutions could be treated in a similar way, but this is not done here as this would also lead to disturbances of a different sort.

As far as rankings at a particular point in time are concerned, any difference between the results in terms of remaining maturity and those based on original maturity has two potential sources. First, if a relevant amount with an original maturity of more than one year is reported in more than one maturity bracket, the distribution across these multiple long-term maturity brackets may be sufficiently different. If only original maturity is looked at, the distribution between different long-term maturity brackets does not matter. But if remaining maturity is approximated, it matters that amounts in the maturity brackets closer to the threshold value of one year sooner reach a remaining maturity of not more than one year. Second, the recent developments of the amounts regarded as long-term based on original maturity may be sufficiently different. Because a recent increase results in a larger share of the overall amount still being long-term also in terms of remaining maturity.

As far as trends are concerned, the distribution across multiple maturity brackets considered long-term based on original maturity matters for the same reason. An increase in the amount in an original maturity bracket closer to the threshold value of one year over time results in a smaller absolute increase in the amount with a remaining maturity of more than one year than a similar increase in a maturity bracket with longer original maturity. However, in relative terms it is the other way round initially.

In terms of levels, lower long-term amounts and higher short-term amounts are to be expected. An original maturity of not more than one year also implies a remaining maturity of not more

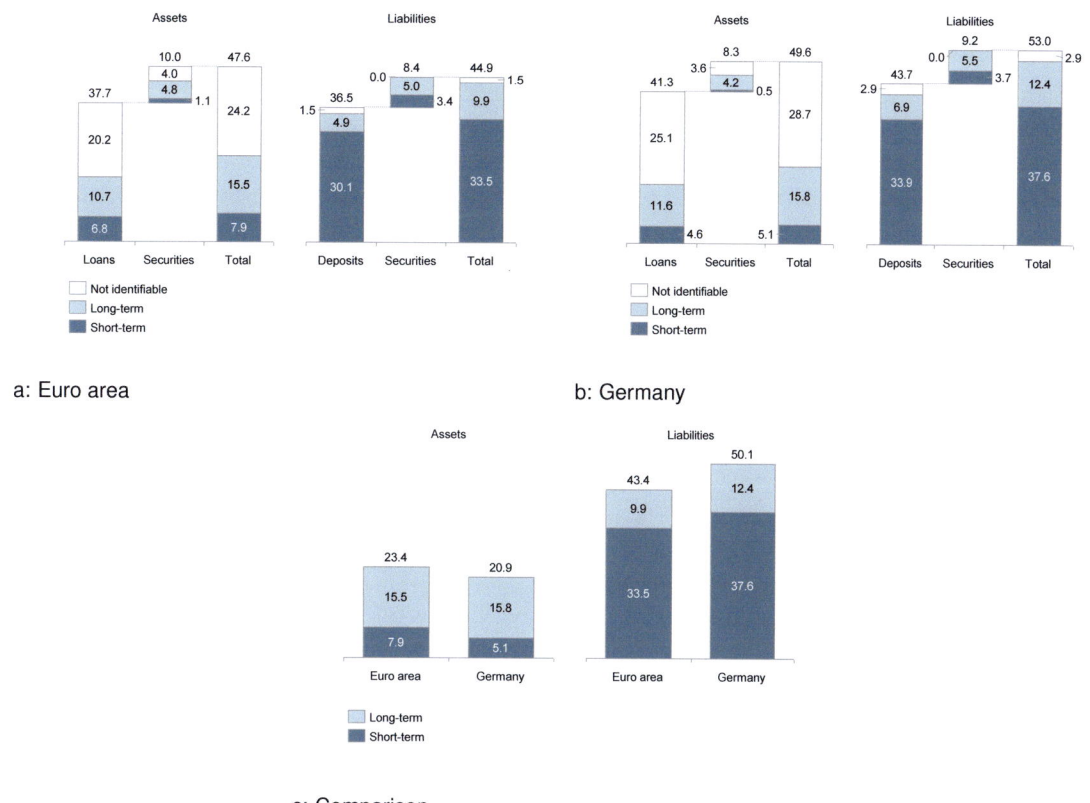

Figure 6.41: Long-term and short-term assets and liabilities in terms of remaining maturity of (a) MFIs in the euro area and (b) MFIs in Germany, plus (c) direct comparison, in percent of total assets (December 2014). Source: ECB, MFI balance sheet statistics; own calculations.

than one year. Hence, all amounts regarded short-term based on original maturity are also to be regarded short-term in terms of remaining maturity. But as discussed above, an original maturity of more than one year does not imply a remaining maturity of more than one year. Because positions with an original maturity of more than one year mature over time and their remaining maturity eventually drops below one year.

Appendix 2: Results for Germany and the euro area

In this Appendix and in the following Appendix 3 the results from applying the above described method are reported in the format of the standard analyses. As it is immediately apparent that the results are overall very similar to the ones based on original maturity in terms of rankings and trends, the focus here is on differences in detail.

With respect to the investigation of the maturity structures of the relevant positions of the balance sheets of MFIs in the euro area and in Germany as of December 2014 one difference is noteworthy. The fractions of identifiable short-term liabilities of MFIs in the euro area and in Germany are no longer only 0.1 percentage points apart with MFIs in Germany with the slightly higher fraction. Now MFIs in the euro area are 2.1 percentage points in front with 77.2%, while MFIs in Germany only have a fraction of identifiable short-term liabilities of 75.1% (see Figure 6.41c). However, with a difference of 9.3 percentage points MFIs in Germany continue to report a much higher fraction of identifiable long-term assets. Hence, this part of the analysis still points to more pronounced term transformation of MFIs in Germany.

With respect to the maturity structure as of December 2014 based only on maturity breakdowns available in the years before 2014, slightly larger differences between the fractions of identifiable long-term loans can be found (see Figure 6.42). For MFIs in the euro area as well as for MFIs in Germany this difference is now larger than one percentage point but still smaller than two percentage points. This suggests that the maturity structure of loans to non-financial corporations is a slightly worse yet still rather accurate measure for the maturity structure of loans to non-financial corporations, the general government, and financial vehicle corporations engaged in securitization combined.

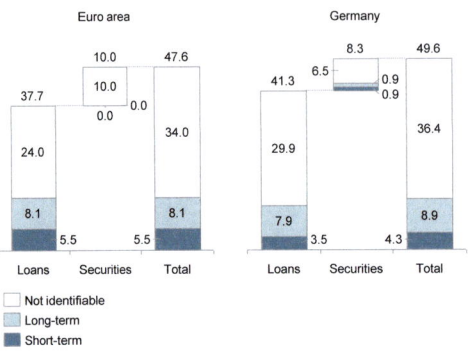

Figure 6.42: Long-term and short-term assets in terms of remaining maturity of MFIs in the euro area and in Germany for which historic data is available, in percent of total assets (December 2014). Source: ECB, MFI balance sheet statistics; own calculations.

As to the development of the maturity structure over time, a few differences can be observed (see Figure 6.43). It is no longer the case that between May 2012 and December 2014 the share of long-term loans stagnates for MFIs in the euro area but increases for MFIs in Germany. Instead, now it hardly changes for both and both are at about the same level. The share of long-term deposits and of long-term debt securities issued now also decreases slightly for MFIs in the euro area between the financial crisis and the current edge. Hence, the evidence is somewhat weaker, but overall remains in favor of stronger trend toward more term transformation of MFIs in Germany compared to MFIs in the euro area as a whole. Overall, the strong recent increase in short-term deposits that MFIs in Germany report remains the dominating factor.

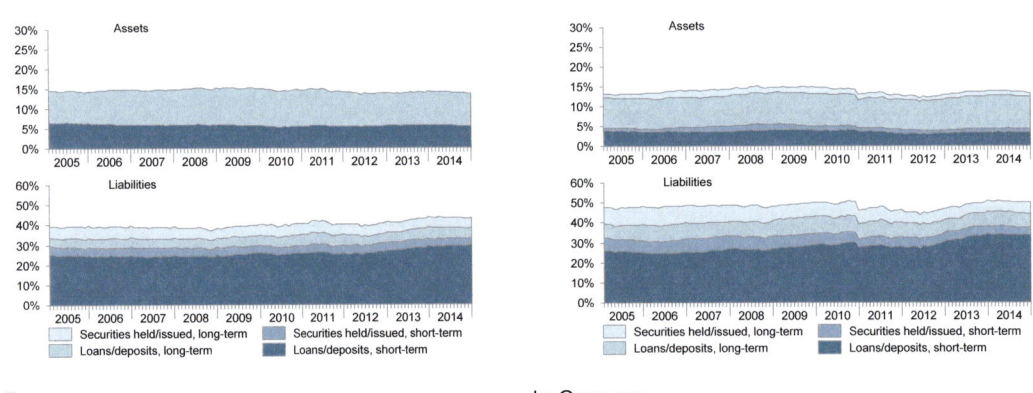

a: Euro area   b: Germany

Figure 6.43: Development of long-term and short-term assets and liabilities in terms of remaining maturity of (a) MFIs in the euro area and (b) MFIs in Germany, in percent of total assets (January 2005 to December 2014). Source: ECB, MFI balance sheet statistics; own calculations.

Concerning the developments of the surpluses of long-term assets, one now finds that since the beginning of 2011 MFIs in Germany have more clearly pulled away from MFIs in the euro area (see Figure 6.44a). Concerning the developments of the surpluses of short-term liabilities, the increase of MFIs in Germany is now less impressive but still remains stronger than that of MFIs in the euro area in particular between mid 2012 and end 2013 (see Figure 6.44b). For the comparison in terms of interest rate risk, the developments of these surpluses hence continue to imply a higher level and a relative increase for MFIs in Germany compared to those in the euro area.

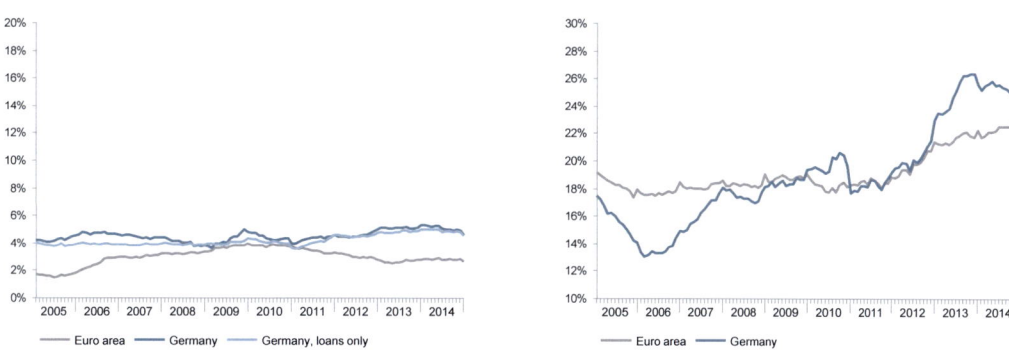

a: Surplus of long-term assets   b: Surplus of short-term liabilities

Figure 6.44: Development of the surplus of (a) long-term assets (b) short-term liabilities in terms of remaining maturity of MFIs in the euro area and MFIs in Germany, in percent of total assets (January 2005 to December 2014). Source: ECB, MFI balance sheet statistics; own calculations.

The developments of the fractions of loans with more than five years remaining maturity looks rather different than those based on original maturity (see Figure 6.45). This can easily be explained. A high lower bound of the original maturity bracket combined with a big width of this bracket implies that the amount with a remaining maturity below the lower bound is affected by reported volume changes only very gradually. The development of the fraction of overnight deposits is necessarily the same and hence omitted.

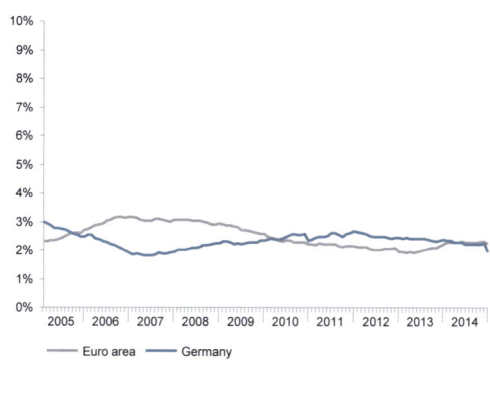

Loans

Figure 6.45: Development of loans with more than 5 years maturity in terms of remaining maturity of MFIs in the euro area and in Germany, in percent of total assets (January 2005 to December 2014). Source: ECB, MFI balance sheet statistics; own calculations.

Appendix 3: Results for types of banks in Germany

Again, the maturity structures of the relevant balance sheet positions as of December 2014 are focused on first (see Figure 6.46). In terms of remaining maturity, Landesbanks and cooperative central institutions now also have a higher share of short-term liabilities than of long-term liabilities. Another noteworthy difference is that expressed as a fraction of all liabilities that can be identified as either long-term or short-term, now large banks have a slightly higher share of short-term liabilities than savings banks and cooperative banks.

With respect to the development of the shares of relevant balance sheet positions that are identifiable as long-term or short-term there are no noteworthy differences between the results based on original maturity and those in terms of remaining maturity at all (see Figure 6.47).

As a consequence, there are hardly any noteworthy differences with respect to the surpluses of long-term assets and of short-term liabilities either (see Figure 6.48). Note that these analyses were introduced in order to magnify differences. And indeed, they uncover some differences in levels. Concerning the surpluses of long-term assets, Landesbanks, cooperative central institutions and regional banks are now closer together in recent years. And concerning the surpluses of short-term liabilities, Landesbanks are now clearly above cooperative central institutions in recent years while large banks are closer to Landesbanks than to regional banks.

Across all types of banks in Germany, the developments of the shares of loans with a remaining maturity of more than five years are very similar to those of loans with the same original maturity (see Figure 6.49).

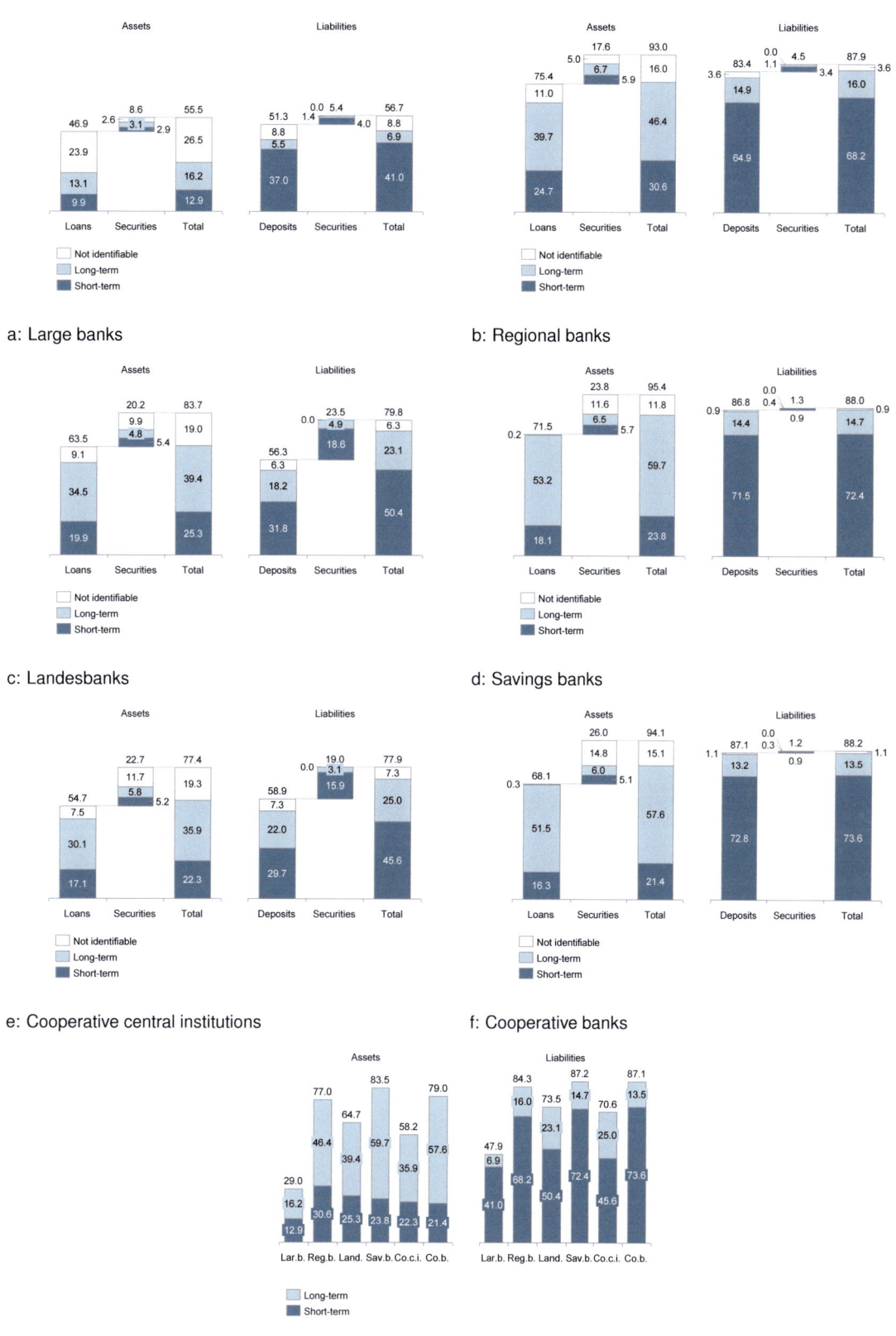

Figure 6.46: Long-term and short-term assets and liabilities in terms of remaining maturity of (a) large banks, (b) regional banks, (c) Landesbanks, (d) savings banks, (e) cooperative central institutions, and (f) cooperative banks in Germany, plus (g) comparison, in percent of total assets (December 2014). Source: BBK, banking statistics (Statistical Supplement 1); own calculations.

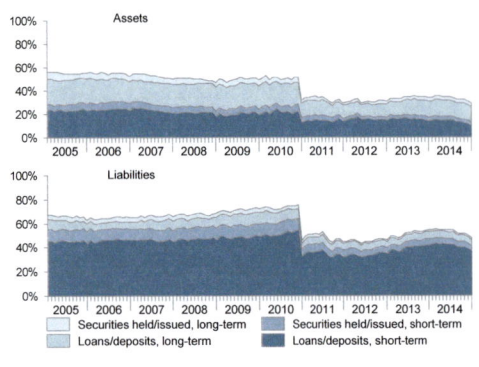

a: Large banks

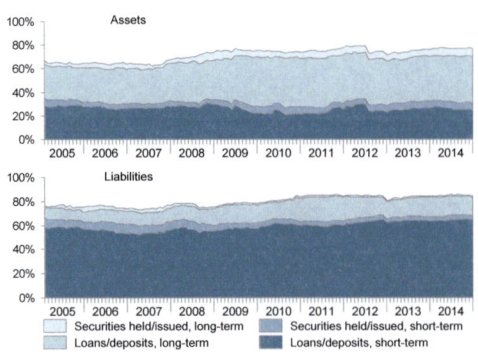

b: Regional banks

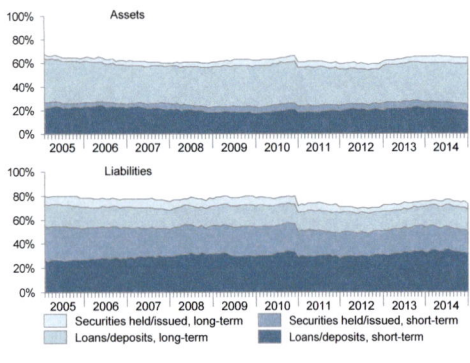

c: Landesbanks

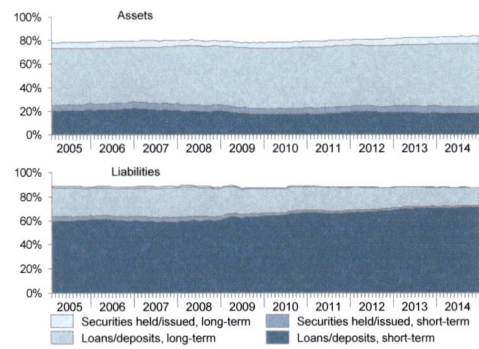

d: Savings banks

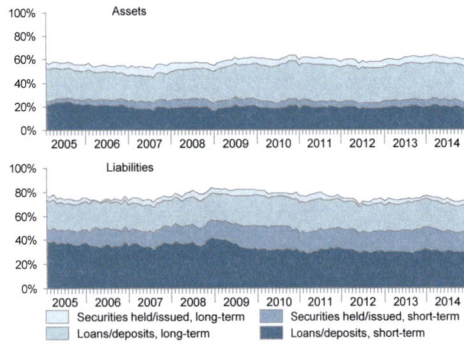

e: Cooperative central institutions

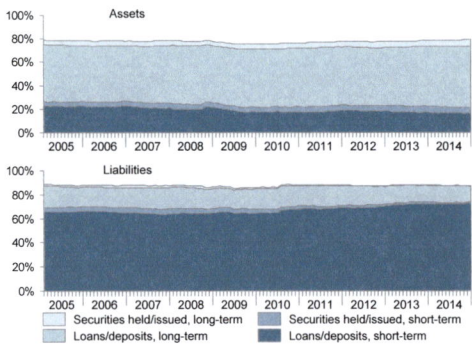

f: Cooperative banks

Figure 6.47: Development of long-term and short-term assets and liabilities in terms of remaining maturity of (a) large banks, (b) regional banks, (c) Landesbanks, (d) savings banks, (e) cooperative central institutions, and (f) cooperative banks in Germany, in percent of total assets (January 2005 to December 2014). Source: BBK, banking statistics (Statistical Supplement 1); own calculations.

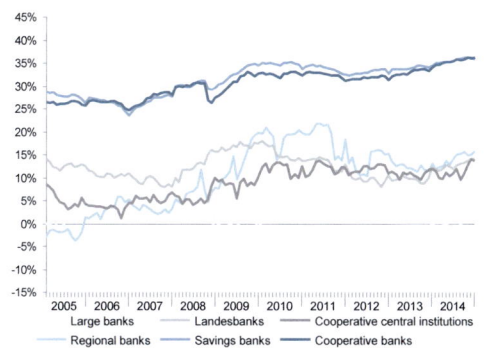

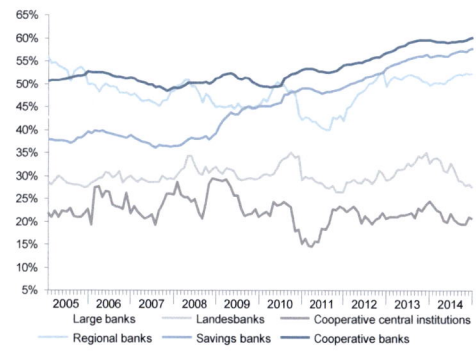

a: Surplus of long-term assets   b: Surplus of short-term liabilities

Figure 6.48: Development of the surplus of (a) long-term assets (b) short-term liabilities in terms of remaining maturity of types of banks in Germany, in percent of total assets (January 2005 to December 2014). Source: BBK, banking statistics (Statistical Supplement 1); own calculations.

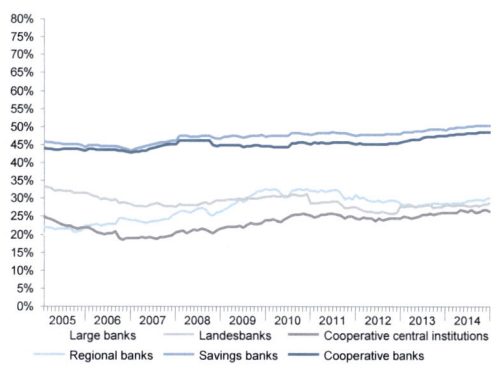

Loans

Figure 6.49: Development of loans with more than 5 years maturity in terms of remaining maturity of types of banks in Germany, in percent of total assets (January 2005 to December 2014). Source: BBK, banking statistics (Statistical Supplement 1); own calculations.

Chapter 7 Supervisory interest rate shock scenarios in Germany: an empirical assessment of adequacy

7.1 Abstract

The Basel interest rate coefficient is a measure of exposure not risk. It quantifies the impact that a certain interest rate change would have, if it occurred. But it does not account for the probability that this interest rate change does indeed occur. The distinction between a measure of exposure and a measure of risk is clear in theory. It is common practice, however, to rely on the Basel interest rate coefficient as the standard yardstick for interest rate risk in the banking book not for exposure. Most prominently, the Deutsche Bundesbank appears to do so. Potential consequences include the misallocation of the scarce resource of supervisory attention as well as wrong hedging incentives for banks and hence the endangerment of financial stability in Germany. The present chapter addresses this threat through a detailed assessment of the interest rate shock scenarios on which the Basel interest rate coefficient has been and currently is based as well as of those scenarios defined by the BCBS (2016) for the future supervisory measurement of banks' banking book exposure to interest rate changes.

7.2 Introduction

The Basel interest rate coefficient does not measure interest rate risk in banks' banking books. Instead, it measures banks' banking book exposure to specific interest rate changes. This difference is important. As a measure of exposure the Basel interest rate coefficient quantifies the impact that a certain interest rate change would have, if it occurred. But it does not account for the probability that this interest rate change actually occurs and therefore it is no measure of interest rate risk.

Even though the distinction between an exposure measure and a risk measure is theoretically clear, this does not seem to be the case in practice. Just like in previous editions, in the 2015 edition of its financial stability review the Deutsche Bundesbank provides some information on the development of the Basel interest rate coefficients of German banks. In particular, it points to an increase of the average Basel coefficient as evidence for an increase of the interest rate risk in German banks' banking books. This way of using the Basel coefficient is commonplace. It is, however, potentially misleading because the probabilities of the materialization of the shock scenarios is not taken into account. Over time, an increase in the potential impact of a particular shock scenario may be seen as indicating an increase in interest rate risk. However, there may be an accompanying decrease of the probability of the materialization of the scenario in question such that the probability weighted impact actually decreases. And also across banks, a comparison based solely on scenario impacts may be misleading, provided more than one shock scenario is considered. Because the probabilities of the different scenarios may differ sufficiently to change the results given the rule of aggregation applied. The latter point is particularly relevant in face of any supervisory threshold values based on the Basel coefficient or its successor above which banks are classified as "outlier banks" or as "banks with elevated interest rate risk". Note that the designation "banks with elevated interest rate risk" is another indicator that supervisors indeed treat the Basel interest rate coefficient as a measure of interest rate risk and not only of exposure. This designation can be found in the official regulations currently in force in Germany which are introduced below.

Even though one would expect that these deficits of a mere exposure measure are rather obvious, in 2016 the Basel Committee on Banking Supervision (BCBS) published new standards for the future regulatory treatment of interest rate risk in the banking book which include new disclosure requirements of the same kind. The new information to be disclosed is a measure of the potential impact certain shock scenarios of interest rate changes would have, if they materialized. Again, the calculations do not account for the probability of the materialization of these scenarios and hence the measure is a measure of exposure and not of risk. In this important respect, the new proposal is no improvement over the Basel interest rate coefficient already in use.

Supervisory attention is a scarce resource and therefore its allocation matters. For this reason it is important to have a undistorted view on the interest rate risk of banks. What is more, relying on inadequate shock scenarios in the supervision of banks' interest rate risk may even lead to an increase of this risk. Because banks have incentives to design their hedging strategies such that they perform optimally under the scenarios. And if these scenarios are inadequate, these hedging strategies may also be inadequate to produce the optimal level of interest rate risk.

In what follows a set of analyses is conducted in order to shed light on the adequacy of the interest rate shock scenarios used historically, currently in use, and to be used in the future in Germany. The shock scenarios are contrasted with the historic development of the term structure in Germany as well as with forecasts of this development. Coming from the other side, the scenarios are evaluated based on their impacts on next year's net interest income of German banks as well as on their current portfolio values.

The Basel interest rate coefficient only measures the impact on the net present value of a bank's banking book. The BCBS (2016) requires not only to measure the impact in terms of some net present value but also to measure the impact on next year's net interest income generated from a bank's banking book.[161] The advantages of this new impact measurement are obvious. Instruments in the banking book are generally not intended to be traded but to be held until maturity. But present value losses resulting from a mere change of interest rates used for discounting future cash flows quantify losses that would only be realized, if the instruments were traded. If the instruments are not traded, however, present value losses quantify opportunity costs only and no actual losses. In contrast, reductions in next year's net interest income may indeed result in actual losses, provided the reductions are large enough.

In what follows, the empirical adequacy of three interest rate shock regimes in Germany is assessed. The first regime lasted from November 2007 to October 2011. The second regime was implemented in November 2011 and is still in force. The third regime is going to replace the second regime in January 2018. The assumption is made that the third regime is going to look exactly like prescribed by the BCBS (2016). In the assessment of empirical adequacy of the shock scenarios close attention is paid to their calibration. Because one important question is what size of shock is adequate and whether the relative sizes of the shocks are adequate. This directly raises the question whether symmetric shocks are adequate. And as quickly becomes apparent, the questions what types of shock scenarios are adequate also rises naturally. These are the main questions addressed in what follows.

7.3   Past and current exposure measures in Germany

Supervisory interest rate shock scenarios for the banking book were introduced in Germany in November 2007 and revised in November 2011. In the first subsection these scenarios are introduced. On top, how they were calibrated is traced and commented on. In the second

---

[161] The new standards defined by the BCBS (2016) include a revision of the threshold beyond which a bank is regarded as an "outlier bank". The components of this revision and their quantitative effects are presented in Appendix 3.

subsection these scenarios are compared to historic term structure changes. For this purpose, a new method is developed.

7.3.1   Past and current shock scenarios

In Germany, the supervisor standardly quantifies banks' interest rate risk in the banking book with the Basel interest rate coefficient. Currently, the Bundesanstalt für Finanzdienstleistungsaufsicht (BaFin) defines the shock scenarios that feature in its calculation as parallel shifts of the term structure upward and downward by 200 basis points. These adjusted scenarios are the result of an international harmonization effort and are in place in Germany since November 2011. Before that, the scenarios in place in Germany were a parallel upward shift by 130 basis points and a parallel downward shift by 190 basis points. These original scenarios had been implemented in November 2007.[162]

The original scenarios were based on the past development of domestic interest rates. They were derived as follows (see BaFin (2007)). The reference point was the current yield of listed Federal Government securities with a remaining maturity of more than three and up to five years. In a first step, the one year interest rate change was calculated as the difference between the current yield today minus the current yield 240 trading days earlier. And in a second step, the 99th and 1st percentiles of these interest rate changes were identified considering a rolling five-year window. In November 2007 the 99th percentile stood at 129 basis points and the 1st percentile at minus 189 to minus 186 basis points. From these values, it only takes minor rounding to get to the 130 and 190 basis points as the sizes for the parallel shifts of the term structure upward and downward, respectively, and hence to the original scenarios.

These original scenarios were meant to be dynamic. It was planned to review them on an annual basis. And it was intended to adjust the sizes of the parallel shifts, if the relevant percentiles had changed by a notable amount. In fact, no adjustments were made until November 2011 when the original scenarios were replaced by the internationally harmonized scenarios (see BaFin (2011)). Already back in 2001 the BCBS had proposed parallel shifts of the term structure upward and downward by 200 basis points as an internationally harmonized alternative to scenarios based on the development of domestic interest rates only (see BCBS (2001))[163]. More precisely, the 200 basis points upward and downward had been introduced as roughly corresponding to the 99th and 1st percentile of the one year interest rate changes considering a rolling five-year window across major currencies. And still before the BaFin announced the original scenarios for Germany, the Committee of European Banking Supervisors (CEBS) had given the guidance to national supervisors to take the 200 basis points upward and downward as the starting point for the definition of their domestic scenarios (see CEBS (2006)). This means that when these internationally harmonized scenarios were finally adopted in Germany in 2011, they already had been around for a while.

In the present context, it is most important to note that in adopting the internationally harmonized scenarios, the direct link to the development of interest rates was broken.[164] Adopting the internationally harmonized scenarios was not simply a change of the starting point. It would, of course, have been possible to define an international basket of securities of certain maturities and to proceed from there as done by the BaFin for the calculation of its original scenarios or in a similarly transparent way. However, nothing like this was done. Instead the 200 basis

---

[162] For Germany the supervisory requirements are set out in two circulars by the BaFin, namely BaFin (2007) and BaFin (2011).

[163] The final version to this consultative document is BCBS (2004).

[164] One might also say that the direct link had practically been broken before when original scenarios were not adjusted as planned. With the introduction of the internationally harmonized scenarios the direct link was then also broken formally.

points upward and downward were established without deducing them precisely. What is more, these scenarios were explicitly defined as static or constant over time, independent of the future development of interest rates. The Deutsche Bundesbank (BBK) even highlighted the increased planning security that comes with static scenarios as a major benefit for banks (see BBK (2012b)).

Figure 7.1 shows the development of the one year interest rate change for Germany on which the BaFin had based its calculation of the original scenarios. The figure also features the relevant percentiles for the calculation of the original scenarios as well as the original scenarios. Furthermore, the figure includes the adjusted scenarios after the international harmonization. It is striking to see just how closely the original scenarios linked in with the relevant percentiles at the time of implementation. It is also obvious that an adjustment of the size of the parallel downward shift was in order since 2009. But three further observations are also important in the present context. First, at the time of adjustment, i.e. when the internationally harmonized scenarios were introduced and when the parallel upward shift was increased from 130 to 200 basis points, the originally relevant 99th percentile had just moved in the opposite direction, namely decreased from 129 to 116 basis points. Second, back in 2001 this 99th percentile had stood at 183 basis points and hence not much below the 200 basis points then initially proposed by the BCBS (2001). Third, considering the longer-term development of the 99th percentile overall, it appears to be following a downward trend.

Focussing on Germany, it makes sense to pay particular attention to the upward shift of the term structure for the following reason. The vast majority of German banks conduct positive term transformation in their banking books, also referred to as borrowing short and lending long.[165] Indeed, for almost all banks the parallel upward shift is the (more) adverse scenario, the effect of which on the present value of the bank's banking book therefore features as the numerator in the bank's Basel interest rate coefficient.[166]

The observations just made on the basis of Figure 7.1 suggest two interrelated conclusions. First, the internationally harmonized scenario for an upward shift of the term structure appears to have been out-of-date already when it was implemented in Germany. Second, the underlying reason for this appears to be that the increases of the interest rate considered here are subject to a long-term downward trend.[167]

7.3.2 Adequacy in light of historic term structure changes

What is most striking about the calibration of the interest rate shock scenarios for the Basel interest rate coefficient is that it was based on the development of one interest rate only. As presented above, the BaFin (2007) based its calibration of the original scenarios on the current yield of listed Federal Government securities with a remaining maturity of more than three and up to five years, that is on one specific average interest rate. And in doing so, the BaFin applied the principles that had been laid down by the BCBS (2004) and which were applied again when the internationally harmonized scenarios were calibrated. However, the shock scenarios in question are not changes of any single interest rate but changes of the entire term structure, namely parallel shifts. And changes of the entire term structure can be characterized and quantified in a substantially more informative way with reference to at least two instead of only one interest

---

[165] Chapter 6 produced a substantial amount of statistical evidence of this.

[166] More precisely, Memmel et al. (2016) find that this is the case for about 95% of their observations of German banks. At issue here are the parallel shocks up and down by 200 basis points.

[167] Of course, using a different procedure it might be possible to reach different conclusions. It might be possible to find some international basket of securities of a certain maturity range and some way of calculating a reference value from the development of the associated interest rate such that an upward shift by 200 basis points still appears as a natural scenario. And it might also even be possible to find some upward changes of certain interest rates which have not become smaller over the last decades. However, no effort of this sort was made by supervisors.

rate, that is with reference to two points on the term structure at different maturities instead of only one.

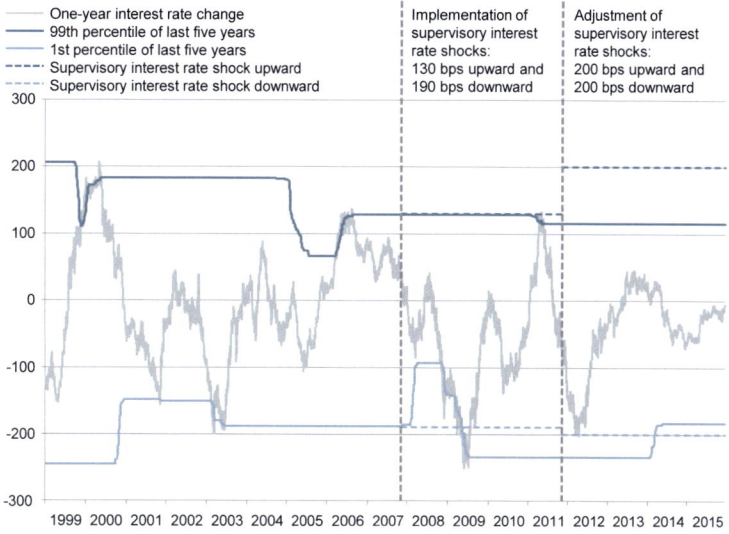

Figure 7.1: Scenarios featured in the calculation of the Basel interest rate coefficient in Germany put in context, i.e. development of the one year change of the current yield of listed Federal Government securities with a remaining maturity of more than three and up to five years, and the relevant percentiles for the calculation of the original scenarios as well as the original scenarios and the adjusted scenarios after the international harmonization. Source: BBK, interest rate data; own calculations.

Introduction to method for two-maturities-assessment

For two interest rates from two points on the term structure at different maturities, the possible changes of these interest rates span a plane. Each point on this plane represents one pair of possible changes of the two interest rates in question.[168] With reference to two interest rates, the most precise characterization of a parallel shift of the term structure is that both interest rates change by the same absolute amount. On the plane, the set of pairs of changes of this type corresponds to the bisecting line of quadrants one and three.[169] However, for the characterization and quantification of actual term structure changes it is reasonable to introduce some tolerance. The tolerance level determines how large the differences between the absolute changes of the two interest rates at a shorter and a longer maturity are allowed to be such that the change of the term structure still counts as a parallel shift. One way to define the tolerance level is in terms of deviation from the average change. Only if the two absolute changes of the interest rates in question are within plus or minus a certain fraction of the average absolute change, the term structure change counts as a parallel shift.[170] The natural lower and upper limit of the tolerance level are 0% and 100%, respectively. This way to define the tolerance level is illustrated in Figure 7.2. On the plane, the tolerance area consists of two wedges that meet in the origin, are symmetric to the bisecting line of quadrants one and three, and are the wider the higher the tolerance level is. Note that at a tolerance level of 100% the two wedges cover the quadrants one

---

[168] More precisely, the relationship between the pairs of possible changes of the interest rates on the one hand and the points on that plane on the other hand is bijective. This means that each pair of possible changes is represented by exactly one point on the plane and each point on the plane represents exactly one pair of possible changes.

[169] As it is common practice, quadrants are counted clockwise starting from the upper right.

[170] Note that by construction, the smaller absolute change is always the same fraction of the average change lower than that average that the larger absolute change is larger.

and three completely.[171] Last but not least, note that the natural way to quantify the size of a parallel shift is to take the average of the absolute changes of the two interest rates referred to.

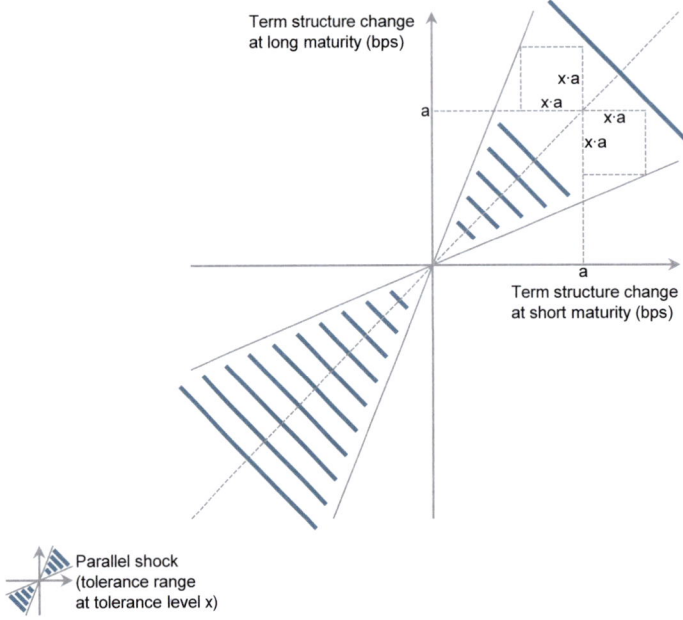

Figure 7.2: The parallel shock tolerance range at tolerance level x is delimited by two straight lines that can be derived from the bisectrix of quadrants one and three with the help of two unit squares with side length equal to x times a at a. Source: own illustration.

First two-maturities-assessment of past and current scenarios

The following assessment refers to the two interest rates from the two points on the term structure at one year and at 10 years maturity. The assessment is based on end-of-month data for the German term structure calculated by the BBK from listed Federal securities.[172] This monthly data goes back to September 1972.[173] And the assessment focusses on changes over 12 months.[174] Taking into account data till December 2015, 508 overlapping changes of the term structure are identified. The absolute changes of the interest rates at one year and at ten years maturity are depicted in Figure 7.3. Before jumping to conclusions about parallel shifts, note that the scales on the two axes differ. One observation can be made right away. There are term structure changes in every quadrant but the majority is in quadrants one and three, meaning that most of the time the interest rates at one year and at ten years maturity have moved in the same direction. In numerical terms, 75% of the term structure changes are of this type. Furthermore, it appears as if the term structure changes were becoming smaller in the course of time. However, as the dimension of time is only depicted in a rather rough way, further checks are in order before endorsing this statement.

---

[171] This is the reason why 100% is the natural upper limit for the tolerance level. Because points in quadrants two and four represent pairs of changes of interest rates in different directions.

[172] Alternatively, you may, for example, use daily data, use a different curve-fitting technique than the standard method introduced by Svensson (1994) building on Nelson and Siegel (1987), and use the interest rates of Pfandbriefe as your primary input.

[173] The corresponding daily data goes back only to the 7th of August 1997.

[174] This corresponds to a one year change given monthly data just like the change over 240 trading days given daily data referred to by the BaFin (2007).

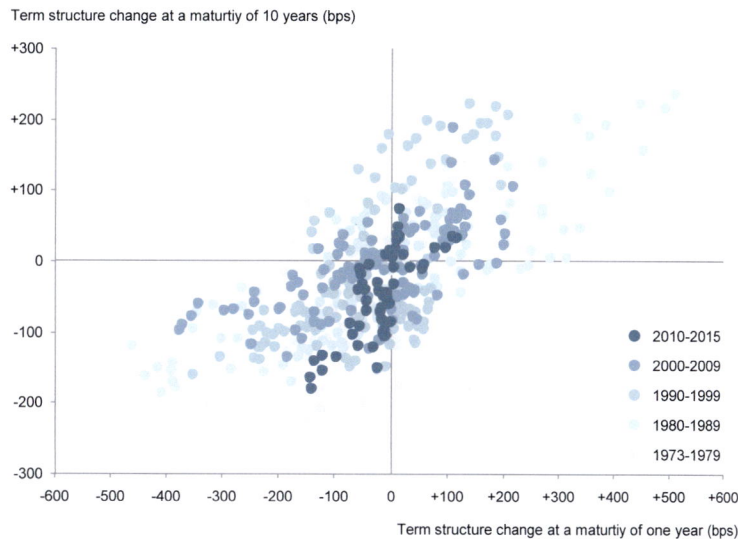

Figure 7.3: Distribution of term structure changes at maturities of one year and 10 years over the last 12 months on a monthly basis between end of September 1973 and end of December 2015. Source: BBK, interest rate data; own calculations.

According to the tolerance introduced above, any of the term structure changes where the interest rates at one year and at ten years maturity move in the same direction may be identified as a parallel shift. Indeed, at a tolerance level of 100% the entire 75% referred to above qualify. This triggers the key question which tolerance level is the appropriate one. What different tolerance levels imply in the actual case at hand is depicted in Figure 7.4. Remember, that here the size of the parallel shift is quantified by the average of the absolute changes of the two interest rates in question. As was to be expected given the distribution of the actual changes of the two interest rates in question, the number of parallel shifts identified increases, if the tolerance level is increased from 5% to 10% to 20% to 50% and finally to 100%. But what is more, the maximum absolute sizes of the parallel shifts up and down identified as such also increase, even if not in every subperiod, at every increase of the tolerance level. In particular, more parallel shifts up and down are identified with absolute sizes of 200 basis points or more.

Of particular interest are the time periods before the German regulator imposed the original scenarios (BaFin (2007)) and then later the internationally harmonized scenarios (BaFin (2011)). As five years has commonly been regarded as the length of an interest-rate-cycle (see for example CEBS (2006) and BaFin (2007)), the length of the periods under investigation is set to five years to begin with. More precisely, the periods from November 2002 to October 2007 and from November 2006 to October 2011 are looked at. Because these periods cover the five years just before the imposition of the original scenarios in November 2007 and of the internationally harmonized scenarios in November 2011 in Germany. Note that these two periods overlap.

Two analyses are undertaken, both for parallel shifts up and down. The first analysis investigates the relationship between the tolerance level and the maximum size of a parallel shift of the respective type identified in the five-year-periods under scrutiny. The second analysis drops the limitation of a certain length of the time period considered and instead investigates the relationship between the tolerance level and the number of months that you have to go back to find an actual parallel shift up or down of at least the size the regulator then imposes. Note that for the second analysis different threshold values for the size are relevant. When looking at the months before the imposition of the original scenarios the relevant threshold values are 130 basis points for parallel shifts up and 190 basis points for parallel shifts down. And when looking at the months before the imposition of the internationally harmonized scenarios the treshold value is 200 basis points for both parallel shifts up and down.

The results of both analyses are displayed in Figure 7.5. Parallel shifts up of the sizes imposed by the regulator cannot be identified in any of the two five-year periods (see Figure 7.5a). In the five years before the introduction of the original scenarios the largest identifiable parallel shift up amounts only to 116.5 basis points. This is markedly less than the 130 basis points that the regulator then imposed. Yet, the largest parallel shift up that can be identified in the five years before the introduction of the internationally harmonized scenarios is even further below the relevant regulatory value of 200 basis points. It amounts to 89.5 basis points and hence to not even half the size featured in the respective regulatory scenario. Concerning parallel shifts down, only in the five years prior to the imposition of the internationally harmonized scenarios a parallel downward shift can be identified that is at least as large as in the respective regulatory scenario (see Figure 7.5b). The tolerance level necessary is very high, though. More specifically, at a tolerance level of at least 58.6% a parallel shift down of 237 basis points is recorded for June 2009 which is above the 200 basis points featured in the regulatory scenario. The largest parallel shift down that can be identified in the five years prior to the introduction of the original scenarios, however, measures only 160.5 basis points, substantially less than the regulatory 190 basis points. Starting from the month in

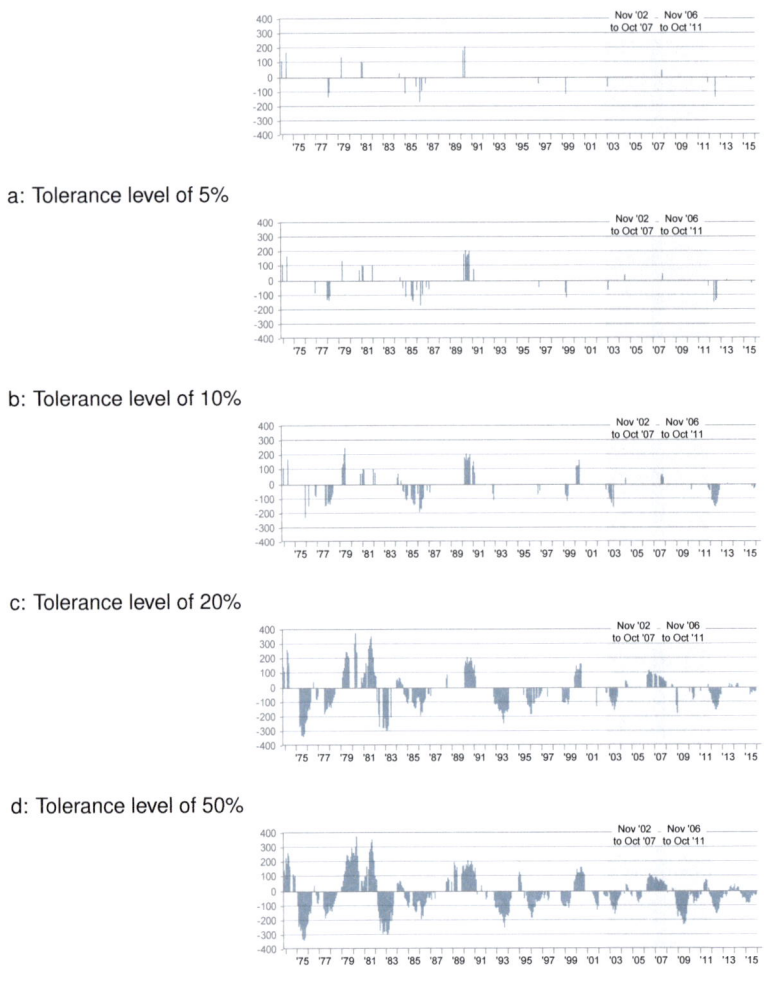

a: Tolerance level of 5%

b: Tolerance level of 10%

c: Tolerance level of 20%

d: Tolerance level of 50%

e: Tolerance level of 100%

Figure 7.4: Parallel shocks over time at a tolerance level of (a) 5%, (b) 10%, (c) 20%, (d) 50%, and (e) 100% with highlighted five-year periods before the introduction of the original and of the internationally harmonized scenarios. Source: BBK, interest rate data; own calculations.

which the original scenarios were imposed (November 2007), it is necessary to go back at least 90 months (seven and a half years) to find an actual parallel shift up of at least 130 basis points and at least 142 months (close to 12 years) for an actual parallel shift down of at least 190 basis points. And starting from the month in which the internationally harmonized scenarios were imposed (November 2011), you even need to go back at least 255 months (21 years and a quarter) to find a parallel shift up of at least 200 basis points (see Figure 7.5c). At least the closest identifiable parallel shift down of at least 200 basis points occurs only 27 months before the imposition of the respective regulatory scenario (see Figure 7.5d).

These findings support the hypothesis that the internationally harmonized scenario for an upward shift of the term structure was out-of-date already when it was implemented in Germany in November 2011. Furthermore, it seems as if while the original scenarios were calibrated with a similar extra buffer, the internationally harmonized scenarios came with very different buffers for Germany. More precisely, the new size of the parallel shock up would have had to be much smaller or that of the parallel shock down much larger for the two sizes to stand in a similar quantitative relationship to the historic development of interest rates in Germany.

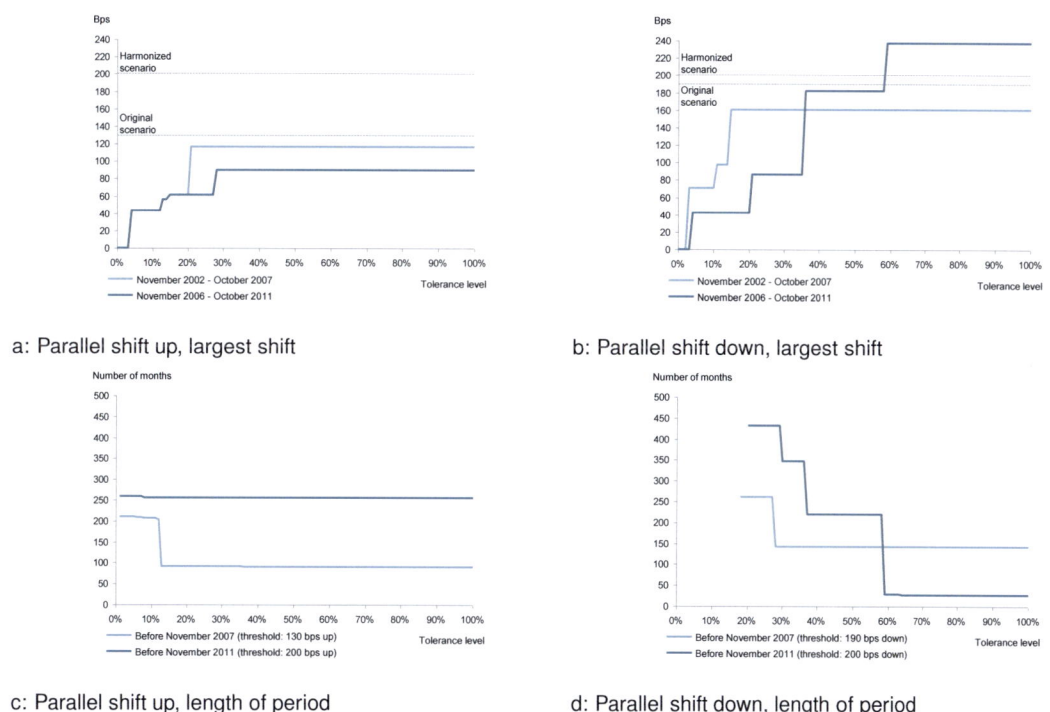

a: Parallel shift up, largest shift

b: Parallel shift down, largest shift

c: Parallel shift up, length of period

d: Parallel shift down, length of period

Figure 7.5: Relationship of the tolerance level to (a and b) the size of the largest parallel shift up and down within the five year periods prior to the imposition of the original scenarios, and (c and d) to the number of months one has to go back to find a parallel shift up or down of the size then imposed by the regulator. Source: BBK, interest rate data; own calculations.

As the previous analyses have shown, some general findings are independent of the particular tolerance level chosen.[175] However, it is also obvious that the tolerance level is a key input parameter for the assessment of the interest rate shock scenarios imposed by the regulator. This is why next an attempt is made to identify one specific tolerance level as particularly appropriate. This challenge is addressed as follows. To begin with, a specific tolerance level is highlighted as a very promising candidate. Thereafter, it is shown that this tolerance level is very close to the one implicitly brought forward by the BCBS (2016).

---

[175] For example, in the five years prior to the introduction of the internationally harmonized scenarios in November 2011 there was not a single parallel upward shift of the size then imposed by the regulator. As can be seen in Figure 7.5a this finding is independent of the tolerance level chosen.

Appropriate tolerance level

The question, what the most appropriate tolerance level is, can in principle be addressed in at least two ways. On the one hand, one might understand it as an empirical question regarding what people, possibly with a certain professional background, would still accept to be a parallel shift. On the other hand, one might understand it as a theoretical question regarding what a workable and attractive delimitation would be. Here, the question is understood in the second way.

Answering this question comes down to determining how large the difference between the absolute changes of the interest rates from the term structure at one year and at ten years maturity is allowed to be, such that the overall term structure change can still sensibly be regarded as a parallel shift rather than as some other type of change. Now, the multiple m, by which the larger absolute change may be larger than the smaller one is a simple function of the tolerance level l:

$$m = \frac{1 + l}{1 - l} \tag{7.1}$$

Note that this function is, of course, not defined for $l = 100\%$. At this extreme tolerance level the smaller absolute change may be zero while the larger one takes any value. A simple plot of this function is helpful (see Figure 7.6). As a multiple of one is obviously too strict, one is inclined to look at the next integer values, namely multiples of two and three. These correspond to tolerance levels of 33.3% and 50% respectively. And as the more conservative choice, 33.3% turns out to be a very promising candidate for the particularly appropriate tolerance level searched for.

Until now, the candidate tolerance level of 33.3% has only been identified. No explicit reason was given to actually select it. Implicitly, Ockham's razor was applied in opting for an integer multiple. But more persuasive efforts are required. To this end, a delimitation of two adjacent shock scenarios brought forward by the BCBS (2016) is anticipated next. Later, these new scenarios are addressed in much greater detail when the adequacy of their sizes is scrutinized in several analyses.

As is presented below, the BCBS (2016) defines six shock scenarios. Besides parallel shocks up and down, it defines short rates shocks up and down as well as a steepener shock and a flattener shock. The short rates shocks are characterized by larger changes of the shorter term rates accompanied by smaller changes of the longer term rates in the same direction. Hence, the short rates shocks up and down are adjacent to the parallel shocks up and down, respectively, as is illustrated in Figure 7.7.[176] And indeed, the definitions for parallel shocks and for short rates shocks brought forward by the BCBS (2016) in the format of formulas allow to identify an implicit tolerance level. For the identification of this implicit tolerance level all that is additionally required is a measure for the goodness of fit.[177] If the sum of squared residuals is selected as a measure, the implicit tolerance level turns out to be about 35.4% (for a detailed derivation of this result see Appendix 1). It should be noted that this tolerance level is sensitive to the maturities considered, which are one year and 10 years in the analysis at hand. Given these maturities and for our analysis of the candidate tolerance levels identified earlier, this implicit tolerance level is much closer to the promising candidate of 33.3%. hence, this finding strongly suggests to use

---

[176] The fact that these two types of shocks are adjacent in the sense depicted is the reason why short rates shocks are relevant for the determination of the implicit tolerance level and the steepener and flattener shocks are not. Note that the characterizing feature of the the steepener and flattener shocks is that short-term and long-term interest rates move in opposite directions. Just like the short rates shocks, the steepener and the flattener shocks are analyzed in much greater detail later.

[177] Given a measure for the goodness of fit, for any pair of changes of the short-term and the long-term interest rate it can be determined whether it can best be described as a short rates shock or as a parallel shock as formalized by the BCBS (2016). Thus, the set of limiting cases can be identified. And as is shown in the appendix, this set corresponds to a certain tolerance level.

this tolerance level going forward. And as will additionally be shown later, this tolerance level also leads to particularly similar shares of shocks up and shocks down being identified as parallel shocks up and down, respectively.

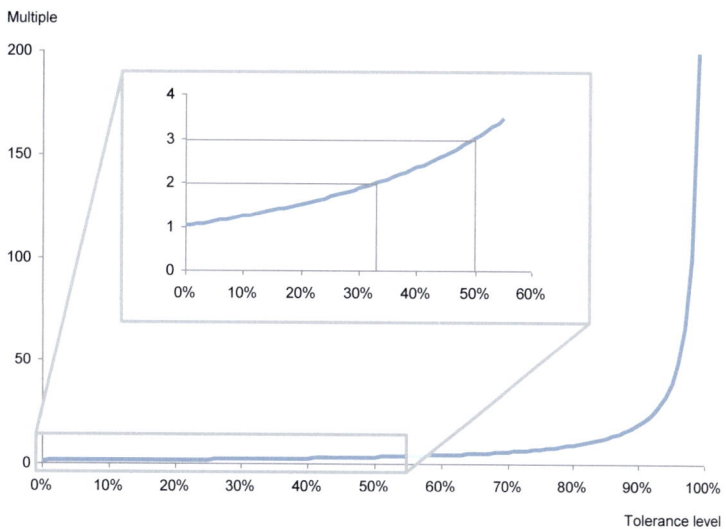

Figure 7.6: The maximum multiple between the smaller and the larger absolute change as a function of the tolerance level. Source: own illustration.

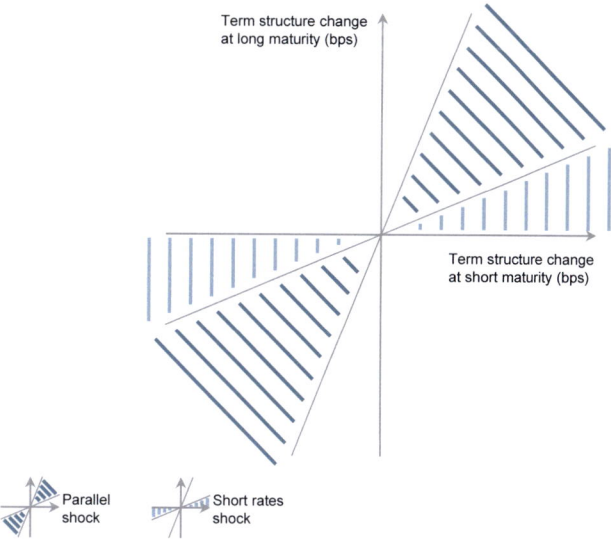

Figure 7.7: The delimitation of the adjacent parallel and short rates shocks define the tolerance level unambiguously because it is symmetric per definition. Source: own illustration.

Second two-maturities-assessment of past and current scenarios

The analysis of the parallel shocks up and down with a tolerance level of 33.3.%, again assuming a five year interest rate cycle (see again CEBS (2006) and BaFin (2007)), and tracking the largest shocks over the length of the cycle, produces three main findings (see Figure 7.8a).[178] First,

---

[178] Note that in the derivation of the sizes of the shocks undertaken by the regulator which was detailed above, not the largest shocks but the 99th and the 1st percentile are tracked over the length of the cycle, i.e. a five-year rolling

153

there appears to be a long-term trend toward smaller parallel shocks both up and down. Second, for recent years much more pronounced parallel shocks down than up can be observed. Third and consequently, while the original supervisory scenarios for parallel shocks up and down in Germany already featured notably larger shifts than indicated by the actual development of the term structure, the internationally harmonized scenarios were substantially further off at the time they were introduced. And most recently, the scenario for a parallel shock up appears to be particularly out of step with the actual developments. Note that all but one of these observations can also be made at a tolerance level of 100% (see Figure 7.8b). The only material difference is that at a tolerance level of 100% the internationally harmonized scenario for a parallel shock down does not feature a larger but a smaller shift than indicated by the actual term structure when introduced. However, as mentioned above, for most German banks the scenario of a parallel shock up is the (more) harmful and hence the relevant one.

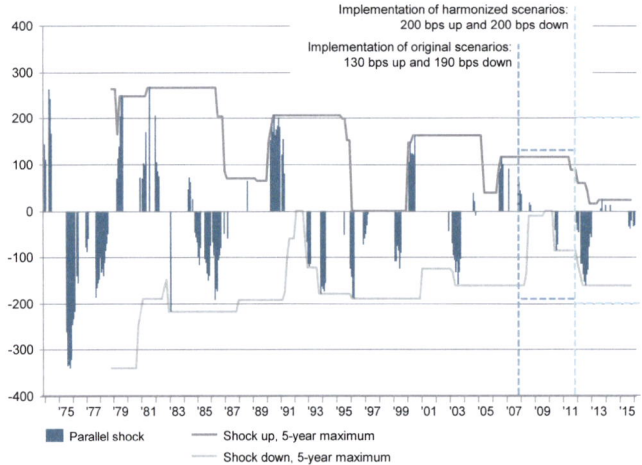

a: Tolerance level of 33.3%

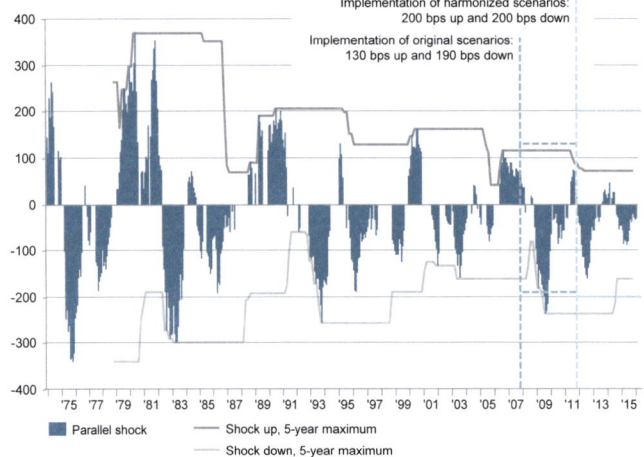

b: Tolerance level of 100%

Figure 7.8: The development of parallel shocks at a tolerance level of (a) 33.3% and (b) 100% plus the relevant supervisory scenarios for Germany. Source: BBK, interest rate data; own calculations.

---

window. Here the extreme values are referred to instead because the focus on monthly data already reduces the number of observations compared to when daily data is used by about 95%. And even though end-of-month data is used here and not averages, this can sensibly be expected to smooth the development.

To sum up, in the light of the historical development of interest rates in Germany, the original scenarios defined by the German supervisor appear to have been rather risk-averse already, that is calibrated with a buffer on top of the historically observable maximum changes of interest rates. The discrepancy between actual interest rate changes and the internationally harmonized scenarios is, however more dramatic. The new size for the parallel shock up is much larger than what can be observed in the five, 10, and even 15 years prior to it being enforced independent of the tolerance level. In contrast, the new size of the parallel shock down is smaller than the maximum during the last 10 years at least at a tolerance level of 100% and already much closer to it at a tolerance level of 33.3%. However, the scenario of a parallel shock up is particularly relevant for German banks as the large majority engages in positive term transformation in the banking book. Hence, the most important finding is that the more relevant scenario has a size much above what the historic development of interest rates suggests. There is a buffer much larger than the one the historic scenarios come with.

7.4 Future exposure measure in Germany

In April 2016 the BCBS (2016) published a new regulatory standards for the future regulatory treatment of banks' interest rate risk in the banking book. These regulatory standards feature six shock scenarios for a term structure change, besides parallel shocks up and down also short rates shocks up and down as well as a steepener and a flattener shock.[179] These shock scenarios are investigated next.

7.4.1 Future shock scenarios

The BCBS's new standards for the future regulatory treatment of banks' interest rate risk in the banking book feature six shock scenarios for a term structure change. Two parallel shocks shift the term structure up and down, respectively, by the same number of basis points at every maturity. Two short rates shocks also shift the term structure up and down, respectively, but the more so the shorter the maturity is. A steepener shock rotates the term structure counterclockwise by decreasing interest rates for shorter maturities and increasing them for longer maturities. And conversely, a flattener shock rotates the term structure clockwise by increasing interest rates for shorter maturities and decreasing them for longer ones.

The formulas that define these six scenarios all produce absolute changes independent of the current level of the relevant interest rates. But these formulas include parameters which are currency specific and the values of which are based on historic averages of the respective reference interest rates.[180] To arrive at the currency-specific parameter values, each currency-specific average reference interest rate is first multiplied with each of three uniform factors to produce provisional values for the parallel, the short, and the long parameter. From these provisional values the final values of each currency-specific parameter-triple are then derived by applying certain caps and floors plus some rounding, or essentially some expert judgement. For the euro the resulting parameters values are 200 basis points (parallel), 250 basis points (short), and 100 basis points (long). The BCBS (2016) allows supervisors to set non-positive floors for the interest rates that result from running the shock scenarios.

---

[179] The preceding consultative document published in June 2015 by the BCBS (2015) had featured the option of introducing capital requirements based on these scenarios (Pillar 1). However, the BCBS (2016) eventually opted for more comprehensive supervision (Pillar 2) and publication requirements (Pillar 3), only. The BCBS (2016) pointed to the complexity and heterogeneity of the risk in question as reasons for its decision.

[180] More precisely, the historic averages are calculated from interest rates from the time period between 2000 and 2015 and across maturities from three months to 20 years. However, national regulators may deviate from this time period when conducting own calibrations (see BCBS (2016)).

The defining formulas for the parallel shock up (Formula (7.2)), the parallel shock down (Formula (7.3)), the short rates shock up (Formula (7.4)), the short rates shock down (Formula (7.5)), the steepener shock (Formula (7.6)), and the flattener shock (Formula (7.7)) feature the parallel ($\delta_{parallel}$), the short (δ_{short}), and the long parameter (δ_{long}) in the following ways, with t being the maturity in years (see BCBS (2016))[181]:

$$\Delta_{parallel\,up}(t) = \delta_{parallel} \tag{7.2}$$

$$\Delta_{parallel\,down}(t) = -\delta_{parallel} \tag{7.3}$$

$$\Delta_{short\,rates\,up}(t) = \delta_{short} \cdot e^{-\frac{t}{4}} \tag{7.4}$$

$$\Delta_{short\,rates\,down}(t) = -\delta_{short} \cdot e^{-\frac{t}{4}} \tag{7.5}$$

$$\Delta_{steepener}(t) = (-0.65) \cdot |\delta_{short} \cdot e^{-\frac{t}{4}}| + (0.9) \cdot |\delta_{long} \cdot (1 - e^{-\frac{t}{4}})| \tag{7.6}$$

$$\Delta_{flattener}(t) = (0.8) \cdot |\delta_{short} \cdot e^{-\frac{t}{4}}| + (-0.6) \cdot |\delta_{long} \cdot (1 - e^{-\frac{t}{4}})| \tag{7.7}$$

One peculiarity about this set of formulas is particularly noteworthy. The parallel shocks up and down as well as the short rates shocks up and down are symmetric, but the steepener and the flattener shock are asymmetric. Another point is also striking. The steepener and the flattener shock are both weighted overlays of a short rates shock and a long rates shock, but in contrast to the former the latter is not also featured separately.

In order to get a better grasp of the formulas that define the shock scenarios for a term structure change, and in particular of how the parameter values affect the results, it helps to visualize the decay rates attached to δ_{short} and δ_{long}, namely $e^{-\frac{t}{4}}$ (decay short) and $1 - e^{-\frac{t}{4}}$ (decay long), respectively. Some example calculations are also helpful. Both the two visualized decay rates up to 10 years maturity, and two example calculations that show how the effect at a certain maturity of a short rates shock up and of a steepener shock depends on the relevant parameters, can be found in Figure 7.9.

In the following assessment, the focus will be on the parameters and on their specific values. The parameter $\delta_{parallel}$ features only in the formulas that define the parallel shocks up and down (Formulas 7.2 and 7.3). Its value corresponds directly to the number of basis points by which the term structure is shifted upward or downward, respectively, at every maturity.

The parameter δ_{short} features in the formulas that define the short rates shocks up and down (Formulas 7.4 and 7.5) as well as in the formulas that define the steepener and the flattener shock (formulas 7.6 and 7.7). In both sets of formulas it is multiplied with the decay rate which is referred to here as decay short. As can easily be calculated and also roughly be seen from the diagram in Figure 7.9 this decay rate takes the value of approximately 0.78 at a maturity of one

---

[181] Note that the BCBS (2016) states that $x = 4$ for the the decay rate $e^{-\frac{t}{x}}$ is the correct value for most currencies but permits that some national supervisors may select a different value for x.

year and of approximately 0.08 at a maturity of 10 years. A short rates shock up or down hence increases or respectively decreases the interest rates by about 78% of the value of the parameter δ_{short} at a maturity of one year and by about 8% of the value of the parameter δ_{short} at a maturity of 10 years. Hence, the shifts have the same sign but very different sizes. All of this is in basis points, of course.

In the formulas for the steepener and the flattener shock the parameter δ_{short} is further multiplied with specific weights, namely -0.65 and 0.8, respectively. Hence, at a maturity of one year the value of δ_{short} enters to about -51% ($= -0.65 \cdot 78\%$) and 62% ($= 0.8 \cdot 78\%$), respectively. And at a maturity of ten years it enters to about -5% ($= -0.65 \cdot 8\%$) and 7% ($= 0.8 \cdot 8\%$), respectively.[182] Along the same lines one finds for the value of δ_{long} that at a maturity of one year it enters to about 20% ($= 0.9 \cdot 22\%$) and -13% ($= -0.6 \cdot 22\%$), respectively. And at a maturity of ten years it enters to about 83% ($= 0.9 \cdot 92\%$) and -55% ($= -0.6 \cdot 92\%$), respectively. All this is again in basis points.

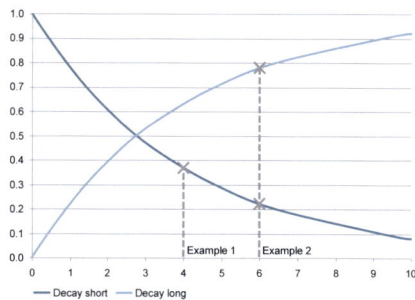

Example calculation 1: short rates shock up

At $t = 4$ we have $e^{-\frac{t}{4}} = 0.37$

Hence, $\Delta_{short\ rates\ up}(4) = \delta_{short} \cdot (0.37)$

Example calculation 2: steepener shock

At $t = 6$ we have $e^{-\frac{t}{4}} = 0.22$ and $(1 - e^{-\frac{t}{4}}) = 0.78$

Hence, $\Delta_{steepener}(6) = (-0.65) \cdot |\delta_{short} \cdot (0.22)|$
$$+ (0.9) \cdot |\delta_{long} \cdot (0.78)|$$
$$= |\delta_{short}| \cdot (-0.15) + |\delta_{long}| \cdot (0.7)$$

Figure 7.9: Decay rates attached to δ_{short} and δ_{long} by the BCBS (2016), referred to as decay short and decay long, with maturity on the horizontal axis plus example calculations for short rates shock up and steepener shock, rounded to two decimal places. Source: BCBS (2016); own calculations.

At every maturity the overall effect of a steepener or a flattener shock depends on the values of both parameters δ_{short} and δ_{long}. But at different levels of maturity the contributions of the two parameters differ. Further note that since these parameters enter with opposing signs into both formulas, their relative sizes determine at which maturities interest rates are shifted downward and at which they are shifted upward. Obviously, the higher the value of the parameter δ_{short} relative to the value of the parameter δ_{long} the higher is the maturity of the pivot points of the steepener and the flattener shock. Figure 7.10 presents the six shock scenarios with the officially prescribed parameter values for the euro zone and for German reference rates.[183] Last but not least, it is noteworthy that the BCBS (2016) plans to review the parameter values on a regular basis. The frequency envisaged is every five years. The planned review is explicitly limited to the parameter values and does not concern other parts of the shock scenarios such as the decay rates or existing or potential new weights. A new weight would for example be one way to erase the symmetry between the parallel shocks up and down.

---

[182] The first number here concerns a steepener shock and the second number a flattener shock.
[183] These reference rates are the estimated zero-coupon default free interest rates as regularly published by the BBK, here for end of January 2000. This reference date is selected for purely illustrative reasons.

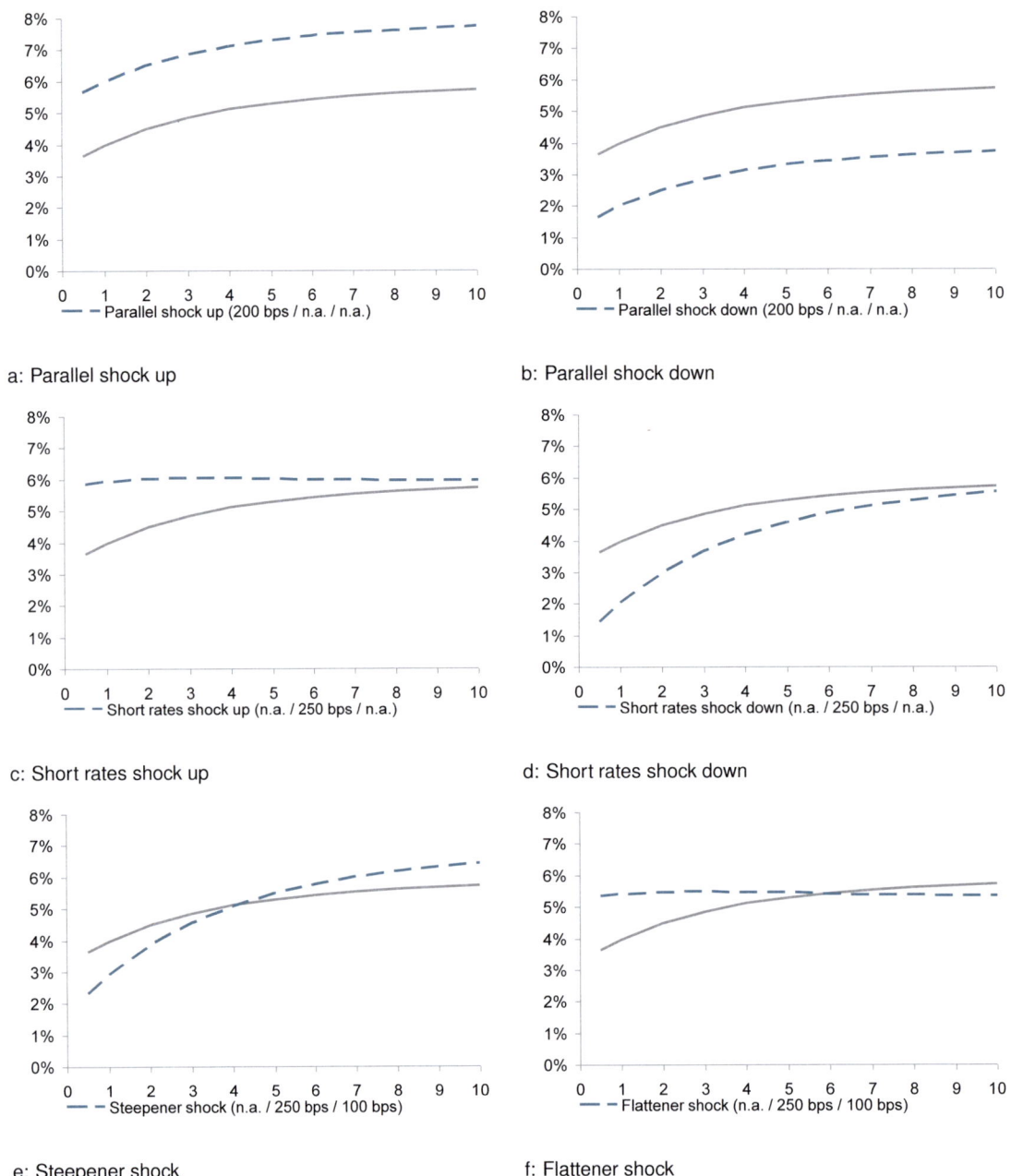

a: Parallel shock up   b: Parallel shock down

c: Short rates shock up   d: Short rates shock down

e: Steepener shock   f: Flattener shock

Figure 7.10: The six shock scenarios as developed by the BCBS (2016), euro zone parameter values (parallel / short / long), German reference interest rates from end of January 2000. Source: BCBS (2016); BBK, interest rate data; own calculations.

7.4.2 Adequacy in light of historic term structure changes

The BCBS (2016) does not make it completely transparent how the parameter values are derived.[184] Since reproducing only the transparent steps would be of limited informative value, this is abstained from. Instead, we directly turn to an independent assessment. In what follows,

---

[184] In particular, there is no detailed technical guidance made available to the calculation of the three uniform factors that are used to produce the preliminary values of the parallel, the short, and the long parameter from the currency-specific average reference interest rates. Independent of the precise values of these factors, the procedure of using uniform factors and multiplying them with currency-specific average interest rates obviously rests on the assumption that the sizes of the relevant shocks are proportional to the levels of interest rates. An assessment of this important assumption is not included in what follows.

the focus is again on Germany. More precisely, we evaluate to what extend the parameter values brought forward for the euro fit the development of German reference interest rates.

In this assessment, the parameter values are subject to review and are so on an individual shock-scenario-basis, meaning that they are treated as if they were scenario-type-specific. This is done in order to address the peculiarity mentioned earlier that the parallel and the short run shocks up and down are supposed to be symmetric while the steepener and the flattener shock are supposed to be asymmetric. Treating the parameter values as scenario-type-specific will produce results that either support or conflict with this setup. Additionally the set of shock scenarios is supplemented by long rates shocks up and down which are defined like the short rates shocks up and down but with what is called here decay long instead of decay short. This picks up on the observation that the steepener and the flattener scenarios include long rates shocks which in contrast to the short rates shocks also included are not featured separately. Including long rates shocks as the potentially best fitting shocks in the assessment will reveal their actual empirical importance. In contrast, the general structures as well as the decay rates are left unchallenged in what follows as in contrast to the specific parameter values they are considered characteristic for the scenarios presented by the BCBS (2016) which are under scrutiny here.[185] As in the analysis conducted before, here end-of-month term structure data calculated by the BBK from listed Federal securities is used and changes over 12 months are taken into consideration.

The following assessment has two parts. In the first part we use the assessment technique developed earlier which focusses on interest rates from the term structure at two different maturities. In short, we refer to this as the "two-maturities-assessment". In the second part we increase the number of different maturities simultaneously considered to eleven, using all the time series the BBK publishes.[186] This we refer to as the "multiple-maturities-assessment". In both parts the longest maturity considered is 10 years. One reason for doing so is that the decay rates are pretty close to their limiting values at this level of maturity. More importantly, however, this maturity range is generally found to be of highest practical importance for banks.

Completion of method for two-maturities-assessment

As presented above, the possible changes of two interest rates from two points on the term structure at different maturities span a plane with each point on this plane corresponding to one specific combination of possible interest rate changes. Now it was already explained above that on this plane, the tolerance area for parallel shocks up and down consists of two wedges meeting in the origin and being centered in quadrants one and three. Last but not least, short rates shocks up and down were already located on the plane in the wedges between the tolerance area for parallel shocks and the axis with the changes at the shorter maturity on it, here the abscissa. Now the remaining two shock types newly introduced by the BCBS (2016) can be located just as easily. All points in quadrant four correspond to steepener shocks. And all points in quadrant two correspond to flattener shocks.[187] The only part of the plane that cannot be associated with a shock type brought forward by the BCBS (2016) in a similar natural way consists of the two wedges between the tolerance area for parallel shocks and the axis with the changes at the longer maturity on it, here the ordinate. But by symmetry one can directly infer that the points in this area are best regarded as corresponding to long rates shocks. And as already announced, long

---

[185] Note that, obviously, considering different parameter values across scenarios here comes down to the same as considering the introduction of new plus the change of existing weights.

[186] Of course it would also be possible to calculate the term structure and its changes at any intermediate maturity since the BBK also publishes the parameters required for doing so. Here, however, the focus is on the time series of term structure interest rates published by the BBK for maturities up to and including 10 years.

[187] This setup effectively presupposes parameter values for the steepener and the flattener shock in each case similar enough such that the pivot point has a maturity between one and 10 years.

rates shocks are included in the assessment even though the BCBS (2016) does not feature them. Hence, the scope of the following assessment is comprehensive in the sense that the entire plane is covered. This is illustrated in Figure 7.11. Before turning to the actual assessment, we take a final look at the impact of the chosen tolerance level for parallel shocks. As in our data we find no perfect parallel shock, a tolerance level of zero implies that not a single term structure change is identified as a parallel shock. In contrast, at a tolerance level of 100% all combinations of changes with the same sign are identified as parallel shocks either up or down, depending on the sign. The higher the tolerance level, the lower are the shares of changes with the same sign that are identified as either short rates or as long rates shocks. Figure 7.12 plots this relationship. It is interesting to see that for shocks up there are more short rates shocks with a larger difference between the changes than long rates shocks but that the opposite is true for shocks down. At higher tolerance level a larger fraction of short-rates shocks up but also a larger fraction of long rates shocks down remains. Besides, an observation can also be made that reinforces the selection of 33.3% as a more adequate tolerance level than 50%. At a tolerance level of 33.3% we find that of the shocks up 43.9% are identified as parallel shocks up and of the shocks down 43.3% are identified as parallel shocks down. The difference is only 0.6 percentage points. In contrast, at a tolerance level of 50% the difference amounts to 6.8 percentage points with 67.6% of the shocks up identified as parallel shocks up but only 60.8% of the shocks down identified as parallel shocks down. Hence, in so far as the similarity of the quantitative effect of the application of the tolerance level to shocks up and down is of any value, this observation clearly favours 33.3%.

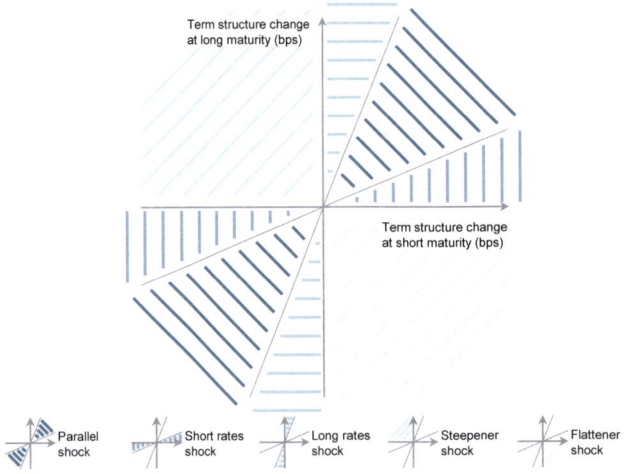

Figure 7.11: Identification of term structure changes on the basis of the signs and the proportion of the changes at short and long maturity. Source: own illustration.

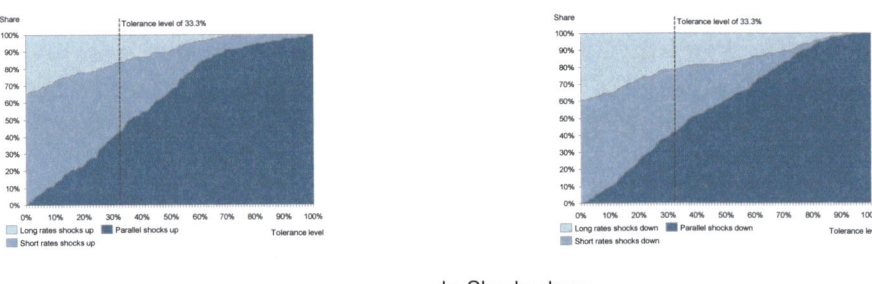

a: Shocks up   b: Shocks down

Figure 7.12: Relationship of the tolerance level to (a) the shares shocks up and (b) the share of shocks down by types of shocks. Source: BBK, interest rate data; own calculations.

Two-maturities-assessment of future scenarios

With parallel, short rates, and long rates shocks up and down plus steepener and flattener shocks, eight different shock types are considered in this assessment. A natural first step is to quantify their relative frequency in the data at hand. For this exercise the tolerance level for parallel shocks is not the only relevant parameter. Another relevant parameter is the time period considered. Last but not least, borderline cases need to be addressed.

As to the tolerance level, the 33.3% are maintained. Regarding the time period covered, the focus remains on the five years up to and including 2015 as our current edge. As discussed above, five years has usually been regarded as the length of one interest rate cycle (see CEBS (2006) and BaFin (2007)). For good measure we also look at the 10 and the 15 year period up to and including 2015, corresponding to two or three lengths of an interest-rate cycle, respectively. Borderline cases in which one of the two interest rate changes is zero are identified either as steepener or as flattener shocks, depending on which change is zero and on the sign of the non-zero change.[188] Simply put, if the point that corresponds to the borderline case in question is on the border of the third quadrant, this borderline case is identified as a steepener shock. If instead the point is on the border of the second quadrant, the borderline case in question is seen as a flattener shock. A case in which both changes are zero would not be an instance of a change. However, such a case is not included in the data anyway. The reason for identifying the borderline cases as steepener or flattener shocks is the following. If the change is precisely zero at one of the two maturities considered, it is natural to expect that a a maturity slightly further away from the other maturity where the non-zero change is observed a non-zero change with a different sign could be observed. For example, if a change of 300 basis points up at 10 years maturity is observed while at one year maturity the interest rate does not change, this might be a pivot point and hence at a maturity of 0.5 years the interest rate can be expected to go down rather than up. Note however, that our data only includes two borderline cases and hence this convention does not affect the results materially.

Looking at the relative frequencies of the shock types, three main observations can be made (see Figure 7.13). First, long rates shocks are comparably frequent in particular during the last five years, and shocks down more so than shocks up. Of the term structure changes observed in this period, 42% can be identified as long rates shocks, namely 32% as long rates shocks down an 10% as long rates shocks up. Second, similar to long rates shocks, parallel shocks are relatively numerous especially in the recent five-year period, and again the shocks down clearly outnumber the shocks up. Of all actual term structure changes 37% are within the tolerance range for parallel shocks, namely 30% for parallel shocks down and 7% for parallel shocks up. Third, while the shares of term structure changes identifiable as steepener or flattener shocks are rather independent of the length of the time period considered, the opposite is true for short rates shocks and particularly for short rates shocks down. Whereas over the last 15 years one in five term structure changes takes the shape of a short rates shock down, not a single term structure change of this sort is observed during the last five years.

In light of these numbers it is hard to understand why long rates shocks are not among the scenarios prescribed by the BCBS (2016). A large and growing share of historic term structure changes is of one of these types. And a long rates shock down is even the most frequently observed type of term structure changes over the last five years. Excluding long rates shocks from the set of new supervisory scenarios could nevertheless be justified, if it was implausible that there was a negative exposure of banks toward these types of shocks. That there indeed is such an exposure is, however, all but implausible. In a scenario where long-term interest rates

---

[188] Note that above where the concept of the tolerance level for parallel shocks up and down is introduced these borderline cases are regarded as potential parallel shocks. They would be regarded as such for a tolerance level of 100%. However, here the tolerance level is set to 33.3%.

increase much more than short-term interest rates, i.e. a long rates shock up, the typical bank engaged in positive term transformation will see the net present value of its assets decrease much more than that of its liabilities. And after a long rates shock down the net interest income of a bank decreases immediately, if only the reduction of long-term interest rates sufficiently larger than that of short-term interest rates.[189] As the impact assessment later shows, even relatively small long rates shocks would indeed have material impacts on German banks. Hence, it remains a clear deficit that the new set of interest rate shock scenarios prescribed by the BCBS (2016) does not include long rates shocks up and down.

The impact assessment below assesses the impacts of the interest rate shocks as calibrated by the BCBS (2016) on German banks. Up to this point, the analysis has not been based to these calibrations except for in the derivation of implied tolerance level for parallel shocks. But what the impact assessment clearly shows is that with this calibration, which will be presented and discussed in great detail hereafter, the parallel shock up, the short rates shock up, and the flattener shock can be identified as consistently harmful for German banks. Consistently here means in terms of current portfolio value as well as in terms of next year's net interest income.[190] Now, of course the term structure changes, the relative frequencies of which are at issue here, are not necessarily of exactly the shape that the official calibration implies. But it nevertheless appears reasonable to have a closer look at the aggregate share of those term structure changes corresponding to the consistently harmful shock scenarios. Together, the shares add up to 31% over the last 15 years, 34% over the last 10 years, but only 23% over the last five years. This suggests that German banks were exposed to a substantially lower share of consistently harmful term structure changes recently than before.

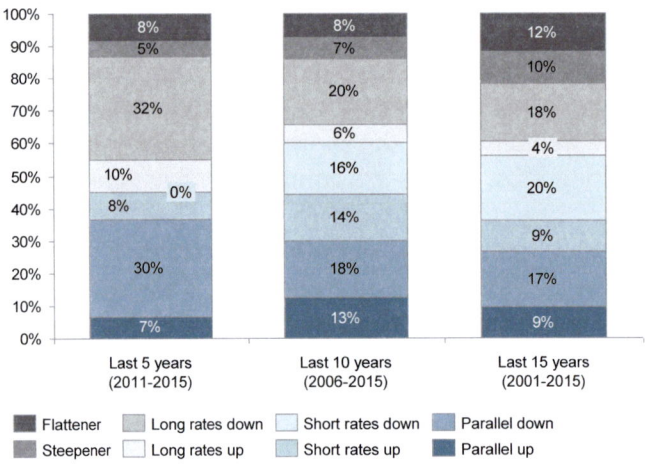

Figure 7.13: Shares of types of changes over five, 10, and 15 years, corresponding to what was traditionally regarded as the length of one, two, and three interest-rate cycles. Source: BBK, interest rate data; own calculations.

---

[189] Note that the net impact of a long rates shock up or down on a bank's net interest income is very sensitive to the precise sizes of the interest rate changes across the term structure as well as to the precise maturity profile of the bank. Because prima facie it is unclear whether the larger change of the interest rates at longer maturities or the smaller share of assets rolled-over in any time period predominates. For example, as a consequence of a long rates shock up a bank may be able to charge much higher interest rates on any new long-term loan it makes. But at the same time, the also increased short-term interest rates might lead to even higher total refinancing costs. Because being engaged in positive term transformation, the bank rolls-over a larger fraction of its liabilities than of its assets in every period.

[190] The long rates shock up is also harmful in terms of current portfolio value and also induces a reduced net interest income. However, the reduction in net interest income is smaller than the reduction that is inflicted on banks if there is no change in interest rates.

After having assessed the relative frequency of the different shock types over the last five, 10, and 15 years, now the focus is on when they occurred precisely and on their sizes. Earlier, when the size of parallel shocks was assessed, their size was measured as the arithmetic average of the two changes of the interest rates at different maturities. In contrast, the following analysis desists from aggregating the two interest rate changes at the two different maturities. Instead, they are simply report both. The reason for doing this is that for the other types of term structure changes no comparably natural aggregate measure is available like the arithmetic mean for parallel shocks.

Of course, the reporting of both simultaneous interest rate changes requires slightly more complex graphs. For this reason, Figure 7.14 features a detailed key with reading examples, the main lessons of which are the following two. First, both interest rate changes are depicted by columns starting from the zero-level with the larger change always being depicted by the darker column, which runs behind the lighter column, if both point in the same direction. Second, the color-coding tells you whether the absolute change at the shorter or that at the longer maturity is larger, with blue colors indicating that the change at the shorter maturity is larger and grey colors indicting that instead the change at the longer maturity is larger. Combining the length of the columns and the color coding, the graph tells you for every term structure change by how much the two interest rates considered changed individually.

As previously, here the focus is on the interest rate from the term structure at a maturity of one year and on that at 10 years. All changes are reported in basis points. Again, for parallel, short rates and long rates shocks, the shocks up and down are reported in a combined graph while for steepener shocks and flattener shocks there is an individual graph each (see Figure 7.14).

Before looking at the sizes of the shocks their timing is looked at a bit closer. Two main observations can be made. First, after the beginning of the financial crisis and till the current edge, there have mainly been short rates shocks down, then parallel shocks down, and then long rates shocks down. Second, as a part of this development, there have been extraordinarily many long rates shocks lately. Over the entire time period covered, which ranges back to the mid 1970s, such a concentration of long rates shocks is unprecedented. The impact assessment later shows that short rates shocks down and parallel shocks down are consistently favourable for German banks. In contrast, the effect of long rates shocks down, at least as calibrated by BCBS (2016), turns out to be positive for the net present value but negative for the net interest income.

This brings us to the sizes of the shocks. With respect to the most recent long rates shocks down, the difference between the sizes of the decreases of the two interest rates is striking. The interest rate at one year maturity hardly went down at all. This suggests that the recent long rates shocks are likely to have had adverse consequences on many banks net interest incomes as their refinancing costs have not been reduced by sizeable amounts while the interest rates on the loans granted have decreased substantially. In contrast, banks' net present value should be expected to have increased as the present value of their assets has increased substantially more than that of their liabilities. Taking a longer term perspective, a trend toward smaller interest rate changes becomes visible, again. This trend is not equally pronounced for all shock types and the time periods for which it can be observed also differ. While for parallel and short rates shocks the trend toward smaller changes seems to have been there since the beginning of the time period covered, for long rates, steepener, and flattener shocks, the trend appears to have kicked in much later during the 1990s or even as late as the turn of the century. Nevertheless, that the shocks become smaller is an empirical fact that needs to be taken into account when calibrating scenarios. Hence, using unchanged scenario calibrations is likely to lead to distortions when these scenarios are used for the measurement of banks interest rate risk.

Next, the sizes of the actual interest rate changes are compared to the changes implied by the formulas and parameter values brought forward by the BCBS (2016). For parallel shocks the value of the parallel parameter directly corresponds to the number of basis points the shock scenario shifts the entire term structure up or down, respectively. For short rates and long rates shocks decay rates come into play which produce shifts of different sizes for interest rates at different maturities. And for steepener and flattener shocks specific weights are included on top which determine how the underlying short rates and long rates shocks overlap. The numeric results for the maturities of interest here are displayed in Table 7.1. Note that per design, parallel, short rates, and long rates shocks up and down are symmetric while, as expected, the steepener and the flattener shock are no horizontal mirror images of one another, not even if one only considers changes at one and 10 years maturity. Remember that the long rates shocks up and down are not brought forward by the BCBS (2016) as independent scenarios. However, the formula and parameter values used here and in what follows are clearly set out in the derivation of the steepener and the flattener shocks.

Three things about the sizes of the changes implied by the BCBS (2016) are noteworthy. First, the parallel shocks come with the largest absolute changes of all scenarios. Second, compared to the steepener shock the flattener shock comes with a substantially larger change of the interest rate at one year maturity but also a much smaller change at 10 years maturity. Third, long rates shocks come with changes of the interest rate at one year maturity of about the same size as the changes at 10 years maturity that short rates shocks come with, but long rates shocks come with much smaller changes at 10 years maturity than short rates shocks at one year maturity. The third observation reminds us of the fact that short rates and long rates shocks are no vertical mirror images of one another. The fact that the absolute changes resulting from long rates shocks calibrated as such remain so far below those of parallel shocks is also reflected in a very evident way in the impact assessment below.

| Change (maturity) | Parallel | | Short rates | | Long rates | | Steepener | Flattener |
	up	down	up	down	up	down		
$\Delta(1)$	200	-200	195	-195	22	-22	-107	142
$\Delta(10)$	200	-200	21	-21	92	-92	69	-39

Table 7.1: Sizes of absolute changes at one year and 10 years maturity implied by formulas and parameter values for the euro area presented by the BCBS (2016) in basis points. Source: BCBS (2016); own calculations.

The whole point of calculating these implied changes is, of course, to contrast them with the changes that can actually be observed. This is done here in two steps. Step one is a categorical analysis. In this analysis the actual interest rate changes observed are categorized according to whether they are smaller or larger than the changes implied by the shock scenarios. Step two is a ratio analysis. In this analysis the ratio is calculated of the largest actual interest change that qualifies as a certain type and the change implied by the respective shock scenario. For both steps the data presented in Figure 7.14 is built on in straightforward ways. Value is added by processing this data in appropriate ways.

For step one, we again look at five, 10, and 15 years up to and including 2015 as our current edge. The results are presented in Figure 7.15. Five particularly interesting lessons can be learnt. First, over the last five years the only two shock scenarios for which actual interest rate changes have been observed that were not too small at both maturities are the scenarios short rates shock up and long rates shock down. 40% of the term structure changes that qualify as short rates shocks up came with a change at 10 years maturity that was at least as large as implied by the official shock scenario, that is 21 basis points. And as to long rates shocks down, of the qualifying actual term structure changes, 16% came with changes that were large enough only at 10 years maturity, 5% with changes large enough only at one year maturity, and 32% with changes that were large enough at both one year and ten years maturity.

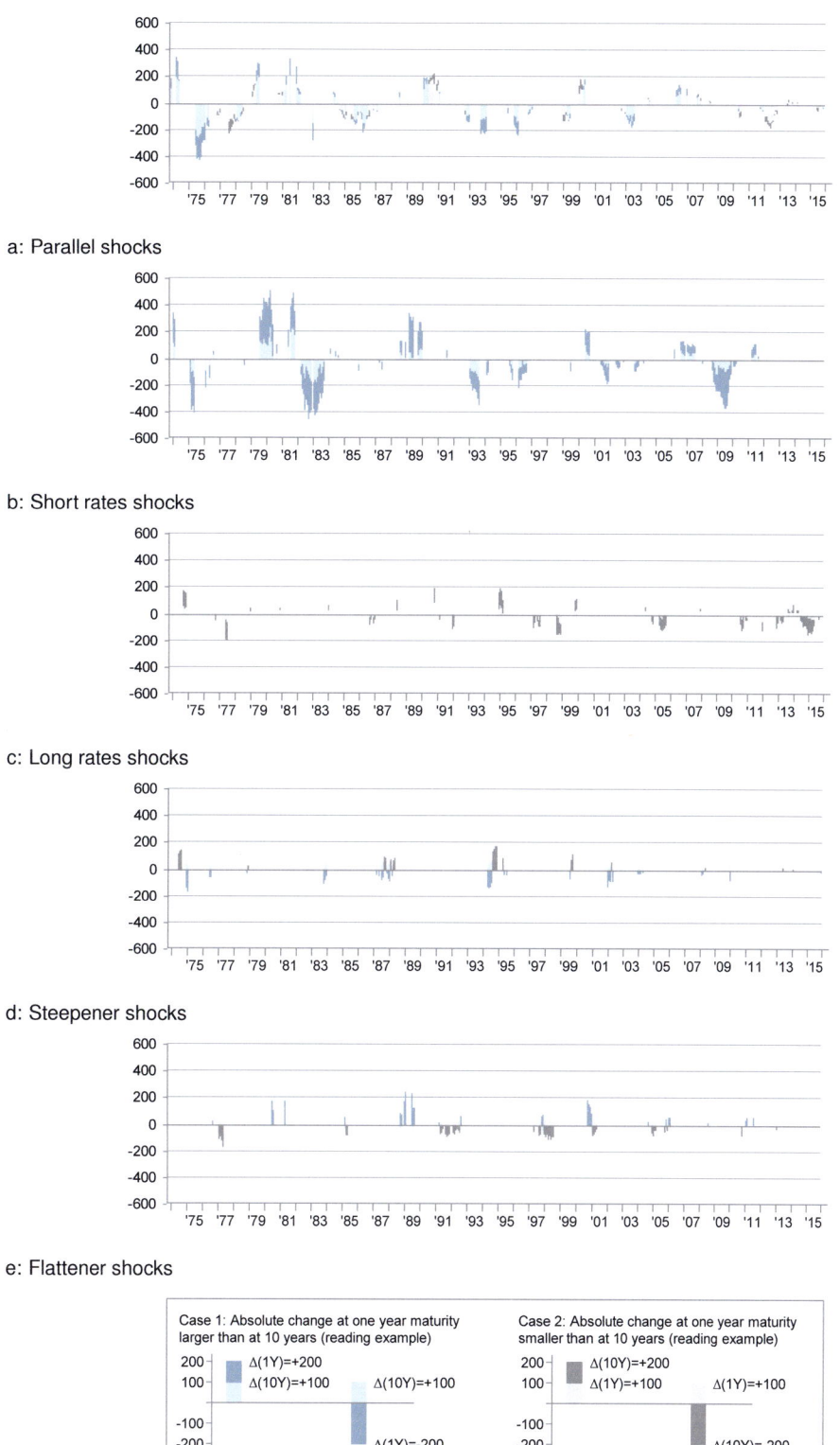

a: Parallel shocks

b: Short rates shocks

c: Long rates shocks

d: Steepener shocks

e: Flattener shocks

Figure 7.14: Absolute changes at maturities of one year or 10 years for (a) parallel shocks, (b) short rates shocks, (c) long rates shocks, (d) steepener shocks, and (e) flattener shocks over time, at a tolerance level of 33.3% and in basis points. Source: BBK, interest rate data; own calculations.

Of course, the result for long rates shocks reflects the small changes implied, which was already noted previously. What is also noteworthy looking at the last five years is that there has not been a single term structure change that qualified as a short rates shock down and this brings us to the second observation. Second, looking back 10 years, over half of the term structure changes that qualified as short rates shocks down turn out to have come with changes large enough at both one year and ten years maturity. Remember that looking back 10 years, 16% of all term structure changes qualify as a short rates shock down (see Figure 7.13). And as was also already noted, it was the beginning of the financial crisis that was accompanied by massive term structure changes of this type (see Figure 7.14). Third, there has not been a single term structure change that qualifies as a parallel shock up or down and that comes with at least one interest rate change which is at least as large as the shock scenario has it. This is true for the last five, 10, and 15 years. And this is only true for these two shock scenario types. This result reflects that the absolute changes these scenarios feature are particularly large, as noted earlier. Note that the results are extraordinarily stable over the different number of years considered for the long rates shock down scenario. And for this scenario type there are actual changes of the term structure in every category and not in one category only. Fourth, the actual term structure changes that qualify as short rates or as long rates shocks tend to be more parallel than the respective scenarios have it. Of the term structure changes that qualify as short rates shocks up not a single one comes with a change of the interest rate at one year maturity that is at least as large as the scenario has it. But in the last five years 40% come with a large enough change of the interest rate at 10 years maturity. For long rates shocks up a similar observation can be made. Looking back 10 years, 14% of the qualifying actual term structure changes come with a change of the interest rate at one year maturity large enough but there is no actual term structure change with a change of the interest rate at 10 years maturity at least as large as the scenario has it. And finally fifth, for short rates shocks up and down, long rates shocks up, steepener shocks, and flattener shocks, the distribution of actual changes of the term structure across categories and over the different number of years considered suggests that the empirical relevance of the shock scenarios is decreasing.

To sum up, based on historic term structure changes a low and decreasing empirical relevance of the official shock scenarios as calibrated by the BCBS (2016) can be observed for Germany. These observations cast doubt on the their appropriateness for the measurement of banks interest rate risk. What is more, it is striking to see that in contrast to the scenarios actually prescribed by the BCBS (2016), the scenario of a long rates shock down is neither of low nor of decreasing empirical relevance. And since, as the impact assessment later shows, this scenario also inflicts substantial harm on German banks net interest income, not including this scenario in the official ones now presents itself as a major lapse.

For step two we again track the largest changes using a five-year rolling window. To be precise, we track three different measures. Measures one and two report the ratios of the largest observed changes of the interest rates at one year and at 10 years maturity divided by the the respective change the shock scenario in question features. For example, a value of 0.5 for one year maturity means that over the five years up to the point in time considered the largest actual change of the interest rate at one year maturity has been 50% of that of the shock scenario. Of course, only interest rate changes that are parts of term structure changes that qualify as the respective shock scenario type are considered. In contrast to measures one and two, measure three takes into account interest rate changes at both maturities. It takes the value of the largest ratio over the last five years, the inverse of which is the smallest coefficient that the actual changes at one particular point in time during these five years need to be multiplied with, such that both are at least as large as the respective shock scenario has it. For example, a value of 0.5 means that within the last five years, there has been one particular change of the term structure with the following two features. First, the change of the interest rate at one year or at 10 years maturity was 50% the size of that of the shock scenario in question. Second, the simultaneous change of the interest rate at the other maturity was at least 50% the size of the same shock scenario. Whenever the largest changes at the two maturities considered do not occur at the same point in time, this third measure does not coincide with that one of the first two measures that currently takes the lower value. Note that since the values of the measures are analyzed over the 15 years up to and including 2015 the data included ranges back 20 years. The results are displayed in Figure 7.16.

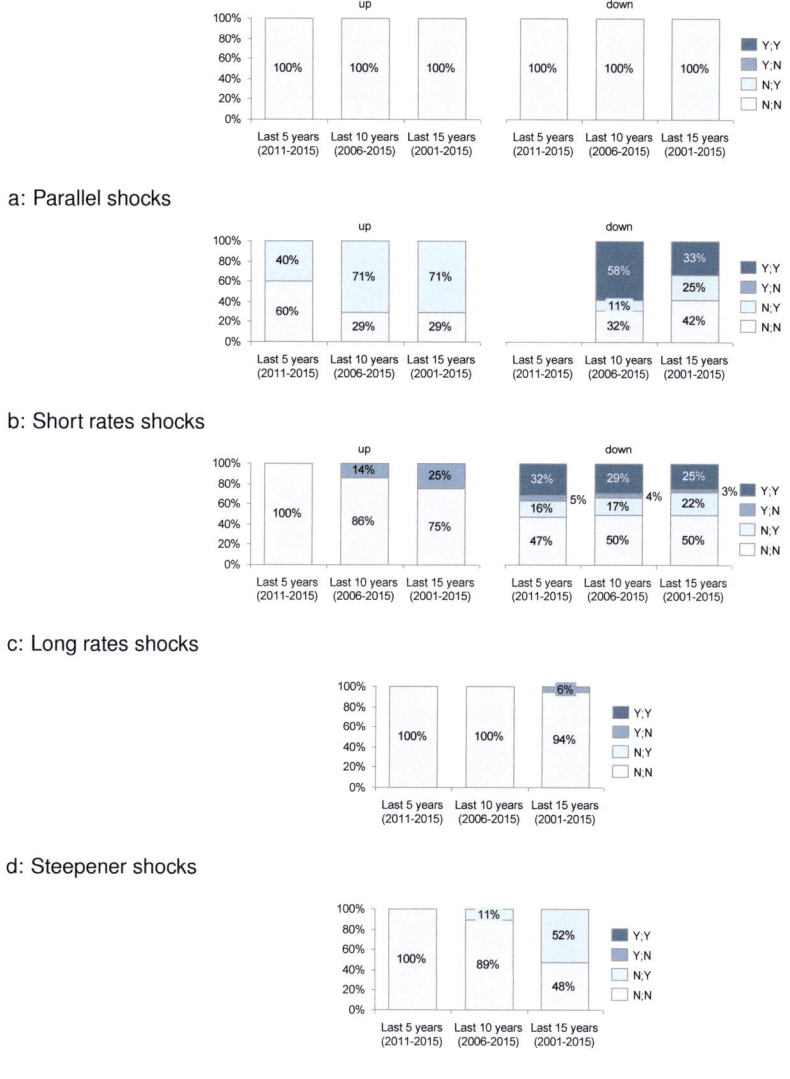

Figure 7.15: Binary assessment whether absolute changes are at least as large as indicated by the BCBS (2016) with "Y" indicating "yes" and "N" indicating "no" for interest rates at one year and at 10 years of maturity in the format (one year;10 years) for (a) parallel shocks, (b) short rates shocks, (c) long rates shocks, (d) steepener shocks, and (e) flattener shocks, at a tolerance level of 33.3%. Source: BBK, interest rate data; own calculations.

The results from the previous analysis can readily be found here, again. For example, for parallel shocks up and down all three measures consistently remain below one. For short rates shocks down all three measures hit zero at the current edge. And for short rates and long rates shocks up, the third measure closely tracks the value of the measure for 1 year and for ten

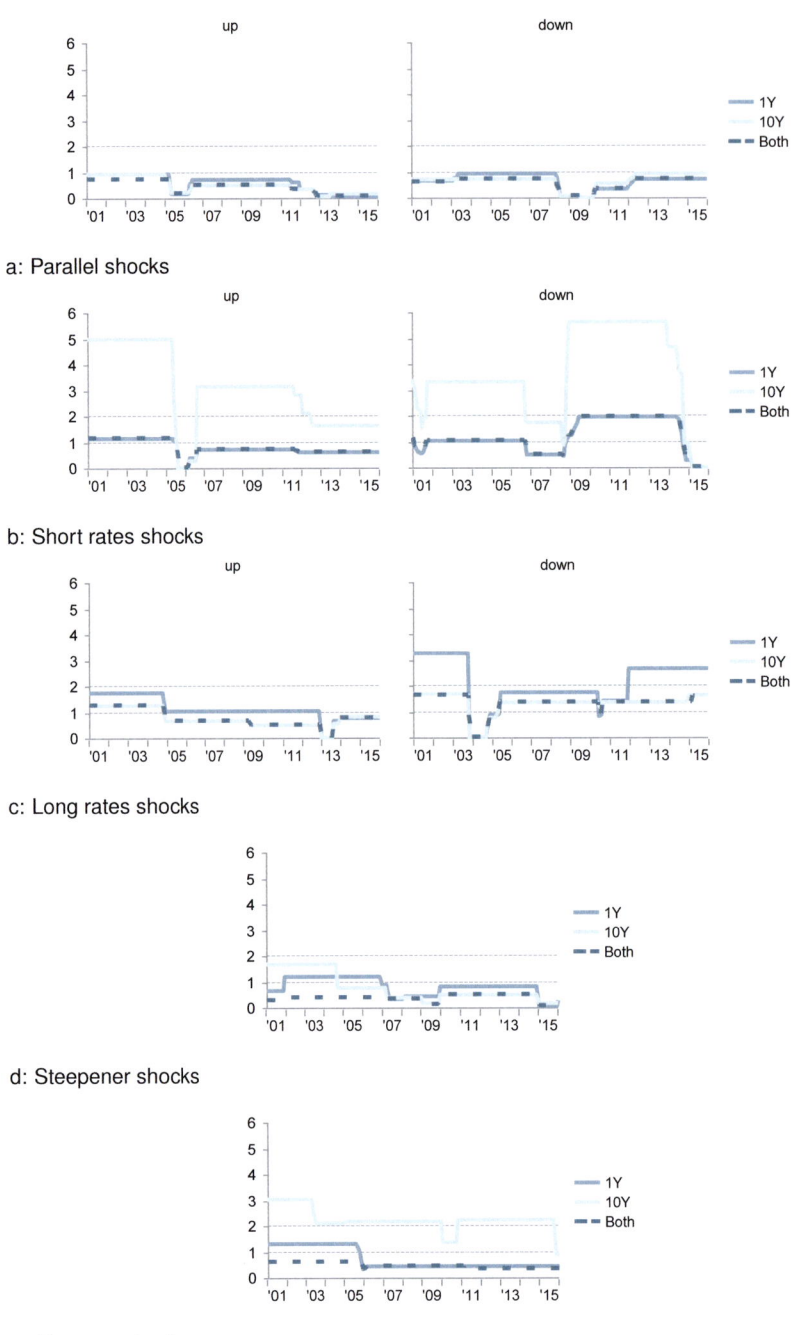

Figure 7.16: Relative assessment absolute changes in terms of changes indicated by the BCBS (2016) for individual interest rates at one year and at 10 years maturity as well as for both interest rates together for (a) parallel shocks, (b) short rates shocks, (c) long rates shocks, (d) steepener shocks, and (e) flattener shocks, at a tolerance level of 33.3%. Source: BCBS (2016); BBK, interest rate data; own calculations.

years maturity, respectively. But the ratios calculated make it possible to make more detailed observations, three of which are particularly important. First, while for parallel shocks up we observe a decline of all three measures particularly in 2011 and 2012, for parallel shocks down we observe an increase of these measures that even starts one year earlier. As a consequence, at the current edge, the measures differ substantially. For parallel shocks up the measures for one year maturity and the combined measure stand at 0.08 and the measure for 10 years maturity stands at 0.16. In contrast, for parallel shocks down the measures for one year maturity and the combined measure stand at 0.71 and the measure for 10 years maturity stands at 0.91. This material difference was not visible in the previous analysis. As it stands, this observation might suggest that the parallel shock down scenario currently mirrors the reality closer than the parallel shock up scenario. However, one also has to note that over the 15 years considered here, for both parallel shocks up and down the measures for the individual interest rate changes have been close to one and the third overall measure around 0.7. This might hence be seen as justifying the symmetry of the two parallel shock scenarios. Highs and lows are just distributed differently across time. Second, the ratios for short rates shocks up and down take rather different values. While for the shock up the third measure that takes into account both interest rates reached a maximum value of only just above 1 (1.12) and never exceeded a value of 1 since 2005, for the shock down it reached a maximum value of close to 2 (1.93) and dropped down from it as recently as 2014. This observation pulls the symmetry of the two scenario types into question as it suggests that the numerical value of the relevant short parameter is much more conservative for shocks up than for shocks down. Third, even though the steepener and the flattener shock are tailored in that the defining formulas include specific weights, only for steepener shocks these weights lead to a comparable fit at one year and at ten years maturity. For flattener shocks, the ratio for 10 years maturity exceeds that for one year by far for large parts of the time period considered. Finally, it is noteworthy that also the detected long rates shocks up and down differ substantially in size. The finding is generally the same as that for short rates shocks. Over the last 10 years there has been at least one shock down which was considerably larger than the calibrated scenario but not a single shock up to which this applies. For long rates shocks this is even true for the last five and even for the last two years. Together with the observation that at least at the current edge the measures for parallel shocks up and down also differ considerably, this puts a question mark on the appropriateness of the symmetry of the scenario calibrations for German banks.

Method for multiple-maturities-assessment

The procedure envisaged for using interest rates from 11 maturity levels is straightforward and involves three main steps. The first step is to assign a type or a number of potential types of shock scenarios to each of these actual changes on the basis of some qualitative criteria. The second step is for each actual change to determine the parameter value or values of the shock scenario that fits best according to some quantitative measure. The third and final step is to contrast the parameter values determined in in the previous steps with the ones brought forward by the BCBS (2016). These three steps are presented in detail in turn before the second part of the assessment is started with.

We begin with a closer look at the first step. This step focusses on the directions of the changes of the term structure. This means that only the signs of the absolute changes of the reference interest rates at the 11 maturity levels considered matter. Based on the signs of the changes at every maturity considered, every overall change, that is every 11-tuple, is identified as a term structure change of a certain type or as one of a number of potential types. The motivation for applying qualitative criteria first is that only using quantitative techniques to determine the type of a term structure change might produce counterintuitive results. For example, it cannot be ruled out that when short and long rates decrease but medium rates increase, of the scenarios considered, a parallel shock up or down with some small parameter value would have the best fit. Such results can be ruled out by applying suitable qualitative criteria first. And being able to rule out counterintuitive results of this type is one of the major benefits of referring to interest rates from 11 instead of only from two maturity levels.[191] Obviously, another way to

---

[191] To be precise, counterintuitive results are, of course, not ruled out in a logical sense. It cannot in principle be ruled out that between two maturities considered something extraordinary happens to the term structure. However,

rule out counterintuitive results of this sort would be to extend the range of considered scenario types. Returning to the example, if appropriate scenarios for a bending of the term structure were included, quantitative techniques might be sufficient to identify the described changes as what could be referred to as a concavity shock. However, as the variety of possible and also of observed series of signs of changes is large, applying qualitative criteria first seems to be the more straightforward solution. The qualitative criteria applied in the assessment here are summarized in Table 7.2. They are defined with reference to what is called here the sign sequence, that is the sequence of different signs observed from the shortest to the longest maturity.[192] The most important intuition that these criteria capture is that parallel, short rates and long rates shocks all require shifts of the term structure in one direction only. If and only if the interest rates at all maturity levels considered increase (decrease), the overall term structure change can be a parallel or short rates or long rates shock up (down). Zero changes are excluded because if a change of zero is measured at one of the maturity levels actually considered, it is likely that at some slightly lower or higher maturity a change with a different sign than those observed elsewhere took place. Naturally, you could also define these qualitative criteria differently. For example, you may be more strict and rule out changes of zero at either extreme end for steepener and flattener shocks.

Sign sequence	Possible scenarios
P	parallel shock up, short rates shock up, long rates shock up
N	parallel shock down, short rates shock down, long rates shock down
NP, NZP, ZP, NZ	steepener shock
PN, PZN, ZN, PZ	flattener shock
other	none

Table 7.2: Sign sequences (P: positive, N: negative, Z: zero, i.e. neither positive nor negative) and possible scenarios for a term structure change. Note that, for example, "NP" stands for all sign sequences for the eleven maturity levels considered here with first only negative signs and then only positive signs, hence, among others, for the sign sequences "NNNNPPPPPPP", "NNNNNNNPPPP", and "NNNNNNNNNNP". Source: own illustration.

The second step involves the largest computational effort but the idea is simple. A certain measure of fit is applied in order to identify for every actually observed term structure change the specific scenario that fits best. For actual changes that were identified as steepener or flattener shocks in the previous step this simply means that the parameter values are determined which produce the calibrated scenario with the best fit. For actual changes that were identified as possibly being best characterized as a parallel or a short rates or a long rates shock up or down the process has two stages. In the first stage, the selected measure of fit is used independently for each of the three potential scenario types in order to determine the parameter value which produces the specific calibrated scenario with the best fit. In the second stage, the same measure of fit is applied to determine which of these three specific calibrated scenarios fits best. In this way, the same measure of fit is used not only for the determination of the parameter values but also for the selection of the scenario type. Actual changes for which none of the scenario types considered comes into question are not analyzed further. In what follows, the sum of squared residuals is used as the measure of fit and the residuals at all 11 maturities considered are included. Only parameter values in full basis points are considered. Other measures of fit are available but the sum of squared residuals is the most established one by far. For this reason it was also already selected above for the determination of the tolerance level for parallel shocks implicit in the shock scenarios as defined by the BCBS (2016).

increasing the number of maturity levels considered from two to 11 while keeping the maturity range covered unchanged, makes it much more unlikely that types of changes of the term structure are misidentified.

[192] Put differently, the sign sequence is the sequence of positive or negative signs that correspond to the sequence of positive or negative changes of the interest rates at the maturity levels considered from 0.5 years to 10 years.

Finally, in the third step the results produced are used for the actual assessment. The overarching question is whether or to what extent the parameter values brought forward by the BCBS (2016) for the euro zone, and hence also for Germany, are appropriate given the historic development of the German term structure. Important topics to be investigated here include the implied symmetry of parallel and short rates shocks as well as the implied negligibility of long rates shocks.

Multiple-maturities-assessment of future scenarios

As done in the assessment based on the interest rates at one year and 10 years maturity only, we start the current assessment with a look at the relative frequencies of term structure changes that are of a certain shock scenario type. Remember that in contrast to the earlier assessment, here no tolerance level needs to be set. Instead, here the sum of squared residuals is decisive for the distinction between parallel, short rates, and long rates shocks. However, a new category needs to be included for the actual term structure changes that do not qualify as one of the shock scenario types considered. We call this category "none".

The relative frequencies over the last five, 10, and 15 years up to and including 2015 are presented in Figure 7.17. The most striking fact about these relative frequencies is that they are rather similar to the ones determined in the earlier assessment based on two maturities only. Three particular similarities are especially noteworthy. First and just like in the earlier assessment, term structure changes that are identified as long rates shocks and parallel shocks turn out to have been particularly frequent during the last 5 years and more so shocks down than shocks up. Second and again just like above, in the last five years there have been no term structure changes that qualify as short rates shocks down even though there has been a fair share over the last 10 and 15 years. Third, the share of term structure changes that cannot be identified to be of any particular type and hence fall in the new category referred to as "none" is negligibly small. There are, of course, also minor differences between the relative frequencies found here and the ones found in the earlier assessment. In particular, the relative frequency of term structure changes that are identified to be of the type flattener shock is a few percentage points higher. Mainly as a consequence of this difference, the aggregated relative frequency of those shock scenario types that are identified as consistently harmful for German banks in the impact assessment below is also higher. Together, the shares of parallel shocks up, short rates shocks up, and flattener shocks add up to 37% (31% in the previous assessment) over the last 15 years, 41% (34%) over the last 10 years, and 27% (23%) over the last five years. However, the development of this share that could be described as "first up, then down below the initial level" (here from 37% up to 41% and then down to 27%) remains unchanged. Hence, the same questions come up regarding the future appropriateness of the shock scenario calibrations as they stand.

Overall, these three similarities cast a favourable light on the previous two-maturities-assessment. Considering only the interest rates at maturities of one and 10 years and simply using a tolerance level of 33.3% for parallel shocks produces very similar relative frequencies of identified shock types as the much more laborious procedure applied here. The application of the qualitative criteria in the first step in the procedure applied here of course more or less corresponds to the classification based on quadrants only in the two-maturities assessment. However, the appropriateness of the tolerance-level of 33.3% is certainly strongly supported here. Yes, the selection of this tolerance level was motivated by the fact that it is pretty close to the one implied by the parallel shock and the short rates shock as defined by the BCBS (2016) if one uses the sum of squared residuals as a measure of fit. But in this calculation only changes of interest rates at one and at ten years maturity were considered and long rates shocks were not accounted for at all because they are not brought forward as official scenarios.

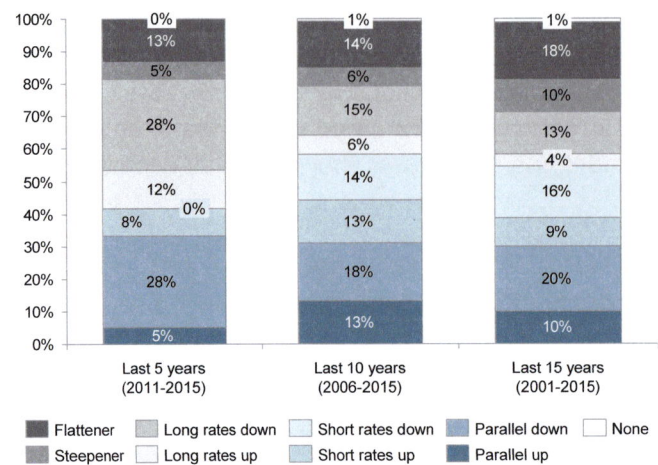

Figure 7.17: Shares of types of changes over five, 10, and 15 years, corresponding to what was traditionally regarded as the length of one, two, and three interest-rate cycles. Source: BBK, interest rate data; own calculations.

Next, the focus is on the precise timing and the development of the sizes of the changes of the maturity structure that have been identified as being of one shock scenario type. In what follows, not the the absolute changes of the interest rates at some selected maturities are looked at. Instead, the values of the relevant parameters that produce the best fit are investigated. For parallel, short rates, and long rates shocks up and down one parameter value summarizes the entire term structure change. For steepener and flattener shocks two parameter values are required. But still, this makes the assessment way more comprehensible than it would be, if all the interest rate changes at the 11 maturities that make up the data basis were tracked individually. Of course, there is also a downside to proceeding in this way. By looking at parameter values only, the structure of the shock scenarios designed by the BCBS (2016), namely the formulas in which these parameters are included, is implicitly accepted. Again, the long rates shocks are also included here even though they are not brought forward as official scenarios.

Remember that the values for the three parameter parallel, short, and long proposed by the BCBS (2016) for the euro are 200, 250, and 100 respectively. The following analysis makes very transparent how the actual term structure changes compare to these values. It is, of course, important to keep in mind that only the parallel parameter is numerically identical to the number of basis points by which the parallel shock scenario shifts the term structure. For the other shock scenarios, the short and the long parameter are multiplied with decay rates and weights to arrive at the envisaged changes of the term structure. Table 7.1 already showed how large parameter values translate into small term structure changes.

The way the BCBS (2016) defines the shock scenarios, they only feature positive parameter values. This is reflected in the following analysis. However, for parallel, short rates, and long rates shocks, the results for shocks up and down are presented in a single graph each. A clear arrangement is achieved by plotting the parameter values for shocks up above and those for shocks down below the abscissa. For steepener and flattener shocks the parameter that enters with a positive weight is plotted above and the one that enters with a negative weight below. As done previously, we again track the highest parameter value using a five-year rolling window. For reasons of simplicity, we track the two parameters of steepener and flattener shocks independently of one another.[193]

The main observations that can be made on the basis of the analysis presented in Figure 7.18 are the following. For parallel shocks it is observed that the five-year maxima of the best fitting

---

[193] This is to say that here no measure comparable to the one what was introduced as the third measure above is employed. Here this would be a measure that takes into account both parameter values.

parameter values of both shocks up and shocks down have indeed been rather close to 200 over large periods of time since the early nineties and even the early eighties, respectively. And while for parallel shocks up the five year maximum is close to zero at the current edge, for parallel shocks down it is still larger than 150. However, there also appears to be a long-run trend toward smaller values of the parallel parameter for both shocks up and down. For short rates shocks a pronounced trend toward smaller values of the short parameter for shocks up is observed while for shocks down the peaks at the beginning of the eighties and after the beginning of the recent financial crisis are found to dominate. Hence, neither for short rates shocks up nor for short rates shocks down does a value of 250 for the short parameter appear as a natural choice. For long rates shocks no clear trend for the size of the long parameter but a historically unprecedented clustering of occurrences, particularly of long rates shocks down, at the current edge is observed. As to the size of the best fitting parameter, one can say that values of above or at least close to double the 100 brought forward have been observed historically and that hence this value would not appear as particularly conservative. Now you might object that long rates shocks are not brought forward as shock scenarios by the BCBS (2016). However, when looking at the best fitting parameter values for steepener and flattener shocks, a similar conclusion is reached. Values for the long parameter of more than or at least close to 200 have occurred multiple times since the seventies. But it is also true that for the long parameter to which a positive weight is attached, that is as it features in the steepener shock, we observe a downward trend since the last peak in the early to mid-nineties. Where a negative weight is attached to the long parameter, that is as it features in the flattener shock, no clear trend is visible. As to steepener shocks, the strong occurences in the early to mid-nineties predominate. More recent occurrences are rare and substantially smaller. Flattener shocks are much more evenly distributed. But the size is also decreasing.

Again, on these findings reasonable doubts as to the appropriateness of the sizes and the symmetries of the prescribed scenarios and of the exclusion of long rates shocks from the set of official shock scenarios can be based. Table 7.3 presents the maxima of the best fitting values of the parallel, the short, and the long parameter for each shock scenario type considered here and for the five, 10, and 15 years up to and including 2015. The results for the five year time frame correspond to the current edge in Figure 7.18. One reason for also considering time frames of 10 and 15 years is, again, that the length of the interest rate cycle might have changed. Looking back 15 years covers a substantial amount of time before the recent financial crisis. Particular attention may again be paid to those shock scenarios that consistently have adverse consequences for German banks, based on the impact assessment below. As noted before, these are the parallel shock up, the short rates shock up, and the flattener shock scenario.

Five findings are particularly noteworthy. First, the numbers confirm the visual impression that there is an overall trend toward more moderate parameter values. The only exception is the long parameter in the long rates up scenario which reached its maximum value within the last five years. Second, comparing the parameter values for up and down for parallel, short rates, and long rates shocks, nothing indicates that these shock scenarios should be symmetric. Between the parameter value measured for the up scenario and that measured for the respective down scenario there is sometimes even a difference in magnitude. Third, the parameter values for steepener shocks do not correspond to those for flattener shocks and the parameter values for either of them hardly square with those for the other shock scenarios. This calls into doubt the appropriateness of the specific weights that feature in the defining formulas of the flattener and the steepener shock. Fourth, interestingly, the values measured for the parallel parameter looking back 10 or 15 years correspond rather closely to the sizes of the asymmetric parallel shocks of the original scenarios introduced in Germany by the BaFin (2007). The 124 measured for the

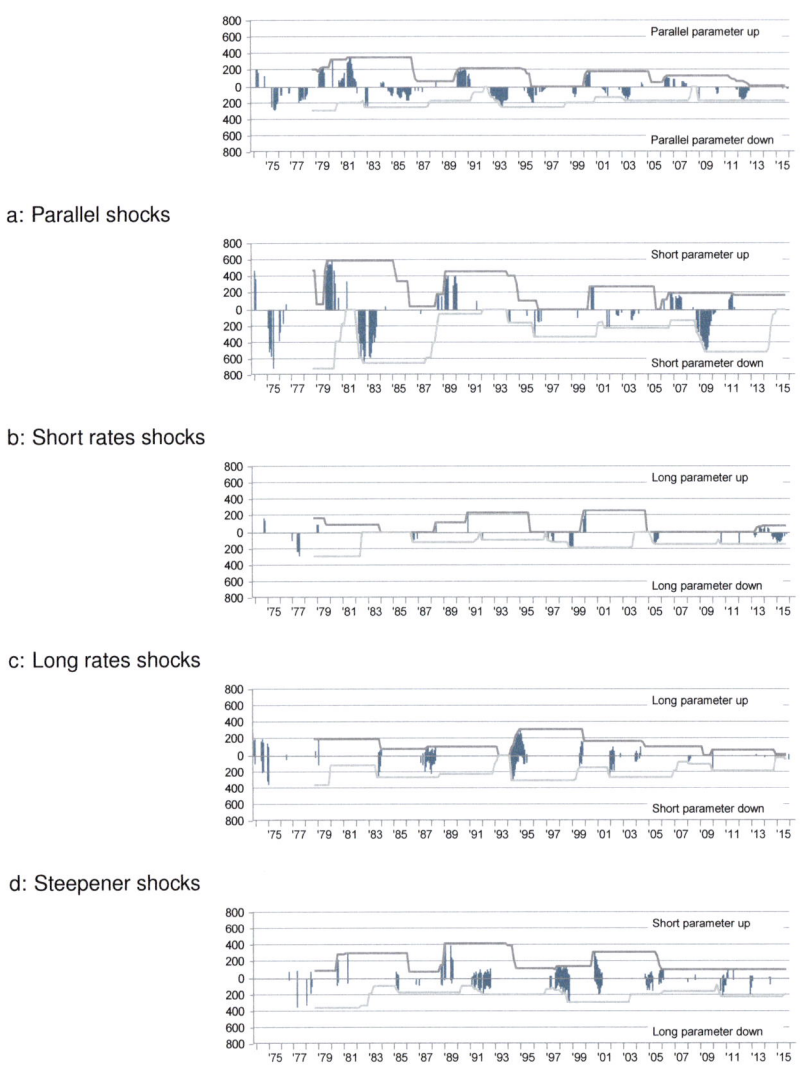

a: Parallel shocks

b: Short rates shocks

c: Long rates shocks

d: Steepener shocks

e: Flattener shocks

Figure 7.18: Best fitting parameter values based on formulas provided by the BCBS (2016) and after qualitative pre-selection of possible shock type for (a) parallel shocks, (b) short rates shocks, (c) long rates shocks, (d) steepener shocks, and (e) flattener shocks. Note that shocks categorized as "none", that is as not of one of the aforementioned types, are not depicted here. Source: BCBS (2016); BBK, interest rate data; own calculations.

shock up is very close to the 130 imposed back then, and so is the 180 measured for the shock down to the 190 imposed. Fifth, the long run parameter measured for scenarios where it governs a decrease in interest rates is consistently much larger than the 100 proposed. This is not only true for the long rates shock down, which is not an official scenario, but even more so for the flattener scenario which is officially brought forward by the BCBS (2016).

Of the many findings this assessment has produced, the following five may plausibly be regarded as the most important ones. First, there is a general trend toward smaller term structure changes in Germany. In isolation, this trend contributes to a decrease of the interest rate risk of banks. Second, the share of actual term structure changes that resemble shock scenario types which are harmful for German banks in terms of current portfolio value as wall as in terms of net interest income has decreased in recent years. In isolation, this development also contributes to a decrease of the interest rate risk of banks. Together, the first and the second finding strongly suggest that the exposure measurement as envisaged by the BCBS (2016) will be a poor indicator for the development of banks' interest rate risk through time. Third, actual term structure changes

Period	Parameter	Parallel		Short rates		Long rates		Steepener	Flattener
		up	down	up	down	up	down		
'11-'15	Parallel	12	176						
	Short			169	0			60	98
	Long					79	149	13	202
'06-'15	Parallel	124	180						
	Short			190	517			187	100
	Long					79	156	59	226
'01-'15	Parallel	124	180						
	Short			190	517			265	116
	Long					79	156	96	226

Table 7.3: Observed best fitting maximum parameter values after qualitative pre-selection and for different periods columns for different types of shocks. Source: BCBS (2016); BBK, interest rate data; own calculations.

neither support the prescribed symmetry of the parallel and the short rates shocks up and down (and also not of the long rates shock up and down) nor the prescribed weights in the steepener and the flattener shocks. Shocks down have been much more pronounced recently and hence the buffers or levels of conservatism or risk-aversion appear to be very different between the shock scenarios as officially calibrated. Fourth, a large and growing number of actual term structure changes resemble long rates shocks. This suggests that the official set of scenarios is incomplete in an important way because it does not include long rates shocks. Together, the third and the fourth finding obviously indicate where the structure and calibration of the scenarios should be adjusted, it they were to be made more empirically relevant for German banks. Fifth, on a meta-level it turns out that an assessment based on interest rates at two maturities already can go a long way compared with an assessment based on eleven.

7.5 Forecasts

Two types of forecasts are covered in what follows, namely qualitative and quantitative forecasts. Qualitative forecasts here mean forecasts about the direction of the future development of interest rates. And quantitative forecasts here refer to forecasts about the precise value of future interest rates. In recent years, the qualitative predictions have mostly suggested that short-term interest rates remain unchanged while long-term interest rates increase. According to these forecasts, banks are more likely to experience a term structure change that is beneficial for next year's net interest income than a change that is harmful. Also of the quantitative forecasts considered here, most of them made during the last five years predicted a long rates shock up or no change. It turns out that neither the qualitative nor the quantitative interest rate forecasts are particularly reliable. Nevertheless, they remain important as they possibly inform banks when making decisions about their exposures. And as forecasts of limited reliability tell them that adverse changes of the term structure are becoming less likely, this might induce excessive risk-taking.

7.5.1 Qualitative forecasts' implications for adequacy

Two prominent qualitative forecasts are introduced subsequently and analysed thereafter. In preparation of analysis, the forecasts are made directly comparable. The analysis then makes use of a classification based on the impact of forecasted term structure changes on next year's net interest income of a prototypical bank engaged in positive term transformation.

Forecasts by the ifo

The Munich based ifo Institut (ifo) publishes a qualitative interest rate forecast for Germany as a part of the results of its World Economic Survey. The ifo conducts this survey on a quarterly basis, surveying economic experts in the first month of each quarter and publishing the results in the second. Concerning the future development of interest rates, the survey asks for the expected developments of short-term and long-term rates over the next six months. For both short-term and long-term interest rates it asks whether you expect them to be "higher" or "about the same" or "lower" in six months time. The survey defines short-term rates as "3-month money market rates" and long-term rates as interest rates of "government bonds with 10 and more years of maturity".

Note that with the three answer options the ifo only asks for the expected direction of the future development of the respective interest rate. This type of question is here classified as qualitative in order to distinguish it from the type of question that asks you to write down the precise future value you expect. The latter type of question is here then classified as quantitative. Of course, the results generated from aggregating the responses to a qualitative question may take a numerical form. But naturally, such a numerical result cannot tell you the precise numerical value of the interest rate that may be expected by the respondents but which they are not asked for.

Now for the purpose of generating aggregated results, the first of the three answer options ("higher") is assigned a point value of nine, the second ("about the same") of five, and the third ("lower") of one. The ifo publishes average point values, with the average for individual countries being calculated simply by dividing the total sum of points from responses for this country by the number of respondents.[194] For general information on the design and evaluation of the survey see ifo (2014), for the standard questionnaire which includes the cited questions on the expected future development of interest rates see ifo (2016).

A quick glance at the plotted data from the last 15 years up to and including 2015 already reveals three important insights (see Figure 7.19). First, over the entire time period covered, the expectations for short-term and long-term interest rates show substantial co-movement. The overall correlation coefficient is as high as 0.86. Second, there are also noteworthy differences in both the signs of the expected changes and in the breadth of consensus. Long-term interest rates have been expected to increase more than 10 times as often as they have been expected to decrease, short-term rates only close to twice as often. The last time long-term interest rates were expected to decline was in 2009 while for short-term rates the last time was as recent as 2015. Hence, in so far as only the sign of the expected change is concerned, the expectations regarding long-term interest rates have been substantially more stable in the last few years than those regarding short-term interest rates. However, the expectations regarding the future development of short-term interest rates have been extremely homogenous at several points in time. Several times there has been a very broad consensus that the short-term interest rates were going to move in a certain direction and this consensus was larger than that regarding long-term interest rates. The more extreme point values for short-term interest rates clearly indicate this. The fact that these values are more extreme than those for long-term interest rates can be explained by the greater uncertainty that expectations about developments further in the future come with. Finally third, over the last few years, the expectations for short-term interest rates have oscillated around the expectation that they remain unchanged. Since the third quarter of 2011, the respective point values have been between 4.4 and 5.9, an unprecedented narrow corridor around the point value of 5.0. Hence, either respondents who expect an increase and respondents who expect a decrease broadly balance out or most of the respondents expect no change. Either way, it is

---

[194] For larger economic regions like the euro area results for individual countries are weighted on the basis of a country's share in world trade volume.

only natural to take these overall weak change expectations as an indicator for low interest rate risk associated with changing sort-term interest rates. With long-term interest rates having been expected to increase consistently over recent years, a bank which is engaged in positive term transformation has been looking into a bright future recently in terms of next year's net interest income. However, it had to worry about its current portfolio value. Clearly further analysis are in order. But beforehand another forecast is introduced.

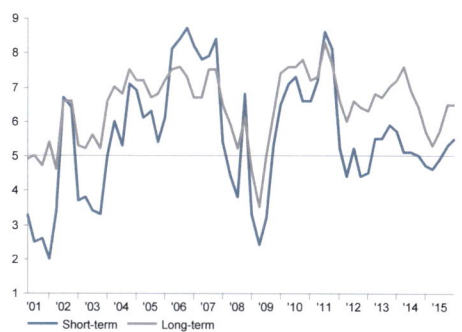

Figure 7.19: ifo six months interest rate forecast point values with values above five indicating an increase and values below a decrease. Source: ifo, World Economic Survey; own calculations.

Forecasts by the ZEW

The Mannheim based Zentrum für Europäische Wirtschaftsforschung (ZEW) publishes a qualitative interest rate forecast for Germany as a part of the results of its Financial Market Survey. The ZEW conducts this survey on a monthly basis, surveying predominantly German economic experts and asking for their expectations regarding financial markets in different parts of the world including Germany. The survey by the ZEW also asks for the expected development of the short-term and long-term interest rates over the next six months. In the questionnaire the ZEW (2016) specifies the short-term interest rate at issue as the three month interbank interest rate and the long-term interest rate as that of government bonds with 10 years maturity. The ZEW publishes the percentages of respondents who responded "increase" or "no change" or "decrease" as well as the "balance" which is defined as the first share minus the third. Note that with these percentages it is possible to calculate an unambiguous point value as it is published by the ifo (see Appendix 2).

Looking at the plotted data from the last 15 years up to and including 2015 as well as the implied point values two lessons on a meta-level can be learnt (see Figure 7.20). First, focussing on the point values greatly simplifies the analysis.[195] Information is lost but clarity is gained. Second, in point values the forecast by the ZEW appears to be rather similar to that of the ifo. Hence, very similar observation to those made above can be made here. Since the ZEW publishes the underlying data also, one very important deeper insight can be uncovered. Namely that at least as far as the forecast of the ZEW is concerned, the recent oscillating of the expectations for short-term interest rates around the expectation that they remain unchanged is the result of a growing share of respondents actually expecting short-term interest rates to remain unchanged. As mentioned above, the same point values could also be the result of a large disagreement with two large and roughly similarly sized groups of respondents expecting an increase and a decrease, respectively. A broad disagreement of this type could be seen as evidence for instability and

---

[195] As Appendix 2 shows, each point value is a simple linear transformation of the balance. For this reason and because the balance is already a measure constructed as a linear transformation of the measures for higher and lower, the balance is not plotted in Figure 7.20.

hence for an increased risk of a change of interest rates. But here the evidence clearly shows that there is no broad disagreement of this sort.

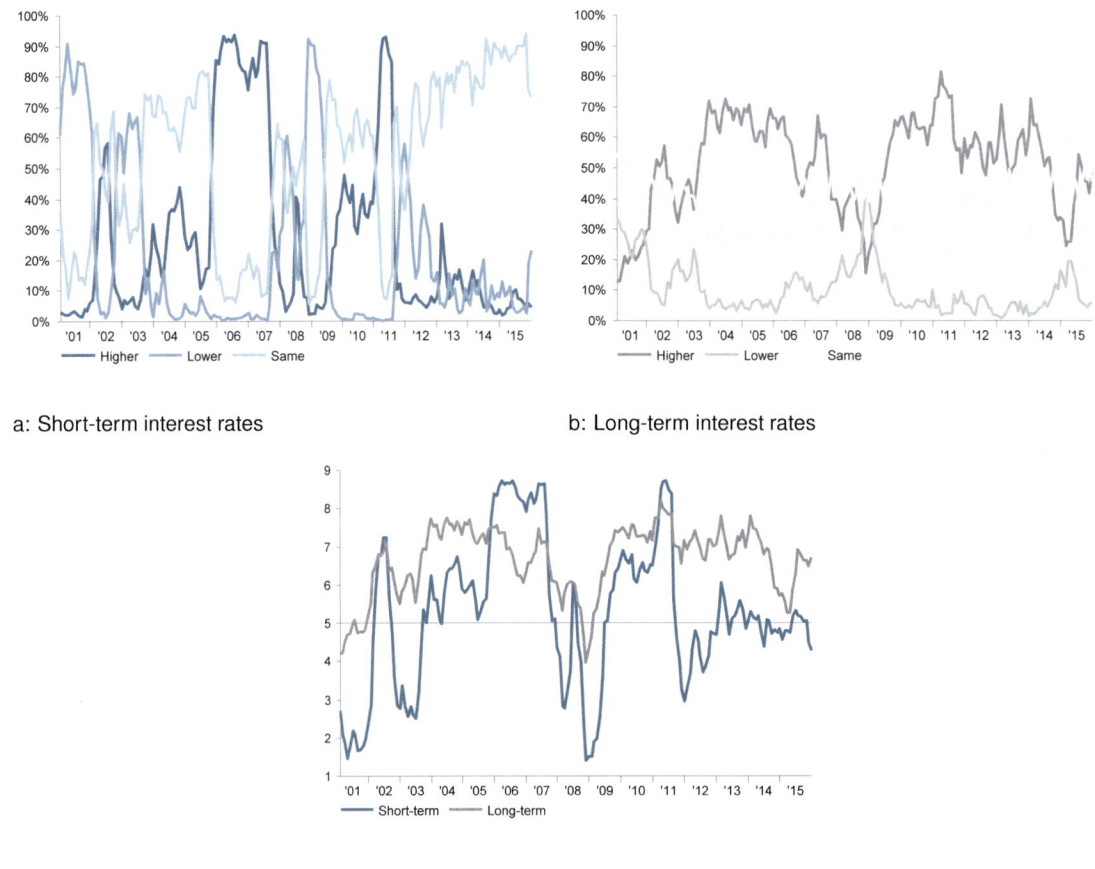

a: Short-term interest rates   b: Long-term interest rates

c: Point values

Figure 7.20: ZEW six months interest rate forecast for (a) short-term and (b) long-term interest rates in percentages of respondents plus (c) translated in point values as published by the ifo. Source: ZEW, Financial Market Survey; own calculations.

Classification by impact on next year's net interest income

Before the analysis or interpretation of the forecasts is turned to, a classification of possible changes may be helpful. One way to interpret the forecasts is to ignore the precise point values and focus instead only on the point values being blow or above or exactly five. The focus is then on the tendency only, namely on whether the interest rate is predicted to go down or up or to remain unchanged. With interest rate forecasts for short-term and for long-term interest rates, there are three times three and hence nine possible combinations of these tendencies, or predicted types of term structure changes. This includes the case of no change of both interest rates.

For the prototypical bank engaged in positive term transformation with a maturity profile that matches the maturities of the interest rates considered here, seven of these types of term structure changes can clearly be identified as beneficial or harmful or neutral for next year's net interest income. The general idea is that at least in the short run a relative decrease (increase) of the short-term against the long-term interest rate increases (decreases) the net interest income because interest expenses decrease (increase) relative to interest earnings. Hence, a term structure change is clearly beneficial, if short-term interest rates decrease and long-term interest rates remain unchanged or even increase and also if short-term interest rates remain unchanged but long-term interest rates increase. And a term structure change is clearly harmful, if short-term interest rates increase and long-term interest rates remain unchanged or even decrease and also if short-term interest rates remain unchanged but long-term interest rates decrease. Finally, the case in which neither short-term nor long-term interest rates change is clearly neutral. Only the net effect of term structure changes which have both the short-term and the long-term interest rate change in the same direction is unclear. The net effect depends on the precise maturity profile of the bank's portfolio as well as on the relative strength of the interest rate changes. Together, these parameters determine whether the increase (decrease) of the short-term interest rates has a larger or a smaller or an effect of the same size as the increase (decrease) of the long-term interest rates. Nevertheless, if one is willing to associate these kinds of changes with parallel changes, one might expect shifts up to be harmful and shifts down to be beneficial. This is most easily explained by the fact that for a bank engaged in positive term transformation liabilities are rolled-over faster than assets. Hence, the effects resulting from changes of the short-term interest rates kick in on the profit and loss account before they are compensated for by the effects resulting from changes of the long-term interest rates. With this in mind, the two remaining types of term structure changes may be identified as likely beneficial and likely harmful. Yet, compared to the other types, a graduation is obviously in order. The graphical illustration in Figure 7.21 features natural designations for the types of term structure changes discussed. Note however, that these designations are not to be confused with the names given to the shock scenarios brought forward by the BCBS (2016). For example, "short rates up" here refers to the case where short-term interest rates increase and long-term interest rates remain unchanged. In contrast, the short rates shock up discussed previously also lets long-term rates increase, though by a smaller absolute amount. The simplistic design of term structure changes categorized here combined with the assumption of a bank with a portfolio the maturity profile of which exactly matches the maturities of the considered interest rates makes the identification of clearly beneficial and harmful term structure changes possible in the first place. A more realistic categorization has to be based on an impact assessment like the one presented later. This impact assessment also assesses the impact of the shock scenarios as calibrated for supervisory purposes on banks' current portfolio value. In the following analysis of the interest rate forecasts, only the categorization based on the impact of next year's net interest income is used. The main reason for preferring this perspective here is that the impact on next year's net interest income already materializes if the bank does not trade the instruments behind its banking-book positions. And the general idea behind classifying positions as banking-book positions and not as trading-book positions instead should be that there is no intention to trade the instruments behind them. In contrast, the impact on the current portfolio value is only realized if the bank actually trades the instruments behind its banking book positions. More generally, instruments behind positions in the banking book are less likely to be traded, because otherwise they would be behind positions in the trading book. This point was already touched on above.

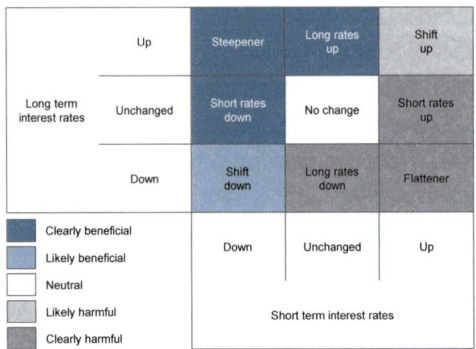

Figure 7.21: Types of forecasts considering tendencies for the development of short and long-term interest rates only classified by impact on next year's net interest income. Source: own illustration.

Forecasts' implications

Turning to the actual forecasts made by the ifo and the ZEW, it turns out they do not cover the full range of types of term structure changes discernable on the basis of tendencies (see Figure 7.22). Over the last 15 years up to and including 2015, neither the ifo nor the ZEW has forecasted a single clearly harmful term structure change in terms of next year's net interest income. In all three time periods covered, namely the last five, the last 10, and the last 15 years, both research institutes have mostly forecasted steepeners and shifts up. Besides, the ifo has also forecasted a few changes of the maturity structure that can be characterized as short rates down, long rates up, and shifts down, the ZEW only also shifts down. The large majority of the forecasts of both research institutes have long-term interest rates going up. Over the last five years, neither the ifo nor the ZEW has forecasted that the long-term interest rate will decrease. The forecasts concerning the short-term interest rate differ more between the two research institutes with the ifo more frequently predicting an increase than the ZEW. However, both have forecasted a decrease of short-term interest rates more frequently over the last five years. In effect, the frequency of the forecast of the clearly beneficial steepener has unanimously increased recently. This might be taken as an indication of reduced interest rate risk for next year's net interest income.[196]

Up until now, the analysis of the forecasts by the ifo and the ZEW was based on tendencies only, that is only on the information whether the point values of the forecasts of the short and the long-term interest rates are below or above or exactly five. Taking into account the precise point values instead adds more information to the analysis. In particular, it becomes possible to assess the ambiguousness the forecasts come with. The general idea is that the closer a given point value is to one or five or nine, the less ambiguous is the forecast that the interest rate in question will decrease or remain unchanged or increase, respectively.

---

[196] Note that the forecasts by the ifo and the ZEW are made with a forecasting horizon of six months only. In contrast, the analyses of the historic term structure changes above consistently investigate changes of interest rates over a period of one year. This one year period can be traced back to BaFin (2007). However, since the forecasts at issue here are qualitative forecasts, this inconsistency is assumed not to have substantial implications for the analyses conducted. Put differently, it is assumed that the responses to the relevant survey questions by the ifo and the ZEW would have been similar, if the forecasting horizon had been one year instead of six months. Because it seems plausible that the directions of the interest rate changes expected by the individual respondents would not change in many cases, if the forecasting horizon was increased in this way.

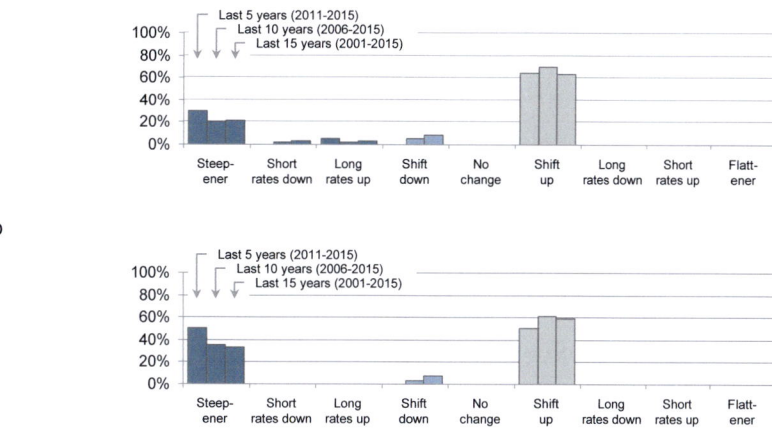

a: ifo

b: ZEW

Figure 7.22: Frequency of predictions by change type for the last five, 10, and 10 years up to and including 2015 by (a) ifo and (b) ZEW. Color-coding as in Figure 7.21. Source: ifo, World Economic Survey; ZEW, Financial Market Survey; own calculations.

For the remaining part of this analysis, the following preparatory steps are taken. First, to every type of term structure change the corresponding prototypical point-tuple is assigned. For example, to a steepener we assign the point-tuple $(1; 9)$ with the 1 for a decrease of the short-term interest rates and the 9 for an increase in the long-term interest rates. Second, for every tuple of actual forecasts of the short and the long-term interest rates we calculate the sum of the absolute distances to the point-tuple of every type of term structure change.[197] For example, the actual forecast $(2;7)$ has a total distance of $3 = 1 + 2$ points to the point-tuple assigned to a steepener. Third, we calculate the probability of every type of term structure change implied by a given forecast as the fraction that the inverse of the corresponding total distance makes up of the sum of inverses of total distances to all types of term structure changes. In our example the implied probability of a steepener would be about 21% as the inverse of the corresponding distance is $1/3$ and all inverses sum to $737/455$.[198] This way, every scenario gets assigned a probability given any forecast.

Tracking the implied probabilities calculated in this way over the last 15 years up to and including 2015 one main lessons can be learnt (see Figure 7.23). There has been no particularly clear trend over the last three to four years. In the first quarter of 2015 the implied probabilities of no term structure change reached their highest values over the last 15 years, namely 50.0% (ifo) and 60.2% (ZEW). However, the implied probabilities of both clearly and likely beneficial and harmful changes of the term structure have since largely returned to their previous levels. Aside from the extreme results for the first quarter of 2015, the beneficial changes have had a consistently higher implied probability than the harmful changes. But there are no particularly clear upward or downward trends over the last three to four years. The only thing that might suggest a trend is about to develop is that while the implied probabilities of the harmful term structure changes have already reached the levels observable prior to the first quarter of 2015, the implied probabilities of the beneficial term structure changes are still a bit lower. The decrease in the implied probability of beneficial term structure changes in the first quarter of 2015 was larger and it still remains to be observed whether they will recover completely.

---

[197] Here the absolute instead of the quadratic distance is used in order to limit the increase of the distance measure toward extreme values, hence toward point values prototypical for a change in interest rate.

[198] Over all forecasts considered, not a single total distance of 0 occurs. Hence we do not run into difficulties trying to divide by zero. A natural way to deal with a case like this would be to assign an implied probability of 100% to the scenario the distance to which is zero.

At the current edge, the implied probabilities of an at least likely beneficial change of the term structure are 39.4% (ifo) and 46.2% (ZEW) but of an at least likely harmful change only 34.1% (ifo) and 30.8% (ZEW). Excluding shifts up and down, which have the most ambiguous effects, the implied probabilities are 34.1% (ifo) and 39.9% (ZEW) on the one hand and only 25.3% (ifo) and 22.8% (ZEW) on the other hand. Note that as the implied probability of a shift up unanimously is larger at the current edge than that of a shift down, and has been so in recent years most of the time, excluding shifts up and down leads to larger gaps between the implied probabilities of likely beneficial and likely harmful changes of the term structure. To sum up, these numbers suggest that in terms of next year's net interest income banks are more likely to experience a beneficial term structure change than a harmful one. Yet, there are first signs for a harmful change becoming more likely.

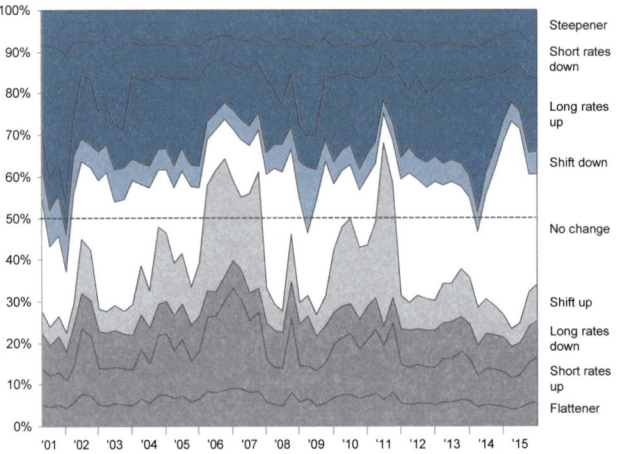

a: ifo

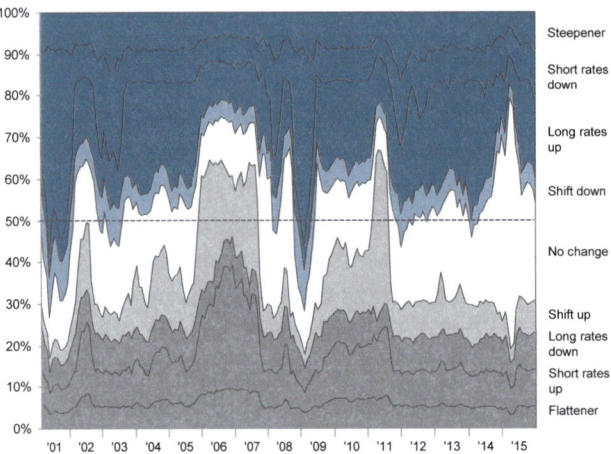

b: ZEW

Figure 7.23: Implied probabilities of term structure changes by (a) ifo and (b) ZEW. Color-coding as in Figure 7.21. Source: ifo, World Economic Survey; ZEW, Financial Market Survey; own calculations.

7.5.2 Quantitative forecasts' implications for adequacy

In the following, the quantitative forecasts published by Consensus Economics are introduced and analyzed. For one part of the analysis a technique is developed that exploits the standard deviations of the respondents' forecasts on top of the means of these individual forecasts.

Forecasts by Consensus Economics

Consensus Economics publishes a quantitative interest rate forecast for Germany. This forecast is available on a monthly basis and through Thomson Reuters Datastream. It covers interest rates at two maturities, namely 3-month money market rates and 10-year government bond yields. And it covers two forecasting horizons, namely three months and one year. In what follows, the focus will be on the forecast with a forecasting horizon of one year only.[199]

Consensus Economics derives what it refers to as the "consensus forecast" as the arithmetic mean of the individual quantitative forecasts of the economic experts it surveys. Consensus Economics does not provide a time series with the number of individual quantitative forecasts, that is the number of respondents. But to get an idea of the magnitude, in the December survey of 2015 a total of 21 individual quantitative forecasts were collected for the 3-month money market rate and a total of 22 for the 10-year government bond yield.

In contrast to the qualitative forecasts provided by the ifo and the ZEW, the quantitative forecast provided by Consensus Economics does not concern changes of interest rates directly. Whereas the ifo and the ZEW ask for future levels relative to the current level or outright for the direction of future change, respectively, Consensus Economics asks for expected absolute levels. But, of course, the implied expected changes can easily be calculated by subtracting the respective current interest rates. In what follows, the 3-month EURIBOR and the 10-year interest rate from the zero-coupon government bond yield curve are regarded as the relevant interest rates. It should be noted, however, that there is minor ambiguity in the survey design concerning the precise interest rates referred to.

Forecasts' implications (means only, part one)

We start the assessment of the implied expected changes of interest rates by simply plotting the data (see Figure 7.24). Already at a brief visual inspection three peculiarities attract attention. First, the large majority of forecasts feature both an increase in the short-term and in the long-term interest rates. Indeed, this is true for about 71% of all forecasts made in the 15 years up to and including 2015 which can hence be found in the first quadrant here. Second, compared to the forecasts made between 2001 and 2005 and those made between 2011 and 2015, those made between 2006 and 2010 show the widest dispersion. Here, clearly the financial crisis left its mark. Third, many of the forecasts which have been made in the last five years feature hardly any change of the short-term interest rate combined with a substantial increase of the long-term interest rate. As is shown next, this is clearly reflected in the frequencies of types of term structure changes forecasted. Since the focus is again on interest rates at two maturities only, the method for the identification of types of term structure changes that was introduced earlier and which prominently features a tolerance level for parallel shocks can be applied again. The fact that earlier we looked at actual term structure changes and now are looking at forecasts of term structure changes does not require any change of the method. The only relevant difference is that the shorter maturity is now three months and hence less than the one year considered above. This could give reason for a higher tolerance level as one might be willing to accept larger differences in the changes of the interest rates and still regard the overall change of the term structure as a parallel shift because the maturities are now further apart. However, to keep things simple the 33.3% tolerance level used earlier is maintained.[200]

---

[199] This accounts for the fact that the change of the term structure over one year is generally regarded as the most appropriate starting point for an assessment of banks' interest rate risk. This fact has already been introduced above.

[200] Note that a slightly higher tolerance level that is still less than 50% would not come with a multiple of an integer value.

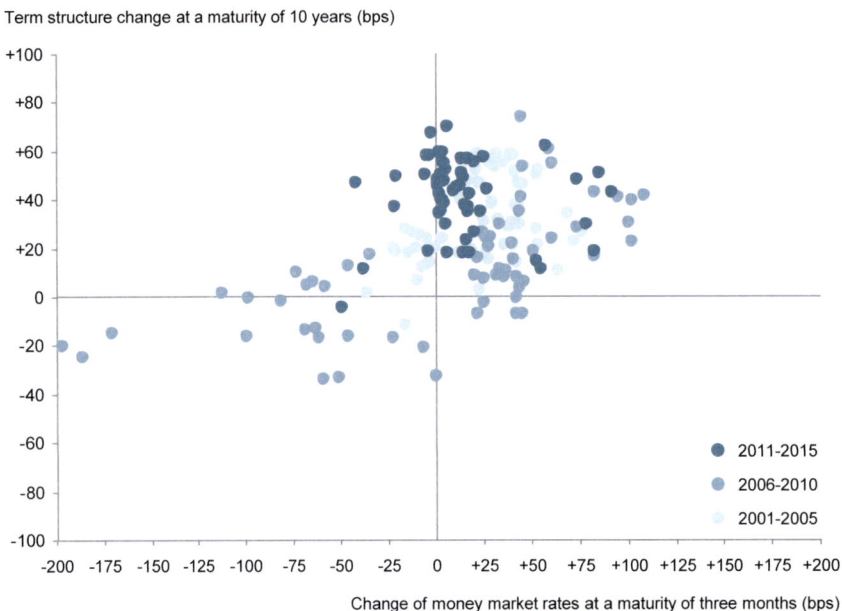

Term structure change at a maturity of 10 years (bps)

Figure 7.24: Distribution of predicted reference rate changes, i.e. of money market rates at 3 months maturity and government bond rates at 10 years maturity over next 12 months. Source: Consensus Economics, interest rate forecasts; BBK, interest rate data; own calculations.

As expected, the first thing one finds when looking at the relative frequencies of the types of term structure changes forecasted is that in the last five years in more than half of the cases a long rates shock up has been predicted (see Figure 7.25). Moreover, that the relative frequency of predictions of this type over the last five years is double that over the last 10 years tells us that all predictions of this type that were made during the last ten years were actually made during the last five years. The second thing to notice is that in the last five years only five types of changes have been predicted at all. Besides long rates shocks up, only parallel shocks up, steepener shocks, as well as short rates shocks up and down have been forecasted. Finally, the third thing that stands out is that there are differences in magnitude between the relative frequencies of forecasts of long rates shocks up and down and also of parallel shocks up and down. In both cases, shocks up have been predicted much more frequently in all three overlapping time periods considered here.

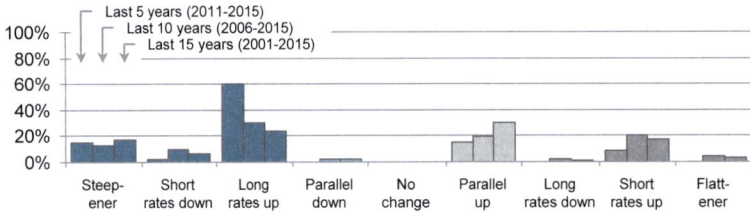

Figure 7.25: Frequency of predictions by change type with a tolerance level of 33.3% for the last five, 10, and 10 years up to and including 2015 by Consensus Economics. Color-coding as in Figure 7.21. Source: Consensus Economics, interest rate forecasts; BBK, interest rate data; own calculations.

If the classification of clearly and likely beneficial and harmful changes introduced in the discussion of the qualitative forecasts is applied again, it may be noticed that the beneficial changes have been forecasted much more frequently in the last five years than in the last 10 or 15 years. And it appears reasonable to say that this indicates a decrease in the interest rate risk in terms of next year's net interest income of the prototypical bank engaged in positive term transformation with the relevant maturities matching those of the interest rates considered here. In numerical terms, the share of predictions of types of term structure changes that are clearly or likely beneficial has been about 49% over the last 15 years, close to 55% over the last 10 years, but even just above 77% over the last five years. As not a single forecast featured no change, the remaining share is always that of predictions of clearly or likely harmful term types of term structure changes.

However, using this simple classification may reasonably be considered problematic given the nature of the forecasts analysed here. The classification was introduced above to enable the analysis of qualitative forecasts. In that context it could be justified as the best you can do. But in the analysis of quantitative forecasts you can clearly do better. That is to say, that using the classification here can only be a first step and the results are only an indication of what the final result may be. Further analyses are in order that exploit the higher informational content of the quantitative forecasts compared to that of the qualitative forecasts.

One last comment may be helpful before engaging in these further analyses. In order to bring about a meaningful analysis of the qualitative forecasts it was required to characterize short and long rates shocks up and down as one-sided changes, i.e. the respective other interest rate was understood to remain unchanged. This made it possible to identify short rates shocks down and long rates shocks up as clearly beneficial and short rates shocks up and long rates shocks down as clearly harmful for next year's net interest income of the prototypical bank engaged in positive term transformation. Of course, with the respective other interest rate changing in the same direction, the net effect is much more sensitive to the precise time horizon of the assessment, even for a bank engaged in positive term transformation and for which the two interest rates under investigation are the effective refinancing and lending rate, respectively. A similar reasoning applies to parallel shocks up and down and note that above we were only able to identify more generally shifts up and down.

Technique for integrated analysis of means and standard deviations

Until now, the analysis of the quantitative forecasts has been based on the "consensus forecasts", that is on the arithmetic means of the individual quantitative forecasts of the economic experts surveyed by Consensus Economics only. But as a further moment we may also include the standard deviation of all these individual forecasts in our analysis. Naturally, a higher standard deviation indicates less agreement and hence less reliability or accuracy of the forecast.[201] Put differently, a higher standard deviation indicates that the implied probability of the realization of values further away from the mean is higher. Hence, for every pair of mean and standard deviation we can establish a ranking of the implied probabilities of the realization of any values in a straightforward way. To this end, we do not need to assume any particular distribution of the individual quantitative forecasts. It is sufficient to assume that the higher the number of standard deviations a certain value is away from the mean, the lower is its implied probability. Note that this measure is symmetric around the mean.

Equipped with this technique, it is possible to assess the implied probability of the stylized scenarios brought forward by the BCBS (2016). We simply track the number of standard deviations that the change in the respective interest rate according to the respective shock scenario is away from the forecasted change. At this point, we do this individually for the two interest rates under investigation and do not introduce an aggregated measure as this requires further distributional assumptions.

---

[201] Note that further below historical forecasts are contrasted with the historic development of interest rates in order to assess the quality of the forecasts as a leading indicator.

Forecasts' implications (means and standard deviations)

The results are rather clear (see Figure 7.26). For parallel, short rates, steepener, and flattener shocks, there has recently been a massive increase in the number of standard deviations that the forecasted change of the 3-month interest rate is away from the respective change featured in the shock scenarios. And according to the reasoning laid out above, this implies a massive decrease in the probability implied in the forecasts made, that the changes of the short-term interest rates that the shock scenarios come with will actually materialize. In comparison, the developments of the distances of the forecasted change of the 10-year interest rate from the changes featured in the different shock scenarios appear almost flat, with the distances remaining much below those recently observed for the changes of the 3-month interest rate. The parallel, the short rates, the steepener, and the flattener shock scenarios are those that feature sizeable changes of the 3-month interest rate between 147 and 235 basis points. The long rates shock scenario, in contrast, features a change of only 6 basis points and the additionally included scenario of no change obviously of zero basis points. For the parallel as well as for the short rates shocks, we can observe that the developments of the numbers of standard deviations between the forecast of the 3-month interest rate and the changes featured in the scenarios up and down are rather similar. As the scenarios of parallel shocks up and down and those of short rates shocks up and down are symmetric this tells us that the increase in the distance must be due to a decrease in the standard deviation rather than to a change in the forecasted interest rate and that this forecasted interest rate must be close to zero. This clearly suggests that in recent years the individual forecasts by the surveyed economic experts have clustered ever closer around zero and that as far as one is willing to trust these experts the forecast of no change has become ever more reliable. This points to decreased interest rate risk.

Now the assessment of the implied probabilities of the realization of the shock scenarios brought forward by the BCBS (2016) is taken one step further in that the 3-month interest rate and the 10-year interest rate are assessed together. As mentioned before, the necessary aggregation requires further distributional assumptions. Here the assumption is made that for each individual interest rate, a t-distribution for the translation of the distance measured in number of standard deviations into the implied probability can be used. Reflecting the number of individual forecasts, a t-distribution with 20 degrees of freedom is used. Concerning the dependence between the interest rates, two extreme cases are considered. Firstly, the case of independence is looked at. In effect, the implied probability of the change of the 3-month interest rate as the respective shock scenario has it is multiplied with that of the 10-year interest rate. Secondly, the case of what is called here complete dependence is looked at where it is assumed that if the less likely interest rate change materializes the more likely one does too. To capture this idea, the smaller of the two implied probabilities is taken as the overall implied probability.

Figure 7.27 presents the relative frequencies of the shock scenarios with the highest implied probability over the last five, ten, and 15 years. It features four subfigures. Because not only the two different options for dependence just outlined are covered. Furthermore results are presented including the long rates shock scenarios and the scenario of no change which are not brought forward by the BCBS (2016) as well as excluding these scenarios. The first lesson that can be learnt is that the results only depend to a very limited extent on which of the two extreme options for dependence is assumed. The reason for this is that the very small implied probabilities of the materialization of the changes of the 3-month interest rate featured in the shock scenarios dominate. These implied probabilities and also their changes differ in magnitudes from the ones of the 10-year interest rates. In contrast, the second lesson that can be learnt is that the results materially depend on whether long rates shocks up and down and the scenario of no change are included or excluded. If they are included, the long rates shock up and the scenario of no change

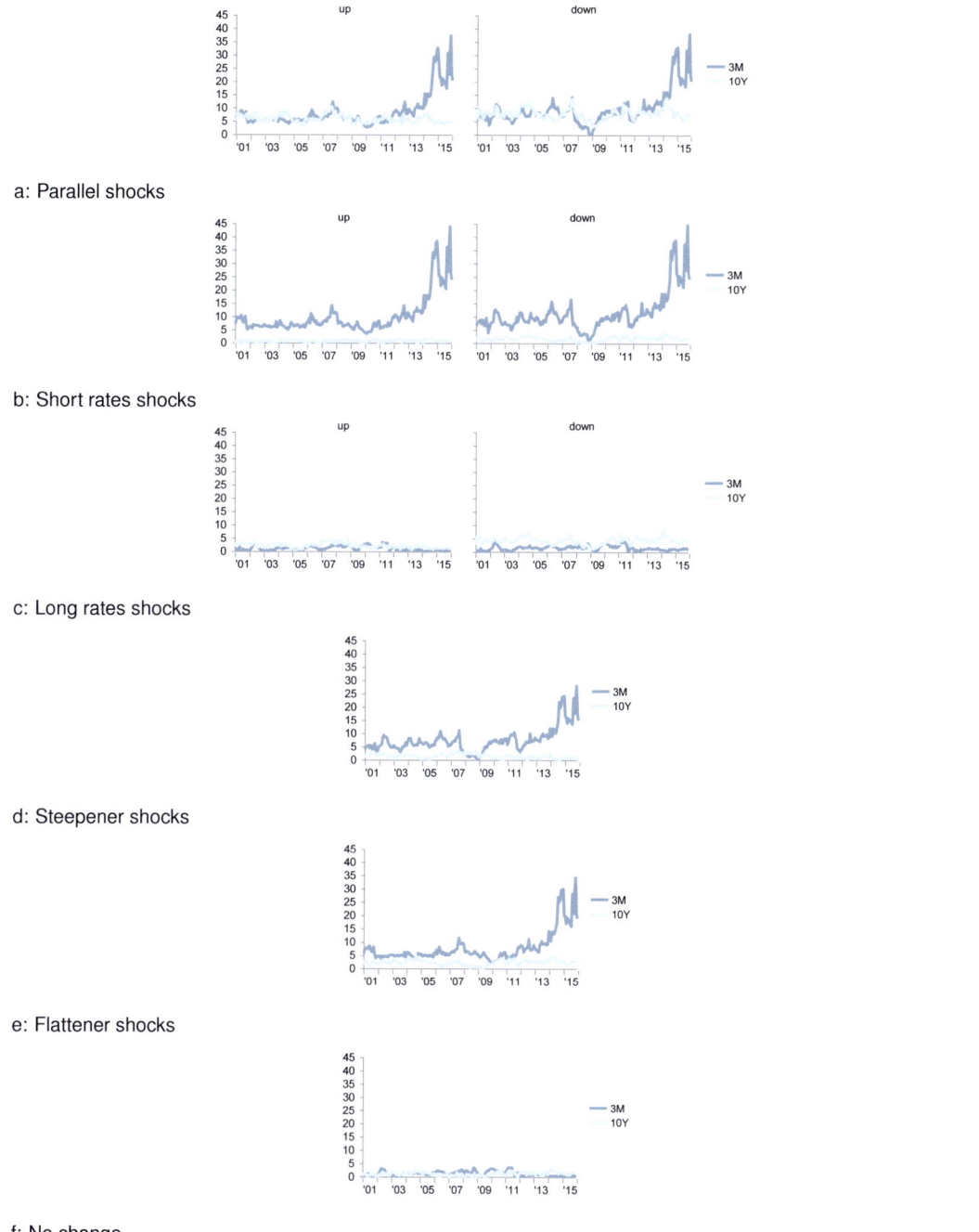

a: Parallel shocks

b: Short rates shocks

c: Long rates shocks

d: Steepener shocks

e: Flattener shocks

f: No change

Figure 7.26: Shocks as defined by the BCBS (2016) versus forecasts by Consensus Economics with the distance measured in number of standard deviations (vertical axis) for (a) parallel shocks, (b) short rates shocks, (c) long rates shocks, (d) steepener shocks, (e) flattener shocks, and (f) no change. Source: BCBS (2016); Consensus Economics, interest rate forecasts; BBK, interest rate data; own calculations.

consistently account for more than 90% of the shock scenarios with the highest implied probability. And over the last five years they even catch 100%, that is every single forecast made during the last five years came with an implied probability of a long rates shock up or of no change that was higher than the implied probability of every other shock scenario. Again, this result obviously reflects the fact that recently the implied probability of any sizeable change of the short-term interest rate has reached unprecedented lows. Now naturally, if long rates shocks and the scenario of no change are excluded, completely different results re obtained. Of the shock scenarios actually brought forward by the BCBS (2016) steepener and flattener shocks turn out to have the highest probabilities implied by the forecasts reported by Consensus Economics over the last 15, 10, and also five years. Over the last five years, the relative frequency of the steepener shock having the highest implied probability increased while that of the flattener shock decreased.

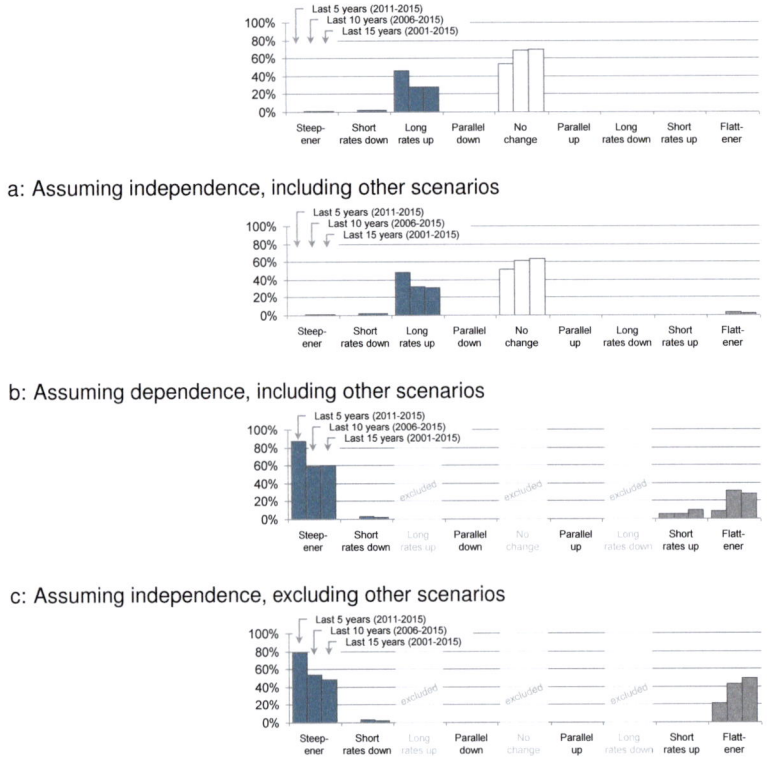

a: Assuming independence, including other scenarios

b: Assuming dependence, including other scenarios

c: Assuming independence, excluding other scenarios

d: Assuming dependence, excluding other scenarios

Figure 7.27: Frequency of predictions by change type for the last five, 10, and 10 years up to and including 2015 by Consensus Economics according to distribution assessment. Color-coding as in Figure 7.21. Source: BCBS (2016); Consensus Economics, interest rate forecasts; BBK, interest rate data; own calculations.

But even though the results are so different, the main driver is the same, namely the low and decreasing implied probability of any material change of the short-term interest rate. Compared to the parallel and the short rates shocks, the steepener and the flattener shock feature smaller absolute changes of the 3-month interest rate. Since larger changes of the short-term interest rates are much more unlikely, that is why the steepener and flattener shock have higher implied probabilities than the other shock scenarios most of the time over the last 15 years. Of the steepener and the flattener shock scenario the steepener comes with a lower absolute change of the 3-month interest rate. And since the implied probability of larger changes decreased severely recently, this explains why the relative frequency of the steepener shock being the most likely increases while that of the flattener shock decreases.

Returning to the results produced when long rates shocks and the scenario of no change are included, it can be noticed that recently the relative frequency of a long rates shock up having the highest implied probability has increased while that of the scenario of no change has decreased. This finding makes it necessary to take a closer look at our explanation of the results so far that they are mostly due to a high and increasing agreement of the surveyed experts that the 3-month interest rate will not change. Now to be precise, the average forecast over the last five years has been a change of 13 basis points up. Hence, it is only natural that a shock scenario which features a change closer to this than the change by zero basis points featured in the scenario of no change may have gained relative frequency. And indeed, the long rates shock up features a change of the 3-month interest rate of 6 basis points. The second closest shock scenario is already the steepener shock which features minus 147 basis points and thus is much further away than the scenario of zero change. Put differently, recently the forecasts for the 3-month interest rate gravitated not to zero but to a positive value very close to zero. And therefore the long rates shock up, which features a very small positive change of the 3-month interest rate, has become more likely relative to the scenario of no change.

The interpretation of the findings just laid out is straightforward. A long rates shock up and a steepener shock as brought forward by the BCBS (2016) belong to those types of shock scenarios that are most naturally seen as beneficial for a bank engaged in positive term transformation at least in terms of next year's net interest income. And hence, the findings suggest German banks' interest rate risk has decreased recently as far as their near future net interest income is concerned. Of course, these results also again may give rise to astonishment at the exclusion of long rates shocks from the official shock scenarios.

Forecasts' implications (means only, part two)

As has been discovered above, if the standard deviation is included in the analysis, the decrease of the standard deviation of the forecast of the 3-month interest rate dominates the results. In the next part of the analysis the focus is again on the means, that is the "consensus forecasts" only. And as done with the historic actual term structure changes, for every historic interest rate forecast it is determined which type of shock scenario with which parameter value, or values in the case of more than one parameter, fits best. As detailed above, a qualitative pre-selection is conducted first and then the scenario with the calibration with the smallest sum of squared residuals is identified. The qualitative pre-selection ensures in particular that if and only if the changes forecasted for the 3-month and the 10-year interest rate have different signs, it is a steepener or a flattener shock the parameters of which then are determined as those with the smallest residual sum of squares. If the changes forecasted have the same signs, the smallest sum of squares does not only determine the parameter value but also whether these changes are overall best described as a parallel or a short rates or a long rates shock. Instead of looking at the difference between the forecasted interest rates and those featured in the shock scenarios brought forward by the BCBS (2016) it is now investigated which shock types and parameter values best capture the forecasts made.

The results of this analysis for the last 15 years are presented in Figure 7.28. Remember that the parameter values defined by the BCBS (2016) are 200 basis points for the parallel parameter, 250 basis points for the short parameter, and 100 basis points for the long parameter. The following assessment addresses one shock scenario type at a time. Looking at the cases for which a parallel shock scenario up or down fits best, it is observed that not in a single month the best fitting parallel parameter does at least reach half the proposed value. The maximum value over the last 15 years is just under 70 basis points, reached in June 2011. What is also noteworthy is that there are only very few occurrences when a parallel shock down best fits the forecasted interest rate changes. And when this is the case, the best fitting parameter value is never larger than 50 basis points. This may be taken to suggest different parameter values for parallel shocks up and down. Concerning the development of the size of the best fitting parameter for parallel shocks up, there seems to be a downward trend since the all-time high in 2011. Looking at instances with a short rates shock fitting best, it is observed that the best fitting parameter values never reach the size proposed. For short rates shock up, the largest best fitting parameter value has been close to 120 basis points and for short rates shocks down about 210.

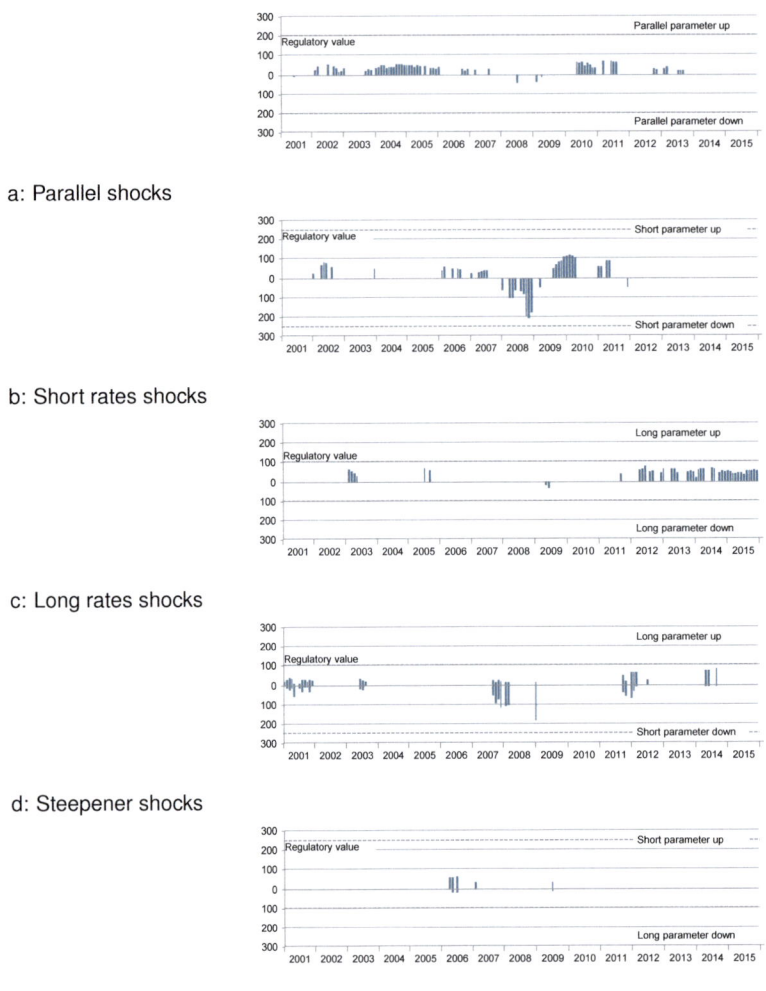

a: Parallel shocks

b: Short rates shocks

c: Long rates shocks

d: Steepener shocks

e: Flattener shocks

Figure 7.28: Best fitting parameter values for forecasts published by Consensus Economics (best fit according to minimal residual sum of squares after qualitative pre-selection). Source: BCBS (2016); Consensus Economics, interest rate forecasts; BBK, interest rate data; own calculations.

Note that the latter value is about 84% of the regulatory value but the former is again below 50%. The 84% are the highest share of the regulatory value that is reached by any parameter in any type of scenario here. However, as it appeared in the second half of 2008 it is clear that the financial crisis left its mark. A recent trend cannot be observed as the most recent forecast for which a short rates shock up or down is the best fitting scenario dates back to December 2011 already. Not surprisingly, looking at long rates shocks, the regulatory parameter value still appears conservative, that is risk-averse, but not far off. For long rates shocks up, the highest value of the best fitting long parameter has been close to 75 basis points and this as recent as in June 2012. Long rates shocks up also make up by far the most frequent best fitting shock scenario over the last few years. In contrast to the long rates shock up, only two forecasts can be found for which a long rates shock down is the best fit. Now it has to be kept in mind that the long rates shocks are not officially proposed as stand-alone shocks by the BCBS (2016). But looking at the proposed steepener shock, it turns out that for that one, too, best fitting values for the long parameter occur which are not very far off from the regulatory value. For a forecast as recently made as in September 2014 the best fitting scenario is a steepener shock with a long parameter of more than 80 basis points. However, the forecast best described as a flattener shock with the largest long parameter only features a long parameter value of just above 20 basis points. The maximum values observed for the short parameter are about 185 basis points in a steepener shock but only just above 60 basis points in a flattener shock. Due to lack of recent occurrences no recent trend of the size of flattener shocks can be identified. As to steepener shocks, it seems as if the decrease of the short-term interest rate was getting smaller while the increase of the long-term interest rate remained largely unchanged. In this way, the shock gets slightly less beneficial for the typical bank engaged in positive term transformation.

In sum, these findings again suggest a decreasing interest rate risk of a bank engaged in positive term transformation, at least in so far as next year's net interest income is concerned. Looking at the most likely harmful shocks, one finds that the parallel shocks up that have been forecasted recently have been decreasing in size while no short rates shocks up and no flattener shocks have been forecasted recently. And as to the most likely beneficial shocks, one finds that most recent forecasts are best described as long rates shocks up and some other recent forecast took the shape of a steepener shock with a particular strong increase of the long-term interest rate.

7.5.3 Accuracy of qualitative and quantitative forecasts

The following assessment of forecast accuracy reveals two important insights. First, the qualitative predictions published by the ifo and the ZEW are rather reliable for the 3-month interest rate but of no value for the 10-year interest rate. Second, the quantitative predictions published by Consensus Economics largely lag the development of actual interest rates and turn out to be severely biased.

Now there are three possible conclusions to be drawn here. The first possible conclusion is that forecasts of interest rates should be disregarded altogether. This would justify the sole focus on the historic development of interest rates in the development of the supervisory shock scenarios. The second possible conclusion is that only the short-term interest rate forecasts should be built on. This would lead to a partial coverage of possible interest rate changes. The third possible conclusion is that even forecasts of long-term interest rates are important to be aware of but only in so far as they potentially influence banks risk-taking behaviour. When banks plan ahead and structure their portfolios they may well also use long-term interest rate forecasts as a guidance.

Note that if banks base their planning on these interest rate forecasts, this could induce excessive risk-taking. Because as has been shown above, the forecasts mostly point toward a decrease of the size and probability of adverse term structure changes at least in terms of next year's net interest income.. And a bank that takes these forecasts at face value is likely to accept larger exposures. This is a strong motivation to look at interest rate forecasts closely.

Qualitative forecasts

Note that the qualitative forecasts of the ifo and the ZEW differ in the precise long-term interest rate that they address. While the ifo addresses the interest rate of government bonds with 10 years or more remaining maturity the ZEW addresses government bonds with exactly 10 years remaining maturity (see the questionnaires by the ifo (2016) and the ZEW (2016)). This should be kept in mind when assessing the accuracy of these forecasts.

To start with, separate assessments of the accuracy of the interest rate forecasts made by the ifo and the ZEW are carried out. In these assessments the same reference interest rates are used, namely the 3-month EURIBOR and the 10-year interest rate from the zero-coupon government bond yield curve. In doing so, the fact that the ifo also addresses the interest rates of government bonds with a remaining maturity of more than 10 years is effectively ignored. The reason for proceeding in this way is that there simply is no benchmark time series for the interest rates of government bonds with 10 and more years of remaining maturity. However, here qualitative forecasts are at issue and these only concern the directions of changes. Hence, this mismatch between the interest rates explicitly referred to by the ifo and the interest rate used in the following analysis to assess the accuracy of the forecasts should be sufficiently irrelevant.

The ifo publishes quarterly forecasts and the ZEW monthly forecasts. The forecasts of both the ifo and the ZEW are based on surveys and the different schedules of these surveys suggest to use slightly different interest rate data for the quality assessment. For the assessment of the quality of the forecasts published by the ifo, the monthly averages of the reference rates are used. Because in every quarter the respondents have the first four weeks to respond. To be precise, the monthly averages from January, April, July, and October are referred to, respectively. For the assessment of the quality of the forecasts published by the ZEW, end-of-month reference rates are used, instead. Because the respondents have to respond in the first days of each month and are asked for the development over the next six months. To capture this, the last value of the respective interest rate from the previous month and the last value six months later are referred to.[202]

There are two commonly used measures for the quality of qualitative forecasts, that is of forecasts of the direction of the development of some variable. The first one is the share of correct forecasts. And the second one is the level of significance at which the null hypothesis of independence between the forecasted and the actual development can be rejected according to Pearson's chi-spared test. The forecasts by the ifo and by the ZEW are looked at separately. For both the forecasts made within the 15 years before and up to 2015 are assessed.

To begin with, the focus is on the forecasts by the ifo. In a first step, the informational content of the point value is reduced to that of a binary variable indicating that the interest rate is forecasted to go down, if the point value is smaller than five, and stay the same or go up, if the point value is equal to or larger than five. For the ifo it turns out that of the 60 quarterly forecasts made, 40 (67%) have been correct about the 3-month interest rate, 21 (35%) about the 10-year interest rate, and 20 (33%) about both interest rates. Pearson's chi squared test tells us that the null hypothesis of independence can be rejected at a significance level below 1% for the 3-month interest rate and for both interest rates but that it cannot be rejected for the 10-year interest rate even at the 10% significance level. Note that this means that you could just as well toss a coin in order to forecast the future development of the 10-year interest rate. Obviously, the share of above 25% of correct forecasts[203] of both interest rates is only due to the share of above 50% correct forecasts of the 3-month interest rate.

A natural thing to suspect is that more extreme point values are more reliable forecasts of interest rate changes. However, it turns out that this in only true for the 3-month interest rate. For the 10-year interest rate, in contrast, a more extreme point value is not a more reliable forecast of the respective change. A look at the scatter plots with the forecast point values on the horizontal axis and the actual changes on the vertical axis already clearly shows this (see Figure 7.29)[204]. For the 3-month interest rate the share of correct forecasts increases from 67% to 76%, if only point values are taken into account that are at least one point away from five. And the share further increases to 94%, if only forecasts that are at least two points away from five are considered. For the 10-year interest rate, however, the share of correct forecasts even drops from 35% to 30%, if all point values that are closer than one point to five are dropped. And the share only partly recovers to 33%, if also the point values closer than two points to five are excluded.

---

[202] For example, a forecast published in February will be contrasted with the actual development of the respective reference rate between the end of January and the end of July of the same year.

[203] Note that for a forecast of the developments of both interest rates you would have to toss two coins.

[204] Note that the color coding of the forecasts is not necessary because obviously exactly the forecasts in the quadrants two and four are incorrect and the forecasts in quadrants one and three are correct. The color coding does not increase the informational content of the figure but makes it more readable.

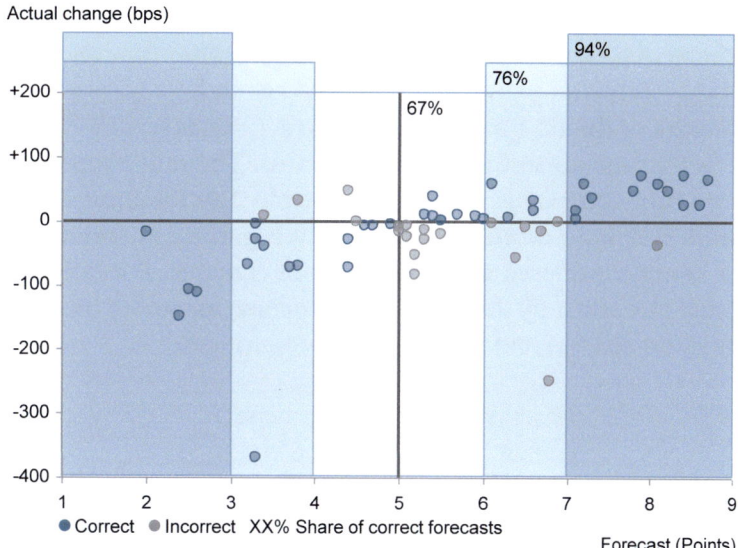

a: 3-month interest rate

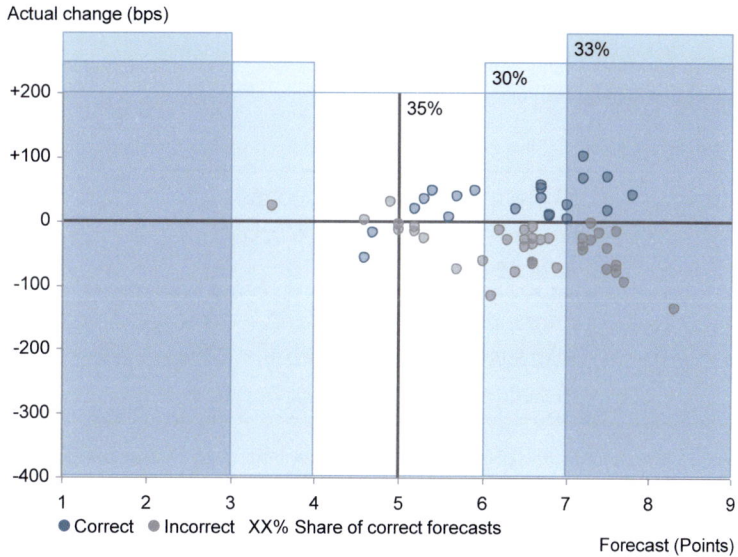

b: 10-year interest rate

Figure 7.29: Forecasts by the ifo (horizontal axis) versus actual changes (vertical axis) with shares of correct forecasts for differently extreme point values. Source: ifo, World Economic Survey; BBK, interest rate data; own calculations.

An alternative to looking at forecasts with extreme point values only is to take only forecasts with extreme point values as forecasts of a change and the forecasts with non-extreme values as forecasts of no change. In this way some tolerance is introduced for the forecasts. If this appears reasonable, it may also appear reasonable to only regard actual changes that are larger than some threshold value as relevant changes and to regard smaller changes as irrelevant or no changes. In this way some tolerance is introduced for the changes of the actual interest rates. Note that introducing tolerance for the changes of the actual interest rates is particularly natural here, given that the neutral answer option on the questionnaire of the ifo is "about the same" and not a phrase like "exactly the same".

The resulting shares of correct forecasts can be found in Table 7.4 for the 3-month interest rate and in Table 7.5 for the 10-year interest rate. At first sight, one particular result for the 10-year interest rate appears promising. If you introduce tolerance for the forecast of two points (meaning that all forecasts between 3 and 7 points are regarded as forecasts of no change) and a tolerance level for the actual change of 50 basis points (meaning that an actual change with an absolute size of less than 50 basis points is considered not to be a relevant change), more than one third of the forecasts of the ifo turn out to be correct, namely 53%.[205] However, Pearson's chi-square test reveals that the appearances are deceptive. The null hypothesis of independence cannot be rejected on any acceptable significance level. The increase in the share of correct forecasts is mostly due simply to more forecasts being regarded as forecasts of no change and more actual changes being considered not to be relevant changes. Put differently, the forecast of the 10-year interest rate published by the ifo does not become any more useful by the introduction of the third category of no change and the respective tolerances.

Share of correct forecasts		Actual change: tolerance in bps		
		0	10	50
Forecast:	0	67%	48%	23%
tolerance	1	47%	57%	55%
in points	2	27%	52%	68%

Table 7.4: Share of correct ifo forecasts of the 3-month interest rate depending on tolerances introduced. Source: ifo, World Economic Survey; BBK, interest rate data; own calculations.

Share of correct forecasts		Actual change: tolerance in bps		
		0	10	50
Forecast:	0	35%	30%	10%
tolerance	1	22%	25%	32%
in points	2	12%	20%	53%

Table 7.5: Share of correct ifo forecasts of the 10-year interest rate depending on tolerances introduced. Source: ifo, World Economic Survey; BBK, interest rate data; own calculations.

Now the focus is on the forecasts of the ZEW. As was to be expected, the results of the assessment of the quality of these forecasts are very similar to the results produced above. Again, the assessment starts with reduced informational content of the point value. The binary variable is looked at which indicates that the interest rate is forecasted to go down, if the point value is smaller than five, and stay the same or go up, if the point value is equal to or larger than five. It can be observed that for the ZEW of the 180 monthly forecasts made, 125 (69%) have been correct about the 3-month interest rate, 64 (36%) about the 10-year interest rate, and 53 (29%) about both interest rates. Pearson's chi squared test tells us that the null hypothesis of independence can be rejected at a significance level below 1% in all three cases. Note, however, that this means that if you want to forecast the development of the 10-year interest rate, you would actually be better off tossing a coin.[206] The forecasts of the 10-year interest rate is significantly more likely to be wrong than to be right.

Just like above, the investigation now turns to the question whether more extreme point values are more reliable forecasts of interest rate changes. But again it turns out that this in only

---

[205] Note that since there are now three categories, namely "increase", "decrease", and "no change", the expected share of correct forecasts given that the forecast is actually completely worthless is one third.

[206] Given these results you would be even better off, if you always expected the change of the 10-year interest rate to have the opposite sign than the sign forecasted.

true for the 3-month interest rate and that for the 10-year interest rate a more extreme point value is not a more reliable forecast of the change. The scatter plots with the forecast point values on the horizontal axis and the actual change on the vertical axis show this clearly (see Figure 7.30). Again, the assessments are restricted to forecasts with point values which are at least one and then which are at least two points away from five. For the 3-month interest rate the share of correct forecasts increases from 69% to 82% and then to 88%. But for the 10-year interest rate it decreases from 36% to 33% and then decreases even further to 30%.

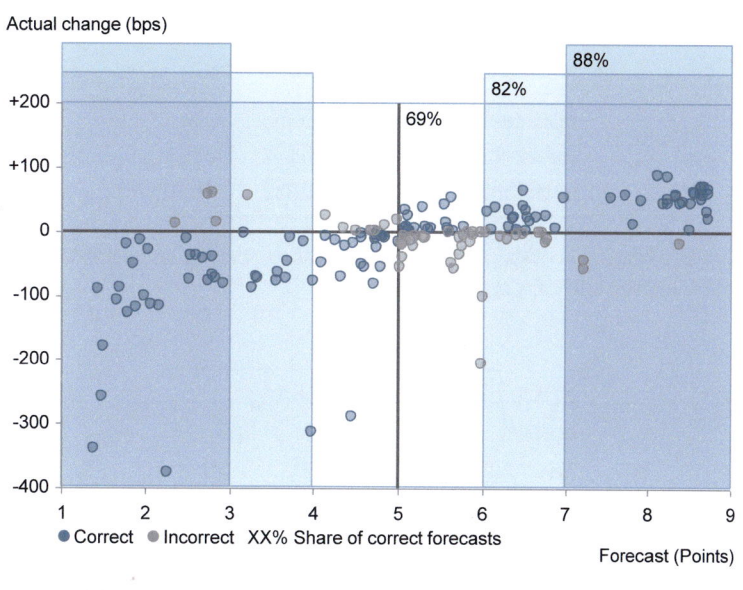

a: 3-month interest rate

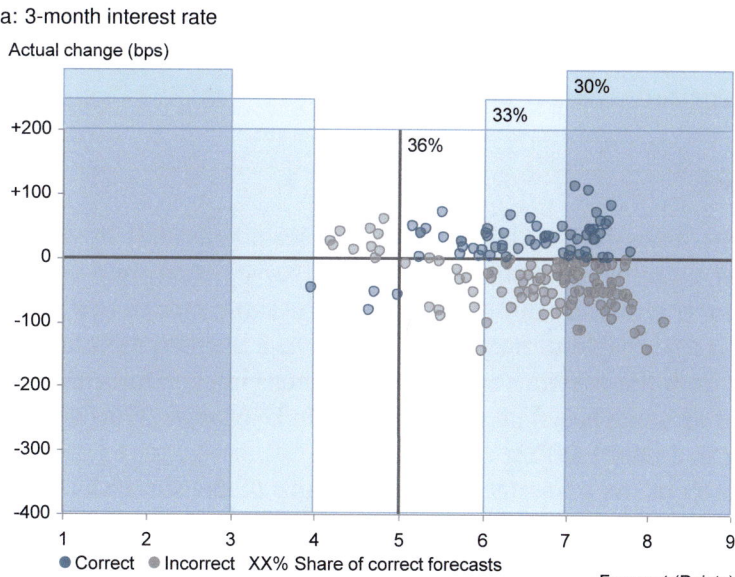

b: 10-year interest rate

Figure 7.30: Forecasts by the ZEW (horizontal axis) versus actual changes (vertical axis) with shares of correct forecasts for differently extreme point values. Source: ZEW, Financial Market Survey; BBK, interest rate data; own calculations.

Just like above, for the next analysis tolerances and the third category of no change are introduced. The results can be found in Table 7.6 for the 3-month interest rate and in Table 7.7 for the 10-year interest rate. If a tolerance of two points for the forecast and of 50 basis points for the actual interest rate change is introduced, the share of correct forecasts of the 10-year interest rate again looks promising that results. Yet again, this result is driven by an increase of the number of forecasts classified as forecasts of no change and of actual changes being categorized as not being a change. If the ZEW predicts an increase, it is more than four times as likely that the 10-year interest rate will decrease than that it will indeed increase. Pearson's chi-square test rejects the null hypothesis of independence at the 5% level but the implied dependence is not the one searched for but precisely the inverse.

Share of correct forecasts		Actual change: tolerance in bps		
		0	10	50
Forecast:	0	69%	52%	29%
tolerance	1	47%	63%	63%
in points	2	29%	58%	74%

Table 7.6: Share of correct ZEW forecasts of the 3-month interest rate depending on tolerances introduced. Source: ZEW, Financial Market Survey; BBK, interest rate data; own calculations.

Share of correct forecasts		Actual change: tolerance in bps		
		0	10	50
Forecast:	0	36%	29%	8%
tolerance	1	26%	25%	21%
in points	2	13%	18%	44%

Table 7.7: Share of correct ZEW forecasts of the 10-year interest rate depending on tolerances introduced. Source: ZEW, Financial Market Survey; BBK, interest rate data; own calculations.

Quantitative forecasts

Now the assessment turns to the quantitative forecasts provided by Consensus Economics. Remember that these monthly forecasts are based on a survey conducted at the beginning of each month which asks for the interest rate at the end of the same month one year later. Accounting for this schedule, it is reasonable to treat each forecast as a thirteen months forecast based on the last available value from the previous month. Along these lines, a forecast published in January 2001 is to be treated as being based on the last value in December 2000 and making a statement about the last value in January 2002.

A natural first step in the assessment of the quality of the forecasts at hand is to contrast the forecasted with the actual interest rates and interest rate changes (see Figure 7.31). Visual inspection immediately suggests that the forecasting errors are not random. And indeed, a simple econometric test strongly supports this finding.[207] Both the forecast of the 3-month interest rate and that of the 10-year interest rate appear to lag the development of the respective actual interest rate. And since both, the 3-month interest rate and the 10-year interest rate decrease most of the time in the period covered, this results in a clear bias in the forecasted changes. Of the 94 actual negative changes of the 3-month interest rate only three had been predicted to

---

[207] A particularly easy to follow application of the econometric standard procedure which involves the use of robust standard errors as introduced by Newey and West (1987) can be found in Bofinger and Schmidt (2003). The only difference is that here no log-values are used. If log-values are used the last 13 observations for the 3-month interest rate have to be dropped as the interest rate is negative. Using log-values and the remaining observations only produces similar results.

be more negative. And also of the 110 actual negative changes of the 10-year interest rate only three had been predicted to be more negative. With respect to banks' interest rate risk, this bias is noteworthy as it suggests that when interest rates fall, these forecasts understate not only the reduction of interest expenses but also of interest earnings.

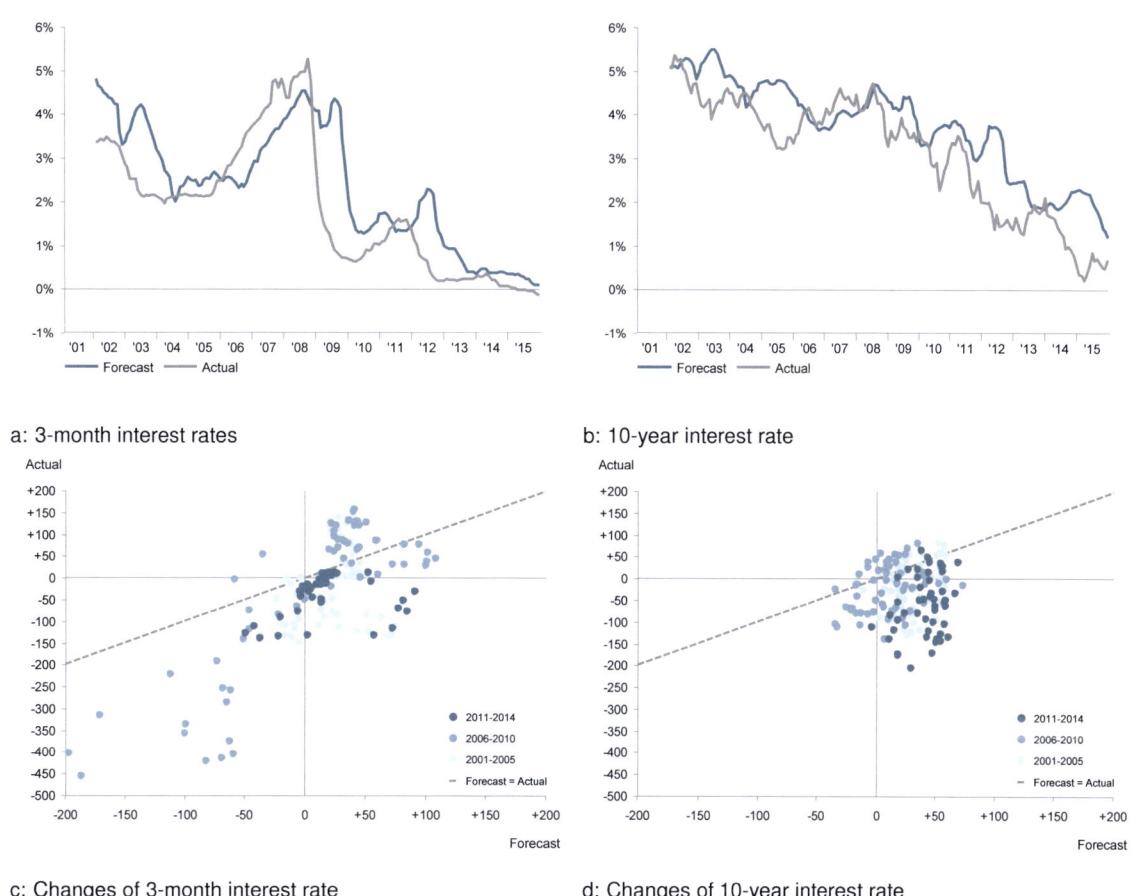

a: 3-month interest rates   b: 10-year interest rate

c: Changes of 3-month interest rate   d: Changes of 10-year interest rate

Figure 7.31: Forecasts by Consensus Economics versus actual interest rates in percent (a, b) and interest rate changes in bps (c, d). Source: Consensus Economics, interest rate forecasts; BBK, interest rate data; own calculations.

7.6   Impact assessment

For the first time, the BCBS (2016) requires banks to disclose the impact of interest rate shock scenarios on an income measure. The requirement supplements the traditional requirement to report scenario impacts on a net present value measure. More precisely, from 2018 on banks[208] are required to report the impacts of certain shock scenarios on next year's net interest income as well as on the economic value of equity. Interestingly, however, the final version of the regulatory standards does not require the disclosure of the impact of all the supervisory shock scenarios developed on a bank's net interest income. Only the impacts of the parallel shocks up and down have to be disclosed. In the consultative version of the standards the BCBS (2015) also prescribed the disclosure of the impacts of the short rates shocks up and down and of the steepener and the flattener shock on next year's net interest income. But these disclosure requirements are missing in the final version. This leads to the worrying outcome that the final disclosure requirement

---

[208] The BCBS (2016) refers to internationally active banks but national supervisors can be expected to increase the scope to non-internationally active banks as they have done in comparable instances in the past.

include the impacts of all six supervisory shock scenarios on a bank's economic value of equity but only the impacts of the parallel shock scenarios on a bank's next year's net interest income. This outcome is worrying for the simple reason that the type of impact measure should not be among the criteria for including or excluding the impact of a certain shock scenario in the disclosure requirements. If a shock scenario meets the criteria such that its impact on a bank's economic value of equity is included in the disclosure requirements, it should also meet the criteria with respect to next year's net interest income.

In what follows it is not investigated how the reduction of the disclosure requirements from the consultative to the final version of the new standards actually came about. However, the impact assessment reveals that the short rates shock up and the flattener shock have more adverse impacts than the parallel shock up on German bank's next year's net interest income. Hence, independent of whether or not the disclosure requirements were reduced as a result of successful lobbying, German banks clearly benefit from this reduction in that it spares them the disclosure of the most severe scenario impacts.

The following impact assessment also simulates the impacts of the long rates shocks up and down which are no official supervisory scenarios. And besides the impact on next year's net interest income also the impact on banks current portfolio value is simulated. The current portfolio value is the best available net present value measure available given the data at hand. Here the key finding is that the parallel shock up consistently has the most adverse impact. On this finding one could base a justification of the sole focus on parallel shocks currently in place in Germany as being conservative, that is as most risk-averse in terms of exposure. In terms of risk, the disclosure of the impacts of the other shock scenarios remains of value, of course. Because the probabilities of the materialization of the different shock scenarios may reasonably be expected to differ based on the analyses provided above.

Two overarching observations can be anticipated, meaning observations about the impacts on both next year's net interest income and current portfolio value. First, the impact of the long rates shocks up and down are mostly smaller than the impacts of the official supervisory shock scenarios but are of the same magnitude. This suggests that excluding the long rates shocks from the set of supervisory shock scenarios, blocks the view on quantitatively important exposures. Hence, also from an impact-perspective, the exclusion of long rates shocks can hardly be justified. Second, the parallel shock up, the short rates shock up, and the flattener shock have consistently adverse impacts. The impacts of these shocks on German banks' next year's net interest income is always worse than that of no change. And their impacts on the current portfolio value of German banks is always negative.

7.6.1 Simulation approach

Prior to the presentation of the results of the impact assessment, the main features of the simulation approach are made transparent. The quality of the publicly available data, on which a simulation of the impact of the scenarios proposed by the BCBS (2016) can be based, is limited in several dimensions.[209] Of the various statistics with more or less relevant informative value, the following impact assessment is based on the MFI interest rate statistics. These statistics contain volumes and interest rates of new business by original maturity for deposits and by initial interest rate fixation period for loans. Making the key assumption that the original maturity and the initial interest rate fixation are always equal, and ignoring repayment, this data can be used to construct a remaining maturity balance sheet with interest rates attached to the individual positions on the asset and on the liability side. Based on this dynamic balance sheet, interest cash flows for every period can be calculated and impacts of shock scenarios simulated.

---

[209] The reader is referred to Chapter 6 for a detailed discussion.

The MFI interest rate statistics cover deposits from and loans to retail customers and non-financial corporations. The data publicly available is monthly data and extends back to January 2003. It consists of business volumes and interest rates of new business for brackets of original maturity for deposits and for brackets of initial interest rate fixation period for loans. For three years before 2003 the BBK provides official estimates of certain interest rates but not of business volumes.

The following impact assessment rests on a remaining maturity balance sheet the individual positions of which each have four attributes, namely business volume, interest rate, original maturity, and remaining maturity. The construction of this balance sheet rests on the aforementioned key assumption that the original maturity and the initial interest rate fixation period are always equal. There is no comprehensive data publicly available that combines information on interest rate fixation and maturity. To construct a balance sheet with the required positions an assumption about the link between interest rate fixation and maturity is always necessary. The key assumption made here appears to be a particularly natural assumption of this sort. Furthermore, there is no appropriate data available on the repayment of loans. Instead of making more or less arbitrary assumptions, repayment is therefore ignored here. Hence, effectively all loans are treated like bullet loans with the repayment of the entire principle due at maturity. Put differently, all loans are treated like issued coupon bonds.

The monthly data is used to construct monthly balance sheets. Each pair of business volume and interest rate reported in the MFI interest rate statistics in any given month is processed as follows. In the month of reporting, as many new balance sheet positions are created as there are months in the original maturity range which equals the bracket of initial interest rate fixation period according to the key assumption. For example, for the pair of business volume and interest rate for new retail loans for consumption with an interest rate fixation period of over one and up to five years 48 new positions are created. Then, these positions are all assigned an equal fraction of the business volume, the reported interest rate, and an original and the same remaining maturity such that all possible original maturities are covered. The level of granularity is that of months. Only in the month of reporting original maturity equals remaining maturity. As next month's balance sheet is constructed, the remaining maturity of all positions created in earlier months is reduced by one month. Positions the maturity of which reaches zero are erased. But when the impact of a scenario is to be assessed, the original maturity of the position erased matters in case the impact on next year's net interest income is at issue. Because in this case the BCBS (2016) dictates a stable balance sheet for the assessment of the impact of the scenarios. This means that maturing positions have to be replaced by positions with the same business volume and the same original maturity which again have a remaining maturity equal to the original maturity. And the original maturity therefore determines the interest rate that is assigned to this position, namely the post-shock interest rate for a new position with this original maturity.

That the business volume is to be distributed uniformly across the possible range of original maturities is, of course, simply assumed. It is also assumed that every maturity range for which no upper limit is provided is as wide as the neighbouring maturity range.[210] The second assumption produces a maturity range of 10 to 15 years for loans to retail customers for house purchase. The upper limit of this maturity range implies a need for 16 years of data prior to the date at which the shock is assumed to occur the impact of which is then to be assessed. Because here net interest income before the shock needs is calculated as a reference point. However, as mentioned earlier, only for 13 years up to and including 2015 data on business volumes and interest rates is provided. Luckily, the interest rate needed is among the ones for which official estimates are provided for three further years back. For the following impact assessment the business volume

---

[210] For a discussion of both assumptions see Chapter 6 and the belonging Appendix 1.

needed is simply set to the average of the three earliest years for which data is available. The results are rather insensitive to changes of this value.[211]

The interest rate shock is simulated to appear between December 2015 and January 2016. The post-shock interest rates are calculated based on the interest rates reported for December 2015. These interest rates are increased or reduced by amounts specific to the maturity range and the scenario under investigation. These amounts are calculated using the formulas provided by the BCBS (2016) and the mid-points of the maturity ranges as inputs. For retail deposits redeemable at notice of more than three months, a maturity mid-point of 12 months is assumed.

One of the biggest challenges in simulating the impact of interest rate shocks on a banks' net interest income is optionality in the form of behavioral options. Behavioral options, the exercise of which plausibly depends on the development of interest rates, are inherent in various banking products. The BCBS (2016) highlights the prepayment of fixed rate loans and the drawing on fixed rate loan commitments as well as the early redemption of term deposits and the withdrawal of non-maturity deposits. Modelling under what conditions bank customers exercise these options is notoriously complex. In fact, this complexity is frequently referred to as one of the major hurdles for the development of a standard approach for the quantification of interest rate risk in the banking book. The BCBS (2016) also brings froward several guidelines for the treatment of behavioral options in internal models. At least for the modelling of the withdrawal of non-maturity deposits quantitative caps are defined that can be accounted for in the simulation with the data at hand to a meaningful extend.[212]

The BCBS (2016) requires that not more than 90% of non-maturity transactional retail deposits are treated as core deposits and that these core deposits do not have an average maturity of more than five years. For non-maturity non-transactional retail deposits the respective caps are 70% and four and a half years. For non-maturity wholesale deposits they are 50% and four years. The BCBS (2016) defines non-maturity deposits as deposits "the depositor is free to withdraw at any time". Of the deposits covered by the MFI interest rate statistics, only the retail and the wholesale overnight deposits have this property. However, with the data at hand it is impossible to distinguish between the transactional and the non-transactional part of the retail overnight deposits. One way forward is tracking the extreme cases.

The implications of the different treatments of non-maturity deposits for the scenario impacts on next year's net interest income are clear. Given the caps just mentioned, the assumption that would permit the smallest impact of an interest rate shock on banks' net interest income would be that 100% of retail overnight deposits are transactional. Conversely, assuming that 100% are non-transactional would permit the largest impact. In order to delimit the interval of possible impacts, below results are reported for assuming that of the retail overnight deposits either 100% are transactional or 100% are non-transactional. In the simulations all caps are used up to the limits. The interest rate shock is passed through completely to non-core deposits and to maturing core deposits but not at all to core deposits that do not mature in the year after the shock. Core deposits are treated as being evenly distributed across all permitted residual maturities. As another limiting case, the case of no special treatment of non-maturity deposits is covered which corresponds to not using any part of the caps implying that there are no core deposits.

In contrast, for the scenario impacts on the net present value of all cash flows from interest sensitive positions, the implications are not clear from the start. Because in this case the BCBS (2016) dictates a run-off balance sheet for the assessment of the impact of the scenarios. Hence,

---

[211] In the final setup introduced below, increasing this assumed business volume by 10% only approximately adds another negative 10 basis points to the results.

[212] The BCBS (2016) also proposes precise increases and decreases of loan prepayment depending on the shock scenario. However, normal prepayment is not reported. Hence, these proposed changes in loan prepayment cannot be accounted for in the simulation in an informative way.

different assumptions about the remaining behavioral maturity of overnight deposits at the time of the interest rate shock imply different amounts of overnight deposits on the liability side of the balance sheet at any point in time in the future. And this implies not only different repayment schedules for the principal but also interest payments that differ by orders of magnitude. For example, a part of the overnight deposits that is assumed to have a remaining behavioral maturity of nine years at the time of the interest rate shock induces nine times the annual interest payment. Hence, which net present value is higher in absolute terms, that of earlier principal repayment and less interest payment or that of later principal repayment and more interest payment, depends on the reference interest rates used for discounting. This is an empirical matter and it is investigated in the following. But it can already be noted that the lower long-term interest rates are, the higher is the net present value of later principal repayment and more interest payment in the future.

One further case discrimination is important. The BCBS (2016) permits national supervisors to set a zero or negative lower bound for post-shock interest rates. Below, results are reported from simulations without a lower bound as well as from simulations with a zero lower bound.

7.6.2 Scenario impacts on next year's net interest income

In the first part of this impact assessment the focus is on the impact on next year's net interest income. It is important to note that even the scenario of no shock may produce a change in net interest income from one year to the next. Because as the monthly balance sheets for 2016 are simulated, positions that were created earlier and hence have older interest rates mature and new positions are created then with the interest rates as of December 2015. Given that interest rates have generally decreased over the past years, it can be expected that even the impact of the scenario of no change is negative comparing 2015 to simulated 2016.

As can also be expected given the current low level of interest rates, with the zero lower bound possible reductions of funding costs are substantially limited. In fact, the results below show that with the zero lower bound the impacts of all but one shock scenarios are worse than the impact of no change.

Covering all the possible combinations of the two case discriminations discussed, six different sets of scenario impacts are simulated (see Figure 7.32). Note that again, no change and the long rates shocks up and down are included as scenarios even though they are not brought forward by the BCBS (2016). Five general observations are particularly noteworthy. First and as anticipated above, the short rates shock up and the flattener shock always have more negative impacts than the parallel shock up. The impact of the short rates shock up is 5.4 to 9.8 percentage points more negative, that of the flattener shock 2.7 to 3.0 percentage points. This observation is highly relevant because it implies that the BCBS (2016) would effectively tighten the regulatory requirements for the average bank if it did not only require the disclosure of the impacts of the parallel shocks up and down on next year's net interest income. Second, in the scenario of no change net interest income is reduced by 5.0% independent of the treatment of non-maturity deposits and of the lower bound on post-shock interest rates. This is easily explained by the facts that interest rates have decreased in recent years and that the average maturity of assets is longer than that of liabilities. Third, without a zero lower bound for post-shock interest rates the impacts of some shock scenarios are positive, with a zero lower bound they are all negative and all but one are even more negative than the impact of no change. The exception is the long rates shock up which, however, has a negative impact independent of the lower bound. Fourth, of all but one of the shock scenarios the absolute size of the impact is largest when there is no special treatment of non-maturity deposits and smallest when all retail overnight deposits are assumed to be transactional. The exception is the long rates shock down for which the weaker decrease of funding costs dominates. Fifth, the ranking of the sizes of the impacts of the shock scenarios is largely independent from the treatment of non-maturity deposits. Without a zero lower bound the prototypical division results with the parallel shock down, the short rates shock down, the long rates shock up and the steepener shock having more advantageous impacts than no change, and with the parallel shock up, the short rates shock up, the long rates shock down and the flattener shock having more adverse impacts. This is what is to be expected for classical positive term transformation.

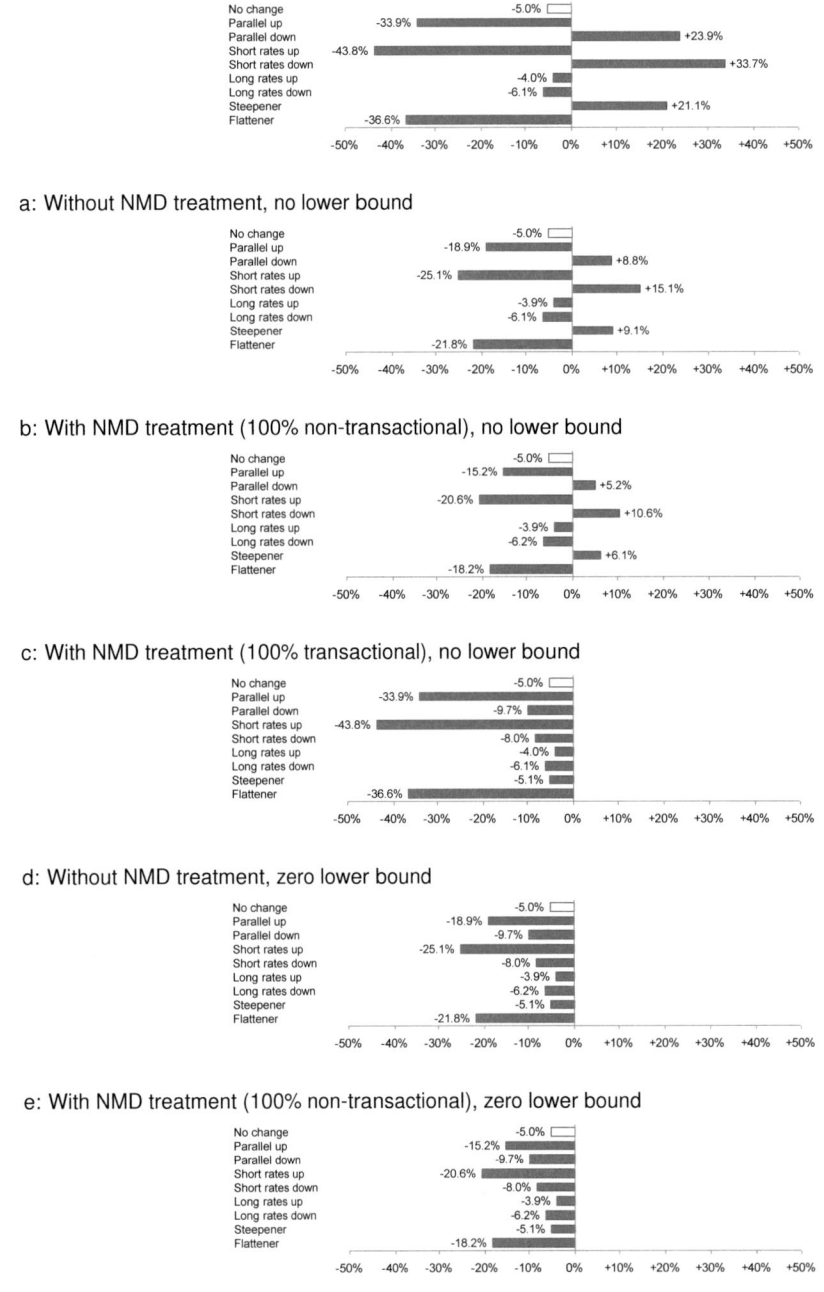

a: Without NMD treatment, no lower bound

b: With NMD treatment (100% non-transactional), no lower bound

c: With NMD treatment (100% transactional), no lower bound

d: Without NMD treatment, zero lower bound

e: With NMD treatment (100% non-transactional), zero lower bound

f: With NMD treatment (100% transactional), zero lower bound

Figure 7.32: Scenario-impact on net interest income without special treatment of non-maturity deposits ("NMD treatment" for short) (a and d) or with NMD treatment and 100% of retail overnight deposits assumed to be non-transactional (b and e) or transactional (c and f) and with no lower bound for post-shock interest rates (a, b, and c) or a zero lower bound (d, e, and f). Source: BCBS (2016); ECB, MFI interest rate statistics; own calculations.

The first of these findings implies that German banks indeed had an incentive to lobby for the reduction of reporting requirements from the consultative version to the final standards. The third finding reveals that as these international standards are implemented by national and supranational regulators, German banks have an incentive to lobby against a zero lower bound for post-shock interest rates. Taking a step back, the magnitudes of the impacts strongly suggest that supervisory resources are well spent on supervising the impact on next year's net interest income.

For a calibration of the results, note that in 2015 for all German banks taken together the net income before taxes amounted to 27.6% of net interest income.[213] Hence, if net interest income decreased by more than 27.6%, net income before taxes would become negative. Looking again at the simulated impacts, without special treatment of non-maturity deposits and without a zero lower bound for post-shock interest rates the parallel shock up, the short rates shock down, and the flattener shock produce decreases of the net interest income beyond this threshold value. With special treatment of non-maturity deposits the impact of the short rates shock up remains close to this threshold value for a high fraction of non-transactional retail overnight deposits. It should not be overlooked, however, that ignoring the repayment of loans potentially distorts the results. With repayment greater than zero the remaining principal amounts of loans granted further in the past are smaller and so are the interest payments earned with them. Hence, the negative effect of replacing old high-interest loans with new low-interest loans is potentially overstated.

Of course, net income before taxes is a purely accounting based measure and does not include the economic cost of capital. Whenever the economic cost of capital is positive, the economic profit is less than the net income before taxes. Hence, a decrease of net interest income that leaves the net income before taxes positive may already push the economic profit below zero.

7.6.3 Scenario impacts on current portfolio value

In the second part of this impact assessment the focus is on the impact on current portfolio value. With this impact the impact on the economic value of equity is approximated to which the BCBS (2016) actually refers. Note that the overall impact of the shock scenarios here results not only from changes of the interest rates that the bank receives and pays but also from changes of the discount rates with which future cash flows are discounted. Impacts are reported relative to the current portfolio value calculated under the assumption that interest rates do not change. Hence, no impact of no change of interest rates is reported.

The impacts of the scenarios are measured with reference to the current portfolio value with no change. A persistent pattern can be observed (see Figure 7.33). Independent of the treatment of non-maturity deposits as well as of the lower bound, the parallel shock up always has the most adverse impact and the parallel shock down always has the most beneficial impact. This points to the paramount importance of long-term interest rates for the calculation of the net present value. The long rates shocks up and down come closest to the parallel shocks for longer maturities but they only approach a parallel shock of 100 basis points. The parallel shocks are twice the size. With a zero lower bound this difference disappears for the shocks down and the overall impacts become rather similar. But the parallel shock up remains unaffected and the most adverse by far.

One more structural difference to the simulated scenario impacts on next year's net interest income remains to be addressed. While the impacts on next year's net interest income generally become smaller when a larger share of core deposits with a longer maturity is assumed, for the impacts on the current portfolio value it is the other way round. As discussed above, assuming a

---

[213] This number can easily be calculated from the numbers published by the BBK in its statistics on German banks' profit and loss accounts.

larger share of core deposits with a longer maturity may in principle increase or decrease the current portfolio value also given no change in interest rates. And the scenario impacts have to be measured relative to this value. Hence, they have to be measured relative to a value which itself depends on the treatment of non-maturity deposits.

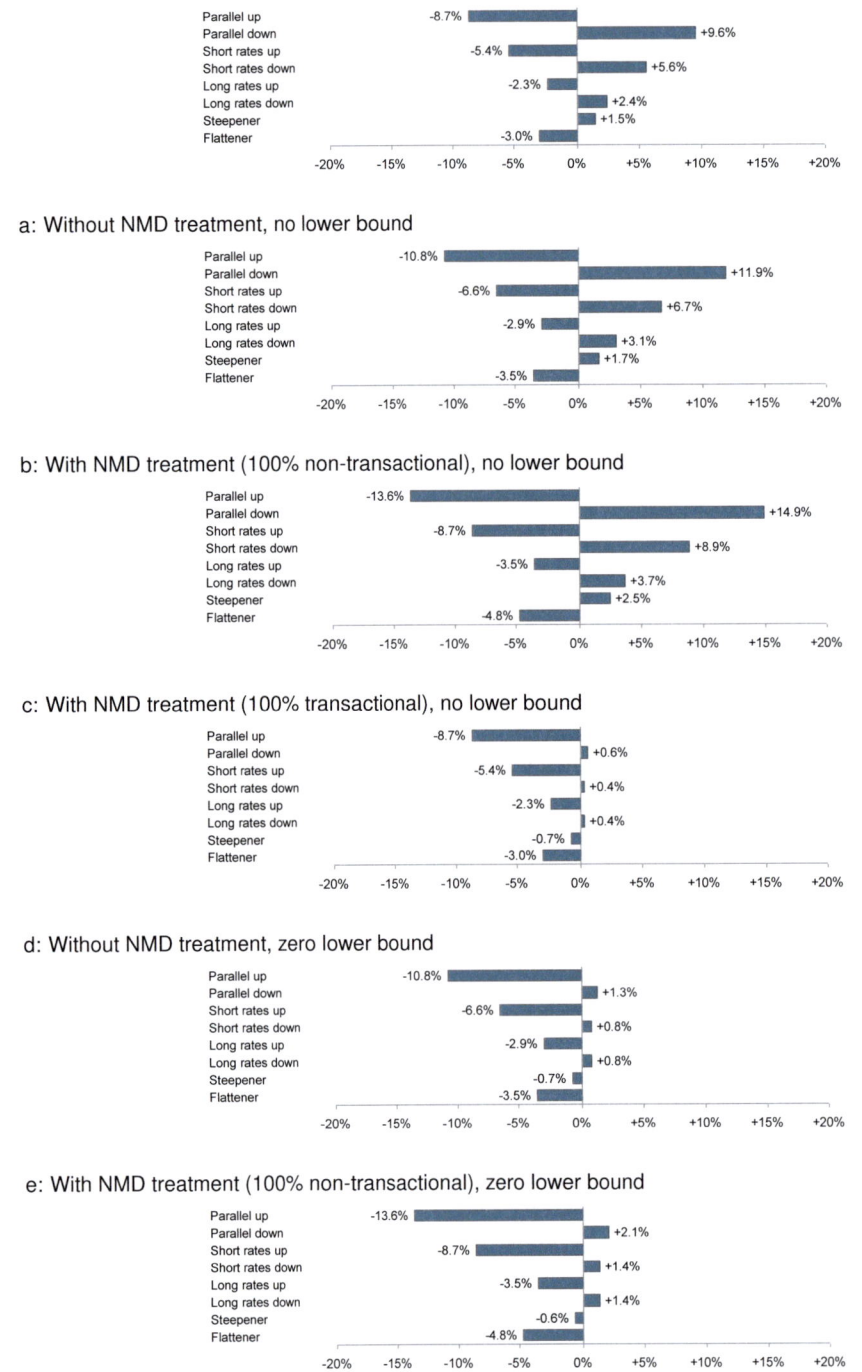

a: Without NMD treatment, no lower bound

b: With NMD treatment (100% non-transactional), no lower bound

c: With NMD treatment (100% transactional), no lower bound

d: Without NMD treatment, zero lower bound

e: With NMD treatment (100% non-transactional), zero lower bound

f: With NMD treatment (100% transactional), zero lower bound

Figure 7.33: Scenario-impact on current portfolio value without special treatment of non-maturity deposits, NMD treatment for short, (a and d) or with NMD treatment and 100% of retail overnight deposits assumed to be non-transactional (b and e) or transactional (c and f) and with no lower bound for post-shock interest rates (a, b, and c) or a zero lower bound (d, e, and f). Source: BCBS (2016); ECB, MFI interest rate statistics; own calculations.

With the actual portfolio numbers at hand and the actual interest rates calculated from traded Government bonds in Germany as of end of December 2015 used for discounting, the impact is however very clear. Compared to the current portfolio value with no special treatment of non-maturity deposits, the special treatment with retail overnight deposits assumed to be 100% non-transactional already results in a decrease of the current portfolio value by 40.9% and that with 100% transactional even in a decrease by 63.5%. The underlying reason is that long-term interest rates used for discounting are so low that when repayments are shifted further into the future, the reduction of the current value of principal repayment is much lower than the increase in current value of total interest payments. And as set out above this increase simply results from higher interest payments being due because more deposits still remain in the portfolio at any point in time until run-off.

Since the reported sizes of the scenario impacts are measured relative to the current portfolio value with no change in interest rates but with the same treatment of non-maturity deposits, this has consequences. Obviously, a given absolute scenario impact is reported as a higher share of the current portfolio value, if this current portfolio value is lower. But, of course, here the absolute sizes of the scenario impacts also depend on the treatment of non-maturity deposits applied. It remains true that the higher the share of core deposits is assumed to be, the smaller is the absolute size of any scenario impact relative to no change. Hence there is not only a reduction of the denominator but also of the numerator. However, for most scenarios the reduction of the denominator obviously dominates.

7.7 Conclusion

The assessment of the adequacy of the past, the current, and the future interest rate shock scenarios based on the historic development of the term structure in Germany has produced three main findings. First, while the sizes of the original interest rate shock scenarios can rather easily be traced to the historic development of interest rates in Germany, the sizes of the internationally harmonized scenarios, in contrast, appear to have been out-of-date already when they were introduced. The symmetry is not motivated at all by developments prior to the introduction. The parallel shock up appears too large while the shock down appears too small. For the parallel shock up, which is commonly regarded as the (more) adverse scenario for most German banks,[214] there appears to be a disproportionate buffer. Second, there is a strong empirical case for including long rates shocks in the set of future supervisory shock scenarios. Additionally, the method developed for the two-maturities-assessment revealed that the inclusion of long rates shocks is sensible already on purely systematic grounds. Because only with long rates shocks up and down, the plane of possible combinations of changes of interest rates at two different maturity levels is covered completely. Third and most importantly, German banks have been exposed to fewer consistently adverse shocks in recent years and overall the size of actual term structure changes has constantly become smaller, leading to most of the proposed calibrations of the official scenarios appearing too large. And just like for the internationally harmonized shock scenarios currently in place, the most recent developments of interest rates do not back the proposed symmetry of the future scenarios empirically.

The investigation of forecasts of the interest rates in Germany has shown three things in particular. First, the qualitative forecasts published by the ifo and the ZEW imply that term structure changes with a likely positive impact on next year's net interest income are more probable than those with a negative impact. This points to limited interest rate risk. However, not all indicators also suggest a downward trend. Second, according to the quantitative forecasts published by Consensus Economics, term structure changes which are likely to be beneficial

---

[214] A quantification of this is included in Chapter 8.

for next year's net interest income become more probable while those which are likely to be adverse become less probable. This points to a decrease of the interest rate risk of German banks measured in terms of near future income. Besides, both the qualitative and the quantitative forecasts imply that long rates shocks are likely. This again suggests to include long rates shocks in the future supervisory shock scenarios. Third, however, forecast accuracy is poor in particular for long-term interest rates and therefore reliable forecasts of changes of the entire term structure are not available. Nevertheless, interest rate forecasts remain important for supervisors to take into account as banks can be expected to base their portfolio planning on these forecasts at least in parts. And given the poor quality of long-term forecasts, interest rate risks of sizes not intended by banks may accumulate.

Finally, the three most important lessons from the impact assessment are the following. First, the short rates shock up and the flattener shock have more adverse impacts on German banks' net interest income in the year after the shock than the parallel shock up. Hence, the reduction of the disclosure requirements from the consultative document BCBS (2015) to the final standards BCBS (2016) for the future regulatory treatment of the interest rate risk in banks' banking books spares banks to disclose the most adverse shock-scenario impacts. Second, the parallel shock up has the most adverse impact on banks' current portfolio value. Nevertheless, the impacts of other shock scenarios are also material and the future disclosure of these impacts is going to provide relevant extra input for the supervision of German banks. Third, also in terms of impact, the long rates shocks up and down do not appear to be reasonably negligible. Extending the range of supervisory shock scenarios hence seems reasonable not only from a systematic standpoint, given the past development of the term structure, and in light of current forecasts thereof, but also because the impacts are sizeable.

Given the long-term development of interest rates, fixed sizes of supervisory interest rate shocks do not appear reasonable. There may be a five year interest rate cycle. But clearly there is a much more long-term trend toward smaller interest rates and interest rate changes, at least in Germany. The most popular way forward is the regular adjustment of the sizes of the supervisory interest rate shocks. This was not only planned by the BaFin (2007) when the original scenarios were introduced, but is now again intended by the BCBS (2016) for the scenarios the future measurement of banks exposure to interest rate changes is to be based on. However, the historic experience of no adjustment in Germany until the internationally harmonized scenarios were introduced by the BaFin (2011) does indicate that adjustments face resistance. Moreover, international harmonization and adjustments based on the development of the national interest rates most relevant for actual banks appear difficult to reconcile. A feasible solution for these problems would be not to prescribe a single calibration but to define a fixed set of multiple calibrations for the interest rate shocks. For example, banks could be required to report the impact not only of parallel shocks up and down by 200 basis points but on top by 50, 100, 150, 250, and 300 basis points. Covering a sufficiently wide range of plausible interest rate changes with sufficient granularity, the reporting requirements for banks could remain unchanged for longer periods of time while the relevance of the reported numbers would remain high and consistency over time would be ensured. But, of course, any regulatory threshold value above which a bank is considered to be an "outlier bank" or to have "elevated interest rate risk" would then need to be defined with respect to a particular shock size. And to which shock size the supervisor refers may then change, depending on which shock is seen as most appropriate given the actual development of interest rates.

Taking a step back, there is a compelling case for national and supranational supervisors to increase the disclosure requirements above the minimum level defined by the BCBS (2016). Long rates shocks should be included among the official supervisory interest rate shock scenarios. Multiple calibrations of all official supervisory shock scenarios should be introduced to cover the entire range of all plausible interest rate changes with sufficient granularity. And finally, the disclosure of the impacts of all supervisory interest rate shock scenarios also on next year's net interest income should be required. Equipped with the data from these enhanced disclosures, a reasonable supervision of banks' interest rate risk in their banking books might be possible within the international regulatory framework.

7.8 Appendices

Appendix 1: Tolerance level implicit in scenario formulas

The tolerance level implicit in the defining formulas for parallel shocks and for short rates shocks brought forward by the BCBS (2016) is derived in three steps. The first and the second step are done separately for the defining formulas for parallel shocks and for short rates shocks in individual assessments. The third step then brings together the results in a joint assessment. The first step is to determine the shock parameter that produces the smallest sum of squared residuals given interest rate changes at any two different maturities. The second step is to use the result from the first step to determine the smallest sum of squared residuals as a function of the two interest rate changes. The third step is to use the results for the defining formulas for both parallel shocks and short rates shocks to determine how different the two interest rate changes may be such that a parallel shocks just still produces the better fit. It turns out, that the permitted difference can be perfectly expressed as a tolerance level. The following calculations are conducted for shocks up only. But obvious symmetries ensure that the results carry over to shocks down. The focus is on two absolute changes of the interest rate from the term structure at different maturities. The maturities in years are referred to as a and b and the corresponding interest rate changes as I_a and I_b, respectively. In what follows, the sum of squared residuals is treated as a function of the relevant shock parameter, $SSR(\delta)$.

Individual assessment one: parallel shock

The BCBS (2016) defines a parallel shock up with t being the maturity as

$$\Delta_{parallel\,up}(t) = \delta_{parallel}.$$

In what follows $parallel$ is abbreviated by pa.

Step 1

The sum of squared residuals can be expressed as

$$SSR_{pa}(\delta_{pa}) = (I_a - \delta_{pa})^2 + (I_b - \delta_{pa})^2.$$

In order to find the minimum of the sum of squares the first derivative is calculated as

$$\frac{\partial SSR_{pa}(\delta_{pa})}{\partial \delta_{pa}} = -2(I_a - \delta_{pa}) - 2(I_b - \delta_{pa}).$$

Obviously, here the necessary condition for a minimum is also sufficient and gives

$$\delta_{pa}^* = \frac{I_a + I_b}{2}.$$

Unsurprisingly, a shock parameter equal to the arithmetic mean produces the best fit.

Step 2

With the optimal value for the shock parameter the sum of squares is

$$SSR_{pa}(\delta_{pa}^*) = (I_a - \frac{I_a + I_b}{2})^2 + (I_b - \frac{I_a + I_b}{2})^2.$$

And simple algebra leads to

$$SSR_{pa}(\delta_{pa}^*) = \frac{1}{2}(I_a - I_b)^2 = \frac{1}{2}(I_a^2 - 2I_aI_b + I_b^2).$$

This result is picked up in step three in the joint assessment.

Individual assessment two: short rates shock

The BCBS (2016) defines a short rates shock up with t being the maturity as

$$\Delta_{short\,rates\,up}(t) = \delta_{short}e^{-\frac{t}{4}}.$$

In what follows *short* is abbreviated by *sr*.

Step 1

Here, the sum of squared residuals can be expressed as

$$SSR_{sr}(\delta_{sr}) = (I_a - \delta_{sr}e^{-\frac{a}{4}})^2 + (I_b - \delta_{sr}e^{-\frac{b}{4}})^2.$$

Again, in order to find the minimum of the sum of squares the first derivative is calculated as

$$\frac{\partial SSR_{sr}(\delta_{sr})}{\partial \delta_{sr}} = -2(I_a - \delta_{sr}e^{-\frac{a}{4}})e^{-\frac{a}{4}} - 2(I_b - \delta_{sr}e^{-\frac{b}{4}})e^{-\frac{b}{4}}.$$

And just like above, the necessary condition for a minimum is also sufficient. It gives

$$\delta_{sr}^* = \frac{I_a e^{-\frac{a}{4}} + I_b e^{-\frac{b}{4}}}{e^{-\frac{a}{2}} + e^{-\frac{b}{2}}}.$$

This shock parameter produces the best fit for the short rates shock.

Step 2

Note that the sum of squared residuals can also be expressed as

$$SSR_{sr}(\delta_{sr}) = \delta_{sr}^2(e^{-\frac{a}{2}} + e^{-\frac{b}{2}}) - 2\delta_{sr}(I_a e^{-\frac{a}{4}} + I_b e^{-\frac{b}{4}}) + I_a^2 + I_b^2.$$

Now using the optimal value for the shock parameter rather directly leads to

$$SSR_{sr}(\delta_{sr}^*) = I_a^2 + I_b^2 - \frac{(I_a e^{-\frac{a}{4}} + I_b e^{-\frac{b}{4}})^2}{e^{-\frac{a}{2}} + e^{-\frac{b}{2}}}.$$

And this is the second result needed for step three in the joint assessment.

Joint assessment: parallel and short rates shock

The objective of the third and final step is to express the critical I_b as a function of I_a. The critical value looked for is the value at which a parallel shock and a short rates shock as defined by the BCBS (2016) fit equally well, provided the shock parameter values are used that minimize the respective sum of squared residuals.

Step 3

The general idea can be expressed by the condition

$$SSR_{pa}(\delta^*_{pa}) = SSR_{sr}(\delta^*_{sr}).$$

Using the results from above, simple algebra gives

$$I_b = I_a \frac{2(e^{-\frac{a}{2}} + e^{-\frac{b}{2}}) - 4e^{-\frac{a+b}{4}} \pm \sqrt{8(e^{-a} + e^{-b}) + 16(e^{-\frac{a+b}{2}} - e^{-\frac{3a+b}{4}} - e^{-\frac{a+3b}{4}})}}{2(e^{-\frac{b}{2}} - e^{-\frac{a}{2}})}.$$

Most importantly, this result has the linear form

$$I_b = I_a c_{a,b}.$$

And $c_{a,b}$ depends only on a and b and here only the negative quare root is relevant.

Finally, with $a = 1$ and $b = 10$ we get $c_{a,b} \approx 0.477$. Graphically, this is the slope of the line through the origin which delimits the tolerance areas for a parallel shock and for a short rates shock. And it corresponds to a tolerance level of about 35.4%.

Appendix 2: Translation of balance reported by the ZEW

In what follows it is shown how the balance of answers reported by the ZEW translates into a point value as it is reported by the ifo. The balance b of answers the ZEW reports is the share of respondents that expect the interest rate in question to be higher in six months time h minus the share of respondents that expect it to be lower l,

$$h - l = b.$$

The remaining share of respondents s expects the interest rate in question to be about the same in six months time,

$$h + l + s = 1.$$

The natural way to calculate a point value p as it is reported by the ifo from h, l, and s is to multiply the shares with the values the ifo attaches to the corresponding answers, namely 9, 1, and 5,

$$9h + 1l + 5s = p.$$

But now using the three equations identified, simple substitution shows that p only depends on b,

$$4b + 5 = p.$$

This functional relationship permits the easiest translation of shares reported by the ZEW into point values as reported by the ifo.

Appendix 3: Changes to threshold for "outlier bank"

The BCBS (2016) revises the regulatory threshold for the change of a bank's economic value of equity beyond which the bank is regarded as an "outlier bank". To be precise, the standards contain two complementary revisions the effects of which both have the same sign. First, the reference value is delimited more exclusively. Instead of a bank's own funds or its total capital, the reference value now is its Tier 1 capital. Second, the relevant fraction is reduced considerably. Instead of 20% it is now a quarter lower at only 15%.

While the quantitative effect of the reduction of the relevant fraction is the same for all banks, the quantitative effect of the more exclusive delimitation of the reference value differs between banks as it depends on what share of the total capital of a bank is made up of Tier 1 capital. If, for example, the Tier 1 capital of a bank accounts for 90% of its total capital and hence is 10% smaller, the quantitative effect is a reduction of the permitted interest rate risk for this bank not to be an "outlier bank" by these 10%. The two quantitative effects both contribute to a reduction of the regulatory threshold and are linked in a multiplicative way. Hence, the total quantitative effect is smaller than the sum of the two individual quantitative effect. In this example, the total reduction equals 32.5% ($= 1 - (1 - 25\%) \cdot (1 - 10\%)$) and hence less than 35.0% ($= 25\% + 10\%$).

To get an idea of the real size of the quantitative effect of the more exclusive delimitation of the reference value and then also of the total quantitative effect for German banks, it is indicative to look at the ten largest savings banks by total assets. In this sample and as of end 2015, the Tier 1 capital accounts for 87.5% of the total capital on average[215].[216] Hence, this individual quantitative effect is a reduction of 12.5%. And the total quantitative effect amounts to a reduction of 34.4% (see Figure 7.34).

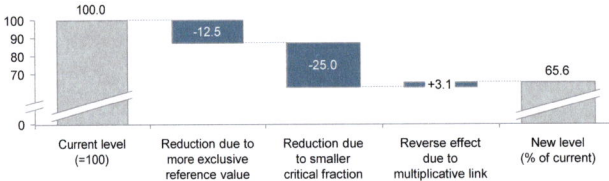

Figure 7.34: Reduction of regulatory threshold beyond which a bank is regarded as an "outlier bank" consisting of two individual reductions due to the more exclusive delimitation of the reference value and the reduction of the relevant fraction and also of a reverse effect due to the multiplicative link. Source: BCBS (2016); Bankscope; own calculations.

---

[215] Here the unweighed average is used because the individual bank's perspective is key.

[216] The ten largest savings banks by total assets as of end 2015 are in this order: Hamburger Sparkasse AG, Sparkasse KölnBonn, Kreissparkasse Köln, Frankfurter Sparkasse, Stadtsparkasse München, Sparkasse Hannover, Ostsächsische Sparkasse Dresden, Mittelbrandenburgische Sparkasse in Potsdam, Nassauische Sparkasse, Die Sparkasse Bremen AG. Note that the Kreissparkasse Köln does not report its total capital (ratio) in its annual report and hence is omitted from the calculation.

Chapter 8 Banks' interest rate risk and search for yield: a theoretical rationale and some empirical evidence

8.1 Preliminary remarks

This chapter presents a co-authored research paper which is the result of a joint research project with Dr. Christoph Memmel and Dr. Atilim Seymen from the Deutsche Bundesbank (BBK).[217] This research paper was already published in the discussion paper series of the BBK as No 22/2016 and is forthcoming in the German Economic Review in 2017. Besides minor editorial amendments, this research paper is complemented in three ways here. The present preliminary remarks locate the research paper in the broader research effort of this dissertation. The Appendices 3 and 4 provide a schematic literature overview in graphical form and complete the descriptive statistics as well as the set of reported regression results, respectively. Finally, the concluding remarks reflect on the strength of the empirical evidence discovered.

Chapter 4 uncovers an important research gap in the monetary economics of the transmission channels and more specifically in the research on the risk-taking channel of monetary policy in so far as it concerns banks' taking of interest rate risk. As laid out above, the existing research on this topic generally links a decrease in short-term interest rates to an increase in banks' taking of interest rate risk. The most common explanation for this link is that a decrease of short-term interest rates leads to an increase in the term spread which implies a higher profitability of term transformation. And this higher profitability then induces banks to engage more heavily in term transformation and as a consequence to take more interest rate risk. However, as discussed above, this understanding of the link between the profitability of term transformation and the taking of interest rate risk by banks is one-dimensional. It omits the dimension of a possible search for yield or gambling for resurrection. Under certain circumstances, banks' may take more interest rate risk as a consequence of a decrease and not of an increase of the profitability of term transformation. And even when these circumstances do not prevail that lead to a change of the sign of the overall effect, besides the positive link between increased profitability and risk-taking there may always be a negative link that reduces the amount of risk-taking induced. The research paper presented in what follows provides a theoretical rationale for banks' search for yield in interest rate risk and presents some empirical evidence from Germany.

In Chapter 5 it is already announced that the following research paper uses an exposure measure closely related to the Basel interest rate coefficient as if it was a comprehensive risk measure. More precisely, the impact that an overnight parallel upward shift of the term structure by 200 basis points would have on the net present value of a bank's banking book is used to measure that bank's interest rate risk from traditional banking. Obviously, the findings of Chapter 7 clearly show that an exposure measure of this sort is of limited value if used as a risk measure for two reasons. First, the probability of the materialization of the parallel upward shift in question appears to be subject to substantial variations over time. Second, other possible term structure changes and the probabilities of their materializations need to be taken into account.

---

[217] The views expressed in this paper and hence also in this chapter are those of the authors and do not necessarily reflect the opinions of the Deutsche Bundesbank. We thank Peter Bofinger, Calebe de Roure, Yalin Gndz, Giulio Nicoletti, Wolfgang Rippin, Benedikt Ruprecht and the participants of the Conference of the International Finance and Banking Society (IFABS 2016, Barcelona), the 33rd annual conference of the French Finance Association (AFFI 2016, Lige), the 6th international conference of the Financial Engineering and Banking Society (FEBS 2016, Málaga) and Bundesbank's research seminar for their helpful comments. In the references at the end of this dissertation this research paper can be found under Memmel et al. (2016).

211

Nevertheless, in using the exposure measure defined in the way described, the research paper follows supervisory practice. But that is not the only reason for doing so.

The investigation of the publicly available statistics in Chapter 6 clearly shows that this data only permits limited insights into banks' taking of interest rate risk. Rankings and trends can be identified. But it appears impossible to quantify the absolute exposure to any term structure change precisely based on this data. The most obvious reason for this is that off-balance sheet items are hardly covered at all by the statistics publicly available. In contrast, the exposure measure used in this research paper covers on- as well as off-balance sheet items. More generally, it is calculated by banks themselves in a process that involves banks' internal data and models and which is subject to supervision by the authorities. Of course, the fact that banks' internal models are involved may provide grounds for criticism. But the fact that much more comprehensive internal data is used than is publicly available can also be expected to increase the precision of the resulting exposure measure. It is unfortunate, of course, that hitherto banks do not disclose similar exposure measures for other shock scenarios.

Furthermore, one of the things that could be learnt from the assessment carried out in Chapter 7 is that a reliable quantification of the absolute probability of the materialization of a certain term structure change still seems to be unavailable. Again, rankings and trends can be identified. But more appears problematic. In the light of this, the use of the described exposure measure in the following research paper, without complementing it by some sort of probability measure for the materialization of the relevant term structure change, presents itself as a conservative choice.

8.2 Abstract

We investigate German banks' exposure to interest rate risk. In finance, higher demand for a risky asset is typically associated with higher expected return. However, employing a utility function which implies both risk-averse and risk-seeking behavior depending on the level of profits, we show that this relationship may get weaker and even change its sign at low profit levels. For the period 2005-2014, we find not only the common positive relationship of higher expected returns and rising interest rate exposure but also that this relationship does become weaker with falling operative income, its sign eventually changing.

8.3 Introduction

Banks bear interest rate risk. This risk stems from traditional banking business activity, in which banks hand out long-term loans and collect short-term deposits. By making use of hedging instruments, banks can decide how much of this risk they want to retain. Many banks do not hedge their interest rate risk completely in practice. In Germany, for example, interest rate risk is one of the most material risks taken by small and medium-sized banks. The interest rate risk is important from an aggregate perspective too, since, due to its high correlation in the cross section of banks, it may have a significant impact on financial stability.[218]

In finance, one typically observes a positive relationship between the demand for a risky asset and its expected return. Hence, banks' interest rate risk is generally expected to decrease if the expected return from bearing the risk falls. Recently, however, a number of German banks seem to have taken more interest rate risk despite falling expected return. In this paper, we first show the theoretical possibility that falling expected returns of interest rate risk may induce the taking of a higher interest rate risk, which we define in this paper as 'search for yield'. We then estimate empirically the critical level of bank profitability below which a negative relationship prevails

---

[218] An extensive discussion of interest rate risk in the German banking sector can be found in BBK (2014a).

between the taking of interest rate risk and its expected return. Put differently, in the current paper we present a theoretical rationale and some empirical evidence for a search for yield in the form of higher risk-taking due to lower profitability.

In economics, it is well known that there exist situations where increasing prices lead to an increase in the demand for the respective good. Counter-intuitive though this may seem, this is not merely a theoretical possibility. There is empirical evidence for the existence of such a phenomenon, for instance in labor economics: An increase in hourly wages (which corresponds to an increase in the opportunity cost and thus the price of leisure) may lead to a decrease in the labor supply and, hence, to an increase in the demand for leisure (e.g. Camerer et al. (1997)). More recently, Domanski et al. (2015) find that the demand curve of German insurance companies for long-term bonds is upward-sloping. In our paper, we also deal with situations where an increase in the price of a good (here: a decline in the expected return of the risky asset) may lead to an increase in the demand for this good. Although the ensuing empirical effects are similar to the foregoing labor market example, a different mechanism is at work in our case: In the labor market example, the income effect dominates the substitution effect. By contrast, in our paper, the effect of a change in expected profits on risk-taking is due to the preference structure: Whereas risk is seen as negative and the decision-makers act in a risk-averse manner in normal times, in times with very low profits, risk becomes something which is desirable and the decision-makers seek risk.

As mentioned above, interest rate risk can easily be hedged and its amount is hence, to a large extent, within the discretion of bank managers. Therefore, the observable level of interest rate risk is a rather accurate reflection of bank managers' underlying incentives. In this paper, we work with a measure for a bank's exposure to interest rate risk which is closely linked to the bank's Basel interest rate coefficient, which is the supervisors' yardstick for the interest rate risk in the banking book. Covering both on- and off-balance sheet items, this coefficient is a rather comprehensive standardized measure of interest rate risk concerning banks' traditional business.[219]

The low interest rate environment is a crucial motivation for our investigation. It is consistently understood as driving down banks' profit margin and, if it persists, as further reducing banks' income in the future.[220] Accordingly, due to low profits, an increasing share of bank managers can be expected to act as if they were risk-prone. In other words, the share of banks which increase their interest rate risk exposure even though the term structure flattens can be expected to rise if the low interest rate environment persists. Since the interest rate risk applies to a large number of banks simultaneously, financial stability risks can ensue, among others, also through this channel in the low interest rate environment. This is a major topical takeaway from our investigation.

We look at German banks' interest rate risk for the period 2005-2014 and find the usual positive relationship between expected returns from term transformation and exposure to the corresponding interest rate risk. In addition, we show that this relationship becomes weaker if a bank's operative income goes down. Eventually, if the operative income falls below a certain threshold, the relationship changes its sign, meaning that the bank starts to increase its exposure to interest rate risk even though the expected returns from term transformation decrease. We find that, depending on the sample specification and estimation methodology, about 0.5% to 8.3% of the observations are below this threshold. This indicates that the prevalence of the search for

---

[219] As will be discussed in detail below, we use the year-to-year change in bank's exposure to interest rate risk, measured as the change in the present value of a bank's banking book due to an overnight upward shift of the term structure by 200 basis points, normalized with the bank's total assets.

[220] The ECB (2015b) expects that, in the current low interest rate environment, the net interest margins of banks are going to remain under pressure. See also Borio et al. (2015) and Busch and Memmel (2015) for empirical evidence on decreased bank profitability as a result of low interest rate levels.

yield in the sense described above has been limited until now. However, this may change if the current low interest rate environment persists.

The paper is structured as follows: In Section 8.4, we provide a review of the literature concerning banks' risk-taking and search for yield, especially in a low interest rate environment. In Section 8.5, we present a theoretical model and its empirical implications. Section 8.6 describes the data and in Section 8.7 we discuss the empirical results. Section 8.8 concludes.

8.4 Literature

Our paper is the first to establish a general link between lower expected return from interest rate risk and increased taking of this risk by banks. We show that there is a threshold level of profitability below which banks search for yield, i.e. below that profitability level banks increase their exposure to interest rate risk although the term structure becomes flatter and thus earning opportunities become smaller.

Research on how interest rates affect banks' risk-taking has gained momentum, not least due to the low interest environment, in recent years. Most recent contributions dealing with the subject are framed as investigations of the risk-taking channel of monetary policy as advanced by, e.g., Borio and Zhu (2012). Theoretical research on how a low interest rate environment affects banks' risk-taking addresses reactions to both lower short-term rates and lower long-term rates as well as a combination of both. Depending on the differing reactions of short-term and long-term rates to the low-interest rate environment, the yield curve may become steeper or flatter, the former (latter) generally leading to a higher (lower) profitability of the lending business due to term transformation. Thus, various possible incentives for risk-taking are conceivable in a low interest environment. Diamond and Rajan (2009) and Acharya and Naqvi (2012), for example, model how lower short-term rates, or open market operations bringing them about, lead to higher liquidity in the form of deposits and thus to a lower probability of punishment in the form of a bank run or a penalty for the manager. Adrian and Shin (2010) explain how an increase in asset values following from lower long-term rates leads to a larger risk-bearing capacity of financial institutions, provided that the balance sheet is marked to market and there is a binding value-at-risk constraint. Adrian and Shin (2011) point out that increased profitability of classical lending business resulting from a steeper yield curve leads to a larger risk-bearing capacity. Fishburn and Porter (1976), who provide the classical discussion of the general link between risk and expected return, point to a what can be called "risk-return slack", i.e. a lower level of risk associated with every given level of expected return. Banks may be inclined to increase their risk due to a risk-return slack. In contrast, Rajan (2005) points out how a decreased profitability of classical lending business, as it results from a flatter yield curve, induces what he calls a search for yield, whereby higher risks are taken in order to counteract decreasing profits.[221]

Note that, reversing the arguments presented in the foregoing paragraph, a low interest environment with a steeper or flatter yield curve can also induce lower risk-taking. How a low interest environment affects risk-taking hence depends on which of its opposite effects on risk-taking is dominant. Dell'Ariccia et al. (2014) develop, for example, a model in which a steepening yield curve generates two opposing effects. Whereas, on the one hand, it leads to higher risk-taking due to a risk-return slack, it lowers, on the other hand, incentives for risk-taking

---

[221] Borio et al. (2015) report evidence for particularly decreased bank profitability as a result of particularly low interest rates and a particularly flat yield curve. Furthermore, a decreased profitability of classical lending business may also be due to a smaller margin contribution from deposits as a result of lower short-term rates as the findings of Ruprecht et al. (2013) and Busch and Memmel (2015) suggest.

due to an inverted search for yield through risk-shifting. In the model of Dell'Ariccia et al., the relative strength of these two channels on risk-taking depends on the leverage of the bank.[222]

It should also be noted that there are possible second-order effects of a low interest environment on risk-taking as well. Adrian and Shin (2011) model, for example, how low short-term rates first lead to increased lending, which in turn leads to higher asset valuations and thus to a larger risk-bearing capacity. Bernanke and Gertler (1989, 1990) show how changes in interest rates reduces the riskiness of borrowers and, if existing borrowers become less risky, a bank might be induced to accept riskier new borrowers. Finally, there are possible effects of low interest rates on the risk-taking of an individual bank which result from the interaction with other banks and the central bank. Most notably, Farhi and Tirole (2012) identify incentives for banks to correlate their risk exposures in order to be bailed-out in the event of failure. Such second-order effects are not investigated in our paper.

Some of the above mentioned mechanisms may affect incentives for both credit risk and interest rate risk exposure. The model of Dell'Ariccia et al. (2014), for example, centers on the decision about the monitoring level of a loan portfolio, which is assumed to be inversely related to the corresponding credit risk, and a steeper yield curve which induces an increased maturity mismatch and hence interest rate risk. Data from lending surveys and credit registers are analyzed by De Nicolo et al. (2010), Paligorova and Santos (2013) and Buch et al. (2014) for the US, by Maddaloni and Peydró (2011) for the US and the euro area, by Jimenez et al. (2014) for Spain and by Ioannidou et al. (2015) for Bolivia. The common outcome of these studies is that lower short-term rates, which are generally associated with a steeper yield curve, lead to increased credit risk-taking by banks.

Search for yield is a crucial aspect of our study. In the existing body of literature, two potential explanations for search for yield have been proposed. The first explanation refers to some sort of risk-shifting as introduced by Jensen and Meckling (1976), elaborated on notably by Stiglitz and Weiss (1981) and Kane (1989) and observed in a recent case study by Landier et al. (2011). Explanations of this type maintain the assumption of perfect rationality and rely on an institutional setup or some appropriate contractual arrangement such as limited liability or bonus incentive schemes. The second explanation relies instead on an assumption of bounded rationality. Explanations of this type feature a behavioural assumption that might be very simple, for example the inability of market participants to account for all available information as suggested by Rajan (2005), or they are more sophisticated, say, along the lines of the prospect theory developed by Kahneman and Tversky (1979).

It should be noted that parts of the existing literature seem to imply a diverse understanding of what constitutes a search for yield. In particular, some studies diagnose a search for yield when lower short-term rates lead to increased risk-taking. For example, when lower short-term rates are accompanied by a steeper yield curve, what might be called search for yield may occur in the form of increased taking of interest rate risk due to increased earning opportunities from term transformation. In contrast, we in this paper understand search for yield as a link between *lower* earning opportunities from taking a certain risk and *increased* taking of that risk. Construed in this way, a shift of risk preferences turns out to be one explanation for search for yield. Our concept as such is a narrow notion of search for yield which is in line with the reasoning of Rajan (2005) who defines search for yield as a reaction to lower earning opportunities that consists in an increase in risk-taking as a means to bolster profitability.

There already exists some empirical research on the link between interest rates and the taking of interest rate risk. Hanson and Stein (2015) find that a steepening of the yield curve due to a decrease in short-term interest rates induces US banks to increase their holdings of long-term

---

[222] A graphical literature overview is provided in Appendix 3.

bonds and thereby to increase their interest rate risk.[223] Memmel (2011), Memmel and Schertler (2013) and Ruprecht et al. (2013) study data from interest rate risk and annual account reporting from Germany with the overall result that a flatter yield curve, implying a lower expected return from interest rate risk, leads to a decreased taking of this risk by banks. Our paper refines the findings of these studies by establishing a general *potential* link between lower expected return from interest rate risk and increased taking of this risk. Namely, we start out by showing the existence of the theoretical possibility that below a threshold level of profitability banks search for yield by increasing their interest rate risk despite, say, a flatter yield curve. Subsequently, we estimate empirically the level of the threshold and the share of banks falling short of it.

8.5 Modeling

8.5.1 Theoretical model

In our theoretical model, we include the search for yield in a bank's taking of interest rate risk by assuming a utility function which is convex below a target rate of return and concave above this rate. Fishburn and Kochenberger (1979) find that a utility function of this form best captures the risk attitude of managers. Laughhunn et al. (1980) present additional evidence for risk-seeking behavior of managers in case of below target returns.

Note that, by assuming a utility function which is symmetric to the reference point, we do not accommodate the assumption of loss aversion common in behavioral economics. This assumption, advanced by Benartzi and Thaler (1995) in the field of behavioural finance, postulates that more disutility results from a loss of a given size than utility from a gain of the same size. In contrast, we focus on an expected utility framework with a symmetric combination of risk seeking below the target rate of return and risk aversion above it. Such a utility function captures the essence of the search for yield behavior we are investigating in the most stripped-down way and without loss of generality of our conclusions. However, it is straightforward to extend our theoretical model to feature loss aversion.

With the empirical specification derived from the following theoretical model, it is possible for the first time to identify the critical value of the expected return below which search for yield dominates the link between expected return from interest rate risk and taking of this risk by banks. Our empirical findings are the first to document this richer picture of banks' interest rate risk-taking.

In the following stylized model, we assume as the bank management's utility function

$$u(\pi) = \arctan(\pi) \tag{8.1}$$

where the first derivative is

$$u'(\pi) = \frac{1}{1 + \pi^2}$$

---

[223] Hanson and Stein (2015) actually go even further and show that this increased demand for long-term bonds leads to an increase in price and by this to a reduction of long-term interest rates also, though to a smaller extend than the initial decrease in short-term interest rates. Chodorow-Reich (2014) reports evidence for increased risk-taking of money market funds seeking to cover administrative costs in a low-interest rate environment.

i.e. the marginal utility is always positive, meaning in economic terms that the bank management is never saturated.[224] For $\pi > 0$, the function is concave, meaning risk aversion, for $\pi < 0$, it is convex which means risk seeking.[225]

The income π of a bank is assumed to be composed of an on-balance sheet part a and a part due to derivatives (interest rate swaps) d where the bank can determine its exposure w:[226]

$$\pi = a + w \cdot d \tag{8.2}$$

with

$$d = \begin{cases} \mu + \sigma & p = 0.5 \\ \mu - \sigma & 1 - p = 0.5 \end{cases} \tag{8.3}$$

where p stands for the probability that the first outcome in (8.3) materializes. Note that with $p = 0.5$ the expected value is μ and σ is a symmetric risk measure. We assume that $\sigma > \mu$ so that there are no arbitrage opportunities and that $\mu > 0$, which means that the risky asset has on average a positive return. Note that d and w can also be interpreted more broadly as describing what may be called the *pure* interest rate risk of off- and on-balance sheet business.

In accordance with standard finance theory, the bank management is assumed to maximize its expected utility; in our paper by choosing the appropriate exposure w. Combining (8.1), (8.2) and (8.3), we can express the expected utility of the bank management as

$$E(u) = 0.5 \cdot \arctan\left(a + w \cdot (\mu + \sigma)\right) + 0.5 \cdot \arctan\left(a + w \cdot (\mu - \sigma)\right). \tag{8.4}$$

Differentiating (8.4) with respect to w, one obtains

$$\frac{dE(u)}{dw} = 0.5 \cdot \frac{(\mu + \sigma)}{1 + (a + w \cdot (\mu + \sigma))^2} + 0.5 \cdot \frac{(\mu - \sigma)}{1 + (a + w \cdot (\mu - \sigma))^2}. \tag{8.5}$$

Setting (8.5) to zero and solving for w,[227] one obtains the optimal exposure w_{opt} as

$$w_{opt} = -\frac{a}{\mu} + \sqrt{\frac{a^2}{\mu^2} + \frac{1 + a^2}{\sigma^2 - \mu^2}}. \tag{8.6}$$

The expected income $E(\pi)$ when using the optimal weights is always positive (combining (8.2) and (8.6)), irrespective of the on-balance sheet income part a, which can be seen from Equation (8.7):

$$\begin{aligned} E(\pi_{opt}) &= a + w_{opt} \cdot \mu \\ &= \sqrt{a^2 + \mu^2 \cdot \frac{1 + a^2}{\sigma^2 - \mu^2}} > 0. \end{aligned} \tag{8.7}$$

The rationale behind this result is as follows. Suppose the expected optimal income $E(\pi_{opt})$ were negative. In this case, the probability mass would be mainly in the convex part of the utility function. Accordingly, the decision-maker would be mainly risk-seeking, not risk-averse,

---

[224] See Appendix 1 for a justification of the qualitative nature of the assumed utility function.

[225] Note that the second derivative of the function reads $u''(\pi) = -2\pi/(1 + \pi^2)^2$. Pratt (1964) mentions this utility function, albeit only the positive part where it is concave.

[226] Note that, for the ease of exposition, the on-balance sheet earnings a are assumed to not have any risk.

[227] See Appendix 2.

meaning that he/she derives a higher expected utility from higher risk. Therefore, a portfolio with negative expected return could not be the optimal one because the decision-maker could in this case always achieve a higher expected utility by increasing the off-balance sheet exposure w (which leads to higher risk and higher expected return). For a sufficiently large derivative exposure w, however, the expected return of the entire bank π would turn positive (even if the on-balance sheet expected return a is negative) because, by assumption, the expected return of the derivative is positive. In this case, the usual trade-off between risk and expected return would apply.

In order to compute the change in the optimal risk exposure in response to changes in the expected return of the risky asset, we calculate the derivative of the optimal amount of the investment in the risky asset with respect to its expected return and obtain

$$\frac{\partial w_{opt}}{\partial \mu} = \frac{a}{\mu^2} \cdot \left(1 - \sqrt{\frac{\frac{a^2}{\mu^2}}{\frac{a^2}{\mu^2} + \frac{1+a^2}{\sigma^2 - \mu^2}}} \right) + \frac{\mu(1+a^2)}{(\sigma^2 - \mu^2)^2} \cdot \frac{1}{\sqrt{\frac{a^2}{\mu^2} + \frac{1+a^2}{\sigma^2 - \mu^2}}}. \tag{8.8}$$

The first summand in (8.8) has the same sign as a, because the term in the brackets is always positive. The second summand is likewise always positive. With this in mind, we rewrite (8.8) as

$$\frac{\partial w_{opt}}{\partial \mu} = x_1(a, \mu, \sigma) + x_2(a, \mu, \sigma) \cdot a \tag{8.9}$$

where $x_1(\cdot)$ and $x_2(\cdot)$ are functions with strictly positive values. With Equation (8.9), we see that the derivative of the optimal weight with respect to the expected return $\frac{\partial w_{opt}}{\partial \mu}$ can be either positive or negative (as in our definition of 'search for yield') and that this derivative is positively related to the bank's on-balance sheet income.

8.5.2 Empirical specification

Equation (8.9) can lead to the following empirical implementation

$$\Delta w_{opt} = (\beta_1 + \beta_2 \cdot a) \Delta \mu \tag{8.10}$$

or – more concretely with indices for time t and bank i –

$$\Delta w_{opt,t,i} = \alpha + \beta_1 \Delta \mu_t + \beta_2 \cdot (a_{t,i} \Delta \mu_t) + \gamma' z_{t,i} + \varepsilon_{t,i} \tag{8.11}$$

where $z_{t,i}$ is a vector including bank-specific and time-variant control variables, $\Delta \mu_t$ is the change in steepness of the yield curve (or the change in the earning opportunities from term transformation), $a_{t,i}$ is the deviation of bank i's operative income from its historic mean and $\Delta w_{opt,t,i}$ is the interest rate risk. Of special interest is the term

$$\beta_1 + \beta_2 \cdot a_{t,i} \tag{8.12}$$

which gives the effect of changes in the earnings opportunities from term transformation (which can be positive or negative). The expression $-\hat{\beta}_1/\hat{\beta}_2$ is an estimate for the critical value a^* where the sign of the effect changes, i.e. for $a_{t,i} > -\hat{\beta}_1/\hat{\beta}_2$, an increase in the earning opportunities from term transformation leads to an increase in the interest rate risk exposure (see Figure 8.1). With the help of the delta method, it is possible to derive the asymptotic distribution of the estimation for the critical value $\hat{a}^* = -\hat{\beta}_1/\hat{\beta}_2$:

$$\sqrt{T \cdot N} \left(\hat{a}^* - a^* \right) \to N\left(0, V\right) \tag{8.13}$$

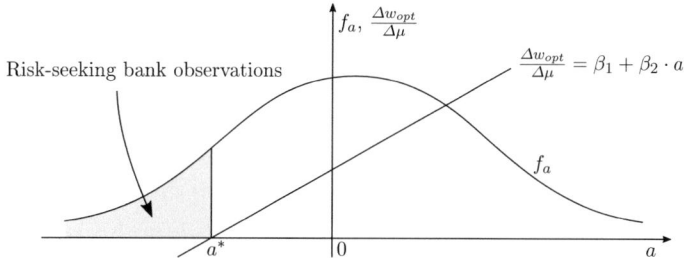

f_a: Prototypical distribution of banks' operating income. a: Deviation of a bank's operative income from its historic mean. a^*: Critical level of a below which banks switch from risk-averse to risk-seeking behaviour. Δw_{opt}: Year-to-year change in a bank's optimal exposure to interest rate risk. $\Delta \mu$: Year-to-year change in the earning opportunities from term transformation.

Figure 8.1: Distribution of banks' operating income and the critical income deviation.

with

$$V = T \cdot N \cdot \left(\frac{var\left(\hat{\beta}_1\right)}{\beta_2^2} - 2 \cdot \frac{cov\left(\hat{\beta}_1, \hat{\beta}_2\right) \cdot \beta_1}{\beta_2^3} + \frac{var\left(\hat{\beta}_2\right) \cdot \beta_1^2}{\beta_2^4} \right) \tag{8.14}$$

where T and N are the numbers of observations in the time and the cross-sectional dimensions, respectively.

8.6 Data

As the dependent variable, named Δw and corresponding to Δw_{opt} in the previous section, we use the year-to-year change in a bank's exposure to a specific interest rate change in our regressions. This exposure has to be reported to the supervisor by each bank in Germany, and banks compute it using their internal risk models. For regulatory purposes, this exposure is defined as the change in the present value of a bank's banking book due to an overnight shift of the term structure. The banks perform the calculation twice, once for a parallel upward shift of 200 basis points and once for a downward shift of the same magnitude, assuming the (more) adverse of the two outcomes for regulatory purposes.[228] As stated just before, each bank determines on its own the exposure to interest rate risk and thereby it has some discretion, for instance concerning the models and assumptions for non-maturity deposits (sight deposits and savings accounts). However, the supervisory authorities examine the models and assumptions behind the calculations and banks cannot change the models and assumptions at discretion. Therefore, we judge the interest rate exposure data as reliable. For reasons of standardization, the present value change is normalized with the banks' regulatory capital (this measure is then called the Basel interest rate coefficient). In this study, we carry out the standardization by using the banks' total assets. This standardization is more convenient for our purposes because the Basel interest rate coefficient includes both the exposure and the loss-absorbing capacity, whereas with our standardization, only the exposure normalized with the size of the bank is expressed.[229]

---

[228] Before 2011, the sizes of the shocks were +130 bp and -190 bp, respectively. To have equal shock sizes across the time, we linearly scaled the shock outcomes to +/-200-bp-shocks, meaning, for instance, that we multiply the losses (in euro) due to a 130-bp-shock by $200/130 = 1.538$.

[229] For the interpretation of the numerical values reported below it is helpful to note that in our sample, the average Basel interest rate coefficient is about 11 times as large as the average interest rate coefficient standardized with total assets.

Another deviation from the regulatory figure is that, in our analysis, we consider only the upward shift in the term structure. We do so because the conventional business model of banking consists in positive term transformation, which means that maturities are longer on the asset side than they are on the liability side. In fact, for 95% of the banks, the upward scenario is the (more) adverse one in our data set. Our empirical analysis covers the period from 2005 to 2014. For the years from 2005 to 2010, reports of banks' exposure to interest rate risk are available only at unsystematic reporting dates, which we treat as follows: Exposures to interest rate risk with reporting dates from January to June are counted as the year-end value of the previous year. Accordingly, values with reporting dates from July to December are counted as year-end values of the current year. From 2011 on, we use the fourth quarter value as the year-end value. Focusing on the direction of the change in banks' exposure to interest rate risk and in order to avoid noise due to extreme values (in spite of the outlier correction mentioned below) in the data, we introduce an alternative dependent variable, which is a dummy variable that takes on the value of one if a bank's exposure to interest rate risk standardized with the bank's total assets has increased in a given year and zero if it has declined or stayed the same. This variable is named $I_{\{\Delta w > 0\}}$.

The main explanatory variables in our regressions are dmu (corresponding to $\Delta \mu_t$ in Equation (8.11)), the year-to-year change in the earning opportunities from interest rate risk, and ert, the deviation of a bank's standardized operating income from its mean operating income over time. More precisely, dmu measures possible earnings from term transformation following an investment strategy that consists in revolvingly investing in 10-year par-yield bonds and of revolvingly issuing par-yield bonds with one year of maturity.[230] ert is defined as the deviation from the mean over time in order to account for differences in bank-specific business models.[231] Furthermore, for the sake of consistency with the theoretical results of the previous subsection, ert is multiplied by the variable dmu, yielding the variable $ertdmu$, which corresponds to the term $a_{t,i}\Delta \mu_t$ in Equation (8.11).[232]

In our regressions, we use several control variables. To measure a bank's credit risk, we look at the write-downs in its credit portfolio and the average riskiness of its assets. The former variable, labeled $writedowns$, is defined as the ratio of a bank's gross write-downs (in a given year) relative to its customer loans. The latter variable, labeled rwa_ta, is the quotient of a bank's risk-weighted assets and total assets. The bank's risk bearing capacity is measured by its regulatory capital ratio, its Tier 1 ratio captured by the variable $Tier1$. According to theory, an increase in this capital ratio should lead to higher risk-taking because of the then larger loss-absorbing capacity. To account for time trends and regulatory changes, the yearly cross-sectional median of the respective variable is subtracted from the variables $writedowns$, rwa_ta, and $Tier1$.[233] Regulatory pressure is captured by the variable reg, which is a dummy variable equaling one if the Basel interest rate coefficient (the measure for a bank's interest rate risk used by supervisory authorities) exceeds 20%, which used to be the regulatory criterion for banks with elevated interest rate risk exposure.

Table 8.1 gives the summary statistics of the dependent variable Δw, i.e. the change in banks' exposure to interest rate risk standardized with its total assets, the main explanatory variables, dmu and $ertdmu$, as well as the control variables $Tier1$, rwa_ta and $writedowns$. Summary statistics of the variable ert are provided only to enable a better understanding of the variable $ertdmu$. For reasons of confidentiality, we do not report summary statistics concerning the dummy variable reg.

---

[230] See Memmel (2008) for details on and Memmel (2011) for an application of this investment strategy.

[231] The main reason to focus on operating income as a measure of profitability is that it is difficult to manipulate for banks.

[232] As one of our robustness checks we additionally include ert by itself as an independent variable. However, the results hardly change and the regression coefficient on ert turns out to be insignificant.

[233] As the variable dmu has no cross-sectional variation, we cannot introduce time dummies.

Variable	Nobs	Mean	Stand. dev.	5th percentile	Median	95th percentile
Δw	6713	0.1109	0.4414	-0.6407	0.1052	0.8487
$I_{\{\Delta w > 0\}}$	6713	0.6204	0.4853	0.0000	1.0000	1.0000
dmu	6713	-0.0538	0.6835	-1.2480	-0.0010	1.9430
ert	6713	-0.0254	0.4644	-0.3794	-0.0291	0.3449
$ertdmu$	6713	-0.0006	0.1629	-0.2702	0.0001	0.2073
$Tier1$	6713	0.0050	0.0496	-0.0394	-0.0045	0.0763
rwa_ta	6713	-0.0019	0.1165	-0.1992	0.0006	0.1810
$writedowns$	6713	0.0316	0.3364	-0.4096	-0.0060	0.5648

Table 8.1: Summary statistics after default outlier treatment. Summary statistics for the two dependent variables, the year-to-year change in a bank's exposure to interest rate risk Δw (present value losses due to a 200 bp parallel shift of the term structure, in percent of total assets) and the dummy variable $I_{\{\Delta w > 0\}}$ which takes the value one in case $\Delta w > 0$, and the main explanatory variables, $dmu, ertdmu, Tier1, rwa\_ta, writedowns$. For completeness, we give the corresponding statistics of the variable ert as well. The summary statistics in this table refer to the sample after applying the default outlier correction as described in the main text. Δw: Year-to-year change in a bank's exposure to interest rate risk, i.e. to a parallel upward shift of the term structure by 200 basis points. dmu: Year-to-year change in the earning opportunities from interest rate risk, i.e. from revolvingly investing in 10-year par-yield bonds and of revolvingly issuing 1-year par-yield bonds. ert: Deviation of a bank's standardized operating income from its mean operating income over time. $ertdmu$: Product of ert and dmu. $Tier1$: Regulatory capital ratio. rwa_ta: Quotient of a bank's risk-weighted assets and total assets. $writedowns$: Ratio of a bank's gross write-downs relative to its customer loans.

We apply an outlier correction to all variables where we cut off the values beyond the first and the 99th percentile as default. The only exception is the continuous variable dmu for which we abstain from any outlier correction because of limited variation and the dummy variable reg. Applying an alternative more extensive outlier correction, we treat the variable $ertdmu$ differently than in the default specification and exclude its values below the 5th percentile and above the 95th percentile from the sample. Our reason for reporting results from both of these alternative treatments in our baseline estimations is that the variable $ertdmu$ has particularly extreme values in the tails. For instance, the ratio of the 99th percentile to the 90th percentile is 5.3 for $ertdmu$, whereas it is 2.2 for the dependent variable Δw and 1.8 for normally distributed variables.[234]

During the ten years under consideration (2005-2014), many mergers took place among the banks in the sample. In our subsection about robustness checks, we try out the following alternative treatment: Two merging banks cease to exist after the year of the merger and a new bank is created in the year after the merger. For our baseline results, however, we proceed as follows: The dominant institution among the two merging banks continues to exist, whereas the subordinate bank ceases operation.

8.7 Empirical results

8.7.1 Baseline models

We estimate four baseline specifications of Equation (8.11), namely with the continuous (I) or the binary (II) dependent variable and each with the default (a) or the more extensive (b) outlier correction. The results (see Table 8.2) show that banks – as expected – increase their interest rate risk exposure when the return from this risk goes up, i.e. in all four specifications the regression coefficient on the variable dmu (year-to-year change in the earning opportunities from

---

[234] These numbers for $ertdmu$ and Δw refer to the sample without any outlier correction applied. The default outlier correction produces similar numbers, namely 5.0 and 1.8, respectively. This suggests that the default outlier correction does not take sufficient care of the fat tail of the distribution of $ertdmu$.

interest rate risk) is positive and highly significant.[235] Focusing on this regression coefficient, the estimates with the continuous dependent variable (specifications Ia and Ib) show that banks increase their exposure to interest rate risk (standardized with total assets) by around 0.06 percentage points on average if the earning opportunities from interest rate risk increase by one standard deviation, meaning that the Basel interest rate coefficient increases by about 0.7 points (see Footnote 13). Regressing on the binary dependent variable instead (specifications IIa and IIb), the probability of the average bank increasing its exposure to interest rate risk in the face of a rise in earning opportunities is estimated to increase by around 5 percentage points.[236] This finding is in line with those of Memmel (2011) and Memmel and Schertler (2013). Note that the positive sign of the regression coefficient on the variable dmu (year-to-year change in the earning opportunities from interest rate risk) suggests that banks actively manage their interest rate risk. The reasoning for this interpretation is as follows. Everything else equal, a flatter yield curve tends to shift loan demand toward longer maturities or interest rate fixation periods. Hence, if banks were passive regarding the level of the interest rate risk, a negative relationship between expected return and interest rate risk would prevail. Accordingly, the positive relationship which we obtain in our regressions is evidence for banks' active management of their interest rate risk.

Dependent variable	Δw (I)		$I_{\{\Delta w > 0\}}$ (II)	
Outlier treatment	default (a)	ext. (b)	default (a)	ext. (b)
dmu	0.0889***	0.0931***	0.3179***	0.3201***
	(0.0092)	(0.0100)	(0.0445)	(0.0485)
$ertdmu$	0.1105**	0.2733***	0.3255*	1.0882***
	(0.0456)	(0.0671)	(0.1755)	(0.2631)
reg	-0.2744***	-0.2787***	-0.5014***	-0.5021***
	(0.0164)	(0.0168)	(0.0553)	(0.0560)
$Tier1$	1.0103**	0.8027*	-0.2371	-0.2476
	(0.4135)	(0.4709)	(0.5857)	(0.6163)
rwa_ta	0.4047**	0.4321**	-0.5469**	-0.4396*
	(0.1738)	(0.1829)	(0.2411)	(0.2473)
$writedowns$	-0.0119	-0.0190	-0.1354*	-0.1875**
	(0.0254)	(0.0268)	(0.0770)	(0.0808)
$constant$	0.1908***	0.1994***	0.6705***	0.6944***
	(0.0051)	(0.0054)	(0.0316)	(0.0325)
$Nobs$	6713	6469	6713	6469
$Banks$	1738	1727		
$R^2 (within)$	7.43%	7.84%		

Table 8.2: Main results. Cluster-robust standard errors in brackets. In the first specification, bank-fixed effects are included. The second specification is a logit-specification. ***, **, and * denote significance at the 1%, 5%, and 10% level, respectively. "default" means that the extreme 1% of the observations (at both ends of the distribution) of the variable $ertdmu$ are treated as outliers, "ext." means that 5% of the observation (at both ends of the distribution) are treated as outliers. Δw: Year-to-year change in a bank's exposure to interest rate risk, i.e. to a parallel upward shift of the term structure by 200 basis points. dmu: Year-to-year change in the earning opportunities from interest rate risk, i.e. from revolvingly investing in 10-year par-yield bonds and of revolvingly issuing 1-year par-yield bonds. ert: Deviation of a bank's standardized operating income from its mean operating income over time. $ertdmu$: Product of ert and dmu. $Tier1$: Regulatory capital ratio. rwa_ta: Quotient of a bank's risk-weighted assets and total assets. $writedowns$: Ratio of a bank's gross write-downs relative to its customer loans.

The regression coefficient on the variable $ertdmu$ (deviation of operating income times the change in earning opportunities from interest rate risk) is significantly positive in all specifications,

---

[235] Note that the significance of the estimated coefficients remain the same when we use clustered standard errors.

[236] This marginal effect is calculated as the difference between the predicted values of the dependent variable with all explanatory variables set to their mean value and with all explanatory variables set to their mean value except for dmu, the year-to-year change in the earning opportunities from interest rate risk, which is set to its mean value plus one standard deviation.

though on different levels. This means that the interest rate risk exposure of a bank with a lower deviation of its operative income from its historic mean shows a weaker response to changes in earning opportunities from interest rate risk (dmu) than a bank with a higher deviation. If the deviation of a bank's operative income from its historic mean is very low, i.e. sufficiently negative, the relationship between exposure and earning opportunities can even change its sign from positive – as it is usually the case – to negative. Table 8.3 gives the level of this critical deviation of operative income a^* below which such a reversal of the relationship is to be expected (see Equation (8.12)). It is striking that the empirical significance and the economic relevance vary with the outlier correction applied. With the default outlier correction, the regression coefficient on $ertdmu$ (deviation of operating income times the change in earning opportunities from interest rate risk) is significant at the 5% level in the specification with the continuous dependent variable and the critical deviation of operative income is below the threshold for around 0.6% of the observations in the sample (specification Ia). Similarly, the specification with the binary dependent variable produces a critical deviation below which 0.5% of the observations can be found, though on an inferior level of significance of 10%. With the more extensive outlier correction, the regression coefficient on $ertdmu$ (deviation of operating income times the change in earning opportunities from interest rate risk) turns out to be significant at the 1% level for both the specification with the continuous and the specification with the binary dependent variable, and more than 5% of the observations in the sample display a deviation of operative income that falls below the critical threshold (specifications Ib and IIb). This shows that the way in which we treat outliers has a significant impact on the percentage of observations (and banks) that are below the critical value. Put differently, with the default outlier correction, an operating income that is close to 1.7 (specification Ia) or 2.0 (specification IIa) standard deviations below the historic mean takes a bank below the critical level, and with the more extensive outlier correction, the factor is less than 0.7 (specification Ib) or 0.6 (specification IIb) standard deviations.

Dependent variable	Δw (I)		$I_{\{\Delta w>0\}}$ (II)	
Outlier treatment	default (a)	ext. (b)	default (a)	ext. (b)
critical operative income $\hat{a}^*$	-0.8040**	-0.3405***	-0.9767*	-0.2942***
	(0.3339)	(0.0883)	(0.5247)	(0.0799)
Share of observations below $\hat{a}^*$	0.6%	5.6%	0.5%	8.3%

Table 8.3: Critical operative income. Robust standard errors in brackets, determined according to Equation (8.14). ***, ** and * denote significance at the 1%, 5%, and 10% level, respectively. "default" means that the extreme 1% of the observations (at both ends of the distribution) of the variable $ertdmu$ are treated as outliers, "ext." means that 5% of the observation (at both ends of the distribution) are treated as outliers. Δw: Year-to-year change in a bank's exposure to interest rate risk, i.e. to a parallel upward shift of the term structure by 200 basis points. In the columns marked this way the results from the estimations with the continuous dependent variable are reported. $I_{\{\Delta w>0\}}$: In the columns marked this way the results from the estimations with the binary dependent variable are reported. $\hat{a}^*$: Estimated critical deviation of a bank's operative income from its historic mean below which the bank is risk-seeking.

With the default outlier correction, we find that a deviation of the operating income relative to total assets from its historic mean by -0.80 percentage points (specification Ia) or -0.98 percentage points (specification IIa) is the threshold. With the more extensive outlier correction, the threshold is estimated to be at -0.34 percentage points (specification Ib) or at -0.29 percentage points (specification IIb). Since the mean operating income relative to total assets amounts to 0.92%, these results imply that mean critical level of operative income is positive. The only exception is the result produced with the default outlier correction and the binary dependent variable (specification IIa), which, however, has the lowest level of significance.

Concerning the control variables, we find that regulatory pressure, measured by the dummy variable reg, has a highly significant impact on the change in the interest rate risk: If a bank is qualified as an outlier, the bank reduces its exposure by 0.3 percentage points (specifications Ia and Ib) (on average) over the next year. According to the specifications with the continuous dependent variable, capital adequacy, measured by the variable $Tier1$, has a significant positive impact, i.e. banks with more capital at hand take a higher interest rate risk. The riskiness, measured by the variable rwa_ta, is estimated to be significant in all four specifications. But the sign of the estimated coefficient varies. With the continuous dependent variable, it is positive (specifications Ia and Ib) and, with the binary dependent variable, it is negative (specification IIa and IIb). As both the dependent variable and this explanatory variable are normalized with total assets, the positive sign can be regarded as an artefact. If total assets decrease, both variables increase mechanically. Noting that a banks' risk-weighted assets mainly reflect credit risk and not interest rate risk, the negative coefficient for rwa_ta (as produced by specification IIa and IIb) suggests that banks have an internal risk budget that they distribute between credit and interest rate risk.[237] The estimation results on the other variable that measures credit risk, $writedowns$, tend to support this assumption. Its effect is significant only in the specifications with the binary dependent variable (specification IIa and IIb), the estimated sign being negative.

8.7.2 Robustness Checks

We run several robustness checks. If not otherwise stated, the results are compared to the ones produced with the baseline specification Ia.[238]

First, we include ert (deviation of operating income) as an additional independent variable in the regression. We do this because the results for the interaction term $ertdmu$ (deviation of operating income times the change in earning opportunities from interest rate risk) might change, if besides dmu (year-to-year change in the earning opportunities from interest rate risk) the second interacted variable ert is separately included in the regression too. The regression coefficient on ert turns out to be insignificant. The regression coefficient on $ertdmu$ hardly changes and its level of significance remains if ert is separately included in the regression. This suggests that our baseline results for $ertdmu$ do not only pick up some spurious regression and justifies the exclusion of ert from our baseline models.

Second, we alternatively use the one year lagged value of the variable ert (deviation of operating income) for the calculation of the independent variable $ertdmu$ (deviation of operating income times the change in earning opportunities from interest rate risk). We do so in order to address a potential endogeneity problem arising from simultaneity, i.e. a two-way determination of the change in a bank's exposure to interest rate risk and its operating income. We find that the regression results hardly differ from the results produced by our baseline model.

Third, we normalize the present value change in a bank's banking book due to an overnight upward shift in the term structure by 200 basis points using the bank's regulatory capital instead of its total assets. As pointed out earlier, this measure is even closer related to the Basel interest rate coefficient. We find that the significance of the variable $ertdmu$ (deviation of operating income times the change in earning opportunities from interest rate risk) vanishes under the default outlier correction and becomes a bit weaker under the more extensive one. The reduction in the significance of the coefficient does not come as a surprise. As noted above, in our baseline models we apply the normalization with total assets in order to disentangle changes in exposure and loss-absorbing capacity. The variable included to capture the latter, namely $Tier1$ (the regulatory capital ratio), becomes insignificant, if the alternative normalization is applied.

Fourth, we apply a different merger treatment as described in Section 8.6: No longer does the dominating bank prevail, but a new bank appears and the two merging banks disappear

---

[237] The canonical reference for this finding is the paper by Schrand and Unal (1998).
[238] All regression results for the robustness checks can be found in Appendix 4.

from the sample after a merger. Due to this different treatment of the mergers, we lose some observations. However, the qualitative results remain, although the significance of the variable *ertdmu* (deviation of operating income times the change in earning opportunities from interest rate risk) becomes slightly weaker.

Fifth, we control for bank size. To this end, we include the logarithm of a bank's total assets normalized by the cross-sectional median for each year as an additional control variable. The regression coefficient on this variable turns out to be negative and highly significant. More importantly, the regression coefficients on the main variables of interest hardly change and their levels of significance remain unaltered.

Sixth, we investigate whether banks applying interest rate derivatives behave differently. We define a dummy variable which takes the value one in each year if a bank reports a positive figure for the nominal derivative volume. This is the case in 48.7% of the observations. We interact this dummy variable with *dmu* (year-to-year change in the earning opportunities from interest rate risk) as well as with *ertdmu* (deviation of operating income times the change in earning opportunities from interest rate risk). We find a positive relationship between expected return and risk for both values of the dummy variable. As noted above, this highly significant relationship suggests that banks' interest rate risk is actively managed in both subsamples. Anecdotal evidence suggests that it is common for smaller banks which do not apply interest rate derivatives to actively manage their interest rate risk by means of bidirectional loans of different maturities with their respective central institutions.[239,240] However, it is only for banks not using interest rate derivatives that we find the variable *ertdmu* to be significant. One possible explanation for the variable *ertdmu* to be significant only for these banks is that banks using interest rate derivatives are likely to use other instruments such as credit default swaps to manage their risk.[241] According to this interpretation, interest rate risk is a viable means of controlling a bank's risk position, although other and possibly more convenient means to that end exist but only banks with an elaborate risk management (here proxied by the use of interest rate derivatives) have access to them.[242]

Seventh, we break up the sample period 2005-2014 into two subperiods, ranging from 2005-2008 and from 2009 on with the low interest rate environment, by interacting the variables of main interest, *dmu* (year-to-year change in the earning opportunities from interest rate risk) and *ertdmu* (deviation of operating income times the change in earning opportunities from interest rate risk), with an appropreately defined dummy variable. We find that the regression coefficients on both variables are significant only for the first subperiod and insignificant for the second. The lack of significance in the second subperiod is likely due to relatively little variation of the variable *dmu*.

Eighth, the empirical specification in Equation (8.11) is a linearization of the relationship derived in Equation (8.9). This relationship is non-linear, which suggests including the term $a_{t,i}^2 \Delta \mu_t$ in the empirical specification (8.11). The corresponding coefficient is positive and significant at the 5% level, suggesting a convex relationship. Note that no real critical operating income can be calculated with the resulting coefficients. Moreover, the estimated coefficients

---

[239] Ehrmann and Worms (2004) have a related study on bank networks in Germany.

[240] Readers who are unfamiliar with the German banking system are referred to the recent overview provided in Chapter 2.1 of Koetter (2013). The three pillars of the German banking system are commercial banks, savings banks, and cooperative banks. Savings banks and cooperative banks have dedicated central institutions. Unlike most savings banks and cooperative banks, their central institutions are active on the capital markets. One of their functions can be described as providing mediated access for savings banks and cooperative banks to these markets.

[241] Gunduz et al. (2015) find that banks apply CDS as an effective tool to control bank risk.

[242] See also Ruprecht et al. (2013), who find that banks with a trading book differ from banks without a trading book with respect to their behavior towards interest rate risk.

other than for the quadratic term are all very similar to the ones that we obtain with the default sample specification.

Ninth, we further restrict the sample to observations with an interest rate exposure that occupies a substantial part of the loss-absorbing capacity. The underlying hypothesis is that banks for which this is not the case do not take interest rate risk as a part of their business model and are, in effect, not subject to the mechanism we investigate. However, we find that restricting the sample to banks with a net present value change in the banking book due to an overnight upward shift in the term structure by 200 basis points normalized with regulatory capital of 5% or 10% does not lead to materially different results. Interestingly, these restrictions reduce the number of observations only by about 4% or 10%, respectively. This shows that our sample is dominated by banks with an interest rate risk exposure that occupies a substantial part of the loss-absorbing capacity. This, in turn, explains why restricting the sample in the way described does not lead to materially different results.

Tenth, for the sake of completeness, we dispense with any outlier correction. Compared to the default outlier correction, the regression coefficients in the estimation with the continuous dependent variable hardly change. The significance of the coefficient of the variable *ertdmu* (deviation of operating income times the change in earning opportunities from interest rate risk) even improves from the 5% to the 1% level.

8.8 Conclusion

In our theoretical model, we allow for the possibility that, in some situations, the bank management may change its risk preference from risk aversion to risk seeking. This behaviour can lead the bank management to increase the bank's risk exposure even if the expected return from the risk is falling. In our empirical study on the interest rate risk exposure of German banks, we observe the usual positive direct relationship between expected return and exposure. Furthermore, we find evidence that in extreme situations, such as the ones with very low profit levels, the relationship is reversed. The reverse relationship is relevant for about 0.5% to 8.3% of the observations, depending on the sample specification and the estimation technique used.

This study is a first attempt to empirically document the search for yield by banks in a narrow sense. We characterize the extreme situations mentioned above as situations in which a banks' operative income falls below a certain threshold. If the low interest rate environment becomes entrenched and banks' earning opportunities are squeezed further, such extreme situations may become more likely.

8.9 Appendices

Appendix 1: Justification of arctan-utility function

Assume that a manager keeps his job if the income π of the bank will exceed a threshold c, which is expressed in the following function:

$$U(\pi, c) = \begin{cases} 1 & \pi > c \\ 0 & otherwise \end{cases} \tag{8.15}$$

The threshold c is stochastic with

$$c \sim N(\mu_c, \sigma_c^2) \tag{8.16}$$

where $\sim N(\cdot)$ means "normally distributed". The expected utility $u(\pi)$ derived from an income π is $u(\pi) = E_c(U(\pi, c))$. Taken together, we obtain

$$
\begin{aligned}
u(\pi) &= E(U(\pi, c)) \\
&= Pr(\pi > c) \\
&= \Phi\left(\frac{\pi - \mu_c}{\sigma_c}\right)
\end{aligned}
\tag{8.17}
$$

where $\Phi(\cdot)$ is the cumulative distribution function of the standard normal distribution. With the introduction of randomness, the non-continuous function (8.15) turned into the manifold differentiable function (8.17). For $\mu_c = 0$ and $\sigma_c = 1$, the expression (8.17) becomes to $u(\pi) = \Phi(\pi)$, which qualitatively corresponds to the assumed utility function (8.1). For reasons of easier handling, we opted for the *arctan* (instead of the cumulative normal distribution Φ) function.

Appendix 2: Solving for w

Setting (8.5) to zero, we get

$$
\begin{aligned}
(\mu - \sigma) \cdot (1 + a^2) + (\mu - \sigma) \cdot 2aw(\mu + \sigma) + (\mu - \sigma) \cdot w^2(\mu + \sigma)^2 \\
+(\mu + \sigma) \cdot (1 + a^2) + (\mu - \sigma) \cdot 2aw(\mu + \sigma) + (\mu + \sigma) \cdot w^2(\mu - \sigma)^2 &= 0.
\end{aligned}
\tag{8.18}
$$

Rearranging gives

$$
w^2 + 2 \cdot \frac{a}{\mu} \cdot w - \frac{1 + a^2}{\sigma^2 - \mu^2} = 0.
\tag{8.19}
$$

(8.19) has two solutions; due to our assumption $\mu > 0$, the solution in (8.6) is the maximum (which we look for) and the other is the minimum. If we tolerated the case $\mu \geq \sigma$, investing in derivates would always lead to a non-negative result and to a strictly positive result with at least probability of 0.5, making arbitrage possible.

Appendix 3: Graphical literature overview

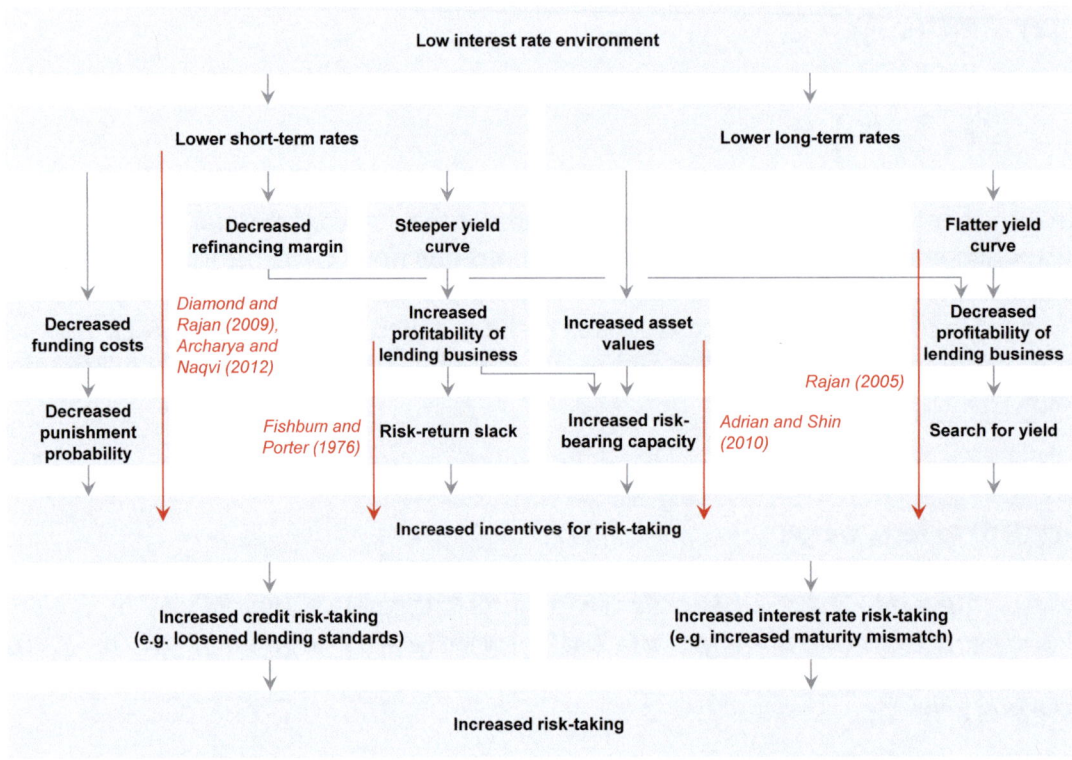

Figure 8.2: Schematic literature overview

Appendix 4: Further descriptive statistics and regression results

Variable	Nobs	Mean	Stand. dev.	5th percentile	Median	95th percentile
Δw	6469	0.1149	0.4387	-0.6285	0.1102	0.8487
$I_{\{\Delta w>0\}}$	6469	0.6248	0.4842	0.0000	1.0000	1.0000
dmu	6469	-0.0601	0.6394	-1.2480	-0.0010	1.9430
ert	6469	-0.0290	0.4350	-0.3581	-0.0294	0.3073
$ertdmu$	6469	0.0019	0.1062	-0.1994	0.0001	0.1610
$Tier1$	6469	0.0047	0.0486	-0.0395	-0.0045	0.0763
rwa_ta	6469	-0.0021	0.1159	-0.1989	0.0006	0.1802
$writedowns$	6469	0.0308	0.3268	-0.4004	-0.0053	0.5519

Table 8.4: Summary statistics after extensive outlier treatment. Summary statistics for the two dependent variables, the year-to-year change in a bank's exposure to interest rate risk Δw (present value losses due to a 200 bp parallel shift of the term structure, in percent of total assets) and the dummy variable $I_{\{\Delta w>0\}}$ which takes the value one in case $\Delta w > 0$, and the main explanatory variables, $dmu, ertdmu, Tier1, rwa\_ta, writedowns$. For completeness, we give the corresponding statistics of the variable ert as well. The summary statistics in this table refer to the sample after applying the extensive outlier treatment as described in the main text. Δw: Year-to-year change in a bank's exposure to interest rate risk, i.e. to a parallel upward shift of the term structure by 200 basis points. dmu: Year-to-year change in the earning opportunities from interest rate risk, i.e. from revolvingly investing in 10-year par-yield bonds and of revolvingly issuing 1-year par-yield bonds. ert: Deviation of a bank's standardized operating income from its mean operating income over time. $ertdmu$: Product of ert and dmu. $Tier1$: Regulatory capital ratio. rwa_ta: Quotient of a bank's risk-weighted assets and total assets. $writedowns$: Ratio of a bank's gross write-downs relative to its customer loans.

Variable	Nobs	Mean	Stand. dev.	5th percentile	Median	95th percentile
Δw	7024	0.0977	0.5194	-0.6975	0.0989	0.8689
$I_{\{\Delta w>0\}}$	7024	0.6129	0.4871	0.0000	1.0000	1.0000
dmu	7024	-0.0542	0.6791	-1.2480	-0.0010	1.9430
ert	7024	-0.0296	0.6218	-0.3938	-0.0292	0.3551
$ertdmu$	7024	-0.0022	0.1914	-0.2740	0.0001	0.2150
$Tier1$	7024	0.0191	0.5818	-0.0411	0.0045	0.0824
rwa_ta	7024	-0.0014	0.1270	-0.2059	0.0005	0.1904
$writedowns$	7024	-4.9800	383.8605	-0.4300	-0.0047	0.6009

Table 8.5: Summary statistics without outlier treatment. The summary statistics in this table refer to the sample without applying any outlier treatment. For details on the variables included see Table 8.4.

Robustness check	First	Second	Third		Fourth	Fifth
Keyword(s)	ert included	ert lagged in $ertdmu$	w relative to capital		merger for new bank	bank size included
Dependent variable	Δw	Δw	Δw_c	Δw_c	Δw	Δw
Outlier treatment	default	default	default	ext.	default	default
dmu	0.0887***	0.0964***	1.1300***	1.1982***	0.0824***	0.0855***
	(0.0092)	(0.0092)	(0.1165)	(0.1272)	(0.0096)	(0.0093)
$ertdmu$	0.1033**	-	0.4756	2.0666**	0.1014**	0.1062**
	(0.0459)	-	(0.5452)	(0.8197)	(0.0482)	(0.0455)
reg	-0.2732***	-0.2825***	-4.0449***	-4.0784***	-0.2854***	-0.2957***
	(0.0165)	(0.01615)	(0.1946)	(0.1964)	(0.0171)	(0.0168)
$Tier1$	0.9189**	1.0112**	-4.3197	-9.2486*	1.0333**	0.2054
	(0.4301)	(0.4041)	(4.8170)	(5.4632)	(0.4198)	(0.4186)
rwa_ta	0.3907**	0.3967**	-4.1049**	-4.6645**	0.5225***	0.1628
	(0.1764)	(0.1718)	(2.0749)	(2.1926)	(0.1816)	(0.1744)
$writedowns$	-0.0097	-0.0126	-0.0304	-0.1284	-0.0101	0.0035
	(0.0255)	(0.0256)	(0.3191)	(0.3214)	(0.0264)	(0.0255)
ert	-0.0201	-	-	-	-	-
	(0.0215)	-	-	-	-	-
$ert_l dmu$	-	0.1661***	-	-	-	-
	-	(0.0348)	-	-	-	-
lta	-	-	-	-	-	-
	-	-	-	-	-	(0.0631)
dmu_d	-	-	-	-	-	-
	-	-	-	-	-	-
dmu_nd	-	-	-	-	-	-
	-	-	-	-	-	-
$ertdmu\_d$	-	-	-	-	-	-
	-	-	-	-	-	-
$ertdmu\_nd$	-	-	-	-	-	-
	-	-	-	-	-	-
dmu_nl	-	-	-	-	-	-
	-	-	-	-	-	-
dmu_l	-	-	-	-	-	-
	-	-	-	-	-	-
$ertdmu\_nl$	-	-	-	-	-	-
	-	-	-	-	-	-
$ertdmu\_l$	-	-	-	-	-	-
	-	-	-	-	-	-
$ert^2 dmu$	-	-	-	-	-	-
	-	-	-	-	-	-
$constant$	0.1903***	0.1992***	1.0903***	2.000***	0.1935***	0.2605***
	(0.0052)	(0.0054)	(0.0606)	(0.0628)	(0.0053)	(0.0117)
$Nobs$	6713	6713	6719	6477	6588	6713
$Banks$	1738	1738	1740	1728	1861	1738
$R^2 (within)$	7.45%	7.79%	10.64%	11.09%	7.49%	8.57%

Table 8.6: Robustness checks 1-5. Cluster-robust standard errors in brackets. ***, **, and * denote significance at the 1%, 5%, and 10% level, respectively. "default" means that the extreme 1% of the observations (at both ends of the distribution) of the variable $ertdmu$ are treated as outliers, "ext." means that 5% of the observation (at both ends of the distribution) are treated as outliers. Δw: Year-to-year change in a bank's exposure to interest rate risk, i.e. to a parallel upward shift of the term structure by 200 basis points relative to total assets. dmu: Year-to-year change in the earning opportunities from interest rate risk, i.e. from revolvingly investing in 10-year par-yield bonds and of revolvingly issuing 1-year par-yield bonds. ert: Deviation of a bank's standardized operating income from its mean operating income over time. $ertdmu$: Product of ert and dmu. $Tier1$: Regulatory capital ratio. rwa_ta: Quotient of a bank's risk-weighted assets and total assets. $writedowns$: Ratio of a bank's gross write-downs relative to its customer loans. $ert_l dmu$: Product of ert from the previous period and dmu. (continued)

Robustness check	Sixth	Seventh	Eighth	Nineth		Tenth
Keyword(s)	use of derivatives	Subperiods 08 | 09	ert^2dmu included	w > 5%	w > 10%	Full sample
Dependent variable	Δw	Δw	Δw	Δw	Δw	Δw
Outlier treatment	default	default	default	default	default	none
dmu	-	-	0.0842***	0.0853***	0.0786***	0.0945***
	-	-	(0.0095)	(0.0093)	(0.0093)	(0.0107)
$ertdmu$	-	-	0.1152**	0.1092**	0.1185**	0.1127***
	-	-	(0.0457)	(0.0474)	(0.0502)	(0.0391)
reg	-0.2753***	-0.3521***	-0.2757***	-0.2816***	-0.3031***	-0.3405***
	(0.0164)	(0.0164)	(0.0164)	(0.0167)	(0.0167)	(0.0198)
$Tier1$	1.0598**	0.5627	1.0307**	1.0559**	1.1231**	0.2502***
	(0.4214)	(0.4040)	(0.4075)	(0.4804)	(0.5052)	(0.0096)
rwa_ta	0.4134**	0.3316**	0.4091**	0.4996***	0.3932**	0.4036**
	(0.1735)	(0.1674)	(0.1733)	(0.1873)	(0.1936)	(0.2020)
$writedowns$	-0.0105	0.0083	-0.0122	-0.0295	-0.0239	0.0003***
	(0.0259)	(0.0247)	(0.0253)	(0.0264)	(0.0274)	0.0000
ert	-	-	-	-	-	-
	-	-	-	-	-	-
$ert_l dmu$	-	-	-	-	-	-
	-	-	-	-	-	-
lta	-	-	-	-	-	-
	-	-	-	-	-	-
dmu_d	0.0835***	-	-	-	-	-
	(0.0123)	-	-	-	-	-
dmu_nd	0.0973***	-	-	-	-	-
	(0.0147)	-	-	-	-	-
$ertdmu\_d$	0.0422	-	-	-	-	-
	(0.0628)	-	-	-	-	-
$ertdmu\_nd$	0.1703***	-	-	-	-	-
	(0.0642)	-	-	-	-	-
dmu_nl	-	0.2932***	-	-	-	-
	-	(0.0168)	-	-	-	-
dmu_l	-	-0.0169	-	-	-	-
	-	(0.0121)	-	-	-	-
$ertdmu\_nl$	-	0.1954***	-	-	-	-
	-	(0.0632)	-	-	-	-
$ertdmu\_l$	-	-0.0039	-	-	-	-
	-	(0.0581)	-	-	-	-
ert^2dmu	-	-	0.0935**	-	-	-
	-	-	(0.0462)	-	-	-
$constant$	0.1924***	0.2642***	0.1919***	0.2113***	0.2422***	0.1969***
	(0.0052)	(0.0072)	(0.0052)	(0.0051)	(0.0054)	(0.0056)
$Nobs$	6666	6713	6713	6466	6067	7024
$Banks$	1731	1738	1738	1673	1613	1786
$R^2(within)$	7.57%	11.18%	7.53%	7.81%	9.20%	8.32%

Table 8.6 (continued): Robustness checks 6-10 Δw_c: Year-to-year change in a bank's exposure to interest rate risk, i.e. to a parallel upward shift of the term structure by 200 basis points relative to regulatory capital. lta: Logarithm of bank's total assets. dmu_d: Product of dmu and a dummy that equals one, if the bank uses derivatives. dmu_nd: Product of dmu and a dummy that equals one, if the bank does not use derivatives. $ertdmu\_d$: Product of $ertdmu$ and a dummy that equals one, if the bank uses derivatives. $ertdmu\_nd$: Product of $ertdmu$ and a dummy that equals one, if the bank does not use derivatives. ert^2dmu: Product of ert squared and $dmu.dmu\_nl$: Product of dmu and a dummy that equals one not in the low interest rate environment (i.e. 2005-2008). dmu_l: Product of dmu and a dummy that equals one in the low interest rate environment (i.e. 2009-2014). $ertdmu\_d$: Product of $ertdmu$ and a dummy that equals one not in the low interest rate environment (i.e. 2005-2008). $ertdmu\_nd$: Product of $ertdmu$ and a dummy that equals one in the low interest rate environment (i.e. 2009-2014).

8.10 Concluding remarks

It is important to make a clear distinction between two empirical findings of the research paper presented here, one more general and one more specific. The more general empirical finding is that there is a not only the already rather well documented positive link between the change in earning opportunities from interest rate risk and the change in a bank's exposure to interest rate risk but there is a complementing negative link as well the strength of which depends on the bank's income. The existence of this negative link can be explained by the motive to search for yield. Now, the more specific empirical finding of the research paper is that there is a threshold for the deviation of a bank's standardized operating income from its mean operating income over time such that below this threshold the overall link between the change in earning opportunities from interest rate risk and the change in the bank's exposure to interest rate risk is no longer positive but negative. Put differently, below this critical income threshold the motive to search for yield becomes dominant.

The reason why it is important to make a clear distinction between these two findings is that it is a prerequisite to see the more general finding clearly. While the more specific finding may be relevant for banks only when there operating income is below the threshold, the more general finding is relevant for all banks at all times. Having provided a theoretical rationale as well as some empirical evidence for this negative link is the principal research contribution here. Having discovered some banks with an operating income below the threshold below which this negative link prevails over the positive link is a nice add-on in comparison. The research paper explains and marshals evidence for the existence of banks' motive to search for yield in interest rate risk. That the paper additionally presents evidence that suggests that this motive is even dominant for certain banks emphasizes its relevance.

Chapter 9 Conclusion

The interest rate risk of banks and in particular that part which is linked to classical banking activities and which can be found in a bank's banking book is a topic of high current relevance. This dissertation covers this topic in depth. It concentrates on Germany where it extends the existing research empirically. This conclusion summarizes the main findings and points to policy implications.

As a first step the most important definitions are provided in Chapter 2. In the discussion of the traditional and the modern understanding of banking key differences are identified. But it is also shown that on the level of the individual bank, on the micro level, important aspects of the traditional understanding resurface in the modern understanding. The most important take-away for the present investigation is that according to the modern understanding, banks are regarded as quintessentially involved in asset transformation and the taking of the associated risks which include interest rate risk.

The review of the microeconomics of banking in Chapter 3 reveals that banks' taking of interest rate risk is hard to explain with reference to transaction costs or asymmetric information only. A richer understanding of interest rate risk is required. With a focus on transaction costs an explanation can be developed for banks' taking of the idiosyncratic part of interest rate risk, provided one accepts that there is such a part. And with a focus on asymmetric information an explanation is available for banks' taking of the systematic part of interest rate risk, provided one agrees that this risk-taking can affect the development of interest rates by influencing the central bank. Now understanding banks as quintessential risk-takers does not mean that these explanations are rejected and replaced by something completely different. On the contrary, it means that these explanations are understood as explanations of an essential part of what banks do. And this is more natural if not the traditional but the modern understanding of banking is taken as a basis. Because then the asset transformation that leads to banks' taking of interest rate risk in the first place is seen not as an incidental byproduct of an intermediation of loanable funds but rather as an essential part of financing through money creation, that is of what banking really is.

The review of the monetary economics of the transmission channels in Chapter 4 uncovers a particularly interesting research gap, namely the theoretic modelling and empirical examination of a search for yield in banks' taking of interest rate risk. In addition to the interest rate channel and the credit channel, the risk-taking channel is now more and more established as a transmission channel of monetary policy. And while most of the research on this newly discovered transmission channel focusses on the influence of monetary policy on banks' taking of credit risk, some research contributions also already address the influence on banks' taking of interest rate risk. However, this influence is largely treated in a one-dimensional way. Lower short-term interest rates are associated with a higher term spread, this in turn with a higher profitability of interest rate risk, and finally this with more taking of interest rate risk by banks. This reasoning is plausible but it is not comprehensive. Most importantly, it does not account for a possible search for yield or gambling for resurrection, that is for a negative link between the profitability of interest rate risk and the amount banks take of it. Theoretically modelling and empirically investigating this additional dimension of the link turns out to be a particularly interesting research gap.

The close-up view on specifics of interest rate risk in economic research in Chapter 5 prepares for the following extensions. Existing empirical results suggest that banks' taking of interest rate risk depends crucially on bank and market characteristics. This motivates a dedicated investigation of German banks and further of different types of these banks. The existing research on German banks' taking of interest rate risk consistently produces evidence of a positive link between the term spread or possible earnings from term transformation and the amount of interest rate risk banks take. But again, the hitherto applied empirical setups are found not even to allow for the additional dimension of a search for yield in interest rate risk, and this motivates research that does. Finally, the relevant data which is generally available for German banks consists of specific exposure estimates provided by banks themselves and of certain parts of the large volume of bank report data.

Chapter 6 addresses the nearly complete lack of specific statistics about the interest rate risk of banks in Germany by analyzing a comprehensive set of publicly available statistics which were not designed to convey this information but from which information about the interest rate risk of banks in Germany can be extracted. The interest rate risk from on-balance sheet term transformation of banks in Germany is found to exceed the average in the euro area already and to be increasing further. Of the different types of banks in Germany, savings banks and cooperative banks are identified as being particularly engaged. Most notably, for banks in Germany a strong shift toward shorter-term funding but also a notable shift toward longer-term lending is observed. In particular, banks in Germany clearly push for more short-term and less long-term deposits by adjusting interest rates. And banks in Germany do comparatively little to counteract the relatively high increase in the demand for long-term loans by adjusting credit standards or terms and conditions.

Chapter 7 empirically assesses the adequacy of past, current, and future supervisory interest rate shock scenarios in Germany on the basis of historic term structure changes, forecasts of term structure changes, and an impact assessment. The main motivation for this assessment is based on the observation that the Basel interest rate coefficient which measures the impact of certain shock scenarios is commonly mistaken for a risk measure. However, it clearly is only an exposure measure since it does not account for the probability of the materialization of the relevant shock scenarios. In the light of historic term structure changes the current scenarios of symmetric parallel shocks up and down appear less adequate than the past asymmetric shock scenarios and the future shock scenarios which also include other types of shocks still appear not to include all the relevant types. In particular, long rates shocks are missing. What is more, the historic term structure changes appear to follow a general trend toward smaller and fewer consistently adverse term structure changes. This suggests a decrease of the probability of the materialization of the respective shock scenarios and hence a decrease of the interest rate risk of German banks everything else equal. The forecasts of term structure changes support the finding that long rates shocks are relevant types of shocks. More importantly, the development of the forecasts of term structure changes also points to a decrease in the interest rate risk at least in so far as it concerns next year's net interest income. However, the accuracy of the forecasts turns out to be limited, particularly for long-term interest rates. Yet, forecasts remain important to be aware of as they might influence banks' risk-taking decisions nevertheless. This would in turn suggest that banks that rely on these forecasts might be taking excessive interest rate risk. Finally, the impact assessment reveals that the impacts of the short rates shock up and of the flattener shock on next year's net interest income are more adverse than that of the parallel shock up. This calls into question the reasonableness of the future requirement to disclose the latter impact but not the former two. In terms of impact on current portfolio value, the parallel shock up turns out to be the most harmful. This may justify why the past and current scenarios feature parallel shocks only since their impact was and is only measured in terms of net present value anyways. Last but not least, the impact assessment reveals the quantitative importance of the impact of long rates shocks. Hence, also from this perspective long rates shocks are relevant.

Chapter 8 presents a theoretical rationale as well as some empirical evidence for banks's search for yield in interest rate risk. It addresses the important research gap identified in the monetary economics of the transmission channels and more specifically in the research on the risk-taking channel of monetary policy in so far as it concerns banks' taking of interest rate risk. The existing research only accounts for the positive link between the term spread and hence the earning opportunities from term transformation on the one hand and banks' taking of interest rate risk on the other hand. For the first time, an additional negative link is modeled theoretically and its existence and relevance are documented empirically. This negative link is identified as banks' search for yield in interest rate risk.

The new results produced in the extensions in Chapters 6, 7, and 8 have direct policy implications. First, the findings obtained from the investigation based on publicly available statistics strongly suggest to supervise the taking of interest rate risk by banks in Germany more closely and to make more use of the existing instruments to discourage them from taking more. In particular, an eye should be kept on the ever shorter-term refinancing. And supervisory attention should be focused on savings banks and cooperative banks. Second, the outcomes of the empirical assessment of their adequacy strongly suggests to use the future exposure measures based on the new interest rate shock scenarios with care and to be aware of them not being risk measures. The set of shock scenarios would gain in comprehensiveness and relevance if long-rates shocks were included. And the disclosure requirements would materially be improved by the requirement also to disclose the impacts of all shock scenarios on next year's net interest income and not only the impacts of the parallel shocks. Third, the empirical proof of a sizeable search for yield in interest rate risk by banks entails that monetary policy needs to account for it. The current low interest rate environment reduces banks' profitability and hence the negative link between the term spread and banks' taking of interest rate risk has to be expected to become more important quantitatively. Hence, a further reduction of long-term interest rates through long-term bond purchases may increasingly induce banks to take more interest rate risk.

Additionally, there are higher-level policy implications. First, taking a step back, the main lessen to be learnt from this effort to extract as much information as reasonably possible about the interest rate risk of banks in Germany from publicly available statistics is that more comprehensive statistics are needed. The availability of hardly any portfolio breakdowns by residual interest rate fixation period is a prime example for the incomprehensiveness of the data currently available. Market discipline would surely be enhanced, if external analysts had the data at their disposal that allowed them to make better estimates of banks' interest rate risk than are currently possible. Second, a practical way to increase the relevance of the estimates of the interest rate risk in their banking books disclosed by banks themselves would be to require banks to disclose the impacts of scenarios not only for one specific calibration but for various calibrations. If these calibrations covered a wide enough range of possible interest rate changes with sufficient granularity, that would lead to much more comprehensive exposure data at the supervisors' disposal. This data could then be complemented with possibly changing probabilities attached to the respective shock scenarios to calculate an actual risk measure. Third, the discovery of banks' search for yield in interest rate risk shows that the incentives of bank managers remain an important topic of banking regulation. It fits in the picture that the publicly available statistics investigated suggest that banks in Germany are increasingly building up negative exposure toward an increase of interest rates at the very short end. In this way banks effectively more and more discourage the increase of the policy rate. Put differently, the longer the turnaround in interest rates is still away, the more harmful it is going to be for banks. Hence, it is high time to take countermeasures, that is to regulate and supervise banks' taking of interest rate risk in a way that guarantees monetary policy the necessary leeway.

The most natural way forward seems to be to introduce capital requirements for interest rate risk in the banking book. This way forward is natural as it is the way in which regulation deals with many other risks banks take. Accordingly, the introduction of capital requirements was one of the two options proposed by the Basel Committee on Banking Supervision (BCBS) in its consultative document that preceded the new regulatory standards. Unsurprisingly, banks and banks' lobby organizations opposed this. They produced two arguments. First, according to the opponents it is technically not feasible to design an appropriate measure of banks' exposures to changes in interest rate risk. Because it is impossible to measure the exposures of different banks in a way that is sufficiently uniform and sensitive at the same time. Second, according to the opponents interest rate risk in the banking book is not one of the types of risk sensibly backed with capital. Because as far as the economic value of equity is concerned, scenario impacts only quantify opportunity costs since instruments belonging to the banking book are not traded and only if they were traded would the reductions of their values be realized. And as far as next year's net interest income is concerned, scenario impacts only quantify volatility of earnings and such a risk may give rise to liquidity requirements if any but not to capital requirements.[243] The final regulatory standards resulting from this consultation process do not include capital requirements. The BCBS justifies this decision only with reference to the first argument brought forward by banks and their lobby organizations. The Bundesanstalt für Finanzdienstleistungsaufsicht (BaFin) seems not to consider any of the two arguments convincing. There is no other explanation as to why the BaFin recently proposed capital requirements which are simply based on the existing Basel interest rate coefficient.[244] But neither the BCBS nor the BaFin provide an answer to the second and more fundamental argument brought forward by the opponents of capital requirements for interest rate risk in the banking book.

To conclude this dissertation, a few observations concerning the fundamental argument against capital requirements for interest rate risk in the banking book are in order. First, to a large extent interest rate risk in the banking book is a systematic risk meaning that when it materializes it does so for many banks as a result of the same development and hence at the same time. Thus, it appears difficult to conceive how appropriate liquidity requirements should be designed. The regulator would in effect have to anticipate what types of assets could be sold at what price and in what amount of time in a situation of widespread stress in the financial system. Capital requirements that require banks to hold some extra capital to lean on in this case appear more appropriate. Second, the reduction of net interest income may be large enough to produce actual losses and hence to reduce the capital of a bank. And the earning opportunities may change in any direction as a result of a change of the term structure but certainly do not have to improve. Given that interest rate risk in the banking book potentially reduces the capital of a bank permanently, if it materializes, capital requirements again appear reasonable. Third, the current situation with no capital requirements and no public disclosures that enable effective market discipline is certainly not sustainable.

---

[243] The responses by banks and their lobby organizations can be found on the homepage of the BCBS.
[244] The relevant regulatory texts are BCBS (2015), BCBS (2016), and BaFin (2016).

References

Abbassi, P.: 2015, Die potenziellen Folgen der (unkonventionellen) Geldpolitik für die Finanzstabilität: ein Literaturüberblick zum Risikoneigungskanal. Internal Document Deutsche Bundesbank.

Acharya, V. V. and Naqvi, H.: 2012, The seeds of a crisis: A theory of bank liquidity and risk-taking oder the business cycle, *Journal of Financial Economics* **106**(2), 349–366.

Acharya, V. V. and Yorulmazer, T.: 2007, Too many to fail - an analysis of time-inconsistency in bank closure policies, *Journal of Financial Intermediation* **16**(1), 1–31.

Adao, B. and Temzelides, T.: 1998, Sequential equilibrium and competition in a Diamond-Dybvig banking model, *Review of Economic Dynamics* **1**(4), 859–877.

Adrian, T. and Shin, H. S.: 2008, Liquidity and financial cycles, *BIS Working Paper* **256**.

Adrian, T. and Shin, H. S.: 2010, Liquidity and leverage, *Journal of Financial Intermediation* **19**(3), 418–437.

Adrian, T. and Shin, H. S.: 2011, Financial intermediaries and monetary economics, *in* B. M. Friedman and M. Woodford (eds), *Handbook of Monetary Economics*, Elsevier.

Akella, S. R. and Chen, S.-J.: 1990, Interest rate sensitivity of bank stock returns: specification effects and structural changes, *The Journal of Financial Research* **13**(2), 147–154.

Akerlof, G. A.: 1970, The market for "lemons": quality uncertainty and the market mechanism, *Quarterly Journal of Economics* **84**(3), 488–500.

Alessandri, P. and Drehmann, M.: 2010, An economic capital model integrating credit and interest rate risk in the banking book, *Journal of Banking and Finance* **34**(4), 730–742.

Ali, M. M. and Greenbaum, S. I.: 1977, A spatial model of the banking industry, *Journal of Finance* **32**(4), 1283–1303.

Allen, F.: 1990, The market for information and the origin of financial intermediation, *Journal of Financial Intermediation* **1**(1), 3–30.

Allen, F. and Gale, D.: 1997, Financial markets, intermediaries, and intertemporal smoothing, *Journal of Political Economy* **105**(3), 523–546.

Allen, F. and Gale, D.: 2000, Bubbles and crises, *Economic Journal* **110**(460), 236–55.

Allen, F. and Gale, D.: 2004, Asset price bubbles and monetary policy, *in* M. Desai and Y. Said (eds), *Global Governance and Financial Crises*, Routledge, pp. 19–42.

Allen, F. and Gale, D.: 2007, *Understanding Financial Crises*, Oxford University Press.

Allen, F. and Rogoff, K.: 2011, Asset prices, financial stability and monetary policy, *Swedish Riksbank Workshop on Housing Markets, Monetary Policy and Financial Stability*.

Allen, F. and Santomero, A. M.: 1998, The theory of financial intermediation, *Journal of Banking and Finance* **21**(11-12), 1461–1485.

References

Allen, F. and Santomero, A. M.: 2001, What do financial intermediaries do?, *Journal of Banking and Finance* **25**(2), 271–294.

Allen, L.: 1988, The determinants of bank interest margins: A note, *Journal of Financial and Quantitative Analysis* **23**(2), 231–235.

Altunbas, Y., Gambacorta, L. and Marques-Ibanez, D.: 2014, Does monetary policy affect bank risk-taking?, *International Journal of Central Banking* **10**(1), 95–136.

Angbazo, L.: 1997, Commercial bank net interest margins, default risk, interest-rate risk, and off-balance sheet banking, *Journal of Banking and Finance* **21**(1), 55–87.

Angeloni, I., Faia, E. and Lo Duca, M.: 2015, Monetary policy and risk taking, *Journal of Economic Dynamics and Control* **52**, 285–307.

Arnold, G.: 2013, *Corporate Financial Management*, fifth edn, Pearson.

Baltensperger, E.: 1972, Economies of scale, firm size, and concentration in banking, *Journal of Money, Credit and Banking* **4**(3), 467–488.

Baltensperger, E.: 1976, The borrower-lender relationship, competitive equilibrium, and the theory of hedonic prices, *American Economic Review* **66**(3), 401–405.

Baltensperger, E.: 1980, Alternative approaches to the theory of the banking firm, *Journal of Monetary Economics* **6**(1), 1–37.

Bank of England: 2014, News release – widening access to the sterling monetary framework: broker-dealers and central counterparties.
URL: *https://www.bankofengland.co.uk/-/media/boe/files/news/2014/november/widening-access-to-the-smf.pdf (2017-12-20)*

Basel Committee on Banking Supervision: 2000, Principles for the management of credit risk.

Basel Committee on Banking Supervision: 2001, Principles for the management and supervision of interest rate risk – consultative document. Bank for International Settlements.

Basel Committee on Banking Supervision: 2004, Principles for the management and supervision of interest rate risk.

Basel Committee on Banking Supervision: 2008, Principles for sound liquidity risk management and supervision.

Basel Committee on Banking Supervision: 2015, Interest rate risk in the banking book – consultative document.

Basel Committee on Banking Supervision: 2016, Interest rate risk in the banking book – standards.

Begenau, J., Piazzesi, M. and Schneider, M.: 2013, Banks' risk exposures. manuscript.

Bell, F. W. and Murphy, N. B.: 1968, *Costs in Commercial Banking: A Quantitative Analysis of Bank Behavior and Its Relation to Bank Regulation*, Boston: Federal Reserve Bank of Boston, Research Report.

Benartzi, S. and Thaler, R. H.: 1995, Myopic loss aversion and the equity premium puzzle, *The Quarterly Journal of Economics* **110**(1), 73–92.

Benati, L. and Goodhart, C.: 2008, Investigating time-variation in the marginal predictive power of the yield spread, *Journal of Economic Dynamics and Control* **32**(4), 1236–1272.

Benston, G. J.: 1964, Branch banking and economies of scale, *Journal of Finance* **20**(2), 312–331.

Benston, G. J.: 1990, *The Separation of Commercial and Investment Banking. The Glass-Steagall Act Revisited and Reconsidered*, Macmillan.

Benston, G. J., Hanweck, G. A. and Humphrey, D. B.: 1982, Scale economies in banking: A restructuring and reassessment, *Journal of Money, Credit and Banking* **14**(2), 435–456.

Benston, G. J. and Smith, C. W.: 1976, A transaction cost approach to the theory of financial intermediation, *Journal of Finance* **31**(2), 215–231.

Berg, J., von Rixtel, A., Ferrando, A., de Bondt, G. and Scopel, S.: 2005, The bank lending survey for the euro area, *European Central Bank: Occasional Paper Series* **23**, 1–90.

Bernanke, B. S.: 1983, Nonmonetary effects of the financial crisis in the propagation of the great depression, *American Economic Review* **73**(3), 257–276.

Bernanke, B. S.: 2007, The financial accelerator and the credit channel. Speech at The Credit Channel of Monetary Policy in the Twenty-First Century Conference, Federal Reserve Bank of Atlanta.

Bernanke, B. S.: n.d., The Taylor rule: a benchmark for monetary policy?, blog post.
    URL: *https://www.brookings.edu/blog/ben-bernanke/2015/04/28/the-taylor-rule-a-benchmark-for-monetary-policy/ (2017-12-20)*

Bernanke, B. S. and Blinder, A. S.: 1988, Credit, money, and aggregate demand, *American Economic Review* **78**(2), 435–439.

Bernanke, B. S. and Gertler, M. L.: 1989, Agency costs, net worth, and business fluctuations, *American Economic Review* **79**(1), 14–31.

Bernanke, B. S. and Gertler, M. L.: 1990, Financial fragility and economic performance, *Quarterly Journal of Economics* **105**(1), 87–114.

Bernanke, B. S. and Gertler, M. L.: 1995, Inside the black box: the credit channel of monetary policy transmission, *Journal of Economic Perspectives* **9**(4), 27–48.

Bernanke, B. S., Gertler, M. L. and Gilchrist, S.: 1996, The financial accelerator and the flight to quality, *Review of Economics and Statistics* **78**(1), 1–15.

Bhattacharya, S. and Thakor, A. V.: 1993, Contemporary banking theory, *Journal of Financial Intermediation* **3**(1), 2–50.

Black, L., Hancock, D. and Passmore, W.: 2007, Bank core deposits and the mitigation of monetary policy. Board of Governors of the Federal Reserve System: Finance and Economics Discussion Series.

Black, L., Hancock, D. and Passmore, W.: 2010, The bank lending channel of monetary policy and its effect on mortgage lending. Board of Governors of the Federal Reserve System: Finance and Economics Discussion Series.

References

Board of Governors of the Federal Reserve System: 2008, Press release: Federal reserve announces two initiatives designed to bolster market liquidity and promote orderly market functioning. URL: *http://www.federalreserve.gov/newsevents/press/monetary/20080316a.htm (2017-12-20)*

Board of Governors of the Federal Reserve System: 2014, Press release. URL: *https://www.federalreserve.gov/newsevents/press/monetary/20141029a.htm (2017-12-20)*

Board of Governors of the Federal Reserve System: 2015, Press release. URL: *https://www.federalreserve.gov/monetarypolicy/files/monetary20151216a1.pdf (2017-12-20)*

Board of Governors of the Federal Reserve System: 2016, Press release. URL: *https://www.federalreserve.gov/monetarypolicy/files/monetary20161214a1.pdf (2017-12-20)*

Bofinger, P.: 2001, *Monetary Policy. Goals, Institutions, Strategies, and Instruments*, Oxford University Press.

Bofinger, P.: 2015, *Grundzüge der Volkswirtschaftslehre: Eine Einführung in die Wissenschaft von Märkten*, Pearson Studium.

Bofinger, P. and Schmidt, R.: 2003, Wie gut sind professionelle Wechselkursprognosen? Eine empirische Analyse für den Euro/US-Dollar-Wechselkurs, *ifo Schnelldienst* **17**.

Borio, C., Gambacorty, L. and Hofmann, B.: 2015, The influence of monetary policy on bank profitability, *BIS Working Paper* **514**.

Borio, C. and Zhu, H.: 2012, Capital regulation, risk-taking and monetary policy: a missing link in the transmission mechanism?, *Journal of Financial Stability* **8**(4), 236–251.

Boyd, J. H. and Prescott, E. C.: 1986, Financial intermediary-coalitions, *Journal of Economic Theory* **38**(2), 211–232.

Bryant, J.: 1980, A model of reserve, bank runs, and deposit insurance, *Journal of Banking and Finance* **4**(4), 315–400.

Buch, C. M., Eickmeier, S. and Prieto, E.: 2014, In search for yield? survey-based evidence on bank risk taking, *Journal of Economic Dynamics and Control* **43**(3), 12–30.

Bundesanstalt für Finanzdienstleistungsaufsicht: 2007, Zinsänderungsrisiken im Anlagebuch; Ermittlung der Auswirkungen einer plötzlichen und unerwarteten Zinsänderung. Rundschreiben 7/2007 (BA).

Bundesanstalt für Finanzdienstleistungsaufsicht: 2011, Zinsänderungsrisiken im Anlagebuch; Ermittlung der Auswirkungen einer plötzlichen und unerwarteten Zinsänderung. Rundschreiben 11/2011 (BA).

Bundesanstalt für Finanzdienstleistungsaufsicht: 2012, Mindestanforderungen an das Risikomanagement - MaRisk. Rundschreiben 10/2012 (BA).

Bundesanstalt für Finanzdienstleistungsaufsicht: 2016, Allgemeinverfügung der BaFin zur Abwehr von Gefahren für die Sicherheit der Finanzmarktstabilität und zur Umsetzung des gebundenen Ermessens in § 10 Absatz 3 Satz 2 Nr. 1 KWG. Entwurf.

Busch, R. and Memmel, C.: 2015, Banks' net interest margin and the level of interest rates. Discussion Paper 16/2015, Deutsche Bundesbank.

Busch, R. and Memmel, C.: 2016, Quantifying the components of the banks' net interest margin, *Financial Markets and Portfolio Management* **30**(4), 371–396.

Calomiris, C. W. and Kahn, C. M.: 1991, The role of demandable debt in structuring optimal banking arrangements, *American Economic Review* **81**(3), 497–513.

Camerer, C., Babcock, L., Loewenstein, G. and Thaler, R.: 1997, Labor supply of New York City cabdrivers: One day at a time, *Quarterly Journal of Economics* **112**(2), 407–441.

Campbel, T. and Kracaw, W. A.: 1980, Information production, market signalling, and the theory of financial intermediation, *Journal of Finance* **35**(4), 863–882.

Carbó, S. and Rodríguez, F.: 2007, The determinants of bank margins in European banking, *Journal of Banking and Finance* **31**(7), 2043–2063.

Cecchetti, S. G.: 1995, Distinguishing theories of the monetary transmission mechanism, *Federal Reserve Bank of St. Louis Review* pp. 83–97.

Cerasi, V. and Daltung, S.: 2000, The optimal size of a bank: Costs and benefits of diversification, *European Economic Review* **44**(9), 1701–1726.

Chance, D. M. and Lane, W. R.: 1980, A re-examination of interest rate sensitivity in the common stocks of financial institutions, *Journal of Financial Research* **3**(1).

Chodorow-Reich, G.: 2014, Effects of unconventional monetars policy on financial institutions, *Brookings Papers on Economic Activity* pp. 155–204.

Choi, J. J., Elyasiani, E. and Kopecky, K. J.: 1992, The sensitivity of bank stock returns to market, interest and exchange rate risk, *Journal of Banking and Finance* **16**(5), 983–1004.

Choudhry, M.: 2012, *The Principles of Banking*, Wiley Finance.

Committee of European Banking Supervisors: 2006, Technical aspects of the management of interest rate risk arising from non-trading activities under the supervisory review process.

Cox, J. C., Ingersoll, J. E. and Ross, S. A.: 1985, A theory of the term structure of interest rates, *Econometrica* **53**(2), 385–407.

Czaja, M.-G., Scholz, H. and Wilkens, M.: 2009, Interest rate risk of German financial institutions: the impact of level, slope, and curvature of the term structure, *Review of Quantitative Finance and Accounting* **33**(1), 1–26.

Czaja, M.-G., Scholz, H. and Wilkens, M.: 2010, Interest rate risk rewards in stock returns on financial corporations: evidence from Germany, *European Financial Management* **16**(1), 124–154.

Dam, L. and Koetter, M.: 2012, Bank bailouts and moral hazard: evidence from Germany, *Review of Financial Studies* **25**(8), 2343–2380.

De Nicolo, G., Dell'Ariccia, G., Laeven, L. and Valencia, F.: 2010, Monetary policy and bank risk taking, *IMF Staff Position Note* **09**, July.

References

Dell'Ariccia, G., Laeven, L. and Marquez, R.: 2014, Real interest rates, leverage, and bank risk-taking, *Journal of Economic Theory* **149**, 65–99.

Dell'Ariccia, G., Laeven, L. and Suarez, G.: 2013, Bank leverage and monetary policy's risk-taking channel: Evidence from the United States, *IMF Working Paper* **143**. forthcoming in the Journal of Finance.

Dell'Ariccia, G. and Marquez, R.: 2006, Lending booms and lending standards, *Journal of Finance* **61**(5), 2511–2546.

Deutsche Bank: 2015, Annual review 2014.

Deutsche Bundesbank: 2002, Bankstellenstatistik 2002.

Deutsche Bundesbank: 2011a, Financial stability review 2011.

Deutsche Bundesbank: 2011b, Monthly report.

Deutsche Bundesbank: 2012a, Monthly report.

Deutsche Bundesbank: 2012b, The role of the "Basel interest rate shock" in the supervisory assessment of interest rate risks in the banking book. Monthly Report June, pp. 51-60.

Deutsche Bundesbank: 2014a, Financial stability review 2014.

Deutsche Bundesbank: 2014b, Monthly balance sheet statistics. Banking statistics guidelines.

Deutsche Bundesbank: 2015, Financial stability review 2015.

Deutsche Bundesbank: 2016, Evolution of the bank lending survey since the onset of the financial crisis. Monthly Report July, pp. 15-40.

Diamond, D. W.: 1984, Financial intermediation and delegated monitoring, *Review of Economic Studies* **51**(3), 393–414.

Diamond, D. W.: 1997, Liquidity, banks, and markets, *Journal of Political Economy* **105**(5), 928–956.

Diamond, D. W. and Dybvig, P. H.: 1983, Bank runs, deposit insurance, and liquidity, *Journal of Political Economy* **91**(3), 401–419.

Diamond, D. W. and Rajan, R. G.: 2001, Liquidity risk, liquidity creation, and financial fragility: a theory of banking, *Journal of Political Economy* **109**(2), 287–327.

Diamond, D. W. and Rajan, R. G.: 2009, Illiquidity and interest rate policy. NBER Working Paper No. 15197.

Directive 2014/49/EU: n.d., Directive 2014/49/EU of the European Parliament and of the Council of 16 april 2014 on deposit guarantee schemes (recast).

Direktive 2004/39/EC: n.d., Direktive 2004/39/EC of the European Parliament and of the Council of 21 April 2004 on on markets in financial instruments amending Council Directives 85/611/EEC and 93/6/EEC and Directive 2000/12/EC of the European Parliament and of the Council and repealing Council Directive 93/22/EEC.

Dodd-Frank Act: 2010, Dodd-frank wall street reform and consumer protection act.

Domanski, D., Shin, H. S. and Sushko, V.: 2015, The hunt for duration: not waving but drowning?, *BIS Working Paper* **519**.

Drees, B., Eckwert, B. and Vardy, F.: 2013, Cheap money and risk taking: opacity versus fundamental risk, *European Economic Review* **62**, 114–129.

Drehmann, M., Sorensen, S. and Stringa, M.: 2010, The integrated impact of credit and interest rate risk on banks: a dynamic framework and stress test application, *Journal of Banking and Finance* **34**(4), 713–729.

Dwyer, G. P. and Samartin, M.: 2009, Why do banks promise to pay par on demand?, *Journal of Financial Stability* **5**(2), 147–169.

EBA/ITS/2013/02: n.d., EBA final draft Implementing Technical Standards on supervisory reporting under Regulation (EU) No 575/2013.

ECB/2014/15: n.d., Guideline of the European Central Bank of 4 April 2014 on monetary and financial statistics (recast).

Edwards, F. R. and Mishkin, F. S.: 1995, The decline of traditional banking: implications for financial stability and regulatory policy, *Federal Reserve Bank of New York Economic Policy Review* **1**(2), 27–45.

Ehrmann, M. and Worms, A.: 2004, Bank networks and monetary policy transmission, *Journal of the European Economic Association* **2**(6), 1148–1171.

Entrop, O., Memmel, C., Ruprecht, B. and Wilkens, M.: 2015, Determinants of bank interest margins: impact of maturity transformation, *Journal of Banking and Finance* **54**(May), 1–19.

Entrop, O., Memmel, C., Wilkens, M. and Zeisler, A.: 2011, Estimating the interest rate risk of banks using time series of accounting-based data, *Working Paper* .

Entrop, O., Wilkens, M. and Zeisler, A.: 2009, Quantifiying the interest rate risk of banks: assumptions do matter, *European Financial Management* **15**(5), 1001–1018.

Estrella, A.: 2005, *The Yield Curve as a Leading Indicator: frequently Asked Questions*, Federal Reserve Bank of New York.

European Central Bank: 1998, Explanatory notes on statistics on the monetary financial institutions sector. Available online at
URL: *http://www.ecb.europa.eu/stats/pdf/money/mfi/mfi_definitions.pdf (2017-12-20)*.

European Central Bank: 2001, Issues related to monetary policy rules. Monthly Bulletin.

European Central Bank: 2003a, A bank lending survey for the euro area. Monthly Bulletin.

European Central Bank: 2003b, Press release: inaugural release of euro area MFI interest rate statistics. Published on 10. December.

European Central Bank: 2004, Annual report 2003.

European Central Bank: 2012, Manual on MFI balance sheet statistics.

European Central Bank: 2015a, Bank lending survey for the euro area, the questionnaire. revised version introduced in April 2015.

References

European Central Bank: 2015b, Financial stability review.

European Central Bank: 2016a, Press release: ECB adjust parameters of its asset purchase programme (APP). Published on 8. December.

European Central Bank: 2016b, Press release: monetary policy decisions. Published on 10. March.

European Central Bank: 2016c, Press release: monetary policy decisions. Published on 8. December.

Faff, R. W. and Howard, P. F.: 1999, Interest rate risk of Australian financial sector companies in a period of regulatory change, *Pacific-Basin Finance Journal* **7**(1), 83–101.

Fama, E. F.: 1980, Banking in the theory of finance, *Journal of Monetary Economics* **6**(1), 39–57.

Fama, E. F.: 1985, What's different about banks?, *Journal of Monetary Economics* **15**(1), 29–39.

Fama, E. F. and French, K. R.: 1992, The cross-section of expected stock returns, *Journal of Finance* **47**(2), 427–465.

Fama, E. F. and French, K. R.: 1993, Common risk factors in the returns on stocks and bonds, *Journal of Financial Economics* **33**(1), 3–56.

Fama, E. F. and French, K. R.: 2004, The capital asset pricing model: theory and evidence, *Journal of Economic Perspectives* **18**(3), 25–46.

Farhi, E. and Tirole, J.: 2012, Collective moral hazard, maturity mismatch, and systematic bailouts, *American Economic Review* **102**(1), 60–93.

Financial Stability Board: 2014, Global shadow banking monitoring report.

Fishburn, P. C. and Kochenberger, G. A.: 1979, Two-piece von Neumann-Morgenstern utility functions, *Decision Sciences* **10**(4), 503–518.

Fishburn, P. C. and Porter, R. B.: 1976, Optimal portfolios with one safe and one risky asset: effects of changes in rate of return and risk, *Management Science* **22**(10), 1064–1073.

Fisher, I.: 1922, *The Purchasing Power of Money*, second edn, New York: The Macmillan Co.

Fisher, I.: 1928, *The Money Illusion*, New York: Adelphi.

Flannery, M. J.: 1994, Debt maturity and the deadweight cost of leverage: optimal financing banking firms, *American Economic Review* **84**(1), 320–331.

Flannery, M. J. and James, C. M.: 1984, The effect of interest rate changes on the common stock returns of financial institutions, *Journal of Finance* **39**(4), 1141–1153.

Fleming, J. M.: 1962, Domestic financial policies under fixed and under floating exchange rates, *IMF Staff Papers* **9**(3), 369–380.

Freedman, C.: 1977, Micro theory of international financial intermediation, *American Economic Review* **67**(1), 172–179.

Freixas, X. and Rochet, J.-C.: 2008, *Microeconomics of Banking*, second edn, MIT Press.

Friedman, M.: 1970, The counter-revolution in monetary theory, *Institute of Economic Affairs Occasional Paper* **33**.

Friedman, M. and Schwartz, A.: 1963, *A Monetary History of the United States, 1867-1960*, Princeton University Press.

Gertler, M. L. and Hubbard, R. G.: 1988, Financial factors in business fluctuations, *NBER Working Paper* **2758**.

Gilbert, R. A.: 1984, Bank market structure and competition: a survey, *Journal of Money, Credit and Banking* **16**(4), 617–645.

Giliberto, M.: 1985, Interest rate sensitivity in the common stocks of financial intermediaries: a methodological note, *Journal of Financial and Quantitative Analysis* **20**(1), 123–126.

Glass-Steagall Act: 1932-3, U.S. Banking Act of 1932 and U.S. Banking Act of 1933.

Gorton, G. B. and Haubrich, J. G.: 1987, Bank deregulation, credit markets, and the control of capital, *Carnegie-Rochester Conference Series on Public Policy* **26**, 289–334.

Gorton, G. and Pennacchi, G.: 1990, Financial intermediaries and liquidity creation, *Journal of Finance* **45**(1), 49–71.

Gorton, G. and Winton, A.: 2003, *Financial Intermediation*, Vol. 1, Elsevier, chapter 8, pp. 431–552.

Graeber, D.: 2014, The truth is out: money is just an IOU, and the banks are rolling in it.
URL: *http://www.theguardian.com/commentisfree/2014/mar/18/truth-money-iou-bank-of-england-austerity (2017-12-20)*

Greenbaum, S. and Thakor, A.: 2007, *Contemporary Financial Intermediation*, second edn, Academic Press.

Gunduz, Y., Ongena, S., Tumer-Alkan, G. and Yu, Y.: 2015, 'Testing the small bang theory of the financial universe' from bank-firm exposures to changes in CDS trading and credit. Available at SSRN: http://ssrn.com/abstract=2607909.

Gurley, J. G. and Shaw, E. S.: 1955, Financial aspects of economic development, *American Economic Review* **45**(4), 515–538.

Gurley, J. G. and Shaw, E. S.: 1956, Financial intermediaries and the saving-investment process, *Journal of Finance* **11**(2), 257–276.

Gurley, J. G. and Shaw, E. S.: 1960, *Money in a Theory of Finance*, Washington, D.C.: Brookings Institution.

Hakenes, H.: 2004, Banks as delegated risk managers, *Journal of Banking and Finance* **28**(10), 2399–2426.

Hanson, S. G. and Stein, J. C.: 2015, Monetary policy and long-term real rates, *Journal of Financial Economics* **115**(3), 429–448.

Haubrich, J. G. and King, R. G.: 1990, Banking and insurance, *Journal of Monetary Economics* **26**(3), 316–386.

References

Hellwig, M.: 1994, Liquidity provision, banking, and the allocation of interest rate risk, *European Economic Review* **38**(7), 1363–1389.

Hellwig, M.: 1998, Banks, markets, and the allocation of risks in an economy, *Journal of Institutional and Theoretical Economics* **154**(1), 328–345.

Hicks, J. R.: 1935, A suggestion for simplifying the theory of money, *Economica* **2**(5), 1–19.

Hicks, J. R.: 1937, Mr. Keynes and the 'classics'; a suggested interpretation, *Econometrica* **5**(2), 147–159.

Hicks, J. R.: 1946, *Value and Capital*, London: Oxford University Press.

Ho, T. S. Y. and Saunders, A.: 1981, The determinants of bank interest margins: theory and empirical evidence, *Journal of Financial and Quantitative Analysis* **16**(4), 581–600.

Holmstrom, B. and Tirole, J.: 1998, Private and public supply of liquidity, *Journal of Political Economy* **106**(1), 1–40.

Hotelling, H.: 1929, Stability in competition, *Economic Journal* **39**(153), 41–57.

Houpt, J. and Embersit, J.: 1991, A method for evaluating interest rate risk in U.S. commercial banks, *Federal Reserve Bulletin* pp. 625–637.

Hubbard, R. G.: 1995, Is there a 'credit channel' for monetary policy?, *Federal Reserve Bank of St. Louis Review* pp. 63–77.

Hull, J. C.: 2012, *Risk Management and Financial Institutions*, John Wiley & Sons, Inc.

ifo Institut: 2014, Ifo world economic survey – Beschreibung und Information. available online at
URL: *https://www.cesifo-group.de/de/dms/ifodoc/docs/facts/survey/WES/Beschreibung_WES_2017.pdf (2017-12-20)*.

ifo Institut: 2016, World economic survey – questionnaire. available online at
URL: *https://www.cesifo-group.de/dms/ifodoc/docs/facts/survey/WES/WES-Sample-Questionnaire/WES_Questionnaire_Sample.pdf (2017-12-20)*.

International Monetary Fund: 2014, Global financial stability report. World Economic and Financial Surveys.

Ioannidou, V., Ongena, S. and Peydró, J.-L.: 2015, Monetary policy, risk taking, and pricing: evidence from a quasi-natural experiment, *Review of Finance* **19**(1), 95–144.

Jacklin, C. J.: 1987, *Contractural Arrangements for Intertemporal Trade*, University of Minnesota Press, chapter Demand Deposits, Trading Restrictions, and Risk Sharing, pp. 26–47.

Jaffee, D. M. and Stiglitz, J. E.: 1990, Credit rationing, *in* B. M. Friedman and F. H. Hahn (eds), *Handbook of Monetary Economics*, Amsterdam: North-Holland, chapter 16, pp. 837–888.

Jakab, Z. and Kumhof, M.: 2015, Banks are not intermediaries of loanable funds – and why this matters, *Bank of England Working Paper* **529**.

James, C. M.: 1987, Some evidence on the uniqueness of bank loans, *Journal of Financial Economics* **19**(2), 217–235.

Jensen, M. C. and Meckling, W. H.: 1976, Theory of the firm: managerial behavior, agency costs and ownership structure, *Journal of Financial Economics* **3**(4), 305–360.

Jimenez, G., Ongena, S. and Peydró, J.-L.: 2014, Hazardous time for monetary policy: What do twenty-three million bank loans say about the effects of monetary policy on credit risk-taking?, *Econometrica* **82**(2), 463–505.

Kahneman, D. and Tversky, A.: 1979, Prospect theory: an analysis of decisions under risk, *Econometrica* **47**(2), 263–291.

Kalish, L. and Gilbert, R. A.: 1973, The influence of bank regulation on the operating efficiency of commercial banks, *Journal of Finance* **28**(5), 1287–1301.

Kane, E. J.: 1989, *The S&L Insurance Mess: How Did it Happen?*, Urban Institute Press.

Kashyap, A. K. and Stein, J. C.: 1995, The impact of monetary policy on bank balance sheets, *Carnegie-Rochester Conference Series on Public Policy* **42**, 151–195.

Kashyap, A. K. and Stein, J. C.: 1997, The role of banks in monetary policy: a survey with implications for the European monetary union, *Federal Reserve Bank of Chicago Economic Perspectives* **21**, 2–18.

Kashyap, A. K. and Stein, J. C.: 2000, What do a million observations on banks say about the transmission of monetary policy?, *American Economic Review* **90**(3), 407–428.

Keuning, S.: 2003, First release of new interest rate statistics, *Presentation by the Director General Statistics* .

Keynes, J. M.: 1930, *A Treatise on Money*, London: Macmillan.

Keynes, J. M.: 1936, *The General Theory of Employment, Interest and Money*, London: Macmillan.

Klein, M. A.: 1971, A theory of the banking firm, *Journal of Money, Credit and Banking* **3**(2), 205–218.

Koetter, M.: 2013, Market structure and competition in German banking. Report commissioned by the Council of Economic Experts and the Monopolies Commission.

Krasa, S. and Villamil, A. P.: 1992, A theory of optimal bank size, *Oxford Economic Papers* **44**(4), 725–749.

Kreditwesengesetz: n.d., In der Fassung der Bekanntmachung vom 9. September 1998 (BGBl. I S. 2776), das zuletzt durch Artikel 339 der Verordnung vom 31. August 2015 (BGBl. I S. 1474) geändert worden ist.

Landier, A., Sraer, D. A. and Thesmar, D.: 2011, The risk-shifting hypothesis: evidence from subprime origination. AFA 2012 Chicago Meetings Paper.

Landier, A., Sraer, D. and Thesmar, D.: 2013, Banks' exposure to interest rate risk and the transmission of monetary policy, *NBER Working Paper* **18857**.

Laughhunn, D. J., Payne, J. W. and Crum, R.: 1980, Managerial risk preferences for below-target returns, *Management Science* **26**(12), 1238–1249.

Leland, H. E. and Pyle, D. H.: 1977, Informational asymmetries, financial structure, and financial intermediation, *Journal of Finance* **32**(2), 371–387.

Lintner, J.: 1965, The valuation of risk assets and the selection of risky investments in stock portfolio and capital budgets, *Review of Economics and Statistics* **47**(1), 13–37.

References

Lloyd, W. P. and Shick, R. A.: 1977, A test of Stone's two-index model of returns, *Journal of Financial and Quantitative Analysis* **12**(3), 363–376.

Lucas, D. J. and McDonald, R. L.: 1992, Bank financing and investment decision with asymmetric information about loan quality, *RAND Journal of Economics* **23**(1), 86–105.

Lucas, R. E.: 1972, Expectations and the neutrality of money, *Journal of Economic Theory* **4**, 103–124.

Lummer, S. L. and McConnell, J. J.: 1989, Further evidence on the bank lending process and the capital-market response to bank loan agreements, *Journal of Financial Economics* **25**(1), 99–122.

Lynge, M. J. and Zumwalt, J. K.: 1980, An empirical study of the interest rate sensitivity of commercial bank returns: a multi-index approach, *Journal of Financial and Quantitative Analysis* **15**(3), 731–742.

Macleod, H. D.: 1855, *The Theory and Practice of Banking*, London: Longmans, Green, Reader, and Dyer.

Maddaloni, A. and Peydró, J.-L.: 2011, Bank risk-taking, securitization, supervision, and low interest rates: evidence from the euro area and the US lending standards, *Review of Financial Studies* **24**(6), 2121–2165.

Maddaloni, A. and Peydró, J.-L.: 2013, Monetary policy, macroprudential policy and banking stability: evidence from the euro area, *International Journal of Central Banking* **9**(1), 121–169.

Madura, J. and Zarruk, E. R.: 1995, Bank exposure to interest rate risk: a global perspective, *Journal of Financial Research* **18**(1), 1–13.

Malinvaud, E.: 1972, The allocation of individual risks in large markets, *Journal of Economic Theory* **4**(2), 312–328.

Maudos, J. and de Guevara, J. F.: 2004, Factors explaining the interest margin in the banking sector of the European Union, *Journal of Banking and Finance* **28**(9), 2259–2281.

McLeay, M., Radia, A. and Thomas, R.: 2014, Money creation in the modern economy, *Bank of England Quarterly Bulletin* **Q1**, 14–27.

Meltzer, A. H.: 1995, Monetary, credit and (other) transmission processes: a monetarist perspective, *Journal of Economic Perspectives* **9**(4), 49–72.

Memmel, C.: 2008, Which interest rate scenario is the worst one for a bank? Evidence from a tracking bank approach for German savings and cooperative banks, *International Journal of Banking, Accounting and Finance* **1**(1), 85–104.

Memmel, C.: 2011, Banks' exposure to interest rate risk, their earnings from term transformation, and the dynamics of the term structure, *Journal of Banking and Finance* **35**, 282–289.

Memmel, C. and Schertler, A.: 2013, Banks' management of the net interest margin: new measures, *Financial Markets and Portfolio Management* **27**(3), 275–297.

Memmel, C., Seymen, A. and Teichert, M.: 2016, Banks' interest rate risk and search for yield: a theoretical rationale and some empirical evidence. Bundesbank Discussion Paper 22/2016, forthcoming in the German Economic Review.

Memmel, C. and Stein, I.: 2008, The prudential database BAKIS, *Schmollers Jahrbuch* **128**, 321–328.

Mersch, Y.: 2014, Monetary policy and economic inequality. Keynote speech at the Corporate Credit Conference in Zurich.

Merton, R. C.: 1973, An intertemporal captal asset pricing model, *Econometrica* **41**(5), 867–887.

Mishkin, F. S.: 1996, The channels of monetary transmission: lessons for monetary policy, *NBER Working Paper* **5464**.

Mishkin, F. S.: 2001, The transmission mechanism and the role of asset prices in monetary policy, *NBER Working Paper* **8617**.

Modigliani, F.: 1971, Monetary policy and consumption: linkages via interest rate and wealth effects in the FMP model, *Federal Reserve Bank of Boston: Conference Series* **5**, 9–84.

Modigliani, F. and Miller, M. H.: 1958, The cost of capital, corporation finance and the theory of investment, *American Economic Review* **48**(3), 261–297.

Monti, M.: 1972, Deposit, credit, and interest rate determination under alternative bank objectives, *in* G. P. Szego and K. Shell (eds), *Mathematical Methods in Investment and Finance*, Amsterdam: North-Holland.

Nelson, C. R. and Siegel, A.: 1987, Parsimonious modeling of yield curves, *Journal of Business* **60**(4), 473–489.

Newey, W. K. and West, K. D.: 1987, A simple positive semi-definite, heteroskedasticity and autocorrelation consistent covariance matrix, *Econometrica* **55**(3), 703–708.

Paligorova, T. and Santos, J. A. C.: 2013, Monetary policy and bank risk-taking: Evidence from the corporate loan market. Available at SSRN 1991471.

Patinkin, D.: 1965, *Money, Interest and Prices*, second edn, New York: Harper and Row.

Patinkin, D.: 1972, On the short-run non-neutrality of money in the quantity theory, *Banca Nazionale del Lavoro Quarterly Review* **100**, 3–22.

Patinkin, D.: 2008, Neutrality of money, *The New Palgrave Dictionary of Economics*, second edn, Palgrave Macmillan.

Patinkin, D. and Steiger, O.: 1989, In search of the 'veil of money' and the 'neutrality of money': a note on the origin of terms, *Scandinavian Journal of Economics* **91**(1), 131–146.

Piketty, T.: 2014, *Capital in the Twenty-First Century*, Harvard University Press.

Porter, R. C.: 1961, A model of bank portfolio selection, *Yale Economic Essays* **1**(2), 323–359.

Pozsar, Z., Adrian, T., Ashcraft, A. and Boesky, H.: 2013, Shadow banking, *Federal Reserve Bank of New York Economic Policy Review* pp. 1–16.

Pratt, J. W.: 1964, Risk aversion in the small and in the large, *Econometrica* **32**(1-2), 122–136.

Pringle, J.: 1974, The capital decision in commercial banks, *Journal of Finance* **29**(3), 779–795.

Purnanandam, A.: 2007, Interest rate derivatives at commercial banks: an empirical investigation, *Journal of Monetary Economics* **54**(6), 1769–1808.

References

Qi, J.: 1994, Bank Liquidity and Stability in an Overlapping Generations Model, *Review of Financial Studies* **7**(2), 389–417.

Rajan, R. G.: 2005, Has financial development made the world riskier? NBER Working Paper No. 11728.

Ramey, V.: 1993, How important is the credit channel in the transmission of monetary policy?, *Carnegie-Rochester Conference Series on Public Policy* **39**, 1–45.

Regulation (EU) No 1071/2013: n.d., Regulation (EU) No 1071/2013 of the European Central Bank of 24 September 2013 concerning the balance sheet of the monetary financial institutions sector (recast).

Regulation (EU) No 575/2013: n.d., Regulation (EU) No 575/2013 of the European Parliament and of the Council of 26 June 2013 on prudential requirements for credit institutions and investment firms and amending Regulation (EU) No 648/2012.

Romer, C. D. and Romer, D. H.: 1989, Does monetary policy matter? A new test in the spirit of Friedman and Schwarz, *NBER Macroeconomic Annual* **4**, 121–170.

Romer, C. D. and Romer, D. H.: 1990, New evidence on the monetary transmission mechanism, *Brookings Papers on Economic Activity* **1**, 149–214.

Ruprecht, B., Kick, T., Entrop, O. and Wilkens, M.: 2013, Market timing, maturity mismatch, and risk management: evidence from the banking industry. Discussion Paper 56/2013, Deutsche Bundesbank.

Samuelson, P. A.: 1945, The effect of interest rate increases on the banking system, *American Economic Review* **35**(1), 16–27.

Santomero, A. M.: 1984, Modeling the banking firm, *Journal of Money, Credit and Banking* **16**(4), 576–602.

Schmidt, R. H., Hackethal, A. and Tyrell, M.: 1999, Disintermediation and the role of banks in Europe: an international comparison, *Journal of Financial Intermediation* **8**(1-2), 36–67.

Scholtens, B. and van Wensveen, D.: 2000, A critique on the theory of financial intermediation, *Journal of Banking and Finance* **24**(8), 1243–1251.

Scholtens, B. and van Wensveen, D.: 2003, The theory of financial intermediation: an essay on what it does not explain, *SUERF - The European Money and Finance Forum in Vienna*.

Schrand, C. and Unal, H.: 1998, Hedging and coordinated risk management: evidence from thrift conversionons, *Journal of Finance* **53**(3), 979–1013.

Schumpeter, J. A.: 1912, *Theorie der wirtschaftlichen Entwicklung*, Leipzig: Duncker und Humblot.

Sealey, C. W. and Lindley, J. T.: 1977, Inputs, outputs, and a theory of production and cost at depository financial institutions, *Journal of Finance* **32**(4), 1251–1266.

Seward, J. K.: 1990, Corporate financial policy and the theory of financial intermediation, *Journal of Finance* **45**(2), 351–377.

Shafir, E., Diamond, P. and Tversky, A.: 1997, Money illusion, *Quarterly Journal of Economics* **112**(2), 341–374.

Sharpe, W. F.: 1964, Capital asset prices: a theory of market equilibrium under conditions of risk, *Journal of Finance* **19**(3), 425–442.

Sidrauski, M.: 1967, Rational coice and patterns of growth in a monetary economy, *American Economic Review* **57**(2), 534–544.

Sierra, G. and Yeager, T.: 2004, What does the Federal Reserve's economic value model tell us about interest rate risk at U.S. community banks?, *Federal Reserve Bank of St. Louis Review* **86**(6), 45–60.

Slovin, M. B., Sushka, M. E. and Poloncheck, J. A.: 1993, The value of bank durability: borrowers as bank stakeholders, *Journal of Finance* **48**(1), 247–266.

Spence, M.: 1973, Job market signaling, *Quarterly Journal of Economics* **87**(3), 355–374.

Stein, J. C.: 1998, An adverse-selection model of bank asset and liability management with implications for the transmission of monetary policy, *RAND Journal of Economics* **29**(3), 466–486.

Stigler, G. J.: 1967, Imperfections in the capital market, *Journal of Political Economy* **75**(3), 287–292.

Stiglitz, J. E.: 1975, The theory of 'screening', education, and the distribution of income, *American Economic Review* **65**(3), 283–300.

Stiglitz, J. E.: 1985, Credit markets and the control of capital, *Journal of Money, Credit and Banking* **17**(2), 133–152.

Stiglitz, J. E. and Weiss, A.: 1981, Credit rationing in markets with imperfect information, *American Economic Review* **71**(3), 393–410.

Stone, B. K.: 1974, Systematic interest-rate risk in a two-index model of returns, *Journal of Financial and Quantitative Analysis* **9**(5), 709–721.

Svensson, L. E. O.: 1994, Estimating and interpreting forward interest rates: Sweden 1992 - 94. IMF Working Paper 114.

Swank, J.: 1996, Theories of the banking firm: a review of the literature, *Bulletin of Economic Research* **48**(3), 173–207.

Taylor, J. B.: 1993, Discretion versus policy rules in practice, *Carnegie-Rochester Conference Series on Public Policy* **39**, 195–214.

Tirole, J.: 2006, *The Theory of Corporate Finance*, Princeton University Press.

Tobin, J.: 1965, Commercial banks as creators of money, *in* W. L. Smith and R. L. Teigen (eds), *Readings in Money, National Income and Stabilization Policy*, Homewood, Illinois: Richard D. Irwin, pp. 156–163.

Tobin, J.: 1969, A general equilibrium approach to monetary policy, *Journal of Money, Credit and Banking* **1**(1), 15–29.

Townsend, R. M.: 1983, Theories of intermediated structures, *Carnegie-Rochester Conference Series on Public Policy* **18**, 221–272.

References

Van Damme, E.: 1994, Banking: a survey of recent microeconomic theory, *Oxford Review of Economic Policy* **10**(4), 14–33.

Viale, A. M., Kolari, J. W. and Fraser, D. R.: 2009, Common risk factors in bank stocks, *Journal of Banking and Finance* **33**(3), 464–472.

von Hayek, F. A.: 1931, *Prices and Production*, London: Routledge and Sons.

von Thadden, E.-L.: 1998, Intermediated versus direct investment: optimal liquidity provision and dynamic incentive compatibility, *Journal of Financial Intermediation* **7**(2), 177–197.

Werner, R. A.: 2014, Can banks individually create money out of nothing? – the theories and the empirical evidence, *International Review of Financial Analysis* **36**, 1–19.

Wheelock, D. C. and Wohar, M. E.: 2009, Can the term spread predict output growth and recessions? A survey of the literature, *Federal Reserve Bank of St. Louis Review* **91**(5), 419–440.

Wicksell, K.: 1906, *Lectures on Political Economy, Volume II: Money*, London: Routledge, Ltd.

Williamson, S. D.: 1987, Costly monitoring, loan contracts, and equilibrium credit rationing, *Quarterly Journal of Economics* **102**(1), 135–146.

Wright, D. and Houpt, J.: 1996, An analysis of commercial bank exposure to interest rate risk, *Federal Reserve Bulletin* pp. 115–128.

Yanelle, M.-O.: 1997, Banking competition and market efficiency, *Review of Economic Studies* **64**(2).

Zentrum für Europäische Wirtschaftsforschung: 2016, Finanzmarkttest. Fragebogen.